Nova Scotia, New Brunswick and Prince Edward Island For Dummies, 2nd Edition

Cheat Sheet

W9-DGB-007

Nova Scotia, New Brunswick, and Prince Edward Island

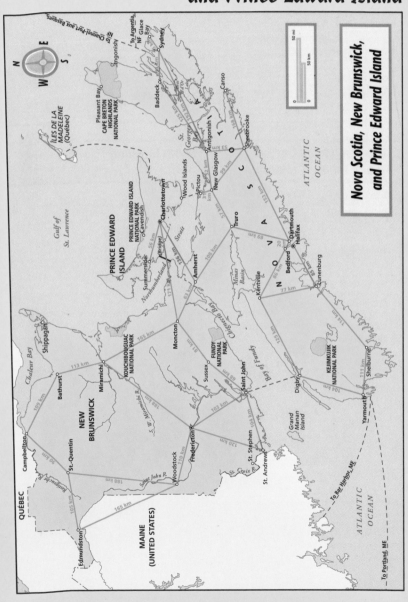

Nova Scotia, New Brunswick, and Prince Edward Island

Prince Edward Island Ferry Schedules

Departing from Wood Islands, Prince Edward Island, to Caribou, Nova Scotia

Date	Time								
May 1–June 15	06:30	09:30	13:00	16:30	19:30				
June 16–June 30	06:30	09:30	11:00	13:00	14:30	16:30	19:30		
July 1–Sept. 6	(06:30)	08:00	09:30	11:00	13:00	14:30	16:30	18:00	19:30
Sept. 7–Oct. 15	06:30	09:30	11:00	13:00	14:30	16:30	19:30		
Oct. 16–Nov. 30	06:30	09:30	13:00	16:30	19:30				
Dec. 1–Dec. 20	08:00	12:00	16:00						

Departing from Caribou, Nova Scotia, to Wood Islands, Prince Edward Island

Date	Time								
May 1–June 15		08:00	11:15	14:45	18:00	21:00			
June 16–June 30	08:00	11:15	12:45	14:45	16:15	18:00	21:00		
July 1–Sept. 6		(08:00)	09:30	11:15	12:45	14:45	16:15	18:00	19:30	21:00
Sept. 7–Oct. 15	08:00	11:15	12:45	14:45	16:15	18:00	21:00		
Oct. 16–Nov. 30	08:00	11:15	14:45	18:00	21:00				
Dec. 1–Dec.20		10:00	14:00	17:30					

( ) Brackets indicate no Sunday departures
* All departures in Atlantic Time

Confederation Bridge Fares

All Vehicles	$40.50
Motorcycle	$16.25
Cyclist	$8.00

Copyright © 2006 John Wiley & Sons Canada, Ltd. All rights reserved. Item 3739-X.
For more information about John Wiley & Sons Canada, Ltd., call 1-800-567-4797.

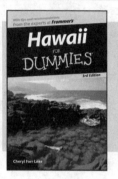
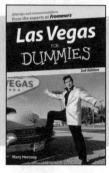
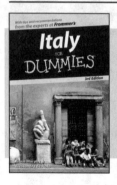

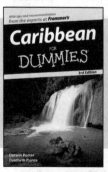
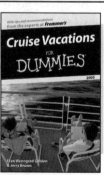

Nova Scotia, New Brunswick & Prince Edward Island

FOR

DUMMIES®

2ND EDITION

by Andrew Hempstead

John Wiley & Sons Canada, Ltd.

Nova Scotia, New Brunswick & Prince Edward Island For Dummies®, 2nd Edition

Published by
John Wiley & Sons Canada, Ltd
6045 Freemont Boulevard
Mississauga, Ontario, L5R 4J3
www.wiley.ca

Library and Archives Canada Cataloguing in Publication

Hempstead, Andrew

Nova Scotia, New Brunswick and Prince Edward Island for

dummies / Andrew Hempstead. — 2nd ed.

Includes index.

ISBN-13: 978-0-470-83739-9

ISBN-10: 0-470-83739-X

1. Maritime Provinces — Guidebooks. I. Title.

FC2024.H44 2006   917.1504'5   C2005-907759-X

Printed in Canada

1 2 3 4 5 TRI 10 09 08 07 06

Distributed in Canada by John Wiley & Sons Canada, Ltd

For general information on John Wiley & Sons Canada, Ltd, including all books published by Wiley Publishing, Inc., please call our warehouse, Tel 1-800-567-4797. For reseller information, including discounts and premium sales, please call our sales department, Tel 416-646-7992. For press review copies, author interviews, or other publicity information, please contact our marketing department, Tel 416-646-4584, Fax 416-236-4448.

For authorization to photocopy items for corporate, personal, or educational use, please contact in writing The Canadian Copyright Licensing Agency (Access Copyright). For an Access Copyright license, visit www.accesscopyright.ca or call toll free, 1-800-893-5777.

About the Author

Andrew Hempstead is a travel writer and photographer who has traveled widely throughout Canada from his home in Banff, Alberta. His research trip for the second edition of this book took him to every corner of the Maritimes, and along the way he found himself searching for fossils along the Bay of Fundy, wine-tasting in Nova Scotia, and golfing the fairways of Prince Edward Island.

In addition to this book, Hempstead has authored guidebooks to Alberta, British Columbia, the Canadian Rockies, and Vancouver, and has co-authored guidebooks to Atlantic Canada, Australia, and New Zealand. His writing and photography have also appeared in many national and international publications.

Author's Acknowledgments

Thanks to the following people for helping out with information and planning at various stages of my research trip: Judy Dougan, Tourism Moncton; Carol Horne and Tracy Stretch, Tourism PEI; Susan Jeffries, Nova Scotia Department of Tourism and Culture; Sally Cummings and Candace MacCullum, Tourism Saint John; and Angela Watson, Fredericton Tourism. Thanks also to staff at information centers, innkeepers, and others on my travels who guided me in the right direction, all of whom contributed to making this book as useful and comprehensive as it could possibly be.

Publisher's Acknowledgments

We're proud of this book; please send us your comments at canadapt@wiley.com. Some of the people who helped bring this book to market include the following:

Acquisitions, Editorial, and Media Development

Associate Editor: Robert Hickey

Copy Editor: Heather Ball, Colborne Communications

Front Cover Photo: © George Hunter/ Superstock

Back Cover Photo: © Andrew Hempstead

Cartoons: Rich Tennant, (www.the5thwave.com)

Composition

Publishing Services Director: Karen Bryan

Publishing Services Manager: Ian Koo

Project Manager: Elizabeth McCurdy

Project Coordinator: Pam Vokey

Layout and Graphics: Wiley Indianapolis Composition Services

Proofreaders: TECHBOOKS Production Services

Indexer: Belle Wong

John Wiley & Sons Canada, Ltd

Bill Zerter, Chief Operating Officer

Robert Harris, General Manager, Professional and Trade Division

Jennifer Smith, Publisher and Vice President, Professional and Trade Division

Publishing and Editorial for Consumer Dummies

Diane Graves Steele, Vice President and Publisher, Consumer Dummies

Joyce Pepple, Acquisitions Director, Consumer Dummies

Kristin A. Cocks, Product Development Director, Consumer Dummies

Michael Spring, Vice President and Publisher, Travel

Kelly Regan, Editorial Director, Travel

Publishing for Technology Dummies

Andy Cummings, Vice President and Publisher, Dummies Technology/General User

Composition Services

Gerry Fahey, Vice President of Production Services

Debbie Stailey, Director of Composition Services

Contents at a Glance

Maps at a Glance

Table of Contents

Introduction

The most common term used to describe the Maritimes as a tourist destination is "underrated." After spending your vacation traveling through Nova Scotia, New Brunswick, and Prince Edward Island, I'm sure you'll agree. This area of Canada possesses a subtle magnetism that is impossible to define — you just have to experience it to understand — and offers spectacular scenery to rival that of many other top destinations. Each of the three provinces has its own distinct character, and yet they come together to create a single destination like no other place on earth.

How do you distill the essence of the Maritimes into one book? That was the challenge I faced as I sorted through my experiences to bring you only the best and most unique accommodations, restaurants, and attractions. And they are just the tip of the iceberg; you won't go wrong at any of the places described in this book, but you will return home from your memorable Maritimes adventure with your own favorites.

About This Book

Nova Scotia, New Brunswick & Prince Edward Island for Dummies, 2nd Edition is a reference guide. It is not designed to be a comprehensive, tell-all guidebook that weighs you down. Each of the three provinces is discussed separately in individual parts, laid out in a logical sequence so you can refer quickly to a particular region, or skip a chapter completely if it is off your route (although you may want to reconsider after reading up on it). History is a big part of the Maritimes and travel, but I only dwell on the past when it is necessary.

Please be advised that travel information is subject to change at any time — and this is especially true of prices. I therefore suggest that you write or call ahead for confirmation when making your travel plans. The authors, editors, and publisher cannot be held responsible for the experiences of readers while traveling. Your safety is important to us; however, so we encourage you to stay alert and be aware of your surroundings. Keep a close eye on cameras, purses, and wallets, all favorite targets of thieves and pickpockets.

Dummies Post-it® Flags

As you're reading this book, you'll find information that you'll want to reference as you plan or enjoy your trip — whether it be a new hotel, a must-see attraction, or a must-try walking tour. Mark these pages with the handy Post-it® Flags included in this book to help make your trip planning easier!

Conventions Used in This Book

To help you get the information you need easily and quickly, I have taken the liberty of using a few conventions throughout this book.

✔ I use the accepted term "Maritimes" to collectively describe the provinces of Nova Scotia, New Brunswick, and Prince Edward Island.

✔ All prices in this book are given in both Canadian and U.S. dollars.

✔ Dollar sign ($) symbols preceding each listing are designed to give you an approximate price for a night's stay in a hotel or a meal in a restaurant. In the hotel section, the rates I quote are the rack rates (the hotel's official rates) for one night for a double room, although after reading Chapter 8, I would hope you never pay this full amount. When recommending restaurants, I give the range of main course prices: appetizers, desserts, drinks, and tips are not included in this amount unless explicitly stated. If a restaurant doesn't serve dinner, the price range refers to the lunch menu. Lobster causes a small problem (not to eat, that's for sure!) — in almost every restaurant it's sold at "Market Price," so my price ranges do not include this Maritimes delicacy.

Here's what the dollar signs represent:

Dollar Signs	Hotel	Restaurant
$	$75 or less	$10 or less
$$	$75–$150	$10–$17.50
$$$	$150–$225	$17.50–$25
$$$$	$225 or more	$25 and up

In this book I often include abbreviations for commonly accepted credit cards. I only include the major ones, so if your particular card is not listed here, it may or may not be accepted. Call ahead to make sure. The credit cards and their corresponding abbreviations are as follows:

AE	American Express
DC	Diners Club

DISC   Discover
MC   MasterCard
V   Visa

Foolish Assumptions

In writing this book, I made some assumptions about you and what your needs might be as a traveler. Here's what I assumed about you:

✔ You may be an experienced traveler who hasn't had much time to explore the Maritimes and wants expert advice when you finally do get a chance to enjoy that particular locale.

✔ You may be an inexperienced traveler looking for guidance when determining whether to take a trip to the Maritimes and how to plan for it.

✔ You're not looking for a book that provides all the information available about the Maritimes or that lists every hotel, restaurant, or attraction available to you. Instead, you're looking for a book that focuses on the places that will give you the best or most unique experience in the Maritimes.

If you fit any of this criteria, then *Nova Scotia, New Brunswick, and Prince Edward Island for Dummies* gives you the information you're looking for!

How This Book Is Organized

Nova Scotia, New Brunswick, and Prince Edward Island for Dummies is divided into six parts. The chapters within each part cover specific topics or regions in detail. You can read each chapter or part without reading the others — after all, there's no need to read about Prince Edward Island if you're heading for Cape Breton Island.

Part 1: Introducing Nova Scotia, New Brunswick, and Prince Edward Island

This part introduces you to the three provinces, and highlights — well, the highlights. I tell you about the best times of year to visit, and describe the top festivals and events. I also propose four itineraries (a one-week trip, a two-week trip, a special trip for families, and another for seafood-lovers). I also offer tips for travelers with special needs, such as seniors and those with disabilities, as well as budget-planning advice that all travelers can use.

Part II: Planning Your Trip to the Maritimes

Call it Trip-Planning 101. Here, I'll lay out the basics and delve into details to help you get started on the right path. By the end of Part II, you will know:

- ✔ The reasons you may or may not use a travel agent to help plan your trip

- ✔ The pros and cons of taking an escorted or package tour

- ✔ The ways to get to the Maritimes, and how to get around after you arrive

- ✔ The different lodging types available to you, and how you can save money when booking a room

- ✔ The useful details, such as the best way to carry your money and what type of travel insurance will meet your particular needs

Parts III, IV, V: The Provinces

These three parts form the bulk of the book, with each one devoted to a separate province. I've then broken the parts down further into chapters that focus on specific regions. In each chapter, you'll find all the information you need to make the most of your visit, including:

- ✔ How to get there

- ✔ Where to stay

- ✔ Where to eat

- ✔ What there is to see and do

Part VI: The Part of Tens

Skip ahead to this part for the best of the Maritimes condensed into a few pages: ten classic Maritimes experiences and my ten favorite seafood restaurants — with ten people you probably didn't know were from the Maritimes thrown in as a bonus.

In the back of this book I've included an *Appendix* — your Quick Concierge — containing lots of handy information you may need when traveling in the Maritimes, like phone numbers and addresses of emergency personnel or area hospitals and pharmacies, lists of local newspapers and magazines, protocol for sending mail or finding taxis, and more. Check out the Appendix when searching for answers to lots of little questions that may come up as you travel. You can find Quick Concierge easily because it's printed on yellow paper.

Icons Used in This Book

I've used five icons throughout this book to call your attention to different types of information. Here's what they mean:

Find out useful advice on things to do and ways to schedule your time when you see the Tip icon.

Watch for the Heads Up icon to identify annoying or potentially dangerous situations such as tourist traps, unsafe neighborhoods, budgetary rip-offs, and other things to beware.

Next to a hotel recommendation, this icon means that the establishment welcomes children. Next to a restaurant, it indicates that kids are offered their own menu. In front of an attraction, it emphasizes somewhere your kids will (hopefully) enjoy.

If you see this icon, you'll know you're about to save some money. It doesn't necessarily mean that something is cheap — just that it is a particularly good value.

This is my favorite icon. When you spot it, you'll know you're in for a special Maritimes welcome.

Where to Go from Here

As you begin to plan your Maritimes vacation, consider my recommendations while keeping your own interests in mind. Pore over maps and plot out an itinerary — the idea is to plan ahead, book your transportation and lodgings, and leave the rest until you get there.

This book is designed to help you juggle the practicalities of advance planning (like the security of knowing you have a comfortable room to retire to) with spontaneity (like a spur-of-the-moment restaurant stop or an exhilarating whale-watching excursion). That way, you won't have to worry about the nit-picky details; you can just relax and enjoy the magnificent Maritimes.

Part I

Introducing Nova Scotia, New Brunswick, and Prince Edward Island

In this part . . .

Okay, it's time to get excited about traveling to the Maritimes! This part breaks it down, nice and easy, by listing the best places to go and sights to see in each province. It'll also highlight the pros and cons of traveling to the region at different times of year, provide four itineraries to help you make the most of your time, and suggest tips for travelers with special needs or those on a budget.

Chapter 1

Discovering the Best of Nova Scotia, New Brunswick, and Prince Edward Island

. . . .

In This Chapter

▶ Focusing in on the best lodgings and restaurants

▶ Exploring the top historic sites

▶ Driving the most scenic highways

. . . .

*M*aritimes' tourist literature is filled with pictures of lighthouses and seafood, and you'll see lots of the former and eat lots of the latter. But in addition, each of the three provinces covered in this book — Nova Scotia, New Brunswick, and Prince Edward Island — offers things that go beyond the ordinary, and this is where this chapter comes in. Here I highlight the best and most unique accommodations, restaurants, attractions, and scenic drives.

In this chapter, I offer a quick rundown of the places to stay, restaurants, historic attractions, and scenic drives that I consider being the best that Canada's Maritime provinces have to offer. In the destination chapters in Parts III, IV, and V, I go into more detail about these experiences and destinations; just look for the "Best of the Best" icon you see here.

The Best Places to Stay

Finding comfortable accommodations with the facilities you require in the price range that fits your budget will go a long way to making your travels enjoyable. With that in mind, here are the best the Maritimes has to offer.

Best splurges

Cities across the Maritimes have a choice of top end hotels. The only real surprise is the cost, which is generally a lot lower than elsewhere in North America.

  ✔ In Halifax, the **Lord Nelson Hotel & Suites** is an excellent choice for upscale lodging within walking distance of downtown. See Chapter 11.

  ✔ **Glenghorm Beach Resort** makes the grade for its Deluxe Suites. These contemporary, casual units are among my favorite rooms in all the Maritimes. See Chapter 14.

  ✔ For top-notch Saint John accommodations, it's hard to go past the old world charm of **Homeport Historic Bed & Breakfast.** See Chapter 16.

  ✔ In a resort town filled with elegant lodgings, none are more lavish than the **Kingsbrae Arms.** See Chapter 16.

  ✔ On the rural eastern portion of Prince Edward Island, **Inn at Bay Fortune** is a once-grand summer estate converted to luxurious lodging. See Chapter 21.

Best historic getaways

The Maritimes is saturated with historic lodgings — some have been taking in guests for a century or more, while others are converted residences.

  ✔ The **Lunenburg Arms Hotel** has undergone serious renovations, converting an old inn into a gracious lodging with character-filled rooms, some with water views. See Chapter 12.

  ✔ In Annapolis Royal, the gracious **Queen Anne Inn** is soaked in Victorian charm. See Chapter 12.

  ✔ Well-priced rooms and a harborside location are the main draws at the 1810 **Consulate Inn,** once home to a United States consulate. See Chapter 13.

  ✔ Along the Acadian Coast, the **Governor's Mansion Inn** offers up plenty of historic atmosphere at a reasonable price. See Chapter 15.

  ✔ In the historic heart of Charlottetown, the **Inns on Great George** oozes the charm of a bygone era. See Chapter 18.

Best ocean outlooks

Sure, a comfortable bed and clean surroundings are important to an enjoyable stay, but there is something especially memorable about waking up to water views, which is what makes the following choices shine.

- ✔ **Prospect Bed & Breakfast** has a delightful ocean setting in a small fishing village, and yet is within an hour's drive of Halifax. See Chapter 11.

- ✔ You really can hear the waves whispering at **Whispering Waves Cottages.** A lobster dinner delivered to your door is a bonus. See Chapter 12.

- ✔ The name says it all — **Water's Edge Inn** combines location with comfortable rooms to be the best choice in Baddeck. See Chapter 14.

- ✔ If you prefer location over luxury, make **Seaside Beach Resort** your base while exploring St. Andrews. See Chapter 16.

- ✔ Staying in a lighthouse guarantees sweeping ocean views, and so it is at **West Point Lighthouse,** where one lucky party gets to stay in the actual light tower while other guests make themselves comfortable in converted living quarters. See Chapter 20.

Best for active travelers

Keeping in mind that not all travelers are on vacation to relax, I present you with the best lodgings for the energetic.

- ✔ Whales and birds are the main attractions out on Brier Island, and the place to mingle with fellow wildlife enthusiasts is **Brier Island Lodge.** See Chapter 12.

- ✔ **Seaboard Bed and Breakfast** is the ideal hangout for surfers drawn to the waves of Lawrencetown Beach. No waves? No problem. Guests have use of canoes and bikes. See Chapter 13.

- ✔ **Glenghorm Beach Resort** has a beachy feel, and activities to match — think sea kayaking, ocean swimming, and sunbathing. See Chapter 14.

- ✔ For resort-style activities such as golf, tennis, and swimming, **Rodd Crowbush Golf & Beach Resort** will not disappoint. See Chapter 21.

The Best Places to Eat

Unless you plan on staying in accommodations with cooking facilities, you'll be eating out a lot on your Maritimes' vacation. But restaurant pricing is reasonable and the choices — in cities and resort areas at least — are varied.

Best seafood

As you'd expect in a region dominated by the ocean, seafood is found on most menus. I've dedicated a full chapter to the subject (see Chapter 23), but here is a quick glance at the best of the best.

Pg. 149

✔ For the plumpest scallops you could ever imagine, go right to the source at **O'Neil's Fundy Fish Market** and order them cooked to go. See Chapter 12. *Nova Scotia, Digby*

Pg. 158

✔ Truro is in the rural heart of Nova Scotia. So **Murphy's**, with its perfectly battered fish and chips, is a welcome surprise. See Chapter 13. *Truro, NS*

Pg. 178

✔ The **Chowder House** is a simple pine-paneled room, but what it lacks in ambience is more than made up for by fresh, inexpensive seafood. See Chapter 14. *Cape Breton, N.S,*

Pg. 178

✔ Order crab and mussels, boiled to order on outdoor gas burners, at the **Muddy Rudder**. Just don't expect table service. See Chapter 14. *Cape Breton, NS*

Pg. 217

✔ At the back of Saint John City Market, **Billy's Seafood Company** is part seafood market, part restaurant, so you can be assured the blackboard menu features the freshest of fresh seafood. See Chapter 16. *Saint John, NB*

Pg. 276

✔ Plan on giving the touristy restaurants in Cavendish a miss and head to the nearby **Blue Mussel Café**, which dishes up fresh, innovative seafood. See Chapter 19. *Cavendish, PEI*

Pg. 276

✔ You should plan on taking in at least one lobster supper while in the Maritimes. My pick is **Fisherman's Wharf Lobster Suppers,** which is halfway between touristy and traditional. See Chapter 19. *Cavendish, PEI*

Pg. 285

✔ Steamed mussels are a common appetizer throughout the Maritimes, but at **Flex Mussels** they are the star of the show, with choices like mussels boiled with roast corn, scallions, kumquats, and bourbon. See Chapter 20. *Summerside, PEI*

Best views

Restaurants with views are notorious for high prices and bad food, but not in the Maritimes, as you'll find out at the following eateries.

✔ **Murphy's on the Water** lives up to its name. This Halifax restaurant, at the end of a wharf extending well into the harbor, offers panoramic views from most tables. See Chapter 11.

✔ Restaurants are few and far between along the Eastern Shore, which makes the **Lobster Shack** even more popular. To make the most of the location, request an outdoor table, order lobster chowder, and watch the Salmon River flow by. See Chapter 13.

✔ You can see the ocean from many Cape Breton Island dining rooms, but none have the intimate atmosphere and creative cooking found at **Seascapes Restaurant**. See Chapter 14.

✔ In the tony town of St. Andrews, **The Gables** is a refreshingly casual seafood restaurant with a deck that extends to the just above the high tide mark. See Chapter 16.

✔ Yes, the **Blue Mussel Café** made the cut when it comes to the Maritimes' best seafood restaurants. But every table has views across delightful Rustico Bay, so I couldn't help but to include it here also. See Chapter 19.

Best pub dining

Forget about nachos and chicken wings. In the Maritimes, pub grub usually includes traditional British cooking or local seafood, and here are the best of the best.

✔ The hordes of university students living in Moncton gravitate to Main Street bars such as the **Pump House Brewery** for inexpensive dining (and drinking). See Chapter 15.

✔ **Captain Dan's** attracts a young, hip crowd of New Brunswickers with its prime waterfront location, well-priced seafood, and live music. See Chapter 15.

✔ In Fredericton, veer off the main street to **Rye's Deli & Bar,** a fancy pub known as much for its food as its beer. See Chapter 17.

✔ On the Charlottetown waterfront, **Peake's Quay** serves standard pub fare but offers a delightful setting and lively atmosphere. See Chapter 19. *PE I*

Best Acadian

Forget about the waistline and plan on dining on down-home hearty Acadian cooking at one of the following establishments.

✔ Rappie pie, an Acadian staple, is the specialty at **Rapure Acadienne.** But you'll need to arrive on an empty stomach — the servings are huge. See Chapter 12.

✔ At **Restaurant Acadian** in Chéticamp, Acadian cuisine is served by waitstaff in traditional dress. See Chapter 14.

✔ **Cajun Jacques** may sound contemporary, but the menu is filled with dishes that date back centuries. See Chapter 20.

Best inexpensive dining

Everyone loves a bargain, but that shouldn't mean eating poorly. So in this section I've included dining establishments where the prices are attractive and the food tasty.

✔ Inhabiting a prime downtown Halifax locale is **Harbourside Market,** where food outlets like **Captain John's** serve up well-priced food in a casual setting. See Chapter 11.

✔ Mahone Bay's **Salt Spray Café** dishes up one of the province's better breakfast deals. Dining on the harbor-front deck makes the low prices even tastier. See Chapter 12. *Mahone Bay, NS*

Pg.113

Pg.135

[handwritten: Pg.242]

✔ The décor is bright and cheery, but it is the prices that will catch your eye at **Chez Cora.** See Chapter 17. *[handwritten: Fredericton, NB]*

[handwritten: Pg.262]

✔ At **Café Diem,** you can check your email while munching away on healthy, inexpensive lunches. See Chapter 18. *[handwritten: Charlottetown, PEI]*

[handwritten: Pg.263]

✔ At the **Lucy Maud Dining Room** you get to indulge in high quality cooking while enjoying top service — thanks to students from the affiliated culinary school. See Chapter 18. *[handwritten: Charlottetown, PEI]*

[handwritten: Pg.298]

✔ The **Bluefin Restaurant** in Souris is notable for its homey atmosphere and inexpensive seafood. See Chapter 21. *[handwritten: Souris, PEI]*

The Best Historic Attractions

Sure, the Maritimes has the usual array of museums filled with predictable collections of pioneer artifacts, but wait! The three provinces also offer an abundance of remarkable sites that delve into the region's long and colorful history.

I don't plan to bore you with too much history in this book. If I mention a museum or historic site, you know it's a good one (or very important), including the following.

✔ **Halifax Citadel National Historic Site,** a nineteenth-century fort that is Canada's most visited National Historic Site, is worth visiting for the sweeping harbor views alone. See Chapter 11.

✔ Halifax played an important role in the aftermath of the *Titanic* tragedy. As a result, there is plenty of related history to explore, from the mainstream (**Maritime Museum of the Atlantic**) to the offbeat (the final resting place of third-class seaman J. Dawson, who was immortalized by a fictionalized character of the same name, played by Leonardo DiCaprio in the movie version of the tragedy). See Chapter 11.

✔ South of Halifax, the entire waterfront core of attractive **Lunenburg,** home port for the famous schooner *Bluenose II,* has been declared a UNESCO World Heritage Site for its unaltered state. See Chapter 12.

✔ The British and French struggled for control of **Annapolis Royal** for almost a century, and many buildings from this era remain along the main street, including Canada's oldest wooden building. Just outside of town is **Port-Royal,** a replica of Canada's first permanent European settlement. See Chapter 12.

✔ The **Alexander Graham Bell National Historic Site** is a top-notch museum commemorating one of the world's best-known inventors. The basement is devoted to learning games for children. See Chapter 14.

✔ The **Fortress of Louisbourg,** Canada's largest historic reconstruction, is also one of its most remote, situated as it is on the northeastern tip of Cape Breton Island. See Chapter 14.

✔ History along the Acadian Coast revolves around the Acadians, a Francophile population who settled the region as early as the 1730s. To fully immerse yourself in the colorful culture of these resilient people, plan on spending time at **Village Historique Acadien.** See Chapter 15.

✔ After fire destroyed much of **Saint John** in 1877, the city was rebuilt in brick and stone, and today these elaborate buildings form the nucleus of a historic downtown precinct. See Chapter 16.

✔ **Kings Landing Historical Settlement** is an outdoor museum that re-creates life as experienced by the Loyalists, who were driven out of America for their loyalty to England after the American Revolution. See Chapter 17.

✔ Canadians take great pride in their heritage, which makes **Charlottetown** a popular destination. It was here in 1864 that the Fathers of Confederation met to discuss uniting the British North American colonies to establish of the Dominion of Canada. The meeting took place at **Province House,** still home to the PEI legislature and open to the public. Charlottetown's top attraction is **Founders' Hall,** which tells the story of Canada from Confederation to modern times. See Chapter 18.

The Best Scenic Drives

In addition to scheduled stops at official attractions, be sure to allow extra time for taking in the scenery along the following routes.

✔ **Best in Nova Scotia:** For rugged scenery coupled with a little bit of history and some Francophone culture, the **Cabot Trail** will not disappoint. The ideal starting point for this 300-km (187-mile) circuit that hits all the hotspots of Cape Breton Island is Baddeck. From this history-filled village, the road cuts across the Margaree Valley to the Gulf of St. Lawrence and Chéticamp, where Acadians go about the business of fishing, making arts and crafts, and filling travelers with hearty cooking. The Cabot Trail then hugs ocean cliffs and cuts through the rugged interior of Cape Breton Highlands National Park to the white sand beaches of Ingonish. See Chapter 14.

✔ **Best in New Brunswick:** The drive along the Fundy Coast is geologically interesting rather than outrageously scenic. It's divided roughly in half by the city of Saint John. Head west from here along **Highway 1** and you'll soon find yourself passing by tranquil lakes and occasional glimpses of the Bay of Fundy before reaching the resort town of St. Andrews. Northeast of Saint John, **Highway 114** passes through Fundy National Park and the fishing village of Alma before reaching Hopewell Rocks, and heading up the Petitcodiac River to Moncton. See Chapter 16.

✔ **Best on Prince Edward Island:** Fill the gas tank and strike out in any direction. Within minutes, you'll be surrounded by the bucolic landscape so vividly described by Lucy Maud Montgomery in *Anne of Green Gables*. Need a little more direction? Take **Highway 1** west from the capital to Summerside, then continue along the coastal Région Évangéline via **Highway 11,** where Acadian culture thrives. As the Northumberland Strait opens to the Gulf of St. Lawrence, rolling green fields along **Highways 11** and **14** come to a stark end at red cliffs that drop precipitously into the ocean. Stop for a slice of Seaweed Pie at Miminegash, before returning to the capital via **Highway 2.** See Chapter 20.

Chapter 2

Digging Deeper into the Canadian Maritimes

- -

In This Chapter

▶ Stepping back into the past

▶ Feasting on local cuisine

▶ Getting a taste for the Maritimes through books and movies

- -

Y ou can spend hours poring over maps and guidebooks while planning your trip to the Maritimes, but learning a little background will help you appreciate the region's finer points. In this chapter, I do my best to condense four centuries of history into a few pages, introduce you to local cuisine, and then round out the chapter with a discussion of books and movies that give you the chance to get even better acquainted with the Maritimes.

History 101: The Main Events

Many centuries before the first Europeans arrived, the Maritimes provided a home for the Mi'Kmaq, coastal dwellers who fished with spears and hook and line, while also collecting shellfish from the shoreline. For food, hunting was less important than fishing, but a hunter still held a great degree of status among members of the group. Canoes with sails were used for summer travel while in winter toboggans (the word toboggan originates from the Mi'Kmaq word *topaghan*) and snowshoes were essential.

Legend has it that a large boulder near Yarmouth (Nova Scotia) was inscribed by the fearsome Viking Leif Eriksson around 1,000 years ago. But the region's first documented European visitor was explorer John Cabot, who spotted Cape Breton Island in 1497. A century later, Frenchman Samuel de Champlain sailed into the Bay of Fundy and established a fur trading post on a small island in the St. Croix River.

Conditions were harsh, so the party relocated to what is now Nova Scotia and built Port-Royal, which is now protected as a National Historic Site, complete with a re-creation of the original fort. The settlement prospered and expanded into what became known as Acadia, or "Peaceful Land."

But French settlement didn't sit well with England, who had colonial aspirations along North America's east coast. The first major conflict between the two occurred in 1613, when the English attacked Port-Royal. This didn't stop Acadian settlements from springing up around the Bay of Fundy, including Grand Pré, which grew into the Acadian capital. The 1713 Treaty of Utrecht, which settled the Queen Anne's War in Europe, gave Acadia to England, which they promptly named Nova Scotia (New Scotland), designating Annapolis Royal as the capital. Having been granted Cape Breton Island and Prince Edward Island in the treaty, the French built the Fortress of Louisbourg, envisioning a major trading center and military base. The French also developed Port la Joye (now Charlottetown, the capital of Prince Edward Island), with the aim of farming the island's rich soils to provide food for Louisbourg. But hostilities between England and France continued, often mirroring events in Europe, such as the Seven Years' War between 1756 and 1763.

In 1755, England began enforcing an oath of allegiance from the Acadians. Those who were noncompliant — around 8,000 — were deported. They were loaded onto ships bound for the English colonies on the eastern seaboard or any place that would accept them. Some ships docked in England, others in France, and others in France's colonies in the Caribbean. In one of the period's few favorable events, the Spanish government offered the refugees free land in Louisiana, and many settled there, where they became known as Cajuns. The poet Henry Wadsworth Longfellow distilled the deportation tragedy in Evangeline, a fictional story of two lovers divided by the events.

After the British had swept the Acadians from their land, prosperous "planters," gentlemen-farmers from New England, were lured to the region with free land grants. Merchants settled in Yarmouth in the 1760s, and other Anglo settlers went to Prince Edward Island. Even the inglorious defeat in the American Revolution benefited the British by helping settlement of the Maritimes. Loyalists (Americans loyal to England) by the thousands poured into Nova Scotia and New Brunswick. Around 14,000 Loyalists settled in Saint John, leading to its incorporation as a city (the first in Canada) in 1785.

One of the more colorful aspects of Maritimes history was privateering. Privateers were government-sanctioned pirates who had permission to capture enemy vessels. They were required by law to take captured vessels to Halifax's Privateers Wharf, where the cargo was auctioned off, a portion of which was handed back to the privateer and his crew.

Maritimes timeline

1497   John Cabot sights Cape Breton Island, and claims it for England.

1604   French explorer Samuel de Champlain establishes a winter camp on an island in the St. Croix River.

1605   Champlain's party moves across the Bay of Fundy, and builds Port-Royal, a fortified settlement overlooking the Annapolis Basin.

1635   Port-Royal is declared the capital of French-speaking Acadia.

1713   After a century of conflict, the Treaty of Utrecht award French Acadia to Great Britain while France falls heir to Cape Breton Island and Prince Edward Island.

1749   The British establish a fortified military base at Halifax Harbour.

1755   Around 8,000 Acadians are deported.

1758   The English capture and destroy the Fortress of Louisbourg.

1776   Even after the signing of the Declaration of Independence, many Americans remained loyal to England. Finding life intolerable, they fled north to the Maritimes, where they were known as Loyalists.

1785   Saint John, New Brunswick, becomes Canada's first incorporated city.

1800   A frozen pond on the outskirts of Windsor, Nova Scotia, hosts the first-ever game of hockey.

1864   The Fathers of Confederation meet in Charlottetown, signing the *British North America Act* and in effect creating the nation of Canada.

1885   The transcontinental railway, extending from Halifax to Vancouver, is completed.

1917   Two ships collide in Halifax Harbour. The ensuing explosion is, for its time, the world's biggest man-made explosion.

1997   The Confederation Bridge opens, providing a road link between Prince Edward Island and the rest of Canada.

In the early 1860s, with the American Civil War raging, England decided it needed to do something to reform its political influence in the New World. This was the impetus for the Fathers of the Confederation coming together at Province House in Charlottetown to discuss a union of colonies. The gathering formed the groundwork for the 1867 *British North American Act*, which established the Dominion of Canada as a confederation of Nova Scotia, New Brunswick, Quebec, and Ontario. Prince Edward Island joined in 1873. The final piece to the jigsaw puzzle was Newfoundland, which became Canada's tenth province by joining the dominion in 1949.

Taste of the Maritimes: Local cuisine

If you're planning on having a true Maritimes experience, you'll have to eat plenty of seafood and you'll have to experience Acadian cooking.

Swimming in seafood

If you love seafood, you'll love the Maritimes, where it is a staple for locals and dominates restaurant menus. Lobsters, crabs, scallops, mussels, clams, halibut, and salmon are all harvested locally. One of the true joys of local seafood is that you don't need to spend a fortune to indulge. For example, fresh boiled lobster is fresh boiled lobster, whether you've picked it up at a market and cooked it yourself, or you've ordered it at the finest restaurant in Halifax. The same goes for other types of seafood. If you have cooking facilities at your accommodation (many cottage complexes do), plan on stocking up on mussels to steam in white wine, scallops to sauté with butter and garlic, and crab to boil in salt water.

But maybe you want someone else to do the cooking. Not a problem. Seafood finds its way onto menus at even the most unassuming restaurant. I purposely avoid recommending chain restaurants in this book, but McDonald's does warrant a mention for its local McLobster burger, which is offered throughout the summer. Moving up one step in style is the down-home atmosphere of a lobster supper in one of the community halls on Prince Edward Island. Other regional highlights include pickled Solomon Gundy herring sold from a roadside cart in New Brunswick and planked Atlantic salmon cooked over an open fire at a resort in Nova Scotia.

Eating Acadian

Not surprisingly, Acadian fare is based on seafood. Two common dishes include chicken *fricot,* a hearty stewlike soup chock-full of chicken, onions, and potatoes; and *poutine râpé,* boiled or deep-fried pork and grated raw potatoes, rolled into a ball and dipped in corn or maple syrup or molasses. Desserts such as sugar pie, apple dumplings, and cinnamon buns appear on most Acadian menus.

Even if you're not invited into an Acadian home, you'll be made to feel welcome at Acadian restaurants along La Côte Acadienne (Nova Scotia), Chéticamp (Nova Scotia), the Acadian Coast (New Brunswick), and Région Évangéline (Prince Edward Island).

Background Check: Recommended Books and Movies

Life on the edge of the world has been the inspiration for many Maritimes books and movies. Here are a few of the better known.

The Maritimes in print

It is impossible to begin a discussion of Maritimes literature any other way than by talking about *Anne of Green Gables,* by Lucy Maud Montgomery (1877–1942). Born and raised around Cavendish, on Prince Edward Island, Montgomery wrote the children's classic in 1908, using her own childhood as inspiration for the tale of a spunky orphan living on a farm at Avonlea. While the book has been turned into a TV drama (*Road to Avonlea*) and a movie, many places described in the novel still exist, including Green Gables House, which is open as a tourist attraction.

His Majesty's Yankees and *The Governor's Lady,* both by Thomas Raddall (1903–1994), do a wonderful job of delving into Nova Scotia's past using fictional characters. *No Great Mischief* (2001), by Alistair MacLeod, is the story of a Scottish clan that settles on Cape Breton Island in the late 1700s. *Island: The Complete Stories* (2001) showcases MacLeod's florid writing style as he describes rural life in Nova Scotia.

Nova Scotian Thomas Chandler Haliburton (1796–1865) is credited with creating the literary character Sam Slick. In *The Clockmaker,* Haliburton first coined phrases such as "it's raining cats and dogs" and "quick as a wink."

New Brunswick's best-known author is Antonine Maillet, a prolific writer whose book *La Sagouine,* about an Acadian fisherman's wife, has been adapted to a summer stage production in her hometown of Bouctouche. If you're interested in Acadia, do pick up a copy of Clive Doucet's *Notes From Exile* (2000), which explores modern day Acadian culture by combining Doucet's own experiences with the 1755 deportation. Heartrending yet gritty, *Mercy Among the Children,* authored by David Adams Richards in 2001, is the story of growing up in a rural town along New Brunswick's Miramichi River.

The Maritimes on the big screen

Canada has a well-respected film industry that produces dozens of excellent movies that are little-known even within Canada. While most are obscure, *Shattered City: The Halifax Explosion* (2003) is worth searching out for its realistic portrayal of what was, at the time (1917), the world's largest man-made explosion. More recently, One More Dead Fish was a compelling docu-drama set in Nova Scotia.

The waterfront precinct of Shelburne was spruced up in 1992 for *Mary Sillman's War,* based on the book *War of Duty,* which was set in Connecticut during the American Revolution. Hollywood producers were so impressed with Shelburne's historic look that they returned with Demi Moore and Robert Duvall to film *The Scarlet Letter.* Modern-day scenes from the 1997 movie *Titanic* were filmed around Halifax. This city has many links to the famous tragedy, including being the resting place of many victims, one of which is J. Dawson, the namesake of Leonardo DiCaprio's character. Halifax Harbour takes a starring role in K-19: *The Widowmaker* (2002), in which Harrison Ford plays a Russian naval captain aboard a nuclear submarine.

Halifax has also stood in for a surprisingly diverse number of cities, including Salt Lake City for the 2005 TV movie *Bring Elizabeth Home: The Elizabeth Smart Story*. Scenes from Leaving Las Vegas (1995) were also filmed in the Nova Scotia capital, as were small parts of *The Shipping News*, which was mostly filmed in Newfoundland. *Beach Girls*, a teen-angst drama starring Rob Lowe, was filmed in numerous coastal communities south of Halifax in 2005. It hadn't hit the big screen as of publication of this book — and I won't be rushing out to see it — but it should give you a good idea of the local scenery.

Based on a poem by Henry Wadsworth Longfellow, *Évangéline* tells the story of a young woman from Grand Pré who was separated by the love of her life during the Acadian deportation. This classic 1929 silent movie (starring Mexican actress Dolores del Rio) was re-released on DVD in 2001.

The setting is supposedly an island off New England, but the Fundy Coast around Saint John did just fine for filming of *Children of a Lesser God*, which won a host of Academy Awards including Best Picture and Best Actress (Marlee Matlin). At the opposite end of the cinematic scale, the backwoods of New Brunswick have provided a backdrop for slasher flicks such as the 1997 hit *I Know What You Did Last Summer* and *Ricky 6* (2000), which was loosely based on the true story of teenaged satanic serial killer from Long Island. Another movie released in 2000 is the thriller *Frozen with Fear*, filmed in and around Fredericton, with Bo Derek as a wife witnessing her husband's murder. Two years earlier, James Wood and Melanie Griffith were in the New Brunswick capital filming the crime thriller *Another Day in Paradise.*

Lucy Maud Montgomery's florid descriptions of utopian Prince Edward Island were bought to the small screen in the 1980s TV series *Road to Avonlea*, as well as numerous movies, including *Happy Christmas, Miss King* (1998). Children will enjoy watching any of these productions, but don't tell them they were filmed in Ontario. One movie that was filmed on the island (but you won't want the kids to watch) is *The Ballad of Jack and Rose*, an R-rated drama about a daughter growing up with her father on a remote commune.

Chapter 3

Deciding Where and When to Go

. . . .

In This Chapter

▶ Describing the regions
▶ Making the most of your time
▶ Sorting out the seasons
▶ Catching the best festivals and events

. . . .

*D*eciding what you want to see and the best time to visit depends on many factors. I begin this chapter with a brief overview of each province, describing spectacular coastal scenery, rural serenity, and the historic appeal of some of North America's oldest towns.

Once you have an idea of *where* you'd like to go on your Maritimes vacation, you need to decide *when* to visit. That's where the second part of this chapter comes to the rescue. I describe the pros and cons of each season and use a table to show monthly temperature differences in a simple format. I end this chapter with a round-up of popular festivals and events (along with a few personal favorites).

Going Everywhere You Want to Be

Even though you can include all three provinces in a week-long vacation, rushing through the Maritimes defeats the purpose of enjoying everything the region has to offer. Instead, plan your travels around your own interests and needs, using this section to find out the highlights of each region. I go into more detail through the travel chapters of this book.

Nova Scotia

Almost cut off from the rest of Canada by the Bay of Fundy, Nova Scotia (see Part III) is compact and easy to get around, which makes visiting the various regions a breeze. You'll never be more than 60km (37 miles) from what best defines the province — the ocean. Picturesque fishing villages, abundant seafood, and the stark beauty of Cape Breton Island are highlights of a visit to Nova Scotia.

Halifax (see Chapter 11), capital of Nova Scotia and largest city in the Maritimes, has history and location as its major draws. Set around a spectacular harbor, the city radiates from a compact downtown core where you find attractions such as **Halifax Citadel National Historic Site,** world-class hotels, fine dining, and a lively nightlife.

In **southwestern Nova Scotia** (see Chapter 12), **Peggy's Cove, Mahone Bay,** and **Lunenburg** get all the attention for their postcard-perfect oceanfront settings, but many other South Shore villages you won't see in the tourist brochures are equally scenic and a lot quieter. Stroll the waterfront sections of **West Dover, Prospect Point,** or **Blue Rocks** to experience Nova Scotia without the crowds. The **Bay of Fundy** is no scenic gem, but with the world's highest tides and resident populations of **whales,** it offers huge attractions.

Beyond the TransCanada Highway, which cuts through **central Nova Scotia** (see Chapter 13), is a wealth of interesting detours. The most intriguing is to watch the **tidal bore** (a wall of water that builds up as the tide comes in against the waters of a river) at **Truro.** You can also drive the **Glooscap Trail** in search of dinosaurs and explore the history of **Pictou** by stepping aboard a replica of the sailing ship that bought the province's first Scottish settlers.

Cape Breton Island (see Chapter 14) is one of Nova Scotia's biggest draws. The island's most spectacular scenery lies within the protection of **Cape Breton Highlands National Park.** The **Cabot Trail,** one of the world's most scenic drives, passes through the park, allowing roadside views of high sea cliffs, endless ocean, white-sand beaches, and occasionally whales frolicking in the water far below.

New Brunswick

The largest of the three Maritimes provinces, New Brunswick (see Part IV) is also the most varied in terms of landscape, and it offers diverse experiences to match. An excellent highway system links the three largest cities — **Moncton, Fredericton** (the capital), and **Saint John** — with other worthwhile destinations close at hand.

The **Acadian Coast** of New Brunswick, northeast of the university town of **Moncton** (see Chapter 15), has long stretches of sandy beaches and some of Canada's warmest ocean water. **Parlee Beach,** near Shediac, is especially popular for its warm water, making it the busiest beach in the Maritimes. If it's solitude you're after, head north to the beaches in **Kouchibouguac National Park.**

The world's highest tides are found in the **Bay of Fundy,** which is bordered to the west by New Brunswick's **Fundy Coast** (see Chapter 16). **Fundy National Park** and **Hopewell Rocks** are the best spots to view the effects of this natural phenomenon. But a coastal drive should also include the historic port city of **Saint John** and the resort town of **St. Andrews,** which oozes old money.

The capital of New Brunswick, **Fredericton** (see Chapter 17) centers on the **Historic Garrison District,** which has changed little since the 1800s, when it was filled with English soldiers defending the Maritimes region from an overland attack. Beyond city limits follow the Saint John River to historic highlights like **Kings Landing Historical Settlement,** and take backs roads that lead to dozens of covered bridges.

Prince Edward Island

Usually referred to simply as PEI, Prince Edward Island (see Part V) is Canada's smallest province, just one-tenth the size of Nova Scotia. It's linked to the mainland by a bridge, but is a world away from the rest of the country in look and feel. The island was immortalized by Lucy Maud Montgomery in her popular *Anne of Green Gables* novel, and in many ways retains the charms she wrote of almost 100 years ago.

The centrally located capital is **Charlottetown** (see Chapter 18), which is chock-full of history, charming bed and breakfasts, and a wide range of restaurants.

Few places in the world are as closely associated with a fictional character as PEI is with Anne of Green Gables. Lucy Maud Montgomery, who wrote the classic in 1908, used her childhood home of **Cavendish** (see Chapter 19) as an inspiration for the young girl who comes to live on a farm in the village of Avonlea. Tens of thousands of fans visit Montgomery-related sites annually, including **Green Gables House,** Montgomery's cousin's farm and the principal setting for the book.

Beyond Charlottetown and Cavendish, don't expect dramatic scenery and stunning natural wonders. Instead, you will be greeted by a gently rolling landscape of cultivated fields surrounded by stark red cliffs that drop into blue ocean. Many of the island's most scenic byways, like coastal Route 14 through **Prince County** (see Chapter 20) are unassuming rural roads. Route 2 leads west from Charlottetown through the pretty farmland of Prince County to **North Cape,** a remote point of land jutting into the Gulf of St. Lawrence.

More bucolic scenery is found in **Kings County** (see Chapter 21), especially south from Route 2. This highway provides access to **Prince Edward Island National Park,** protecting a long sliver of the island's northern coastline that extends west to Cavendish.

Scheduling Your Time

Even though being flexible with your time is fun, it's also important to have at least an idea of where you want to go before striking out across the Maritimes. I've laid out some specific itineraries in Chapter 4, which you can combine with the tips laid out below to create a travel strategy that works best for your own interests and needs.

✔ **Establishing a base.** The vast majority of visitors arriving by air touch down at **Halifax International Airport,** and you should plan on doing the same. Just a short drive (or cab ride) to the region's largest city, the airport is the terminus of flights from across the continent and beyond. If you only have a few days in the region, Halifax is a good base for day trips that could include Peggy's Cove, Lunenburg and Annapolis Royal.

✔ **Deciding whether to drive or fly.** Distances are such that driving is the best way of getting around the Maritimes. From Halifax, it's only a two-hour to New Brunswick, four hours to the farthest point of Prince Edward Island, and five hours to Cape Breton Highlands National Park.

✔ **If your time is limited.** As you will see from the itineraries in Chapter 4, it's possible to hit the highlights in one week, but don't try to fit too much in. Make all accommodation reservations in advance to save wasting time each afternoon and schedule at least one multi-night stop.

✔ **Consider arriving and departing from different airports.** The way airfares are structured these days, there is no real penalty in purchasing two one ways fares. Rental car drop-off charges may be worthwhile when factoring in the time saved in not backtracking.

✔ **Try and avoid cities during the week and resort towns on weekends.** This advice is especially apt in July and August, when locals escape the city for resort areas such as St. Andrews and Cavendish.

Knowing the Secrets of the Seasons

Sure, it may be bright and sunny in one part of the region while raining in another, but as a whole, the Maritimes are under the influence of a single weather pattern whose biggest influencing factor is the Atlantic Ocean. In spring, the cold ocean water creates a lag in the warming of land. In fall, the opposite occurs, as the warmth from the ocean delays the onset of cooler temperatures by a few weeks.

Each of the four seasons is very distinct. Summer is far and away the most pleasant time of year to visit. Unfortunately, the vast majority of visitors and local residents take advantage of this season — more visitors arrive in July and August than during the rest of the year combined.

If possible, plan your trip for either late June or early September. Most attractions are already (or are still) open, the crowds are thinner, and lodgings offer discount prices. If you were to ask me which of these two times of year I prefer, I'd do what all good politicians do and sit on the fence, suggesting I like June for the long hours of daylight and September for the fall colors.

Handy weather information is provided on the following government Web sites:

- ✔ **Environment Canada** (www.weatheroffice.ec.gc.ca) maintains this website with a database of forecasts from across Canada.

- ✔ **Environment Canada Atlantic Region** (www.ns.ec.gc.ca) features general information, such as storm forecasts and details on the hurricane season.

- ✔ **Canadian Hydrographic Service** (www.charts.gc.ca) displays tide charts for the Bay of Fundy.

- ✔ **Marine Services On-Line** (www.marineservices.gc.ca) provides a log of marine forecasts.

The following table shows the average daytime temperatures and precipitation levels in Halifax, which gives you a rough idea for the Maritimes as a whole.

Table 3-1	Halifax's Temperature and Precipitation	
Month	*Daytime Mean Temperature*	*Total Monthly Precipitation*
January	-5°C (22°F)	147 mm (5.8 in)
February	-6°C (21°F)	119 mm (4.7 in)
March	-2°C (29°F)	121 mm (4.8 in)
April	4°C (39°F)	124 mm (4.9 in)
May	9°C (49°F)	111 mm (4.4 in)
June	15°C (59°F)	99 mm (3.9 in)
July	18°C (65°F)	96 mm (3.6 in)
August	18°C (65°F)	109 mm (4.3 in)
September	14°C (57°F)	94 mm (3.7 in)
October	11°C (47°F)	130 mm (5.1 in)
November	3°C (38°F)	155 mm (6.2 in)
December	-3°C (27°F)	168 mm (6.6 in)

As a general rule, the farther inland you go, the greater the temperature differential over the year. For example, Moncton has a hotter average July temperature than Halifax but is generally colder than Halifax in winter.

Spring

As the long days of spring begin to warm the land, the snow melts quickly, giving way to fresh growth and a certain feeling of optimism in the air.

Spring is wonderful because:

- ✔ The crowds of summer have yet to arrive.
- ✔ Gardens are in full bloom.
- ✔ Days are long, with up to 16 hours of daylight.

But this season can also have its drawbacks, such as:

- ✔ Foggy days, especially along the Nova Scotia coast and the Bay of Fundy
- ✔ A lot of rain, especially on Cape Breton Island
- ✔ Cool temperatures that rule out swimming in the ocean or sunbathing

Summer

The climate from mid-June onward makes travel comfortable throughout the Maritimes. Locals and visitors alike take full advantage of long hours of daylight and temperatures that often reach 30°C (86°F). Sea breezes and moderate temperatures along the coast create an agreeable temperature range.

Summer is the busiest travel season for the following reasons:

- ✔ July and August are the sunniest and warmest months.
- ✔ The Maritimes come alive with outdoor activities and festivals.

However, keep these points in mind:

- ✔ Crowds are at their peak.
- ✔ Prices are at their highest and lodging reservations must be made well in advance.

What time is it?

All three provinces are on **Atlantic Standard Time** (AST), which is one hour ahead of Eastern Standard Time, two hours ahead of Central Standard Time, three hours ahead of Mountain Standard Time, and four hours ahead of Pacific Standard Time.

Clocks are moved forward one hour for **Daylight Saving Time** on the first Sunday in April. They are turned back on the last Sunday in October. Starting in 2007, daylight saving will be extended by one month, with clocks being moved forward one hour on the second Sunday in March and turned back on the first Sunday in November.

Fall

The ocean climate creates relatively warm temperatures, prolonging fall in the Maritimes. The famous colors begin appearing in mid-September and often linger well into October.

Fall is a favorite time of year because:

- ✔ Temperatures remain pleasant well into October.
- ✔ Turning leaves put on an incredible display of color.
- ✔ Crowds thin out dramatically.
- ✔ Lodging rates are discounted.

But remember:

- ✔ Many summer-only lodgings begin closing in September, and attractions shorten their operating hours.
- ✔ Daylight hours become shorter.
- ✔ You can get caught up in the tail end of a hurricane (like Juan, which hit Halifax in late Sept 2003, leaving 300,000 people without power).
- ✔ Come October, there's a distinct chill in the air.

Winter

When winter hits the Maritimes, it does so with a vengeance, dumping up to 300 centimeters (118 inches) of snow on some areas in a single season. The biggest 24-hour snowfall recorded in Halifax was in 1960, when 96 centimeters (38 inches) fell.

Winter is wonderful for the following reasons:

- ✔ Crowds are nonexistent.
- ✔ Airlines lower their prices and hotels offer discounted rooms.
- ✔ Winter temperatures are moderated by the Atlantic Ocean.
- ✔ The snow is great for cross-country skiing.

Keep the following in mind, however:

- ✔ Most outdoor attractions are closed.
- ✔ Blizzards can make driving dangerous.
- ✔ Daylight hours are short.

Hitting the Big Events: A Maritimes Calendar

The Maritimes calendar is brimming over throughout summer, so I've focused my efforts there to give you the cream of the crop. However, the other seasons also offer their own special taste of Maritimes culture: Spring and fall bring various festivals and events to the region, while winter is trade show and exhibition time.

The following major annual events are just the tip of the iceberg. Local and regional events take place around the region on a weekly basis, so check individual provincial tourism Web sites (see Appendix) for more information.

May

Nova Scotia

One of the province's most colorful events (literally) is the **Truro Tulip Festival.** Look for tours of private and public gardens, a tulip-themed art display, and an antique fair. Middle week of May. For details, call ☎ 902-895-9258 or visit www.nstulips.com.

Prince Edward Island

Festival Port-Lajoie de Charlottetown is a gathering of Acadian musicians from around Atlantic Canada at venues as varied as the bandstand at Peake's Quay to the ballroom of the Delta Hotel. Second week in May. Call ☎ 902-368-1895 or visit www.festivalacadiendecharlottetown.ca for a schedule and ticket details.

June

Nova Scotia

The **Nova Scotia International Tattoo** is not what you might think. It has nothing to do with body art, but instead brings together military and civilian marching bands for what is billed as the world's largest indoor show. In Halifax over 10 days starting on the last Friday in June. Call ☎ 800-563-1114 or visit www.nstattoo.ca.

July

Virtually every town and city across the Maritimes holds **Canada Day** (July 1) celebrations. The typical schedule may include a free breakfast in the morning, a parade at midday, musicians performing on outdoor stages during the afternoon and evening hours, and finally, a fireworks display. Contact the local information center in the town you plan to visit to see what's going on.

Nova Scotia

The biggest Maritimes music gathering, the **Stan Rogers Folk Festival** (best known as "Stanfest"), is hosted by one of the region's most remote towns, Canso. Over 10,000 fans gather for outdoor performances of all genres by Canada's leading musicians, with Celtic music getting an extra-special welcome. First weekend in July. Call ☎ **888-554-7826** or visit www.stanfest.com for details.

New Brunswick

Shediac Lobster Festival: The name alone is tempting. A local tradition for over half a century, it's a culinary salute to the Maritimes' best-known delicacy. You can enjoy the nightly lobster supper, or compete for prizes in the lobster-eating competition. Kids will love the parade, themed especially for them, as well as appearances by Mr. Lobster, the event mascot. Second week of July. Call ☎ **506-532-1122** or visit the Web site at www.lobsterfestival.nb.ca.

The **Loyalist Heritage Festival** commemorates the founders of Saint John, who came to Canada in 1783. Highlights include an outdoor mock court proceeding and a parade of floats filled with costumed performers. Third weekend of July. Call ☎ **506-632-9018** or go to www.loyalistheritage festival.com for information.

The **New Brunswick Highland Games & Scottish Festival** centers on the grounds of Old Government House in Fredericton. Pipe bands, highland dancing, and heavy-duty sports events like caber-tossing are all sched-uled. Late July. Call ☎ **888-368-4444** or visit www.nbhighlandgames.ca.

Prince Edward Island

Historic St. Mary's Church in Indian River provides the perfect setting for the **Indian River Festival.** Various types of music — chamber ensembles, Celtic, jazz, and more — are featured every Friday and Sunday evening through July and August. Call ☎ **902-836-4933** or visit www.indianriver festival.com for a schedule.

August
Nova Scotia

Hundreds of enthusiasts gather at Mahone Bay for the **Wooden Boat Festival.** Boat-building demonstrations and finished boats cover the Town Wharf, while the harbor is filled with wooden boats of all shapes and sizes. Races take place across the weekend, including the Fast and Furious event, in which teams of two are given just four hours to build their craft. First weekend of August. Call ☎ **902-624-0348** or log on to www.woodenboatfestival.org for details.

The following weekend, the action takes place just down the road at the **Lunenburg Folk Harbour Festival.** Expect traditional and contemporary performances in various venues, including the local Opera House and a downtown gazebo. For details, call ☎ **902-634-3180,** or check out www.folkharbour.com.

Digby Scallop Days celebrate Digby's most famous export. The fun includes scallop-shucking demonstrations and competitions, a parade of scallop boats and, of course, the crowning of the Scallop Queen. Early August. Contact the town office for information, ☎ **888-463-4429**, www.townofdigby.ns.ca.

New Brunswick

Moncton's **Atlantic Seafood Festival** features celebrity chefs from around the world — whose cooking lives up to their fame. Seafood tasting and demonstrations take place at various city venues, along with a Saturday night Cajun street party and a Sunday cooking competition. Middle week of August. Check www.atlanticseafoodfestival.com or call ☎ **866-584-8585** for information.

For over 100 years, Acadians have celebrated their heritage and rich culture on August 15, but it wasn't until 2003 that **National Acadian Day** was officially recognized by federal and provincial governments. Look for celebrations in downtown Saint John and Moncton.

Prince Edward Island

The first weekend in August, the annual **Oyster Festival** is in full swing across the island at Tyne Valley. The crowd is at its loudest during the Canadian Oyster Shucking Championships. Call ☎ **902-831-2848** for information.

The **L.M. Montgomery Festival** in Cavendish celebrates the life of PEI's best-known author. Join a writing workshop on the grounds of Green Gables, enjoy strawberries and ice cream in the garden of Montgomery's childhood home, or have your children participate in a coloring competition at Avonlea School. Second weekend in August. For details, go to www.lmmontgomeryfestival.com.

September

Nova Scotia

New Scotland Days commemorate the arrival of Pictou's first settlers, who traveled from Scotland aboard the *Hector*. Activities include woodworking demonstrations, walking tours, a children's art center, a re-enactment of the arrival of the *Hector,* and a dockside *ceilidh* (a traditional Celtic celebration of singing and dancing). Second weekend of September. Call ☎ **902-485-6057** or go to www.townofpictou.com for details.

New Brunswick

Fredericton's biggest annual event is the **Harvest Jazz & Blues Festival.** Musicians take over downtown, performing on dozens of stages, both indoors and out. Second week in September. Call ☎ **506-454-2583** or visit www.harvestjazzandblues.com.

Prince Edward Island

The **PEI International Shellfish Festival,** centered on the Charlottetown waterfront, is a good place to watch the world's fastest oyster shuckers compete in various events. For C$15 (US$XX) you can give it a go yourself with a dozen oysters and the guidance of a pro. Other event highlights include the International Chowder Championship and boat tours to the shellfish grounds. Third weekend in September. Call ☎ 902-892-0420 or go to www.peishellfish.com for all the details.

October

Nova Scotia

The **Windsor–West Hants Pumpkin Festival** is a crowd-pleasing event that includes a pumpkin weigh-off (first Sat in Oct), where winning weights regularly top 450 kilograms (1,000 pounds), and a "boat" race (second Sun in Oct) where participants compete in huge half pumpkins with the insides scooped out. Call ☎ 902-798-9440 for details, or visit www.worldsbiggestpumpkins.com for a schedule and photos of last year's winners.

Cows and cowboys may seem out of place in Halifax, but the country comes to this port city for the annual **Maritime Fall Fair.** Children will love the Kid's Corral, the Super Dogs, and the large midway. Second week of October. Call ☎ 902-876-1811 or go to www.maritimefallfair.com for a schedule of events.

With the stunning colors of fall as a backdrop, Celtic musicians from around the world descend on Cape Breton Island for the **Celtic Colours International Festival.** Performances take place in bandstands, town halls, and theaters at over 40 island towns. Second week of October. Call ☎ 888-355-7744 or 902-567-3000, or visit www.celtic-colours.com.

New Brunswick

The combination of celebrity chefs and local seafood makes the **Fundy Food Festival** a favorite with foodies. It's hosted at venues through Saint John on the fourth Sunday in October. Call ☎ 506-672-3731 or go to www.fundyfoodfestival.com for details.

November

Nova Scotia

The **Atlantic Christmas Fair,** held at Halifax's Exhibition Park, features over 400 booths filled with antiques and the work of Nova Scotian artisans. First weekend of November. For details, call ☎ 902-463-2561. Similar events take place throughout November across the province, including **Christmas by the Sea,** also the first weekend of November, along the Pictou waterfront.

New Brunswick

The **Silver Wave Film Festival** takes place at various theaters around Fredericton. It focuses primarily on New Brunswick filmmakers, but additional international films fill out a busy screening schedule. Early November. Call ☎ **506-455-1632** or visit www.swfilmfest.com.

The **World Wine & Food Expo,** at the Moncton Coliseum, attracts a blend of connoisseurs and ordinary folks looking to learn more about the world's favorite drink. More than 150 wineries participate, while seminars and foodie shows add to the mix. First weekend in November. Call ☎ **866-846-9463** or 506-532-5333, or visit www.wineexpo.ca.

Prince Edward Island

The **Charlottetown Christmas Parade** is the biggest in Atlantic Canada. It starts downtown at 1 p.m. on the last Saturday in November.

December

Prince Edward Island

Most cities in the Maritimes organize some sort of family-oriented celebration for New Year's Eve. Charlottetown hosts one of the biggest draws, **Capital New Year in the Park,** with lots of games, sleigh rides, and a group countdown to midnight in Victoria Park.

Table 3-2	Public Holidays
Date	*Name*
January 1	New Year's Day
March/April	Good Friday and Easter Monday
Monday preceding May 25	Victoria Day
July 1	Canada Day
First Monday in August	Civic Holiday
First Monday in September	Labor Day
Second Monday in October	Thanksgiving
November 11	Remembrance Day
December 25	Christmas Day
December 26	Boxing Day

Chapter 4

Following an Itinerary: Four Great Trips

● ●

In This Chapter

▶ Hitting the highlights in one week
▶ Exploring the Maritimes in two weeks
▶ Doing the Maritimes with the family
▶ Taking a seafood-themed sojourn

● ●

*E*ven though the Maritimes comprise Canada's three smallest provinces, you can't expect to see everything in a single trip. If you have a specific destination or activity in mind, such as visiting Cape Breton Island for the Celtic Colours International Festival or golfing on Prince Edward Island, then you're well on your way to planning your trip. For those of you who are still pondering the best way to spend your time or which route you should take, this chapter's for you. I'll suggest some itineraries to give you an idea of where you can go and what you can see in the time you have, as well as a trip geared toward families and another specifically designed for seafood lovers.

For each itinerary, I take the liberty of assuming you're flying into Halifax, the transportation hub of the Maritimes, and then renting a vehicle.

Seeing the Maritimes in One Week

If you have one week, you can visit each of the three provinces — but only to hit the highlights.

On **Day 1,** after arriving in **Halifax** (see Chapter 11), plan on making your first stop **Halifax Citadel National Historic Site.** Then wander down to the harbor and enjoy lunch at **Salty's.** Spend the early afternoon browsing the **Historic Properties** or taking in the **Maritime Museum of the Atlantic.** Drive to **Lunenburg** (see Chapter 12), stopping at **Peggy's Cove** to snap the famous **lighthouse** picture without the maddening midday crowds. Spend the night at the **Lunenburg Arms Hotel,** dining in-house on the patio at **Rissers.**

On **Day 2,** strike out early from Lunenburg and cut across southwestern Nova Scotia to **Digby,** walking the docks and then enjoying a scallop lunch at the **Fundy Restaurant.** Catch the ferry across the **Bay of Fundy** to **Saint John** (see Chapter 16). Spend the night at the **Homeport Historic Bed and Breakfast** and ask your friendly hosts for a dinner recommendation.

On the morning of **Day 3,** head north from Saint John to **Moncton** (see Chapter 15). If your mid-morning arrival corresponds with the incoming tide (check at the information center), hang around for the **tidal bore.** Continue north to **Shediac.** Take a dip in the Canada's warmest ocean water at **Parlee Beach.** Cross **Confederation Bridge** to **Prince Edward Island** and continue to **Charlottetown** (see Chapter 18). Dinner at the **Lucy Maud Dining Room,** a couple of drinks at **Peake's Quay,** and a bed at the **Shipwright Inn** are an ideal combination for your first night on the island.

On **Day 4,** drive north from Charlottetown to **Cavendish** (see Chapter 19). Visit the grounds of **Green Gables House** and select other "Anne" attractions; then spend the afternoon at your leisure — maybe exploring adjacent **Prince Edward Island National Park** or golfing at **Green Gables Golf Course.** Skip Cavendish's touristy restaurants and enjoy dinner in nearby North Rustico at the **Blue Mussel Café,** then retire to **Kindred Spirits Country Inn.**

Begin **Day 5** by driving to **Wood Islands** for the ferry trip to **Caribou.** Stop at **Pictou** (see Chapter 13) and visit **Hector Heritage Quay.** Jump aboard Highway 104 and cross Canso Causeway to **Cape Breton Island** (see Chapter 14). Continue along Highway 105 to **Baddeck.** Spend the night at the **Water's Edge Inn.**

On **Day 6,** rise early for the spectacular drive through **Cape Breton Highlands National Park** to **Pleasant Bay,** where you have a mid-morning whale-watching tour booked. Continue along the **Cabot Trail** and take lunch at the **Chowder House** in **Neil's Harbour.** Spend the rest of the afternoon leisurely making your way down the coast to **Glenghorm Beach Resort.**

On **Day 7,** take an early-morning walk along **Ingonish Beach,** or rise at your leisure and begin driving the final stretch of the Cabot Trail to **Baddeck.** Visit the **Alexander Graham Bell National Historic Site,** then enjoy lunch at an outside table at the **Lakeside Café.** Leave the island and stay overnight at **Truro** (see Chapter 13), which is an hour's drive from Halifax International Airport.

Exploring the Maritimes in Two Weeks

On **Day 1,** fly into **Halifax** and spend the remainder of that day along with **Day 2** enjoying Nova Scotia's capital. Chapter 11 provides a detailed sightseeing plan for Halifax.

On **Day 3**, head south from Halifax to **Lunenburg** (see Chapter 12), stopping at **Peggy's Cove** and **Mahone Bay** along the way. That gives you plenty of time to visit the **Fisheries Museum of the Atlantic** and to wander the streets before checking into one of Lunenburg's historic inns.

The destination on **Day 4** is **Shelburne**, an easy two-hour drive from Lunenburg, so rise at your leisure — but be sure to hit the road in time to reach Shelburne's **Charlotte Lane Café** for lunch. Spend some time along the waterfront, watching boat-builders at work. Leave Shelburne and continue south to **Whispering Waves Cottages**, where you can order a lobster dinner delivered to your oceanfront cabin.

On **Day 5**, continue around the coast of southwestern Nova Scotia to La Côte Acadienne, where Acadian traditions live on in the cooking at **Rapure Acadienne** and in the imposing architecture of **Église de Sainte-Marie**. Continue along the Fundy Coast, explore the **Digby** waterfront, and step aboard the *Lady Vanessa* to see what a scallop boat looks like up close. Pick up fresh seafood from **O'Neil's Fundy Fish Market**, then check into the **Mountain Gap Inn** where you can cook up a storm on one of the supplied barbeques.

Plan on catching the first ferry of the morning on **Day 6**, crossing the Bay of Fundy to **Saint John** (see Chapter 16) with enough time to go through the **New Brunswick Museum** before lunching at **Market Square**. Continue down the coastline to **St. Andrews**. It's easy to soak up the village's bustling resort atmosphere by walking along the main street (although if you're staying at the upscale **Inn on the Hiram Walker Estate**, you may not want to leave the grounds).

On **Day 7**, drive to **Fredericton** (see Chapter 17) and join a guided walking tour of downtown sights such as the **Garrison Historic District**; then spend an hour or so on your own exploring the leafy downtown streets of the provincial capital. From Fredericton, follow the **Miramichi River** north to **Miramichi** and hang a right down the **Acadian Coast** (see Chapter 15). With a room booked in **Bouctouche** at **Bellevue sur mer**, you should have time for a beach walk along neighboring **Bouctouche Dune**.

On **Day 8**, take a dip in the warm water off **Parlee Beach** before crossing the **Confederation Bridge** to **Prince Edward Island**. Spend the afternoon catching up with your childhood memories at **Green Gables House** in Cavendish (see Chapter 19). Spend the night in a room overlooking **Rustico Bay** at **Barachois Inn**. Nearby, **Fisherman's Wharf Lobster Suppers** is a good choice for a casual dinner.

Arrive in **Charlottetown** (see Chapter 18) early on **Day 9**, and park at the waterfront information center. A good starting point for exploring Charlottetown is **Province House**, in the heart of the historical precinct. Enjoy a seafood lunch at **Water Prince Corner Shop**, knowing you'd be paying a lot more for the same dishes elsewhere. **Rodd Brudenell River** (see Chapter 21) is a world away from the capital but is easily reached in well under an hour. Make the most of long summer days by fitting in a round of golf at one of the resort's two courses.

On **Day 10,** catch the ferry to **Caribou** and spend the rest of the morning at **Hector Heritage Quay** in **Pictou** (see Chapter 13). Leave Pictou for **Cape Breton Island** (see Chapter 14) and **Baddeck.** Check into the **Dunlop Inn,** and then walk over to the **Alexander Graham Bell National Historic Site.** Have dinner at the **Lynwood Inn Dining Room.**

The next morning, **Day 11,** drive to **Ingonish.** You have two nights here; choose **Glenghorm Beach Resort** for its casual beachside atmosphere, or the **Keltic Lodge** for its historic grandeur. Spend the rest of the day at your leisure, taking a trip with **North River Kayak Tours,** golfing at **Highland Links,** or just doing absolutely nothing at all down on the beach.

Day 12 is a good one. Rise early to beat the crowds along the **Cabot Trail** in **Cape Breton Highlands National Park.** Drive all the way through the park — stopping at lookouts, maybe doing a short hike or two (the Skyline Trail if you're energetic, Benjie's Lake Trail if it's foggy); take a whale-watching tour at Pleasant Bay, and just generally soak up the magnificent scenery. The turnaround point is **Chéticamp.** Back in Ingonish, dine on creative seafood at **Seascapes Restaurant.**

On **Day 13,** drive back to **Halifax** (443km/275 miles). This is the longest day's drive in this itinerary, but it will get you back to your starting point the night before your flight leaves (and give you a few extra hours to shop in Halifax). Book a room at the **Airport Hotel Halifax** for an early morning flight, or downtown at the centrally located **Waverley Inn** for last-minute shopping.

On **Day 14,** catch your plane home.

Enjoying the Maritimes with Kids

The attractions and activities incorporated into this itinerary are designed to appeal to traveling families — a combination of learning experiences and fun times at a leisurely pace. Like the first itinerary, it spans seven days.

As with the first two itineraries, **Day 1** starts in Halifax (see Chapter 11). After getting oriented, plan on lunch at the **Harbourside Market,** where everyone can choose their favorite food (seafood, pizza, and so on). Start your vacation off with a splash on a **Harbour Hopper Tour.** If the weather is colder, head to the **Museum of Natural History,** which has a critter-filled nature center. Drive south to **Mahone Bay** (see Chapter 12) and spend the night at the family-friendly **Ocean Trail Retreat.**

On **Day 2,** visit **Lunenburg** (see Chapter 12), and then backtrack through Halifax to Highway 102, reaching **Hopewell Rocks** (see Chapter 16) by mid-afternoon. This natural attraction has to be explored at low tide; if it's high tide when you arrive, you will need to wait till the following morning. From Hopewell Rocks, drive through **Pictou** (see Chapter 13) to **Pictou Lodge Resort,** where the beach and water sports will keep everyone busy for the rest of the day.

On **Day 3,** catch the ferry to **Prince Edward Island.** It's a one-hour trip, which is enough time to find your way to the upper observation deck and award a prize to the first one in your family to spot the red-and-white lighthouse beside the ferry dock at **Wood Islands** (see Chapter 21). Stop at **Rossignol Estate Winery** for a bottle of island wine, and enjoy it on the deck of your cabin at **Lakeview Cottages** in **Cavendish** (see Chapter 19) while the kids burn off energy in the playground.

On **Day 4,** children (and many grown-ups) familiar with *Anne of Green Gables* will want to spend a full morning at **Green Gables House.** Pick one of the many surrounding commercial attractions for an afternoon of fun — **Avonlea** for Anne fans, **Rainbow Valley** for the under-12's, or **Sandspit** for the older kids. Spend another night in Cavendish.

Day 5 kicks off with a rural drive to **Charlottetown** (see Chapter 18). For a bit of history, a visit to Founders' Hall is a must, while animal lovers may enjoy a trip searching out seals with **Peake's Wharf Boat Tours**. Stop at **Gateway Village** (see Chapter 20) to pick up last-minute souvenirs before crossing **Confederation Bridge** and heading up New Brunswick's **Acadian Coast** (see Chapter 15) to the **Rodd Miramichi River** at **Miramichi.**

Day 6 mixes nature and fun. Take the boardwalk through **Kouchibouguac National Park** to reach a remote stretch of beach with water warm enough for swimming, and then jump back in the car to head to **Moncton.** Let the kids go crazy at **Magic Mountain Water Park,** and then retire to one of the surrounding family-friendly motels, such as **Holiday Inn Express Hotel & Suites.**

On **Day 7,** it's an easy three-hour drive back to Halifax. Depending on your flight time, stagger the drive with a stop to watch the **Tidal Bore** in **Truro** (see Chapter 13) or a visit to **Shubenacadie Wildlife Park.** If your flight doesn't depart until early the next day, make reservations at the **Airport Hotel Halifax.**

Cruising the Coast: In Search of Seafood

Even die-hard seafood lovers like myself might not be able to keep up with the following one-week itinerary word for word. It's designed for true devotees of the ocean and all it offers up. But even if you're not a seafood fanatic, this itinerary will give you some ideas for taking advantage of the Maritimes' best-loved export.

Day 1 begins by heading north from Halifax along the **Eastern Shore** (see Chapter 13). Make your first stop the **Fisherman's Life Museum** in **Jeddore Oyster Pond.** In **Tangier,** drop by **J. Willy Krauch & Sons** to stock up on smoked salmon. If the weather is good, take a stroll along the beach in **Taylor Point Provincial Park** before continuing on to the **Salmon River House Country Inn,** where you dine at the in-house **Lobster Shack.**

On **Day 2,** take Highway 7 to **Antigonish,** then cross to **Cape Breton Island** (see Chapter 14) via the Canso Causeway. At **Baddeck,** check into **Bethune's Boathouse Cottage.** Wander along the waterfront for an afternoon sailing trip aboard the *Elsie,* returning to shore in time for dinner at **Baddeck Lobster Suppers.**

Day 3 starts out with a short drive along St. Ann's Bay to **Ingonish.** Have some cash on hand for mussels and crab at the **Muddy Rudder,** a unique outdoor restaurant where you can watch your lunch being boiled to order. Then hit the fairways of **Highland Links.** An evening walk to **Middle Head** is a perfect way to walk off dinner from the **Atlantic Restaurant.** Spend the night at the **Keltic Lodge.**

Spend the morning of **Day 4** driving the famous **Cabot Trail** through **Cape Breton Highlands National Park.** Wander down to the docks in **Chéticamp** to watch crab boats unloading their precious catch. Head to the **Restaurant Acadian** for a feast of *Croquettes de Morue* (cod fish cakes) served by women in traditional Acadian dress. From Chéticamp, drive to **Pictou** (see Chapter 13). Learn about the traditions of fishing at the **Northumberland Fisheries Museum,** and spend the night in a waterfront room at the **Consulate Inn.**

Day 5 starts with a ferry trip to **Prince Edward Island.** Drive through **Kings County** (see Chapter 21) and catch a tour boat from **Montague** to visit a large **seal colony,** or take a **kayak tour** at Brudenell River **Provincial Park.** Plan on enjoying the most formal meal of your trip (tuck into Malpeque Bay oysters to start, then get serious with the seared Atlantic salmon) and a comfortable night's rest at **Dalvay-by-the-Sea.**

Rise early on **Day 6** for the drive to **Shediac** (see Chapter 15) and book a lobster-fishing trip with **Shediac Bay Cruises.** After the traps are hauled up, the lobsters are boiled for an onboard feast. On the way out of town, have someone snap a shot of you in front of the world's biggest lobster. Drive to **Saint John** and cross the **Bay of Fundy,** then drive along **Digby Neck** (see Chapter 12) to **Brier Island Lodge.**

On **Day 7,** plan on taking an early **whale-watching trip,** returning to **Digby** in time to enjoy a dockside take-out lunch of scallops from **O'Neil's Fundy Fish Market.** This gives you plenty of time to either get back to Halifax for an evening flight home, or to drive only as far as **Annapolis Royal** and stay at the **Garrison House,** where the in-house restaurant does wonders with local seafood.

Part II
Planning Your Trip to the Canadian Maritimes

The 5th Wave   By Rich Tennant

In this part . . .

Y ou know you're going to the Canadian Maritimes, you've done some reading, and you have an idea of where you want to travel; now it's time to start the actual planning. This section deals with the different ways to get there, your transportation options once you arrive, the types of lodging options and the rates you can expect to pay, the best ways to deal with your money while on the road, and assorted odds and ends that are easy to ignore — but good to be reminded about.

Chapter 5

Managing Your Money

- -

In This Chapter

▶ Estimating your costs

▶ Uncovering hidden charges

▶ Learning about the loonie

▶ Carrying your money wisely

▶ Coping with a lost or stolen wallet

- -

L et's kick off this tiresome subject with some good news: It costs less to travel in the Maritimes than anywhere else in Canada. If you're from the United States or Europe, throw in a favorable exchange rate, and you have an inexpensive vacation destination.

Prices in this book are listed in both Canadian and U.S. dollars, with all U.S. dollar amounts rounded out to the nearest US10¢. I did my calculations using an exchange rate of US$1 to C$1.15 (or going the other way, C$1 to US85¢).

 Some accommodations and tour companies quote prices in both Canadian and U.S. dollars. This can sometimes work in your favor, other times not, depending on the exchange rate of the day. Where this is the case, I have stuck with my formula of C$1 equals US85¢.

Planning Your Budget

Budgeting for your Maritimes vacation isn't hard, and a few hours spent with pen and paper before leaving home will prevent any surprises.

To come up with the total amount that you plan to spend, begin with transportation costs, starting from your front door. Include flight costs (see Chapter 6 for tips on how to fly for less), airport shuttles at both ends, and car rental. Then add in gas, hotel rates, meals, admissions to attractions, and the cost of activities you want to participate in (whale-watching or golf, for example).

What things cost in the Maritimes

Double room at Halifax's Lord Nelson Hotel ($$$$) on a weekday	C$250 (US$212.50)
Bed-and-breakfast package for two at the Lord Nelson Hotel ($$$$) on a weekend	C$160 (US$136)
Self-contained unit at Lakeview Lodge & Cottages, Cavendish, PEI, in August	C$120 (US$102)
Self-contained unit at Lakeview Lodge & Cottages, Cavendish, PEI, in September	C$70 (US$59.50)
Dorm bed at Halifax Backpacker's Hostel ($)	C$20 (US$17.10)
Dinner for two without drinks, tax, or tips at da Maurizio ($$$$) Halifax	C$120 (US$102)
Lobster dinner for one (including a full lobster, mussels, and dessert) at Baddeck Lobster Suppers, Cape Breton Island	C$27 (US$23)
A six-pack of Moosehead beer	C$12 (US$10.20)
A pint of Alexander Keith's beer	C$6 (US$5.10)
Greens fees at Brudenell River golf course in July	C$65 (US$55.30)
Greens fees *and* accommodations at Brudenell River golf course in October	C$85 (US$72.30)
Adult admission to Fortress of Louisbourg	C$15(US$12.80)
Whale-watching in the Bay of Fundy	C$35 (US$29.80)
Adult admission to Province House, Charlottetown	free

Transportation

Costs for transportation, which will likely be the single largest cost associated with your trip, are easy to estimate. If you're arriving by air, begin with the cost of your plane ticket. Next, add your car rental costs (Chapter 7 deals with these in detail), including the rental itself, taxes, and gas expenses (C$1–C$1.20 per liter/US$2.20–US$2.80 per gallon) for gas, though prices can fluctuate quite dramatically.

If you are planning to fly from province to province, transportation costs will be an even bigger chunk of your budget.

If you're driving your own vehicle, begin by calculating its fuel consumption. To do this:

1. Fill the gas tank and zero the trip odometer.
2. Drive until the tank is nearly empty.
3. Fill the tank again and note the odometer reading.
4. Divide the distance you've driven by the number of gallons (or liters) it took to fill up the second time. This will give you a miles per gallon (or kilometers per liter) amount.

Lodging

Accommodation costs will be the biggest variable in your budget. Where you stay and, to a lesser degree, *when* you stay are the determining factors. Staying midweek at full-service city hotels is going to take a much bigger bite out of your budget than choosing rooms in rural bed-and-breakfasts with shared bathrooms.

In general, rates are at their peak from late June through mid-September. A month on either side is "shoulder season" (intermediate between high and low). The rest of the year is low season, but many bed-and-breakfasts and inns close down completely through the winter. See Chapter 3 for seasonal specifics and Chapter 8 for lodging categories and costs.

In this book, I use dollar signs ranging from $ to $$$$ to express the approximate cost for a double room in high season (excluding taxes). Hostels and some bed-and-breakfasts outside of cities fall into the $ (under C$75/US$63.70) category. (So do many nondescript roadside motels, but I steer clear of those in this book — you can find them easily enough using the Internet or accommodation guides.) Moving into the $$ range, which runs up to C$150 (US$127.50), you have a choice of most bed-and-breakfasts as well as historic inns. In Halifax, the top end of the $$ category will get you a room within walking distance of the harbor. Moving up to the $$$ (C$150–C$225/US$127.50–US$191.30) and $$$$ (C$225/US$127.80 or more) categories, you will find yourself in a fine city hotel or at an upscale oceanfront resort. Very few standard rooms anywhere in the Maritimes cost more than C$250 (US$212.50).

Dining

Seafood dominates the restaurant menus across the Maritimes (for the highlights, see Chapter 1, or "Cruising the Coast: In Search of Seafood" in Chapter 4) and is generally well priced, even in the top restaurants. If you can do without the niceties associated with fine-dining restaurants, seafood is downright inexpensive. When it comes to dishes like lobster, you're really not sacrificing culinary quality by eating at a cheaper restaurant — it doesn't take a master chef to dunk a lobster in boiling water for a few minutes and prepare a side of melted butter.

Do-it-yourself dining

Wander down to the docks at most coastal towns and you'll find a fish market of sorts, selling everything from filleted fish to live lobsters. If you're staying in a self-contained unit, cooking fresh lobster, crab, or mussels is as easy as boiling up a big pot of salted water (okay, mussels are better when steamed with wine, but you get the idea), at a fraction of the price of dining out. Some accommodations keep a supply of pots especially for their lobster-boiling guests. Many resorts and smaller bed-and-breakfast inns have barbeques, allowing you to get a little more creative in your selection of seafood. Expect to pay around C$10–C$12 (US$8.50–US$10.20) per pound for fresh lobster, crab, or scallops, and around half that amount for mussels and clams.

Attractions

Let's face it, the real reason you're traveling to the Maritimes is to see the sights. So it's a good thing they're so affordable; in fact, they'll probably make up the smallest portion of your overall costs. Small town museums often have no admission fee, or else they request a simple donation to cover costs.

 Count on paying around half-price admissions for children and teens up to the age of 16, while entry for children under the age of six is usually free.

 The definition of "child" can drop to as low as 2 years old when that child fills an actual seat (on a tour boat, for example), so you can't always expect a deal.

 If you plan on visiting lots of national parks and historic sites, consider purchasing an annual pass. After all, the Maritimes have five national parks (out of 39 in all of Canada). A day pass costs from C$5–C$6 (US$4.30–$5.10), while entry to each of the Maritimes' 30 national historic sites ranges from C$3.50–C$15 (US$3–US$12.80). With these factors in mind, you can decide which, if any, of the following annual passes best serve your interests:

> ✔ The **National Parks of Canada Pass,** valid for entry to all Canadian national parks, is C$55 (US$46.80) adults, C$47 (US$40) seniors, C$27 (US$23) children aged 6 to 16, to a maximum of C$109 (US$92.70) per family.
>
> ✔ The **National Historic Sites of Canada Pass** is C$43 (US$36.50) adults, C$37 (US$31.50) seniors, C$22 (US$18.70) children aged 6 to 16, to a maximum of C$85 (US$72.30) per family.

✔ The **Discovery Package** combines annual entry to both national parks and national historic sites for one price — C$69 (US$58.70) adults, C$59 (US$50.15) seniors, C$35 (US$29.80) children aged 6 to 16, to a maximum of C$136 (US$115.60) per family.

Passes can be purchased at all national parks and national historic sites. For more information, click through the Planning Your Visit links on the Parks Canada Web site, www.pc.gc.ca.

Activities and tours

Although your costs can start adding up if your tastes run to guided tours and sporting endeavors, the Maritimes provinces are still a relatively inexpensive destination. A four-hour whale-watching tour in the Bay of Fundy, for example, may cost C$35 (US$29.80), but compared to C$80 (US$68) for a similar trip on the west coast of Canada, it's an excellent value. Golfing is another relative bargain: At Highland Links (Cape Breton Island), which is rated one of the world's top 100 courses, twilight greens fees during peak summer season are a steal at C$70 (US$59.50).

 You can save on some tours, golfing, and big-city options like spa treatments if you book them as part of a hotel package. Hotel Web sites are the best place to search out these deals.

Shopping

Shopping can make or break your budget. You can spend anywhere from C$2 (US1.70) on a fridge magnet to well over C$2,000 (US$1,700) for an oil painting. Original artwork aside, you will find plenty to buy that doesn't break the bank (or stick on your fridge).

Nightlife

Keeping your costs down when it comes to after-dark entertainment is easy. In the Maritimes, it's not about what you wear or which is the hippest nightspot. The quintessential night out involves simply relaxing with a pint of beer while listening to traditional Celtic music at a local bar (that doesn't charge a cover).

Tips on tipping

Tipping in the Maritimes is no different from anywhere else in North America. A good standard tip for service providers such as waiters and cab drivers is 15% to 20%. A smaller tip is enough for a beer at a bar, and C$1–C$2 (US85¢–US$1.70) per bag is a sufficient tip for a city hotel bellhop.

In the Maritimes, you can use a very simple method to calculate an average restaurant tip: In Nova Scotia and New Brunswick, leave the same amount as the HST, and in Prince Edward Island, leave double the amount of the GST. Both of these are clearly marked on the bill.

Cutting Costs — but Not the Fun

Want to cut vacation costs without cutting corners? Don't we all. Look for the Bargain Alert icon throughout this book for hints on keeping costs down. In addition, here are some general money-saving tips:

✔ **Go off season.** Outside of the summer (late June through mid-Sept) high season, you'll find hotel prices almost half the price of peak months. But don't push it — many smaller places close down completely in winter.

✔ **Travel mid-week.** If you can travel on a Tuesday, Wednesday, or Thursday, you may find cheaper flights to the Maritimes. When you ask about airfares, see if you can get a cheaper rate by flying on a different day. For more tips on getting a good fare, see Chapter 6.

✔ **Try a package tour.** For many destinations, you can book airfare, hotel, ground transportation, and even some sightseeing just by making one call to a travel agent or packager — and often you'll pay much less than if you put the trip together yourself. (See Chapter 6 for more on package tours.)

✔ **Reserve a room with a kitchen.** Most motels have a few rooms with cooking facilities, or at the very least a fridge and microwave. Buying supplies for breakfast will save you money (and probably calories).

✔ **Always ask for discount rates.** Membership in the Canadian Automobile Association (CAA, or its American counterpart, AAA), frequent-flier plans, trade unions, the American Association of Retired Persons (AARP), or other groups may qualify you for savings on car rentals, plane tickets, hotel rooms, and even meals. Ask about everything; you may be pleasantly surprised.

✔ **Ask if your kids can stay in the room with you.** A room with two double beds usually doesn't cost any more than one with a queen-size bed, and many hotels won't charge you the additional person rate if the additional person is pint-size and related to you. Even if you have to pay C$10 (US$8.50) or $15 (US$12.80) extra for a roll-away bed, you'll save big bucks by not taking two rooms.

✔ **Try expensive restaurants at lunch instead of dinner.** Lunch usually costs a lot less than what dinner would cost at a top restaurant, and the menu often boasts many of the same specialties.

✔ **Get out of town.** In many places, big savings may be just a short drive or taxi ride away. Hotels just outside the city, across the river, or less conveniently located can be great bargains. Outlying motels often have free parking and lower rates than downtown hotels that offer amenities you may never use. Sure, at a motel you'll be carrying your own bags, but the rooms are often just as comfortable and a whole lot cheaper. See Chapter 8 for more on accommodations.

✔ **Don't rent a gas-guzzler.** Renting a smaller vehicle is cheaper, and you save on gas to boot. Unless you're traveling with kids and need a lot of space, don't go beyond the economy size offered by most rental companies. For more on car rentals, see Chapter 7.

✔ **Don't use exchange bureaus.** Exchange bureaus will give unfavorable rates and then add on a commission. Instead, get your Canadian cash at an ATM, which will always give you the exchange rate of the day.

Handling Money

This section describes the Canadian currency, which is similar to that of the United States, only more colorful and with goofier names. Then, I'll look at how you can use the Canadian banking system to get your money or to pay for purchases using your hometown financial institution. Finally, I'll cover what do to if your money or banking cards are lost or stolen.

Making cents of the loonie

Canadian currency is easy to get used to. Coins come in 1-, 5-, 10-, and 25-cent denominations, as well as $1 and $2. The $1 is a gold-colored coin that depicts the loon (a common species of bird), known as the "loonie." The $2 coin has a silver-colored core with a gold-colored rim and is best known as the "toonie." Bills come in the usual denominations of $5, $10, $20, $50, and $100; they're all the same size but vary in color. The $100 bill can sometimes be difficult to cash at smaller businesses or early in the morning, especially if you're only buying something small, like a cup of coffee.

At press time, the Canadian dollar was roughly equal to US85¢, the conversion rate I used throughout this book. However, exchange rates fluctuate often (and sometimes dramatically), so it's always a good idea to check before you go.

 The best online tool I know of for checking exchange rates is the **Universal Currency Converter** at www.xe.com/ucc.

Doting on debit cards

 Using a debit card (also known as an ATM or banking card) is hands-down the easiest way to manage your money while traveling and is extremely popular in Canada (in fact, Canadians are the world's biggest users of this type of banking). You can use your debit card to withdraw cash at ATMs or to pay for purchases at point-of-sale terminals installed at participating merchant locations (over 300,000 in Canada). The national organization responsible for the network in Canada is **Interac** (similar to the **Cirrus** and **Plus** networks elsewhere in the world), so you'll sometimes hear it referred to as "paying by Interac." Before relying solely on debit and ATMs, check with your bank to find out which Canadian banks honor your card system. The following is a list of the major Canadian banks and the system(s) they use:

- ✔ **Bank of Montreal:** Cirrus
- ✔ **Scotiabank:** Plus
- ✔ **Canada Trust:** Cirrus and Plus
- ✔ **CIBC:** Plus
- ✔ **Royal Bank:** Cirrus and Plus
- ✔ **TD Bank:** Plus

Using ATMs

These days, far more people use ATMs than traveler's checks. Most cities have these handy 24-hour cash machines linked to an international network that almost always includes your financial institution back at home. You can use your debit or credit card to withdraw the money you need every couple of days, which eliminates the insecurity of carrying around a large stash of cash. Of course, many ATMs are little money managers (or dictators, depending on how you look at it), imposing limits on your spending by allowing you to withdraw only a certain amount of money per day.

One important reminder before you go ATM crazy, however: Canadian banks charge a fee of up to C$2 (US$1.70) whenever a non-account holder uses their ATMs. Your own bank may also charge a fee for using an ATM that's not one of their branch locations. In some cases, you may get charged twice. Check out your bank's policy before ruling out traveler's checks altogether, since they may be a cheaper — though certainly less convenient — option for you.

Do not use privately owned ATMs. Also known as white-label ATMs, these banking machines are most often placed in gas stations, corner stores, restaurants, and bars. Fees can be up to C$4 (US$3.40) for a single transaction, in addition to the fee your own bank charges. The businesses that install these machines split the "convenience fee" you pay with the machine owners, making a tidy profit for themselves along the way. Because they are money-makers, some businesses don't use point-of-sale terminals, instead forcing you to withdraw cash from one of these privately owned ATMs hidden away in a corner to pay for your purchase.

Charging ahead with credit cards

Credit cards can be invaluable when traveling: They're a safe way to carry money and they provide a convenient record of all your travel expenses when you arrive home. Of course, the disadvantage is that they're easy to overuse. Credit cards let you indulge in a lot more impulse buying than any other form of payment — taking you as far as your credit limit, which may not bear much relation to your actual financial resources.

You can also get cash advances from your credit card at any ATM if you know your *Personal Identification Number* (PIN). If you've forgotten it or didn't even know you had a PIN, call the phone number on the back of your credit card and ask the bank to send the number to you. You'll then have the number in about five to seven business days. Some banks can give you your PIN over the phone if you tell them your mother's maiden name or provide some other security clearance.

 Use your credit card for a cash advance in emergencies only. Interest rates for cash advances are often significantly higher than rates for credit-card purchases. More importantly, you start paying interest on the advance from the moment you receive the cash. On airline-affiliated credit cards, a cash advance doesn't earn frequent-flier miles.

 Keep in mind that when you use your credit card abroad, most banks assess a 2% fee above the 1% fee charged by Visa or MasterCard or American Express for currency conversion on credit charges. But credit cards still may be the smart way to go when you factor in things like exorbitant ATM fees and higher traveler's check exchange rates (and service fees).

 Some credit card companies recommend that you notify them of any impending trip abroad so that they don't become suspicious when the card is used numerous times in a foreign destination and block your charges. Even if you don't call your credit card company in advance, you can always call the card's toll-free emergency number if a charge is refused — a good reason to carry the phone number with you. But perhaps the most important lesson here is to carry more than one card with you on your trip; a card might not work for any number of reasons, so having a backup is the smart way to go.

Toting traveler's checks

Traveler's checks are something of an anachronism from the days when people wrote personal checks instead of going to an ATM. Because traveler's checks could be replaced if lost or stolen, they were a sound alternative to cash, and as long as vendors continue to accept them, they are still a viable option to cash or banking cards. Service charges are fairly low, or even nonexistent if you know where to go.

The best way to ensure a fair rate of exchange is to purchase your traveler's checks in Canadian dollars. You can get Canadian-currency traveler's checks at most major banks and organizations such as AAA. **American Express** offers denominations of $20, $50, $100, $500, and (for cardholders only) $1,000. You'll pay a service charge ranging from 1% to 4%. You can also get American Express traveler's checks over the phone by calling ☎ 800-221-7282; Amex gold and platinum cardholders who use this number are exempt from the 1% fee. **Visa** offers traveler's checks at Citibank locations throughout the United States, as well as at several other banks. The service charge ranges between 1.5% and 2%; checks come in denominations of $20, $50, $100, $500, and $1,000. Call ☎ 800-732-1322 for information. AAA members can obtain Visa checks without a fee at most AAA offices or by calling ☎ 866-339-3378. **MasterCard** also offers traveler's checks. Call ☎ 800-223-9920 for a location near you.

If you choose to carry traveler's checks, be sure to keep a record of their serial numbers separate from your checks in the event that they are stolen or lost. You'll get a refund faster if you know the numbers.

Taking Taxes into Account

Two taxes are added onto almost every purchase and transaction made in the Maritimes. (Notable exceptions include liquor and gas purchases, which have taxes built into the posted price.) These taxes are collected in different ways. Each province applies a **Provincial Sales Tax** on top of the Canada-wide 7% **Goods and Services (GST) Tax.** In Prince Edward Island, the provincial tax is 10%, for a grand total of 17%. In Nova Scotia and New Brunswick, the provincial tax is 8% and is blended with the GST to create what is known as a **Harmonized Sales Tax** (HST) of 15%. So, since most prices you see quoted do not include tax, you must factor in an extra 15% to 17%, depending on the province, to come up with a final price.

The Halifax Regional Municipality collects a 1.5% **Destination Halifax Marketing Levy,** which will be added to your Halifax hotel bill.

Now for the good news, at least for those visiting from outside Canada: HST that is paid in Nova Scotia and New Brunswick, and GST that is paid in Prince Edward Island, is refundable on accommodations and on most consumer goods (not meals or gas) for foreign visitors. Be aware, though, that you must be very organized in order to claim this refund. First and foremost, keep all your receipts and collect a Proof of Export stamp when leaving the country. To qualify for the rebate, purchases must be at least C$50 each and total over C$200 combined. They must also be dated less than 60 days before your departure from Canada. Rebates can be claimed any time within one year from the date of purchase.

Most visitors apply for the rebate at duty-free shops (at the U.S. border or at Halifax International Airport) when exiting the country. Duty-free shops can rebate up to C$500 on the spot. For rebates more than C$500, you'll need to mail a completed GST rebate form directly to Revenue Canada. These forms are available at city hotels and airports, and online from the Web site noted below. If claiming from outside of Canada, you must have receipts (except for accommodations) validated upon leaving Canada. For more information, contact **Canada Revenue Agency ☎ 800-668-4748** or 902-432-5608; `www.cra-arc.gc.ca`.

Dealing with Loss or Theft

While on vacation, there are few events more stressful than losing your wallet. Though you can rarely prevent this from happening, knowing what to do if it does occur can save you a lot of headaches.

Coping with lost credit cards

Most credit card companies have an emergency toll-free number to call if your card is lost or stolen. They may be able to wire you a cash advance immediately or deliver an emergency credit card in a day or two. Make sure you have the numbers with you (but not in your wallet!) so that, if a theft occurs, you can deal with the situation immediately. Check the following Canadian toll-free emergency numbers and note down those that apply to you:

- ✔ **American Express ☎ 800-668-2639**
- ✔ **Diners Club ☎ 800-363-3333**
- ✔ **Discover ☎ 800-347-2683**
- ✔ **MasterCard ☎ 800-307-7309**
- ✔ **Visa ☎ 800-847-2113**

Be sure to contact all of your credit card companies the minute you discover your wallet has been lost or stolen. You'll also want to file a report at the nearest police precinct. Your credit card company or insurer may require a police report number or record of the loss.

If you need emergency cash over the weekend when all banks and American Express offices are closed, you can have money wired to you via **Western Union (☎ 800-325-6000;** `www.westernunion.ca`). Agents are scattered across all three Maritimes provinces; check the Web site for locations.

Losing your identity

Identity theft and fraud are potential complications of losing your wallet, especially if you've lost your driver's license along with your cash and credit cards. Notify the major credit-reporting bureaus immediately; placing a fraud alert on your records may protect you against liability for criminal activity. **Equifax** has offices around the world, including

Canada (☎ **800-465-7166**; www.Equifax.ca) and the United States (☎ **800-766-0008**; www.equifax.com). **Experian** (☎ **888-397-3742**; www.experian.com) and **TransUnion** (☎ **800-680-7289**; www.trans union.com) are two other U.S. agencies. Finally, if you've lost all forms of photo ID call your airline and explain the situation; they might allow you to board the plane if you have a copy of your passport or birth certificate and a copy of the police report you've filed.

Chapter 6

Getting to the Canadian Maritimes

*T*he first steps in vacation planning can be tough. You have to make a lot of commitments early on — and often back them up with your hard-earned money. You probably have questions: Do you want to be totally independent, either because you're a control freak and can't stand even a single detail being out of your hands, or because you're into spontaneity and hate to have things pre-arranged? Will a self-guided or group tour suit your needs? Which tour company will provide the vacation you're dreaming of? Whatever your goals, this chapter will help you break them down and choose what you really want to do.

If you do decide on a tour, how do you find a deal? I suggest some strategies in the next sections, but every embarkation point and destination province is different, and the tour operators I mention may not offer deals convenient to your city. If that's the case, check with a local travel agent, who will likely have a thorough knowledge of your options and how best to bundle packages, such as escorted tours and airline fares.

Flying to the Maritimes

All Canadian and several major U.S. carriers serve Halifax, the main air hub for the Maritimes. You can also fly into Saint John, Moncton, or Charlottetown. With plenty of competition, prices are usually reasonable and sometimes very good.

Halifax International Airport (www.hiaa.ca), the busiest airport in the Maritimes, handles three million passengers annually in two modern terminals. It is served with direct flights by major Canadian and U.S. airlines (Table 6.1 lists them all) from 30 locations. The Web site www.fly halifax.com is an excellent resource that allows you to search for flights to Halifax from specific destinations and also check flight arrival and departure times.

Table 6-1	Airlines Serving Halifax	
Carrier	*Phone*	*Web Site*
Air Canada	☎ 888-247-2262	www.aircanada.ca
Air Canada Jazz	☎ 888-247-2262	www.flyjazz.com
American Eagle	☎ 800-433-7300	www.aa.com
CanJet	☎ 800-809-7777	www.canjet.com
Continental	☎ 800-784-4444	www.continental.com
Delta	☎ 800-221-1212	www.delta.com
Northwest	☎ 800-225-2525	www.nwa.com
WestJet	☎ 888-937-8538	www.westjet.com

The other major airports are **Greater Moncton International Airport** (www.gma.ca), served by Air Canada, CanJet, and WestJet; **Saint John Airport** (www.saintjohnairport.com), served by Air Canada; www.flypanam.com); **Greater Fredericton Airport** (www.fredericton airport.ca), served by Air Canada; and **Charlottetown Airport** (www.charlottetownairport.ca), served by Air Canada and WestJet.

If you're Maritimes-bound from Europe, your flight will be routed through Toronto or Montreal. Flights originating in Asia and the South Pacific will require a plane-change in Vancouver or Toronto.

Now that you know a little about who flies into the Maritimes, it's time to start searching out the best fares. Read the advice below, then use the worksheet titled "Fare Game: Choosing an Airline" located at the back of this book to do some comparison shopping.

Getting the best deal on your airfare

Competition among major airlines is unlike that of any other industry. Every airline offers virtually the same product (basically, a coach seat is a coach seat is a . . .), yet prices can vary by hundreds of dollars.

Business travelers who need the flexibility of last-minute changes, or those who want to get home before the weekend, pay (or at least their companies pay) the premium rate, known as the *full fare*. But if you can book your ticket far in advance, stay over a Saturday night, and are willing to travel with restrictions such as non-changeable flights, you can save big bucks.

Air Canada has taken a leading role in streamlining their fare system, with five options ranging from a nonrefundable, non-changeable Tango ticket to a flexible Latitude Plus ticket. At the time of publication, a Tango one-way fare from Boston to Halifax was US$149, while the full-fare Latitude Plus option was US$589 for the same flight. The difference shows how it pays to be flexible. Go to www.aircanada.com to see more details, and tools that allow you to see easily which days have the least expensive flights.

The airlines also periodically hold sales, in which they lower the prices on their most popular routes. These fares have advance purchase requirements and date-of-travel restrictions, but you can't beat the prices. As you plan your vacation, keep your eyes open for these sales, which tend to take place in seasons of low travel volume, November to March. You almost never see a sale around the peak summer vacation months of July and August, or around Thanksgiving or Christmas, when many people fly regardless of the fare they have to pay.

Buying from a consolidator

Consolidators, also known as bucket shops, buy seats in bulk and sell them to the public at discounted rates. Several reliable consolidators have worldwide locations and are available on the Internet. In the United States, **STA Travel** (☎ **800-781-4040;** www.statravel.com) is a world leader in student travel. The Canadian equivalent is **Travel Cuts** (☎ **866-246-9762;** www.travelcuts.com). In both cases, you don't need to be a student to take advantage of their good fares. **Flight Centre** is a large consolidator with offices around the world and competitive online fares. Flight Centre contacts are: U.S. ☎ **866-967-5351,** www.flightcentre.us; Canada **877-467-5302,** www.flightcentre.ca; and United Kingdom **0870-499-0040,** www.flightcentre.co.uk. London-based **Trailfinders** (☎ **0845-058-5858;** www.trailfinders.com) always has competitive fares to North America, along with easy-to-understand rental car and hotel packages. They also produce an informative travel magazine, or you can sign up for their e-mail service.

Booking your flight online

If you are simply buying a flight from one point to another, you'll find it hard to beat prices that are available online. Searching out the best online airfares can be more time-consuming than using a travel agent, but it gives you more flexibility and you won't be stuck with any additional charges. Most sites prompt you to enter a departure point and destination along with your dates of travel, so if you're not sure of the specifics of your trip, you can play with the variables until you find the best price. The displayed results usually include a number of flight and fare options.

Travel Web sites

The "big three" online travel agencies are **Expedia** (www.expedia.com), **Travelocity** (www.travelocity.com), and **Orbitz** (www.orbitz.com). For travelers already in Canada, try www.expedia.ca or www.travelocity.ca; U.K. residents can go for www.expedia.co.uk. Each has different business deals with the airlines and may offer different fares on the same flights, so shopping around is wise.

Of the smaller travel agency Web sites, **SideStep** (www.sidestep.com) receives good reviews from users. It's a browser add-on that claims to "search 140 sites at once," although in reality it only beats competitors' fares as often as other sites do.

If you're in no rush to book your vacation, you can sign up for sale alerts at some of the major travel Web sites. Two of the big three, Expedia and Travelocity, will send you an e-mail notification when a cheap fare to your favorite destination becomes available.

Opaque-fare services

If you're willing to give up some control over your flight details, use an *opaque fare service* such as **Priceline** (www.priceline.com) or **Hotwire** (www.hotwire.com). Both offer rock-bottom prices in exchange for travel on an airline that will remain unknown to you until you purchase your ticket. Be assured that the "mystery airlines" are all major, well-known carriers, and the possibility of traveling from Detroit to Halifax via Vancouver is remote. On the other hand, your chances of getting a 6 a.m. or 11 p.m. flight are pretty high. Hotwire tells you flight prices before you buy; Priceline usually has better deals than Hotwire, but you have to play their "name our price" game.

Last-minute specials

Great last-minute deals are available through free weekly e-mail services provided directly by the airlines, including **Air Canada** (www.aircanada.ca). Usually, these deals are announced on a Tuesday or Wednesday, and must be purchased online. Most are only valid for travel that weekend, but some can be booked weeks or months in advance. Sign up for weekly e-mail alerts at airline Web sites, or check mega-sites that compile comprehensive lists of last-minute specials, such as **Smarter Travel** (www.smartertravel.com) and **Webflyer** (www.webflyer.com).

Driving to the Maritimes

You can drive to the Maritimes via numerous highways, all of which enter the region through New Brunswick.

- **Trans-Canada Highway,** which takes on different numbers as it crosses the country, enters New Brunswick near Edmundston as Highway 2. Using this route, it's 1,238km (769 miles) from Montreal and 1,757 kilometers (1,092 miles) to Halifax. Planning on driving across Canada via the Trans-Canada Highway? Gas up. It's 6,187 kilometers (3,846 miles) from Vancouver to Halifax.

✔ **Interstate 95** links Portland and Bangor, Maine, with the Maritimes, crossing the Canadian border west of Fredericton at the Houlton/Woodstock crossing.

✔ **Highway 1** winds its way along the Maine coastline to the Calais/St. Stephen border, crossing in the southern corner of New Brunswick. From this point, it's 90km (56 miles) to Saint John, and a little farther to Fredericton.

✔ **Highway 189** branches off Maine's Highway 1,77km (48 miles) south of Calais. It makes for an interesting approach to New Brunswick. At Lubec, it crosses a bridge to Campobello Island, across the border in New Brunswick. From this point, it's a short ferry ride to Deer Island, and then another to reach the mainland. Both ferries are summer-only.

Arriving by Other Means

Though flying is the primary means of getting to the Maritimes, some people enjoy a road trip, or have mobility issues that make flying impossible, or simply prefer not to fly. Here's the lowdown on traveling to the Maritimes by train, bus, and ferry.

Taking the train

VIA Rail (☎ **888-842-7245** or 416-366-8411; www.viarail.ca) operates the *Ocean* between Montreal and Halifax up to six times weekly, with stops in Moncton and Truro en route. The two classes of travel are Comfort (lots of leg room, reclining seats, reading lights, pillows and blankets, and a Skyline Car complete with bar service) and Easterly (daytime seating, nighttime sleeping room, a domed lounge, and a dining car for passengers in this class). The Comfort Class fare between Montreal and Halifax is C$216 (US$183.60), while the fare in Easterly Class is C$513 (US$436). Discounts of up to 35% are applied to bookings made more than seven days in advance. Children, seniors, and students also enjoy discounted travel.

If you're planning extensive rail travel in Canada, VIA Rail's **Canrailpass** may be a worthwhile investment. It allows for unlimited rail travel across Canada for 12 days over any given 30-day period for C$778 (US$661.30) in high season (June–mid-Oct) and C$486 (US$413.10) the rest of the year.

 While the Canrailpass can be a good deal if you plan to do a lot of rail traveling, it comes with a few hitches: If you travel on the Montreal to Halifax service, for example, it counts as two days of travel. So check to see that the routes you plan to take don't make this pass a not-so-smart investment.

Bussing it in

Greyhound (☎ 800-231-2222; www.greyhound.com) operates passenger buses throughout North America, with only a couple of exceptions and one of these is the Maritimes. The good news for bus travelers is that connections from Greyhound to the local carrier Acadian (see Chapter 7) are seamless at gateway cities that include Montreal, Toronto, and Bangor (Maine). You can also catch a Greyhound bus to Bar Harbor, then jump aboard a ferry to Yarmouth (see the following section), and then rely on Acadian buses to get you around Nova Scotia and beyond.

Acadian honors all Greyhound passes. Therefore, if you have a 10-day Canada Discovery Pass (C$399/US$339.20) or a 21-day Eastern CanAm Discovery Pass (US$409), no additional costs will apply to your travels within the three Maritimes provinces. Check the Greyhound Web site for pass options.

Arriving by ferry

A glance at a map will make it obvious that catching a ferry from Maine to Yarmouth, on the southwestern tip of Nova Scotia, will shorten the journey considerably. **Bay Ferries** (☎ 888-249-7245; www.catferry.com) operate a service between Bar Harbor, Maine, and Yarmouth, twice daily in each direction between mid-May and mid-October. It is North America's fastest car ferry, doing the journey in under three hours (a traditional ferry would take twice as long). Sample one-way fares are US$55 adults, US$50 seniors, US$25 children 5 to 17, US$120 for vehicles up to 7m (20 feet) long. Discounts apply in the shoulder season. Due to the convenience of this service, vessels fill fast in summer. Therefore, reservations are strongly recommended.

Joining an Escorted Tour

Say the words "escorted tour" and you may automatically feel as though you're being forced to choose between your money and your lifestyle. Think again. Times — and tours — have changed.

An **escorted tour** does, obviously, involve an escort, but that doesn't mean it has to be constricting. Escorted tours range from cushy bus trips, where you sit back and let the driver worry about the traffic, to adventures that include biking around Prince Edward Island or sea kayaking on Cape Breton Island — situations where most of us could use a bit of guidance. The main point is you travel with a group, which may be just the thing if you're single and want company. In general, your costs are taken care of after you arrive at your destination, but you have to cover your airfare to get there.

Many people love escorted tours. The tour company takes care of all the details and tells you what to expect at each leg of your journey. You know your costs up front and, in the case of the tame tours, you don't get many surprises. Escorted tours can take you to the maximum number of sights in the minimum amount of time with the least amount of hassle.

If you decide to go with an escorted tour, I strongly recommend purchasing travel insurance, especially if the tour operator asks to you pay up front. But don't buy insurance from the tour operator! If the operator doesn't fulfill its obligation to provide you with the vacation you paid for, there's no reason to think that it will fulfill its insurance obligations either. Get travel insurance through an independent agency. (I tell you more about the ins and outs of travel insurance in Chapter 10.)

When considering an escorted tour, find out if you have to put down a deposit, and ask when final payment is due. In addition, there are a few simple questions you should ask before you buy:

✔ **What is the cancellation policy?** Can the operator cancel the trip if not enough people make reservations? How late can you cancel if you are unable to go? Do you get a refund if you cancel? If they cancel?

✔ **How jam-packed is the schedule?** Does the tour schedule try to fit 25 hours into a 24-hour day, or does it give you ample time to shop or relax by the pool? If starting your day at 7 a.m. to pack in 10 to 12 hours of nonstop sightseeing sounds like a grind, certain tours may not be for you.

✔ **How large is the group?** The larger the group, the more time you'll spend waiting for people to get on and off the bus. Tour operators may be evasive about this, because they may not know the exact size of the group until everybody has made reservations, but they should be able to give you a rough estimate.

✔ **Is there a minimum group size?** Some tours have a minimum size, and may cancel if they don't book enough people. If a quota exists, find out what it is and how close the tour operator is to reaching it. Again, operators may be evasive in their answers, but the information can help you select a tour that's sure to happen.

✔ **What exactly is included?** Don't assume anything. You may have to pay to get yourself to and from the airport. A box lunch may be included in an excursion, but drinks could be extra. Beer may be included, but not wine.

✔ **How much flexibility do you have?** Can you opt out of certain activities, or does the bus leave once a day, with no exceptions? Are all your meals planned in advance? Can you choose your entrée at dinner, or does everybody get the same chicken cutlet?

Picking the right escorted tour is a very personal choice. I won't pretend to know what you like, but here are a few reputable companies (in alphabetical order) to get you started:

✔ **Ambassatours** (☎ **800-565-7173** or 902-423-6242; www.atlantic
tours.com) is the Atlantic Canada arm of the Grayline conglomer-
ate. Typical offerings include a three-day Cape Breton Island tour
for C$820 (US$697) and the Atlantic Maritimes tour that hits the hot
spots in each of the three provinces over eight days for C$2,200
(US$1,870).

✔ **Collette Vacations** (☎ **800-340-5158;** www.collettetours.com)
offers many tours that include the Maritimes. The six-day Best of
New Brunswick tour is US$799 per person, and the Atlantic Coastal
Experience hits all three provinces as well as Maine over 11 days
for US$1,699.

✔ **Horizon & Co.** (☎ **800-387-2977** or 416-585-9911; www.horizon-
holidays.com) is a Canadian tour company with an excellent reputation. Expect to pay around C$5,750 (US$4,887.50) for a 14-day, all-
inclusive tour that visits each of the three provinces.

✔ **VBT** (☎ **800-245-3868;** www.vbt.com) offers a seven-day bike tour
of Prince Edward Island for US$1,495. The biking is easy, and
upscale accommodations and all meals are included.

You can also check ads in the travel section of your local Sunday newspaper or in the back of national travel magazines such as *Travel &
Leisure, Outside, National Geographic Traveler,* and *Condé Nast Traveler.*

Choosing a Package Tour

Unlike escorted tours, **package tours** are simply a way to buy the airfare,
accommodations, and other elements of your trip at the same time and
often at a discounted price. Some companies bundle every aspect of your
trip, including tours to various sights, but most deal just with selected
aspects. This allows you to get a good deal by putting together an airfare
and hotel arrangement, say, or a lodging and greens-fee package. Most
packages tend to leave you a lot of leeway, while saving you money.

For the Maritimes, package tours can be a smart way to go. In many
cases, a package tour that includes airfare, hotel, and transportation to
and from the airport costs less than the price of a hotel alone that you
book yourself. That's because packages are sold in bulk to tour operators, who resell them to the public. It's kind of like purchasing your vacation at a bulk store — except the tour operator is the one who buys the
1,000-count box of garbage bags and resells them ten at a time at a cost
that undercuts the local supermarket.

Package tours can vary as much as those garbage bags, too. In a comparison of any two tours, one may offer a better class of hotels for the
same price, or provide the same hotels for a lower price. Some book
seats on scheduled airline flights; others sell charters. In some packages,
your choice of accommodations and travel days may be limited. Some
let you choose between escorted vacations and independent vacations;

others allow you to add on just a few excursions or escorted day trips (also at discounted prices) without booking an entirely escorted tour.

Here are some recommendations (in alphabetical order) for companies offering package tours:

- ✔ **Air Canada** (☎ **888-247-2262;** www.aircanada.ca), Canada's national airline, offers numerous ways to book package tours incorporating Air Canada flights. **Destina.ca** (☎ **800-563-5633** or 514-845-5633; www.destina.ca) is an online travel site with Maritimes package deals; and **Air Canada Vacations** (www.aircanadavacations.com) offers packages that can be booked through travel agents as well as an online search tool for air-car rental combos.

- ✔ **Hillcrest Vacations** (www.hillcrestvacations.com) combines rail travel with car rental and accommodations for independent travelers. Its Web site has details, but bookings must be made through travel agents.

- ✔ **Liberty Travel** (☎ **888-271-1584;** www.libertytravel.com) is one of the biggest packagers in the Northeast. It offers separate package tours to each of the three Maritimes provinces.

- ✔ **Rodd Hotels & Resorts** (☎ **800-565-7633** or 902-892-7448; www.rodd-hotels.ca) is an upscale Maritimes hotel chain with golf and "leisure" packages that usually include breakfast and passes to local attractions.

- ✔ **VIA Rail** (☎ **888-842-7245** or 514-871-6000; www.viarail.ca) and Canadian tour operators combine forces to offer some interesting packages that originate in Toronto and Montreal. Go to www.trainpackages.ca or click on the "Adventure and Outdoor Activities" link on the Web site for details.

- ✔ **WestJet** (☎ **888-937-8538** or 403-250-5839; www.westjet.com) offers its own flights bundled with car rental-hotel packages throughout the Maritimes.

Several big online travel agencies — **Expedia, Travelocity, Orbitz,** and **Site59** — also do a brisk business in packages.

Chapter 7

Getting Around the Canadian Maritimes

In This Chapter

▶ Exploring the Maritimes by car

▶ Taking the ferry

▶ Flying or riding the rails between provinces

So, you know how you're getting *to* the Maritimes: Now you need to know how to get around. This chapter covers driving (really the only way to explore beyond the downtown core of the major cities) as well as two important ferry routes. If you're willing to shell out big bucks, flying between provinces is an option, as is catching the train, although the latter is limited in its options.

Driving Around

Unless you're on an escorted tour, driving is the best way to get around the Maritimes. All you need is a vehicle, a good set of maps, a full tank of gas, and a sense of adventure.

Motoring in the Maritimes is similar to that in other parts of Canada or in the United States. Major thoroughfares are kept in excellent condition, and all towns and minor highways are well marked. Gas stations are regularly spaced — you'll find one in almost every town — so running out of gas won't be a problem if you keep an eye on the gauge. Expect to pay around C$1–C$1.20 per liter (US$2.20–$2.80 per gallon) for gas, though prices can fluctuate quite dramatically.

 Apart from other drivers, the most important thing to watch for on the roads is wildlife, most commonly deer, moose, and bears, especially if you're driving at dawn or dusk. Areas with lots of animal activity are usually signposted, but it is always best to scan both sides of the road just to make sure. In winter, blowing snow and blizzards can make driving extremely dangerous.

Wearing a seat belt is compulsory in Canada, and the fine for not wearing one is steep. Most drivers voluntarily travel with their headlights on at all times; motorcyclists are required by law to ride with their lights on. Traffic in both directions must stop when school buses have their red lights flashing. Pedestrians have the right of way at crosswalks.

Renting a car

The good news is that every major car rental company is represented in the Maritimes, so you can easily shop around for the best deal. The bad news is that demand is high during the peak summer months (mid-June–early Sept), so prices can be high. Rental car companies and their contact numbers and Web sites are listed in the Appendix.

Getting the best deal

Car rental rates vary even more than airline fares. The price depends on the size of the vehicle, the length of time you keep it, where and when you pick it up and drop it off, where you take it, and a host of other factors. The following tips could help save you hundreds of dollars:

✔ Check your rental car company's weekend rates — they may be lower than the weekday rates. If you're keeping the car for five or more days, a weekly rate may be cheaper than the daily rate.

✔ Ask about drop-off conditions: Some companies may add a drop-off charge if you don't return the car to the same rental location.

✔ Rent your vehicle from some place other than the airport. At Halifax International Airport, for example, a Concession Recovery Fee adds 11.7% to all airport rentals. To save this charge, rent a vehicle at one of dozens of downtown agencies.

✔ Find out whether age is an issue. Many car rental companies add on a fee for drivers under 25, while some don't rent to them at all.

✔ If you see an advertised price in your local newspaper, be sure to ask for that specific rate; otherwise, you may be charged the standard (higher) rate. Don't forget to mention membership in AAA, AARP, and trade unions. These memberships usually entitle you to discounts ranging from 5% to 30%.

✔ Check your frequent-flier accounts. Airlines often team up with rental car companies to offer you incentives to use their services. Not only are your favorite (or at least most-used) airlines likely to have sent you discount coupons, but most car rentals add at least 500 air miles to your account.

✔ As with other aspects of planning your trip, using the Internet can make comparison shopping for a car rental much easier. You can check rates at most of the major agencies' Web sites. Plus, all the major travel sites, such as **Travelocity** (www.travelocity.com), **Expedia** (www.expedia.com), **Orbitz** (www.orbitz.com), and **Smarter Travel** (www.smartertravel.com), have search engines that can dig up discounted car-rental rates. Just enter the car size you want, the pickup and return dates, and the location, and the server returns a price. You can even make the reservation through any of these sites.

Adding up the charges

In addition to the standard rental prices, other optional charges apply to most car rentals (along with some not-so-optional charges, such as taxes). The *Loss Damage Waiver* (LDW), which requires you to pay for damage to the car in a collision, is covered by many credit card companies. Check with your credit card company before you go, to see if you can avoid paying this hefty fee (as much as C$30/US$25.60 a day).

The car rental companies also offer additional *liability insurance* (if you harm others in an accident), *personal accident insurance* (if you harm yourself or your passengers), and *personal effects protection* (if your luggage is stolen from your car). Your insurance policy on your car at home probably covers most of these unlikely occurrences. However, if your own insurance doesn't cover you for rentals or if you don't have auto insurance, definitely consider the additional coverage (ask your car rental agent for more information). Unless you're toting around the Hope diamond (and you wouldn't want to leave that in your car trunk anyway), you can probably skip the personal effects insurance, but driving around without liability or personal accident coverage is never a good idea. Even if you're a good driver, other people may not be, and liability claims can be complicated.

 Most companies also offer *refueling packages*, in which you pay for your initial full tank of gas up front and then return the car with an empty gas tank. The prices can be competitive with local gas prices, but you don't get credit for any gas remaining in the tank. If you reject this option, you pay only for the gas you use, but you have to return the car with a full tank or face charges that are around 50% higher per liter than at the pump to make up for the shortfall. If you tend to run late and a fueling stop may make you miss your plane, you're a good candidate for the fuel-purchase option.

Ferrying Between Provinces

The three provinces are linked not only by road (or bridge, in the case of PEI) but also by ferry. This is a fun, affordable way to travel while cutting down on driving.

Nova Scotia to New Brunswick

The ferry across the Bay of Fundy between Digby, Nova Scotia, and Saint John, New Brunswick can cut a considerable chunk from your driving mileage if your itinerary takes you either up the Maine coast (and you didn't use the ferry systems detailed in Chapter 6) or on a circuitous route through both Nova Scotia and New Brunswick.

The *Princess of Acadia* plies this route year-round, with up to three sailings daily, depending on the season. The trip takes three hours and is C$22–C$37 (US$18.70–US$31.50) for adults, C$18.50–C$26 (US$15.70–US$22.10) for seniors, C$15–C$21 (US$12.80–US$17.90) for children 5–17, and C$75–C$92 (US$63.80–US$78.20) for vehicles under 6.4m (21 feet). Fare variations reflect seasonal pricing (July–early Oct is high season). Contact **Bay Ferries** (☎ **888-249-7245** or 506-649-7777; www.nfl-bay.com) for information and reservations.

Nova Scotia to Prince Edward Island

Although Prince Edward Island is linked to mainland New Brunswick by a bridge, the ferry link between Caribou (north of Pictou, Nova Scotia) and Wood Islands (on the southeastern corner of PEI) is also a viable way of crossing Northumberland Strait.

In July and August, there are eight sailings daily in each direction, with less frequent service in spring and fall. Drifting ice closes the service down completely between mid-December and April. Once the vessel gets going, the crossing takes little more than an hour. The round-trip fare is C$55 (US$46.80) per vehicle including passengers. For walk-on passengers, the cost is C$14 (US$11.90) for adults, C$12 (US$10.20) for seniors; no charge for children under five. For information, contact **Northumberland Ferries** (☎ **902-566-3838**; www.nfl-bay.com). No reservations are taken, so plan on catching a mid-week (except Fri afternoon) or early morning sailing to avoid a long wait.

Getting to Prince Edward Island is free, regardless of whether you cross the Confederation Bridge or take the ferry. The bridge toll and ferry fare are only collected when you leave the island. The bridge toll (C$39.50/ US$33.60) is less expensive than traveling by ferry, so if you cross to the island aboard the ferry and return to the mainland via the bridge, you'll save a bit of money.

To Newfoundland

I didn't forget about Newfoundland when writing this book. It was simply that it was impossible to comprehensively cover the three Maritimes provinces as well as their northern neighbor in the page count I was allotted. (Collectively, the province of Newfoundland and Labrador and the Maritimes provinces are known as Atlantic Canada.)

For those who plan on visiting Newfoundland, this section details ferry routes and rates from Nova Scotia.

Marine Atlantic (☎ **800-341-7981** or 902-794-5200; www.marine-atlantic.ca) operates the following ferries between North Sydney and the Newfoundland docks (reservations are required for all sailings):

✔ **Port aux Basques,** located at the southwestern tip of Newfoundland. This ferry ride takes between five and seven hours, with departures twice daily year-round. Costs are (one-way) C$27 (US$23) for adults, C$25 (US$21.30) for seniors, and C$13.50 (US$11.50) for children 5 to 12. Vehicles up to 20 feet in length cost C$76.50 (US$65), and accommodations range from a dorm bed for C$16 (US$13.60) to C$105 (US$89.30) for an ensuite cabin.

✔ **Argentia,** situated a couple of hours' drive from the capital, St. John's (not to be confused with Saint John, New Brunswick). This route is much longer and more of an adventure, taking around 16 hours and crossing sometimes-rough open ocean. It departs twice a week between mid-June and mid-October. Sample one-way fares are: C$75.50 (US$64.20) adults, C$68 (US$57.80) seniors, C$38 (US$32.30) children 5 to 12, C$18 (US$15.30) reclining chair, C$28 (US$23.80) dorm bed, C$135 (US$114.80) ensuite cabin, and C$157 (US$133.50) for vehicles up to 20 feet in length.

Before leaving home, request an information package from **Newfoundland & Labrador Tourism** (☎ **800-563-6353** or 709-729-2830; www.gov.nf.ca/tourism). The recommended guidebook is *Frommer's Newfoundland and Labrador.*

Getting Around by Other Means

If you aren't on an escorted tour and don't want to drive, your options for travel in the Maritimes are limited to flying between provinces, catching the train along one of two main routes, or taking the bus.

Traveling by plane

Air Canada (☎ **888-247-2262;** www.aircanada.ca) or one of its partners such as Air Canada Jazz flies daily between Halifax, Moncton, Fredericton, Saint John, Charlottetown, and Sydney. At each of these airports, you'll find transportation to downtown, car rental desks, and an information booth or a bank of phones linked to a directory of local accommodations.

Taking the train

VIA Rail (☎ **888-842-7245** or 514-871-6000; www.viarail.ca) service between Montreal and Halifax stops in Truro, Moncton, Miramichi, and Bathurst, making it a viable transportation option. From Moncton, bus connections can be made to Charlottetown, Saint John, and Fredericton. Fares are reasonable, especially if purchased seven or more days in advance.

Catching the bus

As I say in the previous chapter, Greyhound services come close to the Maritimes, but terminate at surrounding cities such as Bangor (Maine), Toronto, and Montreal. From downtown depots in these three places, **Acadian** (☎ **800-567-5151** or 902-454-9321; www.acadianbus.com) provides connecting services to major Maritimes centers and hundreds of towns and villages in between. Acadian services cross the Confederation Bridge to Charlottetown, but beyond the capital there is no public transportation on Prince Edward Island.

Chapter 8

Booking Your Accommodations

In This Chapter
▶ Choosing the best overnight option
▶ Wheeling and dealing for a good night's sleep

*Y*ou'll have an easy time finding accommodations that meet the basic criteria of being clean and comfortable — the Maritimes has all the chain hotels and motels you already know. But unless you're traveling there to have the same experience you can have anywhere else, you should consider my recommended lodgings in Chapters 11 to 23. The chains are sure to lack Maritimes charm, which is why I recommend them only when you have no other options.

Finding the Place That's Right for You

People have different ideas about the type of places they want to stay at, so no lodging I recommend in this book will appeal to everyone. I've included a wide cross-section of options to suit all tastes and budgets — not hard to do, as the Maritimes has everything from big-city luxury hotels to rustic wilderness cabins. And compared to other North American destinations, hotel rooms in the Maritimes are reasonably priced.

 Remember to add taxes to all quoted prices — the 15% Harmonized Sales Tax in Nova Scotia and New Brunswick and 17% worth of taxes on Prince Edward Island. Halifax accommodations also collect a 1.5% **Destination Halifax Marketing Levy**.

Hotels and motels
You'll find a plethora of luxury hotels in the major cities. Most international chains are represented in each province, along with **Fairmont Hotels and Resorts** (www.fairmont.com) and **Delta Hotels** (www.deltahotels.com), both upscale Canadian chains with impeccable credentials. These hotels have rack rates in the top $$$$ (over

C$225/US$191.30) category, but generally offer discounts on weekends or for online bookings.

Reliable mid-priced chains like **Holiday Inn** (www.ichotelsgroup.com) and **Best Western** (www.bestwestern.com) are also plentiful. The Maritimes' own **Rodd Hotels & Resorts** (www.rodd-hotels.ca) is in this same $$ to $$$ price bracket. On the edge of the cities and in smaller towns, you'll find hotels in the middle of the $$ category. Their rooms usually come with fewer amenities and the furnishings may be older.

If you just need somewhere to spend the night or you can't get a room at one of my recommended lodgings, a roadside motel will do. Access to the room is normally from the parking lot. In general, motels don't have attached dining rooms. They are common throughout the Maritimes, other than in Prince Edward Island. Always in the $ or $$ range but rarely over C$100 (US$85), you will find them listed in provincial tourism guides, or look for their brochures displayed in local information centers.

Bed-and-breakfasts

Some travelers plan their vacations around bed-and-breakfasts; others avoid them like the plague. If you fall into the first category, you'll have plenty of scope in the Maritimes. Literally hundreds of homes in each of the three provinces have been converted to bed-and-breakfast accommodations, with a wide range of services and prices to match (anywhere from C$50/US$42.50 to over C$200/US$170 double). By doing some research and asking the right questions, you can easily avoid unpleasant surprises. If you follow my recommendations, you won't have to worry about ending up in a room left vacant by the owner's college-bound kid. My picks are all proper businesses with more than two guest rooms, not individuals looking to rent an extra room to make some quick cash.

Bed-and-breakfasts are a great place to meet fellow travelers, learn more about the area from knowledgeable hosts, and enjoy a hearty breakfast before hitting the road. It is a perceived lack of privacy that puts most people off this type of accommodation. Most North American travelers do not relish the idea of sharing a bathroom with other guests — but this is not the case at all bed-and-breakfasts. Here are the accepted definitions (I use them throughout this book), but it's always best to double-check when reserving so you know exactly what you're getting:

- ✔ **Ensuite bathroom:** A bathroom that is accessed directly from the guest room, and only used by the guests in that room.

- ✔ **Private bathroom:** A bathroom that is for the sole use of one room, but may be down a hallway.

- ✔ **Shared bathroom:** A bathroom that is used by guests in more than one room.

If you're traveling with children or have a disability, it is very important that you make the proprietor aware of your situation before making a reservation. Other guests may not appreciate children (who may be vacationing from their own kids!). Many bed-and-breakfasts are converted residences, so wheelchair access is often limited.

Cottages, cabins, and chalets

This type of accommodation is perfect for families or those who don't need the luxuries of resort living.

The words "cabin" and "cottage" are mostly interchangeable, but "cottage" sounds somehow more inviting (sort of like using "home" instead of "house"). Either way, you can expect a freestanding unit with a bathroom and linen provided. Some may have extras like a kitchen or a private verandah. Generally, a chalet will be a larger unit with more amenities and some attention to décor.

Many cabin resorts pre-date World War II, and became increasingly popular as families began to vacation together in the coastal resort towns. These old cabins, loaded with character, remain; some have been combined with newer and bigger units to suit a wider range of budgets and needs, and feature facilities that may include a restaurant or canoe rentals. For this reason, pricing runs the full spectrum. A good example is **Glenghorm Beach Resort** on Cape Breton Island (www.capebreton resorts.com), where the most basic cabins are at the bottom end of the $$ price range while luxurious chalets cost well into the top $$$$ category at C$395 (US$335.80).

Expect older, more basic cabins to be in the $ category (under C$75/ US$63.80). The addition of cooking facilities doesn't usually affect the price that much, with many self-contained cabins costing around C$100 (US$85). By the time you reach the $$$ category, you will be getting a modern, self-contained cabin with a separate bedroom.

Cabins and cottages are priced seasonally throughout the Maritimes, with peak season in July and August. Many close completely after September, reopening in April or May.

Resorts

While most hotels and motels are set up for overnight stays, resorts are designed to keep you happy for an entire vacation. The Maritimes' top resorts do this well, with golf courses, activity programs, spa services, and a choice of dining rooms. Resorts are generally kid-friendly, with children's programs and menus as well as baby-sitting services.

Of course, you pay for all this pampering. Rack rates at most resorts are in the $$$ to $$$$ range, with decent savings for booking a package that may include meals or greens fees. Resorts are the first to offer discounts outside of summer, so look for bargains in June and September, while the property is still functioning fully. You will find my resort recommendations liberally spread throughout this book, but the Web sites for **Rodd Hotels and Resorts** (www.rodd-hotels.ca), **Cape Breton Resorts** (www.capebretonresorts.com), and **Signature Resorts** (www.signatureresorts.com) are a good place to decide if this type of accommodation seems suited to your needs.

Finding the Best Room at the Best Rate

Some people book a room by calling a hotel, asking for a reservation, and paying whatever price is quoted. That won't be you, though, because after reading this section, you'll know how to find the best rates available.

Uncovering the truth about rack rates

The *rack rate* is the maximum rate a hotel charges for a room. It's the rate you get if you walk in off the street and ask for a room for the night. (You sometimes see these rates printed on the fire/emergency exit diagrams posted on the back of your door.) Hotels are happy to charge you the rack rate, but you can almost always do better. Perhaps the best way to avoid paying the rack rate is surprisingly simple: Just ask for a cheaper or discounted rate. You may be pleasantly surprised.

Some lodgings, especially bed-and-breakfasts and hostels, really mean what they say. The rates they publish are what everyone pays.

Making sure the price is right

In all but the smallest accommodations (mostly bed-and-breakfasts), the rate you pay for a room depends on many factors — chief among them being when you travel and how you make your reservation. The following are some strategies you can use to find the best rate possible.

Shopping early for the greatest choice

If you're planning on traveling to the Maritimes in summer, it's not too early to start making bookings at the beginning of the year. Some chain hotels sell a percentage of rooms at a discounted rate, and when they're gone, they're gone — everyone else pays a higher rate. Booking early won't get you a discount at that quaint little bed-and-breakfast, but it will ensure that you get the room you want, rather than, say, their smallest room with a bathroom down the hallway, which is always last to go.

Traveling off-peak

As shown as an example in the "What things cost in the Maritimes" sidebar in Chapter 5, Lakeview Lodge & Cottages, in Cavendish on Prince Edward Island, rents self-contained cottages for C$125 (US$106.30) in July and August. If you make your booking anytime outside of these two months — even for the first week of September — the rate drops to C$70 (US$59.50), a saving of almost 50%. The difference isn't always this abrupt — many accommodations discount a bit during "shoulder season" (June and Sept), then further discount rates the rest of the year (or close altogether).

Luxury hotels and big resorts often charge less than half their peak rates during the off season, which often puts them in competition with mid-range chain hotels. Check the Web sites of the major chains as well as of Canadian companies such as **Delta Hotels** (www.deltahotels.com) and **Rodd Hotels and Resorts** (www.rodd-hotels.ca), who lead the way in this regard.

See Chapter 3 for more information on what you can expect during different times of year in the Maritimes.

Asking for discounts

Hotels usually offer discounts for people with travel club or other memberships. In most cases, you can expect a 10% to 15% discount simply for flashing your AAA card. Going gray has its advantages too — Best Western offers an automatic 10% discount to all travelers over 55, with upgrades, late check-outs, and complimentary breakfasts thrown in for good measure. Most major hotel chains have loyalty programs, but you usually don't really need to be loyal to reap the benefits. Members of Holiday Inn's Priority Club and Fairmont's President Club, for example, enjoy daily papers, free local calls, late check-outs, and more, simply for signing up.

Guesthouses and bed-and-breakfasts are a little different. You can ask for a discount if you want to stay more than one night or pay with cash, but don't push it.

Surfing the Web for hotel deals

Shopping online for hotels is generally done one of two ways: You can book through the hotel's own Web site or through an independent booking agency (or a fare-service agency like Priceline). These Internet hotel agencies have multiplied in mind-boggling numbers of late, competing for the business of millions of consumers surfing for accommodations around the world. This competitiveness can be a boon to consumers who have the patience and time to shop and compare the online sites for good deals — but shop they must, for prices can vary considerably from site to site. And keep in mind that hotels at the top of a site's listing may be there for no reason other than that they paid money to get the placement.

Web sites of the chain hotels (see the Appendix) are the best place to search out discounted rates ("Web savers," advance bookings, and last-minute deals). Another way to pay less for your room is to have it bundled as a package with an activity like golfing or with passes to a local attraction. See Chapter 6 for discussion on booking a package.

For smaller places, check out **Bed & Breakfast Online** (www.bbcanada.com) and **Innsite** (www.innsite.com), where you'll find a list of independent establishments you might not otherwise find on your own. Although you can't book online through these sites, you can follow the links to individual lodgings' Web sites and book directly with them.

Although the major travel booking sites, such as **Destina.ca** (www.destina.ca), **Travelocity** (www.travelocity.com), **Expedia** (www.expedia.com), and **Orbitz** (www.orbitz.com), offer hotel bookings, you may be better off going directly to the source and booking online with the property itself. Also reliable are **Hotels.com** (www.hotels.com) and **Quikbook.com** (www.quikbook.com). An excellent free program, **TravelAxe** (www.travelaxe.net) can help you search multiple hotel sites at once, even ones you may never have heard of — and conveniently lists the total price of the room, including the taxes and service charges.

More than once, travelers have arrived at the hotel after making reservations through an online intermediary, only to be told that they have no reservation. To be fair, many of the major sites are undergoing improvements in service and ease of use, and Expedia will soon be able to plug directly into the reservations systems of many hotel chains —none of which can be bad news for consumers. In the meantime, it's a good idea to **get a confirmation number** and **make a printout** of any online booking transaction.

Getting the most for your money

Now you know how to wrangle a great price, but how about the quality of the room? When making your reservation, ask a couple of pointed questions to make sure you get the best room in the house. Here are some tips that can help, whatever lodging you choose:

- ✔ **Always ask for a corner room.** They're usually larger, quieter, and have more windows and light than standard rooms, and they don't always cost more.

- ✔ **Avoid renovations.** If the hotel is renovating, request a room away from the work. Of course, they probably won't offer up this information when you're making your reservation, so it's up to you to ask.

- ✔ **Inquire about the location of the hotel's restaurants and bars.** This can go either way — fine if you want to be close to the action,but if sleep is what you're after, the hotel's hot night spots are potential sources of annoying noise.

If you aren't happy with your room when you arrive, talk to the front desk. If they have another room, they should be happy to accommodate you, within reason.

Chapter 9

Catering to Special Travel Needs or Interests

● ●

In This Chapter

▶ Bringing the family

▶ Surfing for seniors' tours

▶ Seeking out accessible travel options

▶ Searching out gay-friendly resources

● ●

*I*f you have special needs or interests, this chapter will make your travel planning a little easier. So many resources are available now, especially online, that whatever your needs, you should be able to find the information and the support you need to ensure that your trip is safe, stress-free, and most of all, fun!

Traveling with Kids: Are We There Yet?

If you have enough trouble getting your kids out of the house in the morning, dragging them thousands of miles away may seem like an insurmountable challenge. But family travel can be immensely rewarding, giving you new ways of seeing the world through more youthful eyes.

Here are a few pre-trip planning tips for families:

  ✔ **Look for the Kid-Friendly icon.** I've marked lodgings, restaurants, and attractions especially suited to children throughout the book.

  ✔ **Read books set in the Maritimes.** Books such as *Anne of Green Gables* are a great introduction to the Maritimes, and kids will love visiting Cavendish after reading about it (as do thousands of adults).

  ✔ **Surf the Internet.** Each of the three provincial tourism Web sites has a section devoted to family travel, including kid-friendly attractions or ideas for entire vacations.

You can find good family-oriented vacation advice on the Internet from Web sites like **Family Travel Forum** (www.familytravel forum.com), a comprehensive site that offers customized trip planning; **Family Travel Network** (www.familytravelnetwork.com), an award-winning site that offers travel features, deals, and tips; **Traveling Internationally with Your Kids** (www.travelwith yourkids.com), a comprehensive site that offers customized trip planning; and **Family Travel Files** (www.familytravelfiles.com), which offers an online magazine and a directory of off-the-beaten-path tours and tour operators for families.

✔ **Pack favorite toys and games.** Something simple from home can act as a security blanket for a child traveling in a strange place.

✔ **Reserve a child-safety seat.** If your kids are small, be sure to arrange a car seat for your rental car.

Seeing the Maritimes in Senior Style: The Age Advantage

Getting older certainly doesn't have to mean slowing down, and it even has money-saving benefits. If you're a senior citizen, mention that fact when you make your travel reservations. Most major chain hotels offer discounts for seniors (at Best Western, those over 55 enjoy a discounted stay). In most cases, people over the age of 60 qualify for reduced admission to theaters, museums, and other attractions, as well as discounted fares on public transportation and access to national parks.

Members of **AARP** (formerly known as the American Association of Retired Persons), 601 E St. NW, Washington, DC 20049 (☎ **888-687-2277** or 202-434-2277; www.aarp.org), get discounts on hotels, airfares, and car rentals. AARP offers members a wide range of benefits, including *AARP: The Magazine* and a monthly newsletter. Anyone over 50 can join. In Canada, **New Outlook** (☎ **800-267-3277**; www.newoutlook.ca) is a program for over-50's that costs C$25 and includes preferred rates at Sears Travel and some hotels, as well as over C$1,000 in Sears coupons.

Elderhostel (☎ **877-426-8056** or 978-323-4141; www.elderhostel.org) arranges study programs for those aged 55 and over (and a spouse or companion of any age) in more than 80 countries around the world, including Canada. The courses in Nova Scotia last five to ten days, and many include accommodations (in modest inns), meals, and tuition.

Here are some recommended publications offering travel resources and discounts for seniors:

✔ *Travel 50 & Beyond*, the quarterly magazine (www.travel50and beyond.com)

  ✔ *Travel Unlimited: Uncommon Adventures for the Mature Traveler* (Avalon Travel Publishing) and its associated Web site, www.travelwithachallenge.com

  ✔ *Unbelievably Good Deals and Great Adventures That You Absolutely Can't Get Unless You're Over 50* (McGraw-Hill)

Accessing the Maritimes: Advice for Travelers with Disabilities

Most disabilities shouldn't stop anyone from traveling. You'll find more options and resources out there than ever before. Many travel agencies offer customized tours and itineraries for travelers with disabilities. **Flying Wheels Travel** (☎ 507-451-5005; www.flyingwheelstravel. com) is a full-service travel agency that caters exclusively to travelers with disabilities. Similarly, **Accessible Journeys** (☎ 800-846-4537 or 610-521-0339; www.disabilitytravel.com) accommodates the travel needs of slow walkers and wheelchair travelers and their families and friends. The **Access-Able Travel Source** (www.access-able.com) is a comprehensive compendium of travel agents who specialize in travel for people with disabilities. The site also has an extensive database of lodgings around the world, including the Maritimes, that are suited to travelers with disabilities.

The following organizations offer assistance to travelers with disabilities:

  ✔ The **Moss Rehab Hospital** (www.mossresourcenet.org) provides a online library of accessible-travel resources.

  ✔ The **Society for Accessible Travel and Hospitality** (☎ 212-447-7284; www.sath.org; annual membership fees: US$45 adults, US$30 seniors and students) offers a wealth of travel resources for people with all types of disabilities, as well as informed recommendations on destinations, access guides, travel agents, tour operators, vehicle rentals, and companion services.

  ✔ The **American Foundation for the Blind** (☎ 800-232-5463; www.afb.org) provides information on traveling with Seeing Eye dogs. In Canada, the **Canadian National Institute for the Blind** (☎ 416-486-2500; www.cnib.ca) offers a wide variety of services from division offices in Halifax (☎ 902-453-1480), Fredericton (☎ 506-458-0060), and Charlottetown (☎ 902-566-2580).

  ✔ Operated by the Canadian government, **Access to Travel** (www.accesstotravel.gc.ca) is an information clearinghouse of accessible travel information.

✔ The community Web site **iCan** (www.icanonline.net) has destination guides and several regular columns on accessible travel specifically targeted to travelers with disabilities.

✔ **Twin Peaks Press** (☎ 360-694-2462; www.pacifier.com/~twin peak/index.htm) offers a catalogue of travel-related books for travelers with special needs. Also check out the quarterly magazine *Emerging Horizons* (US$14.95 per year, US$19.95 outside the U.S.; www.emerginghorizons.com), a quarterly magazine for travelers with special needs. The book *Barrier-Free Travel: A Nuts and Bolts Guide for Wheelers and Slow Walkers* is published by the same company.

Advice for Gay and Lesbian Travelers

The university cities of Halifax, Fredericton, and Charlottetown tend to have the most resources in the Maritimes for gay and lesbian travelers. Even in these centers, you won't find gay or lesbian neighborhoods, but specific hangouts, like nightclubs, coffee shops, and bookstores do exist. Outside of the cities, attitudes are generally conservative but accepting.

A good source of gay- and lesbian-friendly businesses in Halifax, including accommodations and restaurants, is the Web site http://gay.hfxns.org. **Gay Crawler** (www.gaycrawler.com) is a search engine with a searchable database of over 17,000 gay-themed Web sites, many of which are travel-related. The **International Gay & Lesbian Travel Association** (IGLTA; ☎ 800-448-8550 or 954-776-2626; www.iglta.org) is the trade association for the gay and lesbian travel industry, and offers an online directory of gay- and lesbian-friendly travel businesses. A search feature makes finding local businesses easy.

Some companies offer tours and travel itineraries specifically for gay and lesbian travelers. One of these is **Now, Voyager** (☎ 800-255-6951 or 415-626-1169; www.nowvoyager.com), a well-known San Francisco-based gay-owned and -operated travel service.

The following travel guides are available at most travel bookstores and gay and lesbian bookstores, or you can order them from **Giovanni's Room** bookstore, 1145 Pine St., Philadelphia (☎ 215-923-2960; www.giovannisroom.com):

✔ *Out and About* (☎ 800-929-2268 or 415-644-8044; www.gay.com/travel/outandabout) offers guidebooks and a monthly newsletter packed with solid information on the global gay and lesbian scene.

- ✔ *Spartacus International Gay Guide* (Bruno Gmünder Verlag; www.spartacusworld.com/gayguide/) and *Odysseus* (www.odyusa.com) are both good, annual English-language guidebooks focused on gay men.

- ✔ The *Damron* (www.damron.com) guides feature separate annual books for gay men and lesbians.

- ✔ *Gay Travel A to Z: The World of Gay & Lesbian Travel Options at Your Fingertips* (Ferrari International; Box 35575, Phoenix, AZ 85069) is a very good gay and lesbian guidebook series.

Chapter 10

Taking Care of the Remaining Details

● ●

In This Chapter

▶ Securing travel documents

▶ Packing for your trip

▶ Crossing into Canada

▶ Covering your assets with insurance

▶ Staying healthy while you travel

▶ Measuring in metric

● ●

*D*on't you hate that feeling that you've forgotten something but can't remember what it is? In this chapter, I'll discuss a variety of often-overlooked planning elements. So relax and read on — it's all covered.

Getting a Passport

At the time of publication, citizens of the United States do not require a passport for entry to Canada, but as of January 1, 2007, all air and sea travelers will require a passport to travel to and from Canada. From January 1, 2008, all travelers at land border crossings will require a passport. The Web site `http://travel.state.gov/travel/tips/regional/regional_1170.html` details this initiative.

For travelers from other countries, a valid passport is the only form of identification accepted at Canadian borders. For an up-to-date country-by-country listing of passport requirements around the world, go to the "Foreign Entry Requirement" Web page of the U.S. State Department at `http://travel.state.gov/travel/tips/brochures/brochures_1229.html`.

Applying for a U.S. passport

If you're applying for a first-time passport, follow these steps:

1. **Complete a passport application.** You can do this in person at a U.S. passport office; a federal, state, or probate court; or a major post office. To find your regional passport office, either check the **U.S. State Department** Web site (http://travel.state.gov/passport_services.html) or call the **National Passport Information Center** (☎ 877-487-2778) for automated information.

2. **Present a certified birth certificate.** This is proof of citizenship. (It's also a good idea to bring along your driver's license, state or military ID, or social security card.)

3. **Submit two identical passport-sized photos.** They should measure 2 inches by 2 inches in size. You often find businesses that take these photos near a passport office. Note: You can't use a strip from a photo-vending machine because the pictures aren't identical.

4. **Pay a fee.** For people 16 and over, a passport is valid for ten years and costs $85. For those 15 and under, a passport is valid for five years and costs $70.

Allow plenty of time before your trip to apply for a passport; processing normally takes three weeks, but can take longer during busy periods (especially spring).

If you have a passport in your current name that was issued within the past 15 years (and you were over age 16 when it was issued), you can renew the passport by mail for $55. Whether you're applying in person or by mail, you can download passport applications from the U.S. State Department Web site at http://travel.state.gov/passport_services.html. For general information, call the **National Passport Agency** (☎ 202-647-0518). To find your regional passport office, either check the U.S. State Department Web site or call the **National Passport Information Center's** toll-free number (☎ 877-487-2778) for automated information.

Applying for other passports

The following list offers more information for citizens of Australia, New Zealand, and the United Kingdom.

- ✔ **Australians** can visit a local post office or passport office, call the **Australia Passport Information Service** (☎ 131-232 toll-free from Australia), or log on to www.passports.gov.au for details on how and where to apply.

- ✔ **New Zealanders** can pick up a passport application at any New Zealand Passports Office or download it from their Web site. For information, contact the **Passports Office** at ☎ 0800-225-050 in New Zealand or 04-474-8100, or log on to www.passports.govt.nz.

> ✔ **United Kingdom** residents can pick up applications for a standard 10-year passport (5-year passport for children under 16) at passport offices, major post offices, or travel agencies. For information, contact the **United Kingdom Passport Service** (☎ **0870-521-0410;** www.ukpa.gov.uk).

Packing for the Maritimes

To be succinct, pack as lightly as possible but be prepared for a variety of weather conditions. Start by assembling all the clothing you think you'll need. Then put half away, and you'll have an ideal amount for your vacation.

Knowing what to bring

Pack clothing that is comfortable and practical. In summer, a rain jacket, sweater, and a pair of worn-in walking shoes are sufficient accompaniments to your regular casual clothing choices. Pack fragile items between layers of clothes, and pack things that may leak, like shampoo bottles, in sealable bags. You should also remember to bring the following:

> ✔ Tickets, car and hotel confirmations
>
> ✔ Discount membership cards
>
> ✔ Credit and debit cards
>
> ✔ Prescription medications and a copy of your prescriptions in case you lose them or run out

Though these are not really essential (believe it or not, you *can* buy film in the Maritimes, too), here's a list of handy items you'll be glad to have on hand:

> ✔ Open-toed shoes, such as sandals
>
> ✔ Binoculars
>
> ✔ Spare film and batteries for your camera
>
> ✔ Insect repellent
>
> ✔ Extra pair of contacts or glasses and a copy of your prescription

Knowing what not to bring

Disregard everything you've heard about Canada and the cold. In summer, there is absolutely no need to carry a down parka or heavy winter boots (as proof, see Chapter 3 for average Maritimes temperatures). You can make due with comfortable, casual spring and summer clothing. And unless you plan on attending the theater or dining in the finest restaurants, you won't need a suit or formal wear either. Khakis and a golf shirt for men, and dress slacks or a skirt for women, are sufficiently dressy.

Meeting airline baggage requirements

Security measures at airports vary from country to country and even from airport to airport. All major airlines include up-to-date lists of permitted and prohibited items, as well as procedures for boarding flights, on their Web sites. Another option is to go straight to the source:

- ✔ United States: **Transportation Security Administration,** www.tsa.gov/public
- ✔ Canada: **Canadian Air Transport Security Authority,** www. catsa-acsta.gc.ca

If you need to have medical equipment like syringes or oxygen bottles on your person when you fly, contact your airline at least seven days prior to your departure.

Checked bags

Most airlines allow each passenger two pieces of checked luggage at no charge. Maximum weights and dimensions vary with each airline, but Air Canada's guidelines are typical. They allow a maximum measurement (combined length, height, and width) of 158 centimeters (62 inches) for each piece. The weight of each piece must not exceed 32 kilograms (70 pounds) and the two pieces combined may not weigh more than 45 kilograms (100 pounds).

Sporting equipment like golf clubs, skis, and snowboards is allowed at no extra cost, but counts as one of your two checked bags. Larger items like bikes and surfboards incur an extra charge. Air Canada charges C$65 (US$55.30) each way for these items. Contact your airline for more details.

On flights originating in the U.S., checked luggage is often screened by hand. Therefore, make sure your luggage isn't locked when you check in. If you're transporting a gift (as either checked-in or carry-on luggage) and it's wrapped, you may be required to unwrap it. So plan ahead, and carry the wrapping paper separately.

In addition to an identification tag, tying a piece of ribbon to your suitcase makes spotting it on the baggage carousel easy. I've seen a dozen bags come off the same flight with yellow ribbon, so be creative and tie yellow and red, or a combination of colors that represent your country or favorite football team.

Carry-on luggage

Every airline is different when it comes to carry-on luggage allowances, but Air Canada's guidelines, once again, are typical. Each passenger is allowed one carry-on bag that measures less than 55 × 40 × 23 centimeters (21 × 16 × 9 inches) and weighs a maximum of 10 kilograms (22 pounds), and one "personal article" (like a laptop computer or briefcase). Items like cameras and coats are allowed but aren't included in the allowance. Check with your airline (Web sites are easiest) for specifics.

In your carry-on bag, pack valuables like jewelry and cameras; documents such as return tickets and car rental reservations; prescription drugs; and a sweater. Throw in a magazine or good book, a bottle of water, and a snack for good measure.

Keep your boarding pass and photo identification (passport or driver license) handy at all times after checking in your main bags.

Getting through Immigration and Customs

Canada is a welcoming country, but officers at the border are still likely to ask some pointed questions, like the purpose of your stay and what you are bringing into the country.

Crossing the border

U.S. citizens need proof of citizenship for entry into Canada. A passport is best, although a birth certificate, baptismal certificate, or voter registration card *and* photo ID such as driver's license are also acceptable. A driver's license alone isn't considered proof of citizenship, but it may help in a tight spot. From January 1, 2007, all air and sea travelers going to or from Canada, including U.S. citizens, will require a passport. (See Getting a Passport" earlier in this chapter for more information.)

All other foreign visitors require a valid passport and will be asked to produce onward tickets and sufficient funds upon arrival in Canada.

Citizens from some countries are required to apply for a Temporary Resident Visa (TRV) before arriving in Canada (if you're from Britain, a Commonwealth country, or somewhere in Western Europe, you probably don't need a TRV, but check current regulations before leaving home at Web site www.cic.gc.ca). For details, as well as contact information for consulates and embassies around the world, contact **Citizenship and Immigration Canada** (☎ 888-242-2100; www.cic.gc.ca).

If you travel with a passport, keep it with you at all times. The only time you should give it up is at the border for officers to examine. If you lose your passport while in Canada, go directly to the nearest embassy or consulate of your own country. (See the Appendix for embassy and consulate locations in the Maritimes.)

Passing through Customs

Although the amount of loot you can take into Canada is unlimited, the Customs authority does have limits on how much you can bring in for free (to separate the tourists from the importers).

Entering Canada

If you're bringing goods other than clothing and personal effects into Canada, you'll need to fill out a declarations form. Here's the threshold on some common items: 50 cigars, 200 cigarettes, and either 1.14 liters (40 oz) of liquor or wine or one case (12 bottles or cans) of beer. It is not illegal to bring more than the equivalent of C$10,000 (approximately US$8,500) into Canada, but you must report it if you do so.

Temporary visitors are permitted to bring their pet cat or dog into Canada without it being quarantined. The department responsible for overseeing the import of animals is the **Canada Food Inspection Agency** (www.inspection.gc.ca). Check their Web site for current regulations.

Revolvers, pistols, and fully automatic firearms are definitely not allowed, and, needless to say, neither are narcotics. For more information, contact the **Canada Firearms Centre** (☎ 800-731-4000; www.cfc.gc.ca). For more information on general Customs regulations, check with the **Canada Border Services Agency** (☎ 800-461-9999 or 204-983-3500; www.cbsa-asfc.gc.ca).

Returning home

If you're a citizen of the United States, you may bring home US$400 worth of goods duty-free, providing you've been out of the country at least 48 hours. This includes one liter of an alcoholic beverage, 200 cigarettes, and 100 cigars. You may mail up to US$200 worth of goods to yourself (marked "for personal use") and up to US$100 to others (marked "unsolicited gift") once each day. You'll have to pay an import duty on anything over these limits.

If you have further questions, or you'd like a list of specific items that you cannot bring into the United States, check the **Customs & Border Protection** Web site, www.cbp.gov.

Customs regulations are different in every country. Here are some contacts for returning citizens of other countries:

- ✔ **Australian Customs Service** (☎ 1300-363-263; www.customs.gov.au).

- ✔ **HM Revenue & Customs** (☎ 0845-010-9000; www.hmrc.gov.uk) for the United Kingdom.

- ✔ **New Zealand Customs Service** (☎ 0800-428-786; www.customs.govt.nz).

Keeping Up with Airline Security

With the federalization of airport security, security procedures at U.S. airports are more stable and consistent than ever. Generally, you'll be fine if you arrive at the airport **1 hour** before a domestic flight and

2 hours before an international flight; if you show up late, tell an airline employee and he or she will probably whisk you to the front of the line.

Bring a **current, government-issued photo ID** such as a driver's license or passport. Keep your ID ready to show at check-in, the security checkpoint, and sometimes even the gate. (Children under 18 do not need government-issued photo IDs for domestic flights, but they do for international flights to most countries.)

In 2003, the Transportation Security Administration (TSA) phased out **gate check-in** at all U.S. airports. And **E-tickets** have made paper tickets nearly obsolete. Passengers with E-tickets can beat the ticket-counter lines by using airport **electronic kiosks** or even **online check-in** from your home computer. Online check-in involves logging on to your airlines' Web site, accessing your reservation, and printing out your boarding pass — and the airline may even offer you bonus miles to do so! If you're using a kiosk at the airport, bring the credit card you used to book the ticket or your frequent-flier card. Print out your boarding pass from the kiosk and simply proceed to the security checkpoint with your pass and a photo ID. If you're checking bags or looking to snag an exit-row seat, you will be able to do so using most airline kiosks. Even the smaller airlines are employing the kiosk system, but always call your airline to make sure these alternatives are available. **Curbside check-in** is also a good way to avoid lines, although a few airlines still ban curbside check-in, so call before you go.

Security checkpoint lines are getting shorter than they were during 2001 and 2002, but some doozies remain. If you have trouble standing for long periods of time, tell an airline employee; the airline will provide a wheelchair. Speed up security by **not wearing metal objects** such as big belt buckles. If you've got metallic body parts, a note from your doctor can prevent a long chat with the security screeners. Keep in mind that only **ticketed passengers** are allowed past security, except for folks escorting passengers with disabilities or children.

Federalization has stabilized **what you can carry on** and **what you can't**. The general rules are that sharp things are out, nail clippers are okay, and food and beverages must be passed through the X-ray machine — but security screeners can't make you drink from your coffee cup. Bring food in your carry-on rather than checking it, as explosive-detection machines used on checked luggage have been known to mistake food (especially chocolate, for some reason) for bombs. Travelers in the U.S. are allowed one carry-on bag, plus a "personal item" such as a purse, briefcase, or laptop bag. Carry-on hoarders can stuff all sorts of things into a laptop bag; as long as it has a laptop in it, it's still considered a personal item. The TSA has issued a list of restricted items; check its Web site (www.tsa.gov/public/index.jsp) for details.

Airport screeners may decide that your checked luggage needs to be searched by hand. You can now purchase luggage locks that allow screeners to open and re-lock a checked bag if hand-searching is necessary. Look for Travel Sentry certified locks at luggage or travel shops and Brookstone stores (you can buy them online at www.brookstone.com). These locks, approved by the TSA, can be opened by luggage inspectors with a special code or key. For more information on the locks, visit www.travelsentry.org. If you use something other than TSA-approved locks, your lock will be cut off your suitcase if a TSA agent needs to hand-search your luggage.

Playing It Safe with Travel and Medical Insurance

Three kinds of travel insurance are available: trip cancellation, medical, and lost luggage. Here's my advice on all three:

✔ **Trip cancellation insurance** is a good idea if you signed up for an escorted tour and paid a large portion of your vacation expenses up front (for information on escorted tours, see Chapter 6). Trip cancellation insurance covers three types of emergencies: death or sickness that prevents you from traveling, bankruptcy of a tour operator or airline, or a disaster that prevents you from getting to your destination.

✔ For travel overseas, most health plans (including Medicare and Medicaid) do *not* provide coverage, and the ones that do often require you to pay for services up front and reimburse you only after you return home. As a safety net, you may want to buy travel **medical insurance,** particularly if you're traveling to a remote or high-risk area where emergnecy evacuation is a possible scenario. If you require additional medical insurance, try **MEDEX Assistance** (☎ 410-453-6300; www.medexassist.com) or **Travel Assistance International** (☎ 800-821-2828; www.travelassistance.com; for general information on services, call the company's Worldwide Assistance Services, Inc., at ☎ 800-777-8710).

✔ **Lost luggage insurance** is not necessary for most travelers. Your homeowner's or renter's insurance should cover stolen luggage if you have off-premises theft coverage. Check your existing policies before you buy any additional coverage. If an airline flying between Canada and the U.S. or other international destination loses your luggage, the airline is responsible for paying US$20 per kilogram to a maximum of US$1,280. On flights within Canada, this liability is limited to C$1,500 (US$1,275) for checked baggage. In either case, the carrier's liability does not exceed your loss.

Some credit cards (American Express and certain gold and platinum Visa and MasterCards, for example) offer automatic flight insurance against death or dismemberment in case of an airplane crash — if you charged the cost of your ticket, that is.

If you're interested in purchasing travel insurance, try one of the following companies:

- ✔ **Access America** (☎ 800-729-6021; `www.accessamerica.com`)

- ✔ **Travel Guard International** (☎ 800-826-4919; `www.travelguard.com`)

- ✔ **Travel Insured International** (☎ 800-243-3174; `www.travelinsured.com`)

- ✔ **Travelex Insurance Services** (☎ 888-457-4602; `www.travelex-insurance.com`)

 Don't pay for more insurance than you need. For example, if you need only trip cancellation insurance, don't buy coverage for lost or stolen property. Trip cancellation insurance costs about 6% to 8% of the total value of your vacation.

Staying Healthy When You Travel

Getting sick will ruin your vacation, so I *strongly* advise against it (of course, last time I checked, the bugs weren't listening to me any more than they probably listen to you).

 If you have health insurance, be sure to carry your insurance card in your wallet. Most U.S. health insurance plans and HMOs cover at least part of the out-of-country hospital visits and procedures if insureds become ill or are injured while out of the country. Most require that you pay the bills up front at the time of care, issuing a refund only after you return and file all the paperwork.

Talk to your doctor before leaving on a trip if you have a serious and/or chronic illness. For conditions such as epilepsy, diabetes, or heart problems, wear a **MedicAlert Identification Tag** (☎ 888-633-4298 or 209-668-3333; `www.medicalert.org`), which immediately alerts doctors to your condition and gives them access to your records through MedicAlert's 24-hour hotline. Contact the **International Association for Medical Assistance to Travelers** (IAMAT; ☎ 716-754-4883 or, in Canada, 416-652-0137; `www.iamat.org`) for tips on travel and health concerns. The United States **Centers for Disease Control and Prevention** (☎ 800-311-3435; `www.cdc.gov`) provides up-to-date information on health hazards by region or country and offers tips on food safety.

Staying Connected by Cellphone or E-mail

Communications in the Maritimes have come a long way since the distress signal from the Titanic was received at a remote cable station in Canso, Nova Scotia. Today, the three provinces are connected to the outside world with the latest and greatest technology, making calling home a breeze.

Using a cellphone in Canada

Just because your cellphone works at home doesn't mean it'll work in Canada. The three letters that define global **wireless capabilities** are GSM (Global System for Mobiles), a big, seamless network that makes for easy cross-border cellphone use in and between around 100 countries worldwide, including Canada. In the U.S., T-Mobile, AT&T Wireless, and Cingular use this quasi-universal system; in Canada, Microcell (Fido) and some Rogers customers are GSM, and all Europeans and most Australians use GSM.

If your cellphone is on a GSM system, and you have a world-capable multiband phone such as many Sony Ericsson, Motorola, or Samsung models, you can make and receive calls throughout built-up areas of the Maritimes. Just call your wireless operator and ask for "international roaming" to be activated on your account. Unfortunately, per-minute charges can be high — usually C$1.50–C$2 (US$1.30–US$1.70) in Canada.

That's why it's important to buy an "unlocked" world phone from the get-go. Many cellphone operators sell "locked" phones that restrict you from using any other removable computer memory phone chip card (called a **SIM card**) other than the ones they supply. Having an unlocked phone allows you to go to a retailer within Canada and install a cheap, prepaid SIM card. (Show your phone to the salesperson; not all phones work on all networks.) You'll get a local phone number — and much, much lower calling rates. Getting an already locked phone unlocked can be a complicated process, but it can be done; just call your cellular operator and say you'll be going abroad for several months and want to use the phone with a local provider. Within the United States, **InTouch USA** (☎ **800-872-7626;** www.intouchglobal.com) sells Canadian-specific SIM cards.

For many, **renting** a phone that is set up to work in Canada is most convenient. While you can rent from within Canada (through car rental companies is often easiest), I suggest renting the phone before you leave home. That way you can give loved ones and business associates your new number, make sure the phone works, and takes the phone wherever you go. In the United States, two recommended wireless rental companies are **InTouch USA** (☎ **800-872-7626;** www.intouchglobal.com) and **RoadPost** (☎ **888-290-1606** or 905-272-5665; www.roadpost.com). Give them your itinerary, and they'll tell you what wireless products you need. InTouch will also, for free, advise you on whether your existing phone will work overseas; simply call ☎ **703-222-7161** between 9 a.m. and 4 p.m. EST, or go to http://intouchglobal.com/travel.htm.

Rogers (☎ 877-764-3772 or 416-935-5555; www.rogers.ca) is a Canadian wireless provider with outlets throughout the Maritimes, including in downtown Halifax at 6169 Quinpool Rd. (☎ 902-423-5653). This company sells SIM cards, cellphone accessories, and pay-as-you-go phones.

If you're venturing deep into the Canadian wilderness, you may want to consider renting a **satellite phone ("satphones"),** which are different from cellphones in that they connect to satellites rather than ground-based towers. A satphone is more costly than a cellphone but works where there's no cellular signal and no towers. Unfortunately, you'll pay at least $2 per minute to use the phone, and it only works where you can see the horizon (i.e., usually not indoors). In North America, you can rent Iridium satellite phones from **RoadPost** (☎ 888-290-1606 or 905-272-5665; www.roadpost.com) from US$100 per week. InTouch USA offers a wider range of satphones but at higher rates. As of this writing, satphones were very expensive to buy.

Accessing the Internet away from home

Travelers have any number of ways to check their e-mail and access the Internet on the road. Of course, using your own laptop — or even a PDA (personal digital assistant) or electronic organizer with a modem — gives you the most flexibility. But even if you don't have a computer, you can still access your e-mail and even your office computer from cyber-cafés. Although there's no definitive directory for cybercafés — these are independent businesses, after all — three places to start looking are at www.cybercaptive.com and www.cybercafe.com. In Halifax, the most centrally located of these are **Ceilidh Connection**, at 1672 Barrington St. (☎ 902-422-9800), and **Paper Chase News Café**, at 5228 Blowers St. (☎ 902-423-0750).

The **Community Access Program** (http://cap.ic.gc.ca) is a network of public access Internet computers across Canada, including in schools, libraries, and community centers. Halifax alone has 30 CAP facilities. Call ☎ 866-569-8428 or go to www.hrca.ns.ca for locations. All libraries in all three provinces have free Internet access.

In addition to public facilities, most major hotels have in-room modem access, wireless Internet, or a business center where guests can get online. Most bed and breakfasts allow their guests access to a computer. Airports across the Maritimes are well connected. All have **Internet kiosks** or **modem-equipped pay phones,** which you'll also see in shopping malls, hotel lobbies, and tourist information offices. They give you basic Web access for a per-minute fee that's usually higher than cyber-café prices. The kiosks' clunkiness and high prices mean they should be avoided whenever possible.

To retrieve your e-mail, ask your **Internet Service Provider (ISP)** if it has a Web-based interface tied to your existing e-mail account. If your ISP doesn't have such an interface, you can use the free **mail2web** service (www.mail2web.com) to view and reply to your home e-mail. For more flexibility, you may want to open a free, Web-based e-mail account with **Yahoo! Mail** (http://mail.yahoo.com). (Microsoft's Hotmail is another popular option, but Hotmail has severe spam problems.) Your home ISP may be able to forward your e-mail to the Web-based account automatically.

If you need to access files on your office computer, look into a service called **GoToMyPC** (www.gotomypc.com). The service provides a Web-based interface for you to access and manipulate a distant PC from anywhere — even a cybercafé — provided your "target" PC is on and has an always-on connection to the Internet (such as with Road Runner cable). The service offers top-quality security, but if you're worried about hackers, use your own laptop rather than a cybercafé computer to access the GoToMyPC system.

If you're bringing your own computer, the buzzword in computer access to familiarize yourself with is **Wi-fi** (wireless fidelity), and more and more hotels, cafés, and retailers are signing on as wireless "hotspots" from where you can get high-speed connection without cable wires, networking hardware, or a phone line. You can get Wi-fi connection one of several ways. Many laptops sold in the last year have built-in Wi-fi capability (an 802.11b wireless Ethernet connection). Mac owners have their own networking technology, Apple AirPort. For those with older computers, you can plug an 802.11b/**Wi-fi card** (around US$50) into your laptop. You sign up for wireless access service much as you do cellphone service, through a plan offered by one of several commercial companies that have made wireless service available in airports, hotel lobbies, and coffee shops, primarily in the U.S. and Canada. The three major U.S. wi-fi suppliers are **T-Mobile Hotspot** (www.t-mobile.com/hotspot), **Boingo** (www.boingo.com), **Wayport** (www.wayport.com), with ever-expanding networks that include Canada. The companies' pricing policies can be byzantine, with a variety of monthly, per-connection, and per-minute plans, but in general you pay around $30 a month for limited access — and as more and more companies jump on the wireless bandwagon, prices are likely to get even more competitive.

Major Internet Service Providers (ISP) have Canadian **local access numbers**, allowing you to go online by simply placing a local call. Check your ISP's Web site or call its toll-free number and ask how you can use your current account away from home, and how much it will cost. If you're traveling outside the reach of your ISP, the **iPass** network has dial-up numbers in most of the world's countries. You'll have to sign up with an iPass provider, who will then tell you how to set up your computer for your destination(s). For a list of iPass providers, go to www.ipass.com and click on "Individual Purchase." One solid provider is **i2roam** (☎ **866-811-6209** or 920-235-0475; www.i2roam.com).

Travelers from the U.S. need not worry about adapters, converters, and cables when traveling to Canada, as all systems are compatible. For travelers from other parts of the world, bring a **connection kit** of the right power (120 volts) and phone adapters, a spare phone cord, and a spare Ethernet network cable — or find out whether your hotel supplies them to guests.

Sizing Things Up: Converting to Canadian

Well, actually, it's converting to **metric**. This section is only relevant to readers from countries that have not adopted the global measurement system — the United States, Liberia, and Myanmar.

Metric works on the decimal system, which means that all measurements have a base of 10. The basic unit of measurement is a meter (a little longer than one yard), which can be divided into 100 centimeters (2.5 centimeters equals 1 inch) or 1,000 millimeters. One thousand meters equals one kilometer (approximately 0.6 miles).

Learning the difference between kilometers and miles when driving is probably the most important conversion you'll need to know. All speed limits and distance signs in Canada are posted in kilometers. If the sign dictates a limit of 100, that means 60 mph. At the pump, gas is sold in liters. Approximately 3.8 liters equals one U.S. gallon.

In 1975, rain began falling in Canada in millimeters and snow in centimeters. And, while you'll still hear older Canadians talk in Fahrenheit, **Celsius** is the official scale of measuring temperature, with water freezing at 0°C and boiling at 100°C. To convert from Celsius to Fahrenheit, multiply by 1.8 and then add 32.

The only Canadian holdouts to metric conversion are golfers (golf courses are measured in yards), seamen (boat speeds are measured in knots and distances in nautical miles), and grocery stores (bulk retail food like fresh vegetables is priced in ounces and pounds — but weighed at the cash register in metric).

Part III
Nova Scotia

The 5th Wave

By Rich Tennant

"We had it in the guest bedroom, and then in the hallway, but for now we're leaving it in here until we figure out which room it seems to want to be in."

In this part . . .

Life in Nova Scotia revolves around the ocean, and chances are, so will your travels in this East Coast province. In this part, I'll unveil the best of Halifax with tips on the top sights, the best places to stay, and dining experiences you won't want to miss. But don't despair, I'll also cover the spectacular Cabot Trail on Cape Breton Island and famous shipbuilding towns such as Lunenburg. Nova Scotia offers more than spectacular scenery and quaint seaside towns, so I've thrown in a few bonus tips, like where to see the world's largest pumpkins and which outdoor restaurant boils its lobster on barbeques — just to make sure you don't miss a thing!

Chapter 11

Halifax

• •

In This Chapter

▶ Getting to Halifax

▶ Finding your way around the city

▶ Choosing the best places to stay and dine

▶ Sightseeing, shopping, and spending a night on the town

▶ Taking side trips out of the city

• •

*H*alifax may look like any other city as you approach the runway, but after you've landed, there's no doubt you're in the Maritimes. This port city does a wonderful job of combining work and play. Although large chunks of shoreline are taken up by industrial endeavors, a prime stretch of waterfront is the epicenter for locals and visitors alike. Museums, boutiques, restaurants, and pubs fill historic waterfront warehouses, with a seawall promenade winding past tour boats, tall ships — and even the occasional seal!

Although the harbor dominates the landscape, it's easy to see past the working port areas to uninhabited islands, with glimpses of the Atlantic Ocean in the distance. Overlooking the harbor is a compact downtown core, with no point more than a few blocks from the water. Here, you find all the trappings of a modern metropolis, delicately interspersed with rows of 200-year-old stone buildings and abundant green space. Downtown is first and foremost a business core, but the streets are perpetually alive with friendly faces and the catchy sounds of traditional east coast music waft out from darkened drinking holes.

Plan on spending two (preferably three) days in Halifax. Maritime weather will have some bearing on what you do, so check the forecast and plan your time at indoor attractions to coincide with rainy spells.

Getting There

Halifax is a transportation hub for all of the Maritimes. Most visitors arrive by plane at Halifax International Airport or drive into the city on one of four major highways.

Nova Scotia

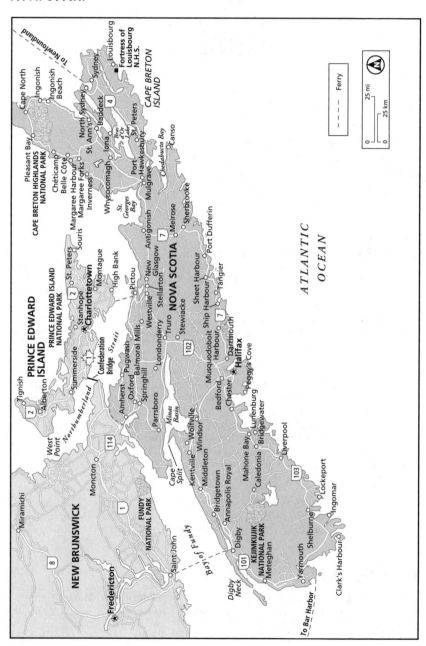

Halifax

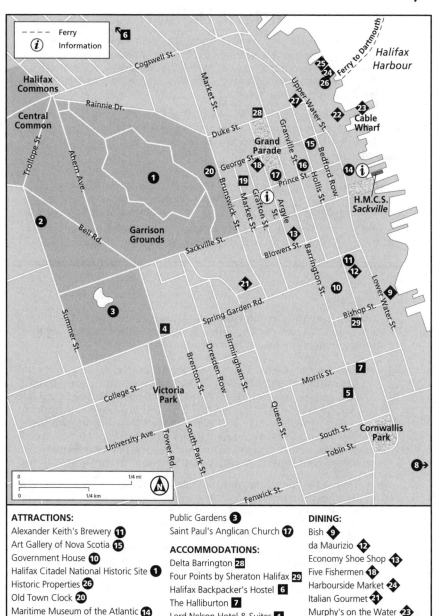

ATTRACTIONS:
Alexander Keith's Brewery **11**
Art Gallery of Nova Scotia **15**
Government House **10**
Halifax Citadel National Historic Site **1**
Historic Properties **26**
Old Town Clock **20**
Maritime Museum of the Atlantic **14**
Museum of Natural History **2**
Pier 21 **8**
Province House **16**

Public Gardens **3**
Saint Paul's Anglican Church **17**

ACCOMMODATIONS:
Delta Barrington **28**
Four Points by Sheraton Halifax **29**
Halifax Backpacker's Hostel **6**
The Halliburton **7**
Lord Nelson Hotel & Suites **4**
Prince George Hotel **19**
Waverley Inn **5**

DINING:
Bish **9**
da Maurizio **12**
Economy Shoe Shop **13**
Five Fishermen **18**
Harbourside Market **24**
Italian Gourmet **21**
Murphy's on the Water **23**
Salty's Bar & Grill **25**
Stayner's Wharf Pub & Grill **22**
Sweet Basil Bistro **27**

Historic Halifax

The sight of arriving immigrant ships and the echoes of horse-drawn carts down cobbled streets may be long gone, but the port city of Halifax retains its historic appeal. Nowhere are the city's nautical traditions better preserved than at the Maritime Museum of the Atlantic, which is flanked by Canada's oldest waterfront warehouses, aptly named the Historic Properties.

But behind the museum and old buildings lies Halifax's colorful history. Now home to popular boutiques and restaurants, Halifax's stone warehouses once stored pirate booty. The British government commissioned private vessels to cruise against their enemies (usually the French or the U.S.) and called it "privateering" — really just a pleasant name for piracy.

The story of Halifax is punctuated by intriguing footnotes like this. The 1997 movie *Titanic* brought renewed attention to the world's best-known maritime disaster and its numerous Halifax links, most of which are actively promoted as tourist attractions. Other links are more subtle, such as the Five Fishermen restaurant, located in a former funeral home where the *Titanic's* first-class passengers were embalmed.

By plane

Traveling from **Halifax International Airport** to the heart of downtown takes around 40 minutes by road, but allow slightly longer during the morning rush hour. Public transportation options are

- ✔ **Bus.** Because Metro Transit buses don't reach the airport, try the **Airporter** (☎ 902-873-2091), which offers service between the airport and major downtown hotels. The fare is C$14 (US$11.90) one-way, C$24 (US$20.40) round-trip. The first bus leaves the airport at 6 a.m., the last at 1 a.m. Heading back to the airport, shuttles depart from most accommodations up to 20 times daily between 5:30 a.m. and 10 p.m. (plan on catching a bus at least 90 minutes before your flight departs). You don't need advance reservations.

- ✔ **Taxi.** After collecting your baggage from the carousels, head through the exit doors to the lineup of taxis out front. The set fare to downtown is C$43 (US$36.60).

Most of the major **car-rental** companies have check-in counters near the baggage carousels and vehicles can be picked up in a parking lot within easy walking distance. The exception is Discount, which operates out of the nearby Airport Hotel; if your reservation is with this company, call for a pickup at the hotel phone bank in front of the information booth.

The Web site www.flyhalifax.com is filled with helpful information, including links to airlines serving Halifax and a real-time flight tracker.

By car

Highway 102 cuts across Nova Scotia from New Brunswick, bringing you right into the heart of Halifax. Allow three hours non-stop from the border. You may discover plenty of worthwhile stops en route, but the only one you *must* make is at the tollgates east of Amherst (C$3/US$2.60). As Halifax looms on the horizon, Highway 118 branches left off Highway 102. This alternate route draws traffic into the city of Dartmouth, but also provides a final approach to downtown.

Two highways lead into Halifax from the west: **Highway 101** from along the Bay of Fundy; and **Highway 103,** which runs along the South Shore from Yarmouth. Both routes pick up ferry traffic from further afield. Ferries from Saint John (New Brunswick) terminate at Digby, a three-hour drive along Highway 101 to Halifax. Travelers arriving by ferry at Yarmouth from either Portland or Bar Harbor, both in Maine, are faced with a four-hour drive on Highway 103.

By train or bus

If you choose to travel into Halifax by train, **VIA Rail** runs into Nova Scotia from Montreal, with the service terminating in Halifax at 1161 Hollis Street (☎ 888-842-7245; www.via.ca), on the southern edge of downtown.

Acadian (☎ 902-454-9321; www.acadianbus.com) provides bus service to Halifax from Moncton (New Brunswick), where connections can be made from Montreal or Maine. These two cities are the closest that **Greyhound** services get to the Maritimes. Through tickets to Halifax can be purchased from Greyhound and connections are seamless. Acadian also runs buses to Halifax from points throughout the province, including the ferry ports of Yarmouth and Digby. The Halifax bus depot is in the VIA Rail station, at 1161 Hollis Street and is open daily 6:30 a.m. to 7 p.m.

Orienting Yourself in Halifax

Most of Halifax's attractions and major hotels are within walking distance of the touristy downtown waterfront precinct between Cogswell Street in the north and South Street in, you guessed it, the south. The main thoroughfare along this 10-block stretch is Water Street. This narrow, winding road set back slightly from the harbor is dotted with public parking lots (that's a hint — downtown is compact enough that most sights can be seen on foot).

Halifax is small and easy to navigate. The city center clings to a hilly peninsula within Halifax Harbour. From here, built-up areas spread in all directions.

Downtown

Most attractions, accommodations, and restaurants are within walking distance of each other in the downtown core. The basic grid pattern of streets laid out over 200 years ago remains, bounded very roughly by the harbor to the east and Citadel Hill to the west, with Cogswell Street and Spring Garden Road creating man-made boundaries to the north and south respectively. Water Street, as you may suspect, runs along the harborfront. South of Sackville Street, it's known as Lower Water Street, while to the north it's Upper Water Street. Between Water Street and the harbor are numerous pay parking lots, the Maritime Museum of the Atlantic, restaurants, and gift shops.

Dartmouth

Two bridges and a ferry service link downtown Halifax with Dartmouth, across the harbor to the east. Although Dartmouth has its own distinct industrial, business, and residential districts, it is not a separate city, but combines with Halifax to form the Halifax Regional Municipality. Less picturesque than Halifax, it offers parks, lakes, and a few eccentric attractions — head here if Quaker history, ocean research, or rocks from around the world are your thing.

Bedford and Sackville

Bedford is a picturesque community at the head of Bedford Basin and north of Halifax proper. Settled as early as 1749, its streets are lined with well-kept middle- and upper-class homes, many with views back down the harbor. If you detour into Bedford, be sure to find your way down to the water's edge, much of it protected by parkland.

There's little reason to visit Sackville, north of Bedford, but a quick overview may be helpful for highway travelers entering Halifax from the north along Highway 102. If you're heading for the city, follow Highway 102 through Sackville. Don't be tempted by "Halifax via the bridges" signage, which detour through Dartmouth and make the approach to downtown confusing.

Getting around Halifax

Although downtown can get congested with traffic, this has more to do with the narrow, hilly streets than any great volume of vehicles. The best advice I can give you is to not plan on driving at all. Public transportation schedules and routes are designed to get residents to and from work so, aside from the ferry to Dartmouth, you can leave this form of transportation to the locals.

Driving (and parking)

If you're staying downtown, park your car and walk. Your best bet is the city-operated parking lots along Upper and Lower Water Streets.

With admission to Halifax Citadel, you can include parking for an additional C$3.25 (US$2.80). Therefore, you can visit this top-of-the-town attraction early in the day, then leave your vehicle there while you spend the rest of the day exploring downtown. Just remember, it's an uphill walk (or an inexpensive cab ride) at the end of the day and keep your Citadel entry receipt.

If Halifax International Airport is the starting point of your Maritimes adventure, reserve your vehicle to be picked up at a downtown location just before heading out of the city. Not only will you save a few days' rental charge, you won't pay the airport rental surcharge.

On foot

Downtown Halifax is a great place to get around on foot. You can easily do without a vehicle and not miss any of the popular attractions. If you're staying downtown, then the main information center and all the best restaurants are within easy reach. If you tire of walking, jump aboard a tour bus or take to the water for a break. Only a few attractions are out of reach by walking — save these up and visit them in one go.

Catching cabs

Cabs are easy to hail anywhere in the downtown area, especially along Upper and Lower Water Streets, or head for one of the major hotels where taxis wait. Rates begin at C$2.50 (US$2.10), increasing based on time and distance to around C$7 (US$6) for a trip across downtown. Cab companies include:

- ✔ Casino Taxi (☎ **902-425-6666**)
- ✔ Co-op Taxi (☎ **902-444-0001**)
- ✔ Maritime Taxi (☎ **902-456-4248**)
- ✔ Yellow Cab (☎ **902-420-0000**)

Transit tips

Metro Transit (☎ **902-490-6600**) provides inexpensive bus and ferry transportation to all parts of the city. The fare for any single sector is C$2 (US$1.70) adults, C$1.40 (US$1.20) children, exact change only. The main transit interchange is at the corner of Upper Water and George Streets. Call or pick up a schedule from the information center.

From June to September, Metro Transit and the Downtown Halifax Business Commission sponsor a free shuttle service known as **Fred** (short for "free rides everywhere downtown"). Hop on and ride the loop through Lower Water Street, Spring Garden Road, South Park Street, and South Street for a free tour of the downtown core.

Staying in Halifax

The following recommendations are a cross-section of accommodation choices in various price categories. Prices fluctuate with supply and demand. Most downtown hotels cater to business travelers, with rack rates matching Monday to Friday work schedules. Weekend packages are offered year-round, but look for the best deals outside of the summer tourist season. As always, hotel Web sites are the best places to start searching out deals.

Ask about additional charges for parking and local calls, since they may not be included in your room's rate.

To the rate quoted, count on 16.5% in taxes being added to your final hotel bill.

First-Choice Lodgings

Airport Hotel Halifax
$$ Airport

As the name suggests, this hotel is right by the airport, 40km (25 miles) north of downtown. A free shuttle transports guests between the two terminals and the hotel 24 hours a day. The exterior and public areas are a little tired, but spacious, comfortable rooms provide a relaxing stay before or after a long flight. Aside from the adjacent aircraft museum, this property is isolated — meaning you're stuck eating at the in-house restaurant (so-so food at best). On the plus side, facilities include indoor and outdoor pools, a small fitness room, and a lounge that opens to a pleasant patio.

60 Bell Blvd. (take Exit 6 from Highway 102). ☎ *800-667-3333 or 902-873-3000.* www. atlific.com. *Parking: Above ground, free. Rack rates: C$95–C$140 (US$80.80– US$119) double. AE, DC, MC, V. Wheelchair-accessible rooms.*

Halifax Backpacker's Hostel
$ Downtown

A 10-minute walk north of the waterfront, this renovated residence is perfectly suited to budget travelers who don't mind being a little away from the night-time action offered by the Hostelling International hostel (on Barrington St.). Facilities include a well-equipped communal kitchen, a lounge room with television and lots of games, Internet access, and a small garden. Bike rentals are C$15 (US$12.75) for a full day. The Airport Shuttle drops hostel guests at the nearby Citadel Hotel.

See map p. 103. 2193 Gottingen St. (north of Cogswell St.). ☎ *888-431-3170 or 902-431-3170.* www.halifaxbackpackers.com. *Parking: Streetside. Rack rates: C$20 (US$17.10) dormitory bed, C$50 (US$42.50) double, C$80 (US$68) family room. AE, MC, V.*

The Halliburton
$$–$$$$ **Downtown**

Three adjoining townhouses, one dating to 1809, make up this well-located accommodation. The inn has 29 guest rooms, each elegantly decked out in period antiques, with in-room coffee and super-comfortable beds topped out with goose-down duvets. Most are at the lower end of the price range; the one-bedroom suite comes with its own wood-burning fireplace (C$225/US$191.30). If you've chosen one of the other rooms, plan on relaxing in the inviting lounge, which also has a fireplace, or in the private garden courtyard. **Stories**, the downstairs restaurant, serves up a complimentary breakfast and the dinner menu features local seafood and game prepared with a European flare.

See map p. 103. 5184 Morris St. (between Barrington and Hollis sts.). ☎ *902-420-0658. Fax: 902-423-2324.* www.halliburton.ns.ca. *Rack Rates: C$140–C$350 (US$119–US$297.50) double. AE, DC, MC, V.*

Inn on the Lake
$$$–$$$$ **Waverly**

Set on 2 hectares (5 acres) of lakefront parkland north of Halifax, this country-style retreat is a world away from the bustle of city living (although I have heard complaints about highway noise). You can sunbathe on a white-sand beach, lounge on chairs surrounded by well-manicured gardens, or crank up the energy level on the tennis courts and then cool off in the large outdoor pool. Some of the standard rooms have poolside patios, while others have lake-view balconies. Upgrade for C$20 (US$17.10) to a Deluxe Room and enjoy a king-size bed, jetted tub, a balcony, and Internet access. Dining options include pool side snacks, an English-style pub, or a more formal dining room. The inn is a 10-minute drive from the airport, a short free shuttle ride away.

3009 Lake Thomas Dr. (take Exit 5 from Hwy 102). ☎ *800-463-6465 or 902-861-3480. Fax: 902-861-4883.* www.innonthelake.com. *Rack rates: C$169–C$320 (US$143.65–US$272). AE, MC, V.*

Lord Nelson Hotel & Suites
$$$$ **Downtown**

Dating to 1928, this landmark hotel has a reputation as one of Halifax's finest. Standard rooms are large and elegantly furnished; bathrooms are particularly well equipped. Amenities include a business center, in-room Internet access, free local calls, a concierge, and a British-style pub with good, inexpensive food. Despite its size (243 rooms), service and attention to detail is flawless. As is so often the case, disregard the rack rates and book online to snatch deals such as a room, parking, breakfast, and a city tour for two for around C$160 (US$136). Make sure you request a room with views of the adjacent Public Gardens.

See map p. 103. 1515 South Park St. (at Spring Garden Rd.). ☎ *800-565-2020 or 902-423-6331. Fax: 902-423-7148.* www.lordnelsonhotel.com. *Parking: C$8 (US$6.80) per day. Rack rates: C$250–C$420 (US$212.50–US$357). AE, DISC, MC, V.*

Prince George Hotel
$$$$ Downtown

This place, halfway between the waterfront and Citadel Hill, is my fave among downtown hotels. Even the standard guest rooms are spacious and well appointed with lots of stylish mahogany furniture. For a few extra dollars, you can opt for a Crown Service room, with upgrades like a CD player, evening turndown service, and breakfast delivered to your door. Other in-house amenities include a bistro-style restaurant, a smallish indoor pool, and a business center. Service is also a step above what you'd expect from a hotel. Don't be scared off by the rack rates — the hotel Web site offers rooms for well under C$200 (US$170) year-round, making them an excellent downtown deal.

See map p. 103. 1725 Market St. ☎ *800-565-1567 or 902-425-1986. Fax: 902-429-6048.* www.princegeorgehotel.com. *Rack rates: C$269–C$475 (US$228.65–US$403.75) double. AE, DISC, MC, V.*

Prospect Bed & Breakfast
$$ Prospect

If you have your own transportation, an overnight stay in seaside Prospect, near Peggy's Cove, is a delightful escape from city living. Housed in a 150-year-old covent, five guest rooms each have a private bathroom and the more expensive ones also have a fireplace. The ocean is nearly always in sight, from your bedroom window, from the dining room, and from the Adirondack chairs scattered around the grounds, or wander down to the private beach and dip your toes in the Atlantic. Hot breakfast and afternoon tea are included in the price of your stay.

1758 Prospect Bay Rd., Prospect. ☎ *800-725-8732 or 902-423-1102.* www.nsinns. com. *Parking: Free. Rack Rates: C$125–C$145 (US$106.25–US$123.25) double. AE, MC, V.*

Waverley Inn
$$–$$$ Downtown

Originally home to a society couple, Halifax's grandest residence was converted to the Waverley Inn in 1876 and has been taking guests ever since. All rooms come with extravagant Victorian touches such as four-poster beds and lace curtains, while more modern conveniences include wireless Internet. Some rooms have jetted tubs. A deck catches the afternoon sun and the parlor is a wonderful place to relax in the evening. Continental breakfast and afternoon tea are included in the rates.

See map p. 103. 1266 Barrington St. ☎ 800-565-9346 or 902-423-9346. Fax: 902-425-0167. www.waverleyinn.com. *Parking: Free. Rack Rates: C$135–C$240 (US$114.80–US$204) double. AE, DISC, MC, V.*

Runner-up lodgings

Delta Barrington

$$$ **Downtown** The Delta Barrington is ideally located one block from the harbor. Rooms are smallish but well appointed. An upgrade to Signature Club (bigger room, continental breakfast, etc) only costs a few extra dollars. *See map p. 103. 1875 Barrington St. ☎ 877-814-7706 or 902-429-7410. Fax: 902-420-6524.* www.deltahotels.com.

Four Points by Sheraton Halifax

$$$$ **Downtown** One of Halifax's most modern hotels, this glass-sided property features stylish rooms with work desks and large televisions. Other amenities include room service, an indoor pool, and a fitness room. *See map p. 103. 1496 Hollis St. ☎ 800-368-7764 or 902-423-4444. Fax: 902-423-2327.* www.sheraton.com.

Fountain View Guest House

$ **Near Citadel Hill** In a renovated residence, seven guest rooms share three bathrooms and parking is on the street, but at under C$50 (US$42.50) for double occupancy, no one complains. *2138 Robie St. ☎ 902-422-4169.*

Travelers Motel

$–$$ **North of Downtown** An inexpensive choice along the old highway linking downtown to the airport, this park-at-your-door motel has basic guest rooms and a few cabins rented in summer only. *773 Bedford Hwy. ☎ 800-565-3394 or 902-835-3394. Fax: 902-835-6887.* www.travelersmotel.ca.

Dining in Halifax

The eateries along the harbor are the easiest to find and have the best views. Considering their prime tourist locale, these restaurants are surprisingly popular with Haligonians, both during the weekday lunch hour and for an evening meal, and the reasonable prices are a pleasant treat. If you're in the city for more than one night, I encourage you to get adventurous and move away from the waterfront, where you find pockets of restaurants along Argyle Street and Spring Garden Road.

Halifax has a good range of coffee houses, but the chains you're familiar with (Starbucks, Second Cup, and others) are almost non-existent. Instead, head to **Perk's,** at 1781 Lower Water St. (☎ **902-429-9367**). Located right beside the harbor, it offers all the usual coffee concoctions, as well as light meals such as seafood salad croissants.

Bish
$$$–$$$$ **Downtown** **GLOBAL**

Aside from the unusual name, a few things make Bish stand apart from Halifax's other waterfront restaurants — it's well away from the crush of the Historic Properties, the setting is elegant, and the menu offers a lot more than seafood. The cooking itself is excellent. The ginger lacquered pork tenderloin brushed with apple sauce stars as a main course; there's seafood if you must, with choices such as arctic char amandine, a delicate-tasting fish from northern waters baked in a almond-based sauce.

See map p. 103. 1475 Lower Water St. (Bishop's Landing). ☎ *902-425-7993. Reservations recommended. Main courses: C$28–C$33 (US$23.80–US$28.10). AE, DC, DISC, MC, V. Open: Mon–Sat 5:30–10 p.m.*

da Maurizio
$$$$ **Downtown** **ITALIAN**

Halifax's finest Italian restaurant, da Maurizio, is in the historic Alexander Keith's Brewery building, across from the waterfront. Little has been done to alter the structure, yet the dining room is pleasing to the eye, with clean, simple lines set off by exposed red brick and lots of richly finished woods. Begin with *astice Alla Isabella* (poached lobster topped with avocado aioli), then get serious with upscale pasta presentations or main courses like *veal scaloppine* (thin slices of veal in a port-based demi-glaze). *Crème brulée* with fresh fruit is a fitting way to end this decadent splurge. The wine list has many Italian choices, while sensibly also including bottles from around the world.

See map p. 103. 1496 Lower Water St. ☎ *902-423-0859. Reservations recommended. Main courses: C$28–C$32 (US$23.80–US$27.20). AE, DC, DISC, MC, V. Open: Mon–Sat 5–10 p.m.*

Economy Shoe Shop
$–$$$ **Downtown** **CONTEMPORARY**

First things first. The unusual name is derived from an old neon sign the owners hung out front when they didn't have the budget for proper signage. Since those simple times, the "Shoe" has become one of Halifax's most popular hangouts and expanded to include four dining rooms, each with a different theme and ambience. One of these, Backstage, has a distinct Bohemian vibe and a Monastery-like setting of arched walls. Diamond is another funky space, this one the domain of music fans who gather around a juke box packed with an eclectic collection of tunes. The Belgian Bar is so named for the European beers on tap, but with its high glass ceiling and tropical setting, its also a great place to feel more cheerful than the outside weather may allow. Finally, there's the restaurant's original space, with tables spilling onto the sidewalk. Each room has a similar menu, with lots of choices that are perfect for sharing.

See map p. 103. 1663 Argyle St. ☎ *902-423-8845. Reservations not necessary. Main courses: C$11–C$24 (US$9.40–US$20.40). AE, DC, DISC, MC, V. Open: Daily 11 a.m.–2 a.m.*

In the market for a cheap meal?

One of the best places to find inexpensive food is **Harbourside Market,** occupying a prime waterfront spot within the Historic Properties complex at 1869 Upper Water Street. Seating is inside or out, with the outdoor tables sitting right above the water. This glorified food court is anchored by **Captain John's** (☎ 902-420-9255), where choices range from a halibut burger (C$8.50/US$7.20) to a full lobster with all the trimmings (C$22/US$18.70). Looking for something to share? Try the mussels, steamed in a tomato broth (C$8/US$6.80). Across the way is **Brisket Boardwalk Deli** (☎ 902-423-7625) with healthy wraps, soups, and sandwiches. The market even has its own brew-pub, **John Shippey's** (☎ 902-423-7386), which serves up draft (C$6/US$5.10 a pint) brewed on site and offers table service inside and at one outside corner. The food outlets are open daily 11 a.m. to 9:30 p.m.

Five Fishermen
$$–$$$ Downtown   SEAFOOD

Five Fishermen is one of Halifax's better seafood restaurants, and the only one housed in a building that once served as a funeral home for some of the Titanic's doomed passengers. Table settings are spread through a number of different rooms (one recreates a cruise ship's dining room), all with high ceilings and lots of brass and dark woodwork. You can't go wrong with any of the seafood or steak choices, although I imagine the baked medley of seafood covered in a lobster butter sauce would be hard to top. Take a break from seafood with any of the Alberta beef dishes, or enjoy the best of both worlds by ordering a half-lobster side. Don't be put off by the price of main courses — they include unlimited salad and steamed mussels.

Little Fish, in the same building (☎ 902-425-4025), is an inexpensive off-shoot of the Five Fishermen, with seafood mains under C$20 (US$17.10). It's open weekdays for lunch, with innovative choices like po' boys stuffed with oysters.

See map p. 103. 1740 Argyle St. ☎ 902-422-4421. Reservations recommended. Main courses: C$29–C$34 (US$24.70–US$28.90). AE, DC, DISC, MC, V. Open: Daily from 5 p.m.

Italian Gourmet
$–$$ Spring Garden Road   DELI

Spend the morning at Citadel Hill and the Public Gardens, and then walk down Spring Garden Road back toward the harbor to reach this hidden gem, which is my favorite city lunch spot. It part café and mostly deli, with a long counter along one side filled with goodies such as vegetarian quiche, salmon rolls, and gourmet soups. Across the room is another counter, where you order coffee concoctions, chai lattes, and the creamiest hot chocolate you could imagine.

See map p. 103. 5431 Doyle St., ☎ *902-423-7880. Reservations not necessary. Lunches: C$4.50–C$11 (US$3.80–US$9.40). AE, DC, DISC, MC, V. Open: Mon–Sat 9 a.m.–7 p.m., Sun 10 a.m.–6 p.m.*

Murphy's on the Water
$–$$$ Downtown   SEAFOOD

Located on a wharf jutting into Halifax Harbour, the panoramic water views from this restaurant's outside seating area at the very end of the building can't be beat. Though the menu isn't the city's most upscale offering, combined with the location, dining here will not dissappoint. Keep it simple and stick to classics like clam linguini or seafood bouillabaisse. Aside from a few additional dinner entrées, the same menu is offered all day, meaning you can order a burger for dinner or share a platter of Nova Scotian seafood for lunch.

See map p. 103. 1751 Lower Water St. ☎ *902-420-1015. Reservations accepted. Main courses: C$8.50–C$27 (US$7.20–US$23). AE, DC, MC, V. Open: Daily 11 a.m.–10 p.m.*

Salty's Bar & Grill
$–$$$ Downtown   SEAFOOD

This popular waterfront eatery is in the heart of the action at the front of the Historic Properties complex. The most sought-after seating is out on the wharf, where, for the price of a bowl of clam chowder, you can watch the watery world of Halifax Harbour go by. The menu is typical pub fare, but with lots of local seafood. Considering the location, it's great value, with choices ranging from simple salads (under C$8/US$6.80) to entrées like baked salmon casserole (C$13/US$11.10). This inexpensive menu is available for both lunch and dinner. An upstairs dining room uses the same menu until 5 p.m., and then things get creative (and more expensive) with a menu that features dishes such as blackened halibut doused in a mango salsa and rack of lamb roasted in a herb crust. Of course, steamed lobster is available anytime. Salty's is a good choice for families looking for waterfront dining — the kid's menu is C$5 (US$4.30), including drink and dessert.

See map p. 103. 1869 Upper Water St. ☎ *902-423-6818. Reservations recommended for the upstairs restaurant after 5 p.m. Main courses: C$8–C$28 (US$6.80–US$23.80). AE, DC, DISC, MC, V. Open: Daily 11 a.m.–11 p.m.*

Stayner's Wharf Pub & Grill
$–$$ Downtown   SEAFOOD/PUB FARE

Head to Stayner's for all the usual East Coast pub fare, like fish and chips or mashed potatoes topped with roasted onions. It's also a good choice if you're in the mood for a more refined take on seafood favorites (think baked salmon glazed with maple syrup or Digby scallops fried in lemon herb butter), but don't want to spend a fortune.

See map p. 103. 5075 George St. ☎ *902-492-1800. Reservations not necessary. Main courses: C$8.50–C$18 (US$7.20–US$15.30). MC, V. Open: Daily 11 a.m.–11:30 p.m.*

Sweet Basil Bistro
$$–$$$ Downtown   ITALIAN/ASIAN

Casual and brightly decorated, this funky dining room is in a historic brick building across from the Historic Properties. It's the perfect spot for an inexpensive meal when you want a break from seafood. The menu features lots of fresh, healthy cooking with classic pastas balanced by lighter choices. Vegetarians will love the ravioli filled with roasted squash and hazelnut cream, or the daily crêpe special, which is often meatless. After 5 p.m., the menu expands to include creative dishes like Slash 'N' Burn Salmon — blackened salmon served with a ginger and basil fritter. Save room for a banana split doused in rum and sprinkled with coconut.

See map p. 103. 1866 Upper Water St. ☎ *902-425-2133. Reservations recommended. Main courses: C$15–C$24 (US$12.80–US$20.40). AE, DC, MC, V. Open: Daily 11:30 a.m.–10 p.m.*

Exploring Halifax

In this section, I start out by discussing the major attractions of Halifax and surrounding areas such as Dartmouth. If you like having someone else doing the driving, the section on guided tours will be of special interest while I also include itineraries to make sure you miss nothing.

In addition to the interest of the attractions themselves, sightseeing in Halifax has two things go for it — most downtown sights are within walking distance of each other and entry fees are well-priced.

The top attractions

Alexander Keith's Brewery
Downtown

When Alexander Keith arrived in Halifax from Scotland, he put his experience brewing beer for British troops in India to work, establishing a brewery on the the Halifax harborfront in 1820. Keith's signature beer, India Pale Ale, is still brewed at what is now North America's oldest working brewery, along with other English-style ales and seasonal brews. Led by costumed guides, brewery tours are as much about the history of the city as they are about the brewing process, making them popular with everyone. (And the two free mugs of beer presented at the end of the tour have nothing to do with it.)

Keith's legacy is celebrated by the raising of mugs across city pubs, often for no particular reason. Keith's birthday, October 5, is celebrated more

---

The Great Explosion

On December 6, 1917, Halifax was scarred by the largest man-made explosion prior to the atomic age. The *Mount Blanc,* a French munitions ship, collided with a Belgian relief ship in the middle of Halifax Harbour. The accident itself wasn't major, but it started a fire aboard the *Mont Blanc* and the crew, well aware of the cargo on board, took to the water in lifeboats. As crowds gathered toward the waterfront to watch the spectacle, the ship exploded, leveling over 100 hectares (250 acres) at the northern end of Halifax.

The force of the blast was almost incomprehensible: It was felt on Cape Breton Island and heard as far away as Prince Edward Island. The initial explosion was followed by fire, much of it fueled by coal stored in cellars for the approaching winter. The final death toll was 2,000, with an additional 10,000 injured.

Fort Needham Memorial Park, a few blocks north of downtown along Gottingen Street, is dedicated to the disaster. From the 14-bell carillon in the center of the park, you can gaze down to the harbor and the exact spot where the explosion occurred.

---

officially at nearby Pier 22 with Nova Scotian music, marching bands, dancing, and, you guessed it — lots of India Pale Ale.

See map p. 103. 1496 Lower Water St. ☎ *902-455-1474.* www.keiths.ca. *Admission: C$10 (US$8.50) adults, C$8 (US$6.80) seniors and children. Open: Tours depart every 30 minutes June–Aug Mon–Sat 11 a.m.–8 p.m., Sun noon–5 p.m.; Nov–Apr Fri 5–8 p.m., Sat noon–8 p.m., and Sun noon–4 p.m.*

Art Gallery of Nova Scotia
Downtown

Much of the art you see in Maritimes' galleries depicts lighthouses and fishing boats. This gallery proves that regional artists have a much broader range of subject matter. The 5,000-strong permanent collection is displayed in two buildings seperated by a courtyard. A highlight is the colorful folk art of Maude Lewis. The gallery also hosts touring and temporary exhibits and is home to a small café serving up tasty lunches.

See map p. 103. 1741 Hollis St. ☎ *902-424-7542.* www.agns.gov.ns.ca. *Admission C$10 (US$8.50) adults, C$8 (US$6.80) seniors, C$2 (US$1.70) children. Open: Daily 10 a.m.–5 p.m. (until 9 p.m. Thurs).*

Fairview Cemetery
Fairview

You can read the names and moving tributes on some of the 121 headstones at the back of Fairview Cemetery, but most only have numbers. All, however, have the same date — April 15, 1912. Halifax was the port where many bodies from the *Titanic* were bought for identification. Victims were identifiied by number, in the order they were pulled from the cold waters of the North Atlantic. Graves of the unknown victims are marked with these numbers.

For almost a century, these tombstones lay quietly at the back of the Fairview Cemetery, visited only by the occasional visitor. Everything changed with the release of the 1997 movie *Titanic*. Suddenly, the final resting place of victim number 227, Joseph Dawson, became very popular. He coincidently shared a name with third-class seaman Jack Dawson (portrayed by Leonardo DiCaprio in the movie) and has, as a result, garnered his own share of the actor's fan base. The grave is impossible to miss — just look for the fresh flowers left by weeping teenage girls.

Cemetery entrances are on Connaught and Chisholm Avenues. Admission: Free.

Government House
Downtown

Completed in 1805, this house has been the official residence of Nova Scotia's Lieutenant-Governor longer than any other North American governemnt residence. Built of Nova Scotian stone, it has been extensively restored inside and out and although access is restricted, feel free to admire the exterior from surrounding gardens.

See map p. 103. 1451 Barrington St. Not open to the public.

Halifax Citadel National Historic Site
Downtown

I recommend starting your exploration of Halifax at the top, literally, by visiting Citadel Hill, which sits atop a high point of land overlooking the harbor. The original fortifications, built in 1749, have been replaced numerous times, with the most recent renovations completed in 1856 as a deterant to a percieved threat from the United States. The fort was decommisioned in 1906, but has continued to serve as a proud symbol of the Canadian military ever since. History comes alive at the Citadel in summer through the haunting reverberations of bagpipers, a variety of interpretive programs, and colorful kilted soldiers following shouted marching orders. Indoor exhibits are tucked away in rooms built into the walls. A good starting point is the Fortress Halifax display, which tells the story of the complex. Other highlights are the schoolroom and the adjacent magazines, where gunpowder and cannon charges were stored. A trail follows the top of the casement, encircling the courtyard and passing cannon emplacements. Looking outward, views extend across downtown to the harbor. In the middle of the courtyard, the two-story Cavalier Building holds an information center, a café, and a gift shop.

The Old Town Clock, below the Citadel's George Street entrance, is a city landmark.

See map p. 103. Enter off Sackville St., immediately west of Brunswick St. and follow signs to public parking at the rear of the fortifications. On foot, walk up George St.

from the waterfront. ☎ *902-426-5080. Admission: C$10 (US$8.50) adults, C$8.50 (US$7.20) seniors, C$5 (US$4.30) children; fees are reduced during shoulder seasons and admission is free Nov–early May. Open: July–Aug 9 a.m.–6 p.m.; Sept–June 9 a.m.–5 p.m. Although the grounds are open year-round, no services are available Nov–May.*

Maritime Museum of the Atlantic
Downtown

Everyone will find something of interest at this museum, one of Halifax's premier attractions. The exhibits in this restored waterfront warehouse include numerous vessels that once plied the coastline, as well as displays exploring Nova Scotia's seafaring legacy through chronicles of shipwrecks, the Canadian Navy, the Great Explosion, Sable Island, and the fishing industry. Because of Halifax's numerous links to the *Titanic*, a good portion of the museum is dedicated to the tragedy. A highlight is *Titanic 3D*, a 15-minute documentary taken at the wreck site, shown at regular intervals throughout the day.

Moored at the wharf in front of the museum is the 1913 hydrographic steamer ***Acadia,*** which spent most of its life charting the ocean floor. Parts of the ship are open for public inspection, including the deck area and the chart room. At the next wharf is the ***HMCS Sackville***, a speedy escort used during WWII. Admission to both vessels is free with a museum ticket.

See map p. 103. 1675 Lower Water St. ☎ *902-424-7490.* www.museum.gov.ns.ca/mma. *Admission: A very worthwhile C$8 (US$6.80) adults, C$7 (US$6) seniors, C$4 (US$3.40) children. Open: May–Oct 9:30 a.m.–5:30 p.m. (until 8 p.m. Tues); Nov–Apr Tues–Sat 9:30 a.m.–5:30 p.m., Sun 1–5:30 p.m.*

McNab's Island
Halifax Harbour

On McNab's Island you'll find an 1888 fort built to defend Halifax Harbour from seaborne attacks. It's also a provincial park that provides a quick escape from the bustle of the city. You can enjoy numerous hiking trails leading to lookouts with views back across to the city, sandy beaches, a lighthouse, and an abandoned farm. Bring your own picnic lunch and drinks to one of the many designated day-use areas.

Titanic tourism

A brochure detailing Titanic-related sights is available at the Maritime Museum and local visitor centers. Included are details and driving directions to Fairview Cemetery, along with Mount Olivet Cemetery, the final resting place of John Clarke, one of the *Titanic* band members famous for continuing to play as the ship was sinking.

Access is by McNab's Island Ferry, ☎ *902-465-4563, which departs on demand from Fisherman's Cove; C$10 (US$8.50) round-trip. Admission: Free.*

Museum of Natural History
Downtown

Natural history comes alive at this musuem, situated west of Citadel Hill. The skeleton of a pilot whale and dinosaur fossils take center stage in the main gallery, with geology, anthropology, human history, and Acadian culture displays filling out an interesting facility. Some exhibits change with the season (it was the geology behind the Fundy tides when I last visited) while the critter-filled Nature Centre is where younger children gravitate.

See map p. 103. 1747 Summer St. ☎ *902-424-7353.* www.nature.museum.gov.ns.ca. *Admission: C$5 (US$4.30) adults, C$4.50 (US$3.80) seniors, C$3 (US$2.60) children. Open: June–mid-Oct Mon–Sat 9:30 a.m.–5:30 p.m., daily the rest of the year.*

Pier 21
Downtown

Between 1928 and 1971, over one million immigrants first stepped foot in Canada at Pier 21. This historic locale has since been turned into a museum dedicated to these people and the trials and tribulations they encountered on the journey to Canada. The Exhibition Hall is filled with interactive displays that trace the immigration process. Even if you're not researching your roots, plan on spending a little time here, especially at the compelling audiovisual presentations that relate personal immigrant stories. The Research Centre sounds more scholarly than it is. Computers and microfilm hold a database of ship arrivals and some passenger lists (1925–1935).

See map p. 103. 1055 Marginal Rd. ☎ *902-425-7770.* www.pier21.ca. *Admission: C$8 (US$6.80) adults, C$7 (US$6) seniors, C$4.50 (US$3.80) children. Open: May–Nov 9:30 a.m.–5:30 p.m.; Dec–April Tues–Fri 10 a.m.–5 p.m., Sat noon–5 p.m.*

Point Pleasant Park
Downtown

At the southern end of the downtown peninsula, 75 hecatres (180 acres) of prime waterfront is protected by this expansive park. The local ecosystem changed forever in September 2003, when Hurricane Juan swept through the park, destroying 75,000 trees, but it is still an enjoyable place to go walking or biking, or enjoy lunch at one of many picnic area. You can stroll along the km (25 miles) of trails that lace the park, or check out the view from the centrally located Prince of Wales Martello Tower, built in 1862 to defend the city from attack.

2 kilometers (1.2 miles) south along Marginal or Young Aves. from downtown; parking is plentiful, or take Bus 9 from Scotia Centre. Open: Daylight hours. Admission: Free.

Province House
Downtown

Famously described by Charles Dickens in 1842 as "like looking at Westminster through the wrong end of the telescope," this small, symmetrical tree-shaded building is Canada's oldest seat of government, having been used as the meeting place of the provincial legislature since 1819. Inside the rather dour sandstone building are a number of inspiring exterior features, including ornamental plasterwork.

See map p. 103. 1726 Hollis St. ☎ *902-424-4661.* gov.ns.ca/legislature. *Admission: Free. Open: July–Aug Mon–Fri 9 a.m.–5 p.m., Sat–Sun 10 a.m.–4 p.m.; Sept–June Mon–Fri 9 a.m.–4 p.m.*

Public Gardens
Downtown

Generally regarded as North America's finest original Victorian garden, this 7-hectare (17-acre) greenspace was created as a private garden in 1753, just four years after the founding of Halifax. Carefully tended rose bushes bloom in formal Victorian-style beds, rhododendrons grow so lush they form a canopy over the path, and small streams link ponds inhabited by ducks and swans. In the center of the gardens, an old-fashioned bandstand hosts free Sunday afternoon concerts, but any sunny afternoon of the week is a perfect opportunity to while away some time here. Across Sackville Street from the north side of the gardens stands a sandstone cottage, the home of gardener Richard Power, who designed the original layout.

See map p. 103. Bordered by Sackville St, Summer St, South Park St, and Spring Garden Rd. The main entrance is at the corner of the latter two streets. Admission: Free. Open: May–Nov daylight hours.

Saint Paul's Anglican Church
Downtown

Founded in 1749, Saint Paul's was the first cathedral built outside Great Britain. Grand, white, and dotted with stained glass windows, it's now surrounded by modern highrises. Above the north-facing porch is a piece of metal embedded during the explosion of the *Mont Blanc* (see "The Great Explosion" sidebar).

See map p. 103. 1749 Argyle St. ☎ *902-429-2240.* www.stpaulshalifax.org. *Admission: Free. Open: Mon–Fri 9 a.m.–4 p.m.*

Crossing the harbor to Dartmouth

Dating to 1750 (just one year after Halifax was founded), the city of Dartmouth lies across Halifax Harbour from downtown. The working waterfront is dominated by industrial complexes with a population of 65,000 sprawling through to city limits. The city itself lacks the charm of Halifax, but it has plenty of things to see and do.

Getting there and around

The ferry from downtown Halifax terminates at the **Alderney Gate** quayside complex. A small visitor's booth (☎ **902-490-4433**) dispenses information on local attractions and transit routes and schedules for buses headed to the sights listed below. You'll also find numerous shops, an indoor play park, a library with free Internet access, and a Saturday market (7 a.m.–2 p.m.).

From Alderney Gate, a short harborfront walking trail offers views back across the water to Halifax and the impossible-to-miss Imperial Oil refinery. In the adjacent Ferry Terminal Park is the World Peace Pavilion, which includes stones of substance from over 60 countries, including chunks of the Berlin Wall and the Great Wall of China.

Bedford Institute of Oceanography
Dartmouth

This government facility beside the MacKay Bridge is definitely worth checking out. It is Canada's largest ocean research center, targeting a wide range of disciplines, from ocean surveillance techniques for the Department of Defense to monitoring cod fisheries for the Department of Fisheries and Oceans. The public is welcome to take a guided tour of the facility that includes a glimpse of the latest 3D underwater mapping technology. Within the institute, you can also visit the Sea Pavilion, home to a series of touch tanks holding sea life collected from the Nova Scotia coastline, while another interesting display depicts the *Titanic* on the ocean floor.

1 Challenger Dr. ☎ *902-426-2373.* bio.gc.ca. *Admission: Free. Guided tours: May–Aug Mon–Fri 9 a.m.–4 p.m.*

Cole Harbour Heritage Farm Museum
Dartmouth

Children will love this little piece of country life, even though it's surrounded by suburbia. Geese, ducks, and rabbits roam freely around the property while sheep and cows are fenced. The original farmhouse has been converted to a tearoom and you can see "smithies" at work in the blacksmith shop.

471 Poplar Dr. ☎ *902-434-0222. Admission: Donation. Open: mid-May–mid-Oct Mon–Sat 10 a.m.–4 p.m., Sun noon–4 p.m.*

Downtown Museums
Dartmouth

Within walking distance of Alderney Gate, **Quaker House**, 59 Ochterloney Street at Edward Street (☎ **902-464-5823**) is a good little museum open Tuesday to Sunday mid-June through August 10 a.m. to 5 p.m. Quakers were drawn to Nova Scotia from New England for the whaling industry and this 1786 home tells their story. Costumed guides lead visitors out back to a herb and vegetable garden planted with the same varieties that were planted there over 200 years ago. Admission is C$2 (US$1.70). Keep your receipt, because entry to nearby **Evergreen House** is included. It's a just few blocks away, at 26 Newcastle Street (☎ 902-464-2300); hours are the same as at Quaker House. Displays catalogue the human history of the Dartmouth region, including a solid collection of antiques.

Fisherman's Cove
South of Dartmouth

Jump aboard bus 60 at Alderney Gate to reach this photogenic fishing village, 7km (4.3 miles) south of Dartmouth. Though many of the buildings along the wharf have been renovated or are made to look weathered, an authentic atmosphere prevails, with fishing boats bringing in daily catches of lobster, crab, salmon, and halibut. At the **Fisherman's Cove Marine Interpretive Centre,** at the entrance to wharf (☎ 902-465-6093) learn about the history of the village and view local marinelife in the aquariums. Admission is C$2 (US$1.70). The waterfront itself is the main attraction, but you can find plenty of activities, including a sandy beach and kayak rentals.

Seeing Halifax by guided tour

If your time in Halifax is limited, joining a guided tour ensures you see all the major attractions. You can get an overview of the city in a variety of ways — by land, sea, or a combination of the two. But even if you only have one day in town, plan on spending at least some of it exploring on foot. A trip out onto the harbor is also a must.

By bus

For a quick, complete tour of the city, **Ambassatours** (☎ 800-565-7173 or 902-423-6242; www.atlantictours.com) offers a three-hour Deluxe Historic Halifax Tour for C$36 (US$30.60) adults, C$33 (US$28) seniors, C$18 (US$15.30) children. A kilted guide provides a running commentary as a trolley car whizzes you around the city. While this tour provides a good overview, you may not get to linger as long as you'd like at some of the best stops — Citadel Hill alone (one of the stops; admission included) easily deserves a two-hour visit. Departures are May to October daily at 9 a.m. and 1 p.m. from major downtown hotels. Another Ambassatours option is a one-hour downtown loop tour aboard an old British-style double-decker bus. You can get on and off as you please at any of ten stops. Tickets are valid for two days and cost C$43 (US$36.55) adults, C$39 (US$33.15) seniors, C$21 (US$17.85) children. Buses depart every 30 minutes from 9 a.m. mid-June to October. The main ticketing office for these tours is a kiosk in front of the Maritime Museum on Upper Water Street.

By boat

One the most pleasurable ways to get a feel for Halifax is from sea level. Jump on a commuter ferry, ride a tugboat with personality, or sail off into the sunset aboard one of the world's most famous yachts. However you do it, get out on the water for a true feel of this seaside town!

The least expensive way to enjoy Halifax Harbour is from the upper deck of the passenger ferry between Halifax and Dartmouth. Operated by **Metro Transit** (☎ 902-490-4000), ferries depart for Dartmouth every 30 minutes between 6:30 a.m. and 9:30 p.m. from the terminal at the foot of Duke Street. The 12-minute trip costs just C$2 (US$1.70) each way.

For a wide variety of tour boat options, head to Cable Wharf at 1751 Lower Water St. and the **Murphy's on the Water** (☎ 902-420-1015; www.murphysonthewater.com) ticket kiosk. The *Harbour Queen* stern-wheeler departs for a two-hour cruise daily at 10 a.m. and 2 p.m. costing C$19.95 (US$17); daily at 4:30 p.m. for a 90-minute cruise costing C$15.95 (US$13.60); daily at 6:30 p.m. for a two-hour dinner cruise costing C$39.95 (US$34); and Friday and Saturday at 9:30 p.m. for a two and a half-hour party cruise complete with live music for C$17.95 (US$15.30). Murphy's also offers nature cruises, fishing trips, and boats to Peggy's Cove.

If the *Bluenose II* is away from Halifax, or you miss one of the precious few spots when this famous schooner is in town (see "The *Bluenose*" sidebar in the Lunenburg section of the following chapter), the *Mar II* is a good alternative. Operated by Murphy's (see above), this wooden ketch that has circumnavigated the world now departs Cable Wharf five to six times daily for a 90-minute sailing trip. The cost is C$19.95 (US$17) per person.

By amphibious craft

I'm sure that the engineers who developed the *Larc V* for transporting supplies and troops in the Vietnam War never imagined one of their boats would end up as a colorfully painted tourist attraction. But that's what's happened in Halifax with **Harbour Hopper Tours,** whose amphibious vehicles will drive you around the streets of Halifax and then plunge into the water for a harbor cruise. You'll find the ticket kiosk on Cable Wharf (☎ 902-490-8687). May through October, the bus (or is that boat?) departs up to 20 times daily between 9 a.m. and 9:30 p.m. Rides are C$22.50 (US$19.10) adults, C$21.50 (US$18.30) seniors, C$13.95 children (US$11.90).

Suggested one-, two-, and three-day itineraries

Here are some of the best ways to spend one, two, or three days in Halifax, assuming you're visiting in summer (along with almost everyone else). For details on the attractions, restaurants, and activities mentioned in these itineraries, see the corresponding sections earlier in this chapter.

One-day itinerary

If you have just a single day in Halifax, start at the top and hit **Halifax Citadel National Historic Site** as soon as it opens (9 a.m.) to get a taste of the city's colorful past. Spend an hour exploring this fort, then head across to the Public Gardens (the Museum of Natural History is the family alternative). Admire heritage buildings such as **Province House** on the walk down to the harbor. At lunchtime, choose from the many stands at Harbourside Marketplace (it's hard to bypass the seafood — splurge and share a lobster platter for two) and find a table outside. Afterward, spend an hour or so at the **Maritime Museum of the Atlantic.** Plan on catching the 4:30 p.m. *Mar II* departure. After returning to the dock, it's a short walk to Salty's, where your reservation ensures a waterfront table.

Two-day itinerary

If you have two days in Halifax, you can follow the approach of the one-day itinerary and then plan on rising early for a walk through **Point Pleasant Park** on the morning of the second day. Kick off your official sightseeing with a tour through **Alexander Keith's Brewery** and then wander along the waterfront to **Pier 21.** After lunch, move away from the water and browse the shops of George Street and then stop by the Art Gallery of Nova Scotia. Take a break from seafood at da Maurizio, then if you're still feeling active, head to the **Lower Deck** and catch one of the regular bands entertaining the crowd with traditional Maritimes music.

Three-day itinerary

For the first two days, follow the two-day itinerary. If you happen to be in Halifax on Saturday, squeeze in a visit to **Halifax Farmers' Market,** wandering through stands of fresh produce and local arts and crafts. Plan on spending most of your third day on the Dartmouth side of the harbor, visiting the **Bedford Institute of Oceanography,** or keep the kids happy by stopping by **Cole Harbour Heritage Farm Museum.** At **Fisherman's Cove,** all ages will enjoy soaking up the salty sights and smells of a working village, but probably not as much as tucking into a feast of seafood from one of the local eateries. Back in the city, enjoy dinner at the Economy Shoe Shop, then head over to **Henry House** for a pint or two of the Granite Brewery's Peculiar Ale. If you're feeling up to it, catch a cab to Spring Garden Road and the Thirsty Duck to dance the night away to traditional Celtic music.

Shopping

Shopping in Halifax tends to center around the waterfront, with a couple of notable exceptions. You can buy a wide variety of Maritimes creations — everything from ceramic fishermen to one-of-a-kind art-works. The city has a number of excellent art galleries, as well as quirky shops.

Checking out the scene

Shopping hours in Halifax are generally longer than elsewhere in the Maritimes, but vary greatly depending on the clientele. The touristy waterfront area is busy every day of the week, while many shops (and some restaurants) in the business district follow business hours, closing in the early evening and not opening at all on weekends.

 Don't forget that you must add the 15% harmonized sales tax to all quoted prices (actually, it's done at the cash register). That's the bad news. The good news is that you may be able to get a portion back via the Visitor Rebate Program. (See Chapter 5 for more information.)

What to look for

Although Halifax is not renowned for any particular specialty items, these Maritime cultural products find their way into Halifax's many shops:

- ✔ **Seafood.** The only sensible thing to do with seafood is to eat it, and that's what you'll probably find yourself doing most of time. Some seafood, such as smoked salmon, is prepared to last, allowing you to take it home to hungry relatives. At the airport, you can choose a lobster from the tank and have it boxed specially for airplane travel.

- ✔ **Books and music.** Most bookstores have sections dedicated to Atlantic Canada literature. Secondhand and antiquarian bookstores often have large collections of nautical non-fiction. Traditional folk music is also abundant in music stores as well as nearly all souvenir shops, which often have listening stations so you can get a taste of the music before you buy.

- ✔ **Tacky souvenirs.** Whether it's a lighthouse Christmas decoration, a city-branded T-shirt, or a fluffy moose that you're after, there's no lack of touristy shops to fulfill your needs. Start your search in the Historic Properties along Upper Water Street.

Where to find it

This section details some of my favorite Halifax shopping experiences.

Arts and crafts

Jennifer's of Nova Scotia, 5635 Spring Garden Rd. (☎ **902-425-3119**) is Nova Scotian all over. Pottery, fabric patchwork, jewelry, soaps, and just about everything else is handcrafted. Many items are seasonal, focusing on such occasions as Easter or Christmas.

You'll find a selection of crafty shops along pedestrian-only Granville Mall. One of these is **Pewter House,** 1875 Granville St. (☎ **902-423-8843**). Pewter products are crafted in the delightfully named village of Pugwash, on Nova Scotia's northern shore, and sold at this outlet in Halifax.

Clothing

Island Beach Co. started out selling T-shirts from an old log church, but has since grown into a 30-store chain with outlets across Atlantic

Canada. Head to their stores at 1903 Barrington St. (☎ **902-423-0908**) and 1781 Lower Water St. (☎ **902-422-4060**) in downtown Halifax for casual, contemporary clothing in a subtly themed nautical setting.

If you're in the market for a kilt, or maybe a length of tartan to make your own, **Plaid Place**, in Barrington Place Shops at 1903 Barrington St. (☎ **902-429-6872**) is a good choice. They also stock other plaid clothing such as ties, scarves, and sweaters. The range of children's tartan products is especially impressive.

Antiques

Urban Cottage, at street level of the 1911 Old Merchant's Bank at 1819 Granville St. (☎ **902-423-3010**), offers an eclectic mix of antiques from around the world.

At **henhouse,** south of downtown at 5533 Young St. (☎ **902-423-4499**) antiques are mixed with beautiful hand-built furniture constructed using traditional techniques. They also sell hand-dyed cotton linens, ceramic kitchenware, and porcelain dog dishes.

Crystal

It's difficult to miss **NovaScotian Crystal,** along the waterfront at 5080 George St. (☎ **888-977-2797** or 902-492-0416), when crowds gather to watch artisans turn molten crystal into delicate masterpieces using century-old techniques. The factory doors open for public inspection daily between 8 a.m. and 4:30 p.m., but the most intriguing part of the process — glass-blowing — takes place Tuesday, Thursday, and Saturday. The adjacent shop sells a wide variety of unique pieces such as glasses, vases, and paperweights.

Camping and sporting gear

Halifax's largest outdoor retailer is **Mountain Equipment Co-op,** 1550 Granville St. (☎ **902-421-2667**). MEC, as it's best known, is a co-operative owned by its members, similar to the American R.E.I. stores. Expect a range of high-quality clothing and camping gear, canoes and kayaks, field guides and maps, and a huge number of accessories.

Sport Chek is a big-box sporting goods retailer offering popular brand names at reasonable prices with over 100 stores across Canada. The store features a wide variety of sporting goods for different recreational pursuits, including golfing and mountain biking; the selection of footwear is particularly strong. In Halifax, Sport Chek is in the Halifax Shopping Centre at 1001 Mumford Rd. (☎ **902-455-2528**).

Halifax Farmers' Market

North America's oldest farmers' market takes place every Saturday in a courtyard at the Alexander Keith's Brewery (1496 Lower Water St.; ☎ **902-492-4043**). Hundreds of stands are filled with local produce and crafty creations. Search out Nova Scotian maple syrup, homemade meat pies, and specialty soaps. The market operates every Saturday 7 a.m. to 1 p.m.

Nightlife

Mainly due to a healthy population of students, Halifax has a huge number of pubs and nightclubs. Beer aficionados will love the selection of local brews, most available on tap. Live music is a big part of the local nightlife scene, with bands playing every night of the week somewhere in town. Local bands to watch for include the Kilkenny Krew, the Navigators, McGinty, and Sloan.

Most pubs open at 11 a.m. and close at midnight through the week and at 1 a.m. on weekends. Nightclubs generally stay open later, closing between 2 a.m. and 4 a.m.

For complete listings of everything that's happening after dark, pick up the free *Coast* newspaper (www.thecoast.ca), where you'll find a full schedule of music, stage, and film performances as well as club listings. Another source of information is the waterfront visitor center, where a map is dedicated to city drinking holes.

Pubbing and clubbing it

There's no better place to start this exploration of the local bar scene than down at the harborfront. The **Lower Deck,** in the Privateer's Warehouse at 1869 Upper Water St. (☎ 902-425-1501), is part of a three-story restaurant complex, with a few tables spread out on the adjacent wharf. It's the quintessential Halifax pub — good tunes, lots of local beer on tap, and smart, friendly service. Bands belt out traditional east coast music nightly from 9:30 p.m., with afternoon patio parties scheduled on summer Saturday afternoons from 3 p.m. It's popular with locals, so arrive early to get the best seats. **John Shippey's Brewing Company** (☎ 902-423-7386) is tucked into a corner of the Harbourside Market at 1869 Upper Water Street. Beer is brewed on-site, with large brew tanks filling a glass-walled loft. As part of the food court, the beer is served at tables spread inside and outside along the dock. A few are set aside for brewery patrons, with table service available. I recommend the Piper's Pale Ale, a light and refreshing beer that is the perfect accompaniment to a seafood meal. Continuing along the harborfront, **Stayner's Wharf,** 5075 George St. (☎ 902-492-1800) is as popular for its food as it is for its beer. Monday and Tuesday nights are dedicated to improv comedy, and Thursday to jazz, while Maritimes music draws weekend crowds. Continuing south along the harbor is the **Stag's Head Tavern,** within Keith's Brewery on Lower Water Street (☎ 902-455-1474). Come here to relax with a pint of India Pale Ale and listen to traditional Maritimes music.

Local brews

Finding an authentic pint in Halifax is easy and I really encourage you to forego the big brewery products familiar to most of us (through advertising as much as anything else) and try local brews.

Best-known is **Alexander Keith's** India Pale Ale, brewed in Halifax since 1820 (see "Exploring Halifax," above, for tour information) and available on draught throughout the city and at liquor stores across Canada. This beer has a distinctive "hoppy" flavor, a hangover (pun intended) from the original recipe. The style of beer was developed in Britain, with extra hops added to preserve the beer during its long journey to troops stationed in India (hence the name).

Propeller and **Garrison** are known as microbreweries. Their output is a fraction of Keith's; look for these beers on tap at many pubs and in local liquor stores.

Ingredients are sourced from as far away as England for **Granite Brewery's** Peculiar Ale. This darker ale has a smooth, malty-sweet taste and is usually served only slightly below room temperature.

The **Granite Brewery,** two blocks from the water at 1662 Barrington St. (☎ 902-422-4954), pours beer from its in-house brewery in a relaxed, upmarket atmosphere. Upstairs is **Ginger's Tavern,** which is the reincarnation of a pub of the same name that was popular in Halifax during the 1980s. On any given night, it could be the same 1980s crowd, too, listing to the same music. Just down the road, Granite Brewery's original location is now **Henry House,** 1222 Barrington St. (☎ 902-423-5660), with a pub downstairs and a restaurant upstairs. It is as authentic as any of the British-style pubs in town, with an exposed brick and beam interior, cozy nooks, private booths, muted lighting, comfortable seating, and of course the Granite's popular Peculiar Ale on tap.

The **Thirsty Duck,** 5472 Spring Garden Rd. (☎ 902-422-1548) is best noted for its sunken rooftop patio, a pleasant escape from the noisy street below. The decibel level does go up on weekends, when crowds gather and bands strum their stuff inside. ("The Duck," as it's usually known, gets its name from a pond in the nearby Public Gardens where ducks gather for a refreshing drink.) Two blocks west, **Your Father's Moustache,** 5686 Spring Garden Rd. (☎ 902-423-6766) is a big, bright pub, with a rooftop patio complete with its own bar. Admiring the ocean-themed mural behind the main stage is a good excuse to visit.

Other bars and nightclubs

Dome, 1746 Grafton St. (☎ 902-422-6907), is Halifax's largest dance club. It also features a separate bar area and a room dedicated to live music on weekends. **Bitter End,** 1570 Argyle St. (☎ 902-425-3039) is a hip hangout that tries for a European air of elegance. The drink selection is impressive (good martinis and Caesars), cool contemporary art hangs on the walls, and candles create a distinctive atmosphere that sets this pub apart from those detailed above. **Velvet Olive,** below Citadel Hill at 1770 Market St. (☎ **902-492-2233**), features a DJ spinning disco and funk on Thursday while on Friday and Saturday, lighter "dinner music" plays until 10 p.m. when a band hits the stage. Crowds thin during the week, when you can expect drink specials and promotions such as theme nights. An extensive menu includes delicious Thai dishes under C$20 (US$17.10) and irresistible desserts like smooth chocolate silk for C$7.50 (US$6.40).

Reflections, at 5184 Sackville St. (☎ **902-422-2957**) has a reputation as Halifax's premier venue for gays and lesbians, but is also popular with the adventurous mainstream crowd. Through the working week, expect game and theme nights as well as karaoke, while on weekends a DJ spins the latest dance hits.

The arts

Halifax more than makes up for its lack of major theater companies with semi-professional theater groups and a packed schedule of summer arts festivals.

Theater

The **Neptune Theatre** calls a historic theater at 1593 Argyle St. (☎ **902-429-7070**) home. The main season runs October to May with a smattering of performances ranging from classic to contemporary throughout the summer. Tickets range from C$15 to C$50 (US$12.80–US$42.50).

For lighter theater fare (historically themed musical comedy anyone?) that comes with a substantial three-course meal, make reservations for the **Grafton Street Dinner Theatre**, at 1741 Grafton St. (☎ **902-425-1961**). Tickets are adults C$36 (US$30.60), children C$17.50 (US$14.90); plan to be seated by 6:45 p.m.

Fast Facts

ATMs

Most banks, along with a growing number of grocery stores and gas stations, have ATMs.

Emergencies

Dial ☎ **911** for all emergencies.

Hospital

The **Halifax Infirmary** (☎ **902-473-3383**) is the 24-hour emergency department of the **Queen Elizabeth II Health Services Centre,** at 1796 Summer St.

Information

Tourism Halifax operates the International Vistor Centre at 1598 Argyle St. (☎ **902-490-5946;** www.halifaxinfo.com). **Tourism Nova Scotia** (☎ **902-425-5782;** www.novascotia.com) has an information booth by the baggage carousels at Halifax International Airport and another on the waterfront at 1655 Lower Water St.

Internet Access

Downtown, **Ceilidh Connection**, at 1672 Barrington Street (☎ **902-422-9800**) has a bank of public computers with high-speed connections.

Police

For emergencies, dial ☎ **911.**

Post Office

The main post office is between Sackville and Prince Sts. at 1680 Bedford Row.

Restrooms

Along the waterfront, public restrooms are located in the Harbourside Marketplace and the ferry terminal. The public restrooms in hotel lobbies are also a good bet.

Taxis

See "Orienting Yourself," earlier in this chapter, for a discussion on using local taxis. One company is **Yellow Cab** (☎ **902-420-0000**).

Transit Info

Public buses are operated by **Metro Transit** (☎ **902-490-6600**). See "Orienting Yourself," earlier in this chapter for details.

Weather

Environment Canada maintains a Web site at www.weatheroffice.ec.gc.ca with a link to Halifax's forecast.

Chapter 12

Southwestern Nova Scotia

● ●

In This Chapter

▶ Sightseeing in Peggy's Cove

▶ Strolling the streets of Mahone Bay

▶ Exploring Lunenburg

▶ Stepping back in time at Shelburne

▶ Soaking up Acadian culture

▶ Brushing up on the history of Annapolis Royal

● ●

*T*he southwestern portion of Nova Scotia has a raw magnetism unlike anywhere else in Canada. You'll find an endless line of picturesque seaside villages clinging to the rocky shorelines of sheltered bays. The region is mostly rugged and often remote, yet it holds some of Canada's oldest towns. Unhurried and unchanged for decades, they are living proof of Nova Scotia's nautical traditions.

Glance at a map of Nova Scotia and you'll see that the southwestern part of the province is encircled by a single highway that is rarely more than a few kilometers from the ocean. If you drive along this route, beginning and ending in Halifax, you'll get more than a taste of Maritimes history and charm. In this section, I'll explore some of the notable towns you'll encounter on the way.

The further you travel from Halifax, the less touristy it becomes. This is a good thing when it comes to crowds, but it also means you should plan ahead by making accommodation reservations in advance and carrying a small amount of cash — just in case that craft shop with the wooden whale doesn't accept credit cards.

Peggy's Cove

Less than an hour's drive southwest of Halifax is Peggy's Cove, a village of just 60 people, renowned for its postcard-perfect composition. On the way there you'll encounter several towns — including Prospect, East Dover, and West Dover — that are worth a look.

Taking a tour to Peggy's Cove

If you don't have your own vehicle (or even if you do), consider taking a tour to Peggy's Cove. **Ambassatours** (☎ **902-425-9999;** www.atlantictours.com) offers transportation that includes a running commentary for C$39 (US$33.30) adults, C$35 (US$29.80) seniors, C$20 (US$17.10) children. It's a flexible tour, with the option to return at your own leisure on buses scheduled to leave Peggy's Cove for Halifax every 90 minutes. An alternative to the bus is a return trip by boat, with the captain searching out whales, dolphins and puffins. This option is an additional C$69.95 (US$59.50) for adults, C$59.95 (US$51) for seniors and children.

Getting there

Finding your way out of Halifax and onto Highway 103 along the South Shore is simply a matter of map-reading — follow Cogswell Street to Quinpool Road then merge across to Highway 3 (Margaret's Bay Rd.) at the large traffic circle. After 3km (1.9 miles), Highway 333 to the left is signposted to Peggy's Cove. Take this route, and you quickly leave the city behind; miss the turn, and you end up on Highway 103, which zips down the coast on an inland route that misses some of Nova Scotia's best scenery.

Between Halifax and Peggy's Cove, Highway 333 passes a turn-off to **East Dover** before reaching **West Dover.** Both are quintessential fishing villages, comprising smartly kept homes separated from the ocean by a rocky shoreline. Even if you don't stop to wander the wharves, at least slow down and soak up the atmosphere.

Staying in Peggy's Cove

Peggy's Cove Bed and Breakfast
$$ **Peggy's Cove**

Peggy's Cove has just three guest rooms, and they're all ensconced in this restored fisherman's home overlooking the famously photogenic harbor. The building has been thoroughly spruced up, given a coat of yellow paint on the exterior, and had a lovely deck added to the rear. The rooms are comfortable and each has an ensuite.

19 Church Rd. ☎ *800-725-8732 or 902-423-1102. Fax: 902-423-8329.* www.nsinns.com. *Rack rates: C$125–C$145 (US$106.25–US$123.30). MC, V.*

Exploring Peggy's Cove

Ocean views from the approach to Peggy's Cove are impressive. But don't be tempted to drive to the end of the road. Instead, leave your vehicle in the parking lot to the left as you enter the village. From this point, the road narrows and descends to the harbor, with its boats, nets, and lobster traps. At the end of the road are a restaurant that tries hard not be touristy and an octagonal **lighthouse,** surrounded by rounded granite boulders, that is the center of attention for most visitors. It's also the only lighthouse in North America to have a post office.

Beyond the turnoff into Peggy's Cove is the touching **Swissair Memorial,** dedicated to the 229 passengers and crew who lost their lives when Swissair Flight 111 crashed into the ocean, within sight of land, off Peggy's Cove on the night of September 2, 1998.

Because the village is popular with tour buses, it can get extremely busy after 9 a.m., especially when the cruise-ship crowd is docked in Halifax. Plan on an early morning excursion to miss the worst of the crowds and also to have the best light for photographing the "world's most pho-tographed lighthouse." Of course, if you'd rather join the tourists than fight them, see the sidebar "Taking a Tour to Peggy's Cove."

Mahone Bay

Picturesque Mahone Bay is a small village with a big-time reputation for its charmingly restored private homes and businesses set around a narrow inlet filled with boats. The narrow main street wends its way around the water, passing art galleries, craft shops, cafés, and restau-rants housed in historic buildings, many dating from the days when Mahone Bay was a major shipbuilding center. At the head of the inlet, the towering spires of three adjacent churches make for one of Canada's most photographed scenes.

Getting there

Follow Highway 103 southwest from Halifax for 80km (50 miles) and take Exit 10 to reach Mahone Bay. Parking is permitted along the streets, but a better option is the parking lot opposite the churches just before downtown.

Staying in Mahone Bay

While day-trippers from Halifax fill the streets of Mahone Bay, only those smart enough to have made advance reservations are able to take advantage of the limited number of guest rooms in the village.

Mahone Bay Bed and Breakfast
$$ Mahone Bay

Watch the world go by from the verandah of this distinctive yellow and white inn along the main street. Constructed in 1860 by a shipbuilder, it's a solid old home that has been spruced up with "gingerbread" trim — elaborate swirls of wood below the roofline and around the verandah. Beyond the photogenic exterior are four adequate guest rooms, two with ensuites and two with private bathrooms down the hall. Bathrobes are a nice touch, and rates include a full breakfast.

558 Main St. ☎ *866-239-6252 or 902-624-6388. Fax: 902-624-0023. Rack rates: C$85–C$125 (US$72.50–US$106.60) double. MC, V. Open: May–Oct.*

Nature's Cottage
$$ Mahone Bay

Set on almost 1 hectare (2.5 acres) of forest across from the water, guests can find plenty of space to relax in the gardens, in an outdoor hot tub, or on a private dock. My favorite of the four guest rooms is the Safari Room, with strikingly earthy décor, African furnishings, and a private bathroom. Above the garage, the Loft has a private entrance, cooking facilities, and television/VCR combo.

906 Main St. (toward Lunenburg). ☎ *877-607-5699 or 902-624-0196.* www.natures cottagebb.com.*Rack rates: C$90–C$150 (US$76.50–US$127.50) double. AE, MC, V.*

Ocean Trail Retreat
$$ Mahone Bay

You won't find a better setting than this sprawling resort high above Mahone Bay. What the resort's hilltop motel rooms lack in cutting-edge décor, they make up for with stunning water views (two of the rooms have balconies) and reasonable prices. For a splurge, book the Balcony Suite that comes with a jetted tub, expansive deck with barbeque, and full kitchen. Closer to the water, the two-bedroom chalets are more comfortable and each has a kitchen, separate living area with gas fireplace, and a balcony. The outdoor pool is a bonus for children. ☎ *888-624-8824 or 902-624-8824. Fax: 902-624-8899.* www.oceantrailretreat.com. *Rack rates: C$109–C$200 (US$92.65–US$170) double. Minimum stay applies on some units in July and Aug. AE, MC, V. Open: Apr–Nov.*

Dining in Mahone Bay

Innlet Café
$$–$$$ Mahone Bay   SEAFOOD

Slightly sperated from the main strip of shops, the Innlet Café takes full advantage of its location, with big windows and a patio to take full advantage of views extending down Mahone Bay. The kitchen takes full advantage of local seafood, and then presents it in hearty European dishes. I had the Skibbereen (seafood stew with Irish cream), doing well to also finish a slice of rich mud cake.

249 Edgewater St. ☎ *902-624-6363. Main courses: C$11.50–C$20 (US$9.80–US$17.10). MC, V. Open: Apr–Dec daily 11 a.m.–9 p.m.*

Salt Spray Café
$–$$ **Mahone Bay** SEAFOOD/CANADIAN

The Salt Spray is my all-time favorite breakfast spot in Nova Scotia. Sitting on the back deck soaked in morning sun with the ternary of harborside churches reflecting on the water is simply divine. The food is tasty and very well priced, too. Typically, breakfast for two, with all the trappings, will cost well under C$20 (US$17.10), *including* tip. The rest of the day, the menu features soups, salads, and healthy sandwiches, with emphasis on the seafood, of course.

621 South Main St. ☎ 902-624-9902. Main courses: C$8.50–C$14 (US$7.20–US$11.90). MC, V. Open: Daily 7:30 a.m.–6 p.m.

Exploring Mahone Bay

You could easily walk from one end of Mahone Bay to the other in 10 minutes, but that's not the point. Instead, plan on spending at least two hours admiring the fine architecture and making the following stops (listed from the parking lot in front of the churches):

- **Jo-Anns Deli:** Located at 9 Edgewater St. (☎ **902-624-6305;** May–Oct daily 9 a.m.–6 p.m.), this is the place to pick up picnic supplies like baked goodies and healthy wraps, as well as jams and preserves. Of special note are the blueberry scones (delicious!) and the bag of carrots (not for general consumption) used as a counterweight for the front door.

- **Tea Brewery:** On Main St. opposite the end of Clairmont St., the Tea Brewery (☎ **902-624-0566;** daily 9:30 a.m.–5:30 p.m.) is crammed with teas and tea-brewing paraphernalia from around the world. Two tables and a selection of cakes may tempt you to linger longer.

- **Bandstand:** Behind the grocery store parking lot, you'll find a flower-encircled waterfront bandstand. From this vantage point, you can take the classic Mahone Bay photo of the three churches reflected on the water.

- **Mahone Bay Trading Company:** Opposite the bandstand on Main St. (☎ **902-624-8425**). Walk past the potting soil and laundry detergent in this general store to admire the massive boat-shaped counter. It's open Monday to Saturday 10 a.m. to 6 p.m., Sunday 11 a.m. to 5 p.m.

- **Amos Pewter:** The ancient art of casting, spinning, and finishing pewter can be viewed at this waterfront workshop at 589 Main St. (☎ **902-624-9547;** www.amospewter.com). Open: June to August Monday to Saturday 10 a.m. to 6 p.m., Sunday 10 a.m. to 5 p.m.

- **Mahone Bay Settler's Museum:** Admission is free to this small museum in a 150-year-old home across from Amos Pewter. Displays trace the history of the local shipbuilding industry and highlight local architecture. It's at 578 Main St. (☎ **902-624-6263**). Open:

June to early September Tuesday to Saturday 10 a.m. to 5 p.m., Sunday 1 to 5 p.m.

✔ **Redden's Fine Whale Sculptures Studio:** Stop by the studio of Susan Redden, at 788 Main St. (☎ **902-624-1232;** June–Sept), to admire her mahogany carvings, which reflect the enchanting personality of whales and dolphins through clean, polished lines.

Lunenburg

A stay in Lunenburg, famous for its colorful, perfectly preserved private homes and commercial buildings overlooking a bustling harbor, is a Maritimes highlight.

Lunenburg successfully juggles an active working harbor with a prosperous tourism industry — and does it well. The town brims with excellent accommodations, lively restaurants, and artsy shops.

Getting there

Lunenburg is 92km (57 miles) southwest of Halifax. To drive from the capital, take Highway 103 to Exit 10 (if you want to visit Mahone Bay) or Exit 11. From either of these exits, it's a 10-minute drive along well-signposted rural roads to Lunenburg.

Orienting yourself in Lunenburg

Commercial enterprises are concentrated on four main streets: Bluenose Drive, along the waterfront, Pelham Street, and Montague Street. Both streets running parallel to Bluenose are of most interest, with restaurants, boutiques, and craft shops; Lincoln Street, one block up from Pelham Street, is the original thoroughfare.

Charming Chester

In the late 1700s, Chester, north of Mahone Bay along Highway 3, was an infamous hub of pirates, privateers, and smugglers. The village matured over time into a resort town dominated by imposing waterfront mansions and sprawling summer estates. Today, Chester still has a distinctive moneyed feel. Local real estate is among the highest priced east of Montreal; well-heeled guests stay at upscale lodges such as **Haddon Hall Resort Inn** (☎ **902-275-3577;** www.haddonhallinn.com), and yachters from around the world tie up at the local marina. Through it all, the community itself remains very approachable — children splash around in a tidal swimming pool beside million-dollar boats, locals mix with Hollywood stars on the waterfront deck of the **Captain's House** pub (☎ **902-275-3501**), and a mid-August yachting regatta attracts as many spectators as boat owners.

The location of the **Lunenburg Visitor Information Centre** (take Pelham St. east through town) on Blockhouse Hill Road (☎ 902-634-8100) affords good views, but is a little inconvenient for arriving visitors. It's open May through October 9 a.m. to 8 p.m. The Web site www.explore lunenburg.ca has lots of information on the town's history and links to tourist services.

Staying in Lunenburg

A couple of factors make staying in Lunenburg more expensive than elsewhere in the province — most lodgings are in grand old homes (no chain motels here) and demand is high for a limited number of rooms. Reservations are a must in July and August, but also recommended for June and September.

Captain Westhaver Bed and Breakfast
$–$$ Lunenburg

Backed by quiet gardens with a rural outlook, this lodge offers three clean, simple rooms that share a bathroom. My favorite room is Hollyhock, which opens to a private sundeck. Built in 1910 for a sea captain, the home's historic character shines through best in the comfy parlor or out on the wide verandah overlooking a private garden.

102 Dufferin St. ☎ *902-634-4937. Fax: 902-634-8640. Rack rates: C$70–C$80 (US$59.50–US$68) double. MC, V.*

Lunenburg Arms Hotel
$$–$$$$ Lunenburg

This gracious 18th-century hotel has been renovated inside and out, yet retains its historic character. Original hardwood floors combine well with modern amenities such as plush mattresses and high-speed Internet access to create a memorable stay. Bathrooms are well appointed and all 26 guest rooms are air-conditioned. Only some have harbor views (404 is the least expensive room with a view of the water). Breakfast (extra) is served in the downstairs restaurant, and you'll find it easy to relax in the adjacent lounge.

94 Pelham St. ☎ *800-679-4950 or 902-640-4040. Fax: 902-640-4041.* www.lunenburg arms.com. *Rack rates: C$140–C$260 (US$119–US$221) double. AE, MC, V.*

Lunenburg Inn
$$–$$$ Lunenburg

An attractive Victorian home in a leafy setting, this bed and breakfast is away from the bustle of Old Town yet within a five-minute walk of the waterfront. Built in 1893, the inn features seven guest rooms, some opening to a second-floor sundeck, all richly decorated with lots of polished wood. The two suites are extra-large and come with jetted tubs. This inn has five rate levels over a six-month season, with rooms dipping as low as C$90 (US$76.50) in April. Rates include a cooked breakfast.

26 Dufferin St. ☎ *800-565-3963 or 902-634-3963. Fax: 902-634-9419.* www.lunenburg inn.com. *Rack rates: C$145–C$185 (US$123.30–US$157.30) double. MC, V. Open: Apr–Sept.*

Lunenburg Oceanview Chalets
$$–$$$$ Lunenburg

I've included this one because it's a better option for families than the historic downtown inns, which make up the bulk of Lunenburg's lodgings. The complex comprises six newish log chalets, each with a full kitchen, a fireplace, separate bedrooms, and a deck with gas barbeque. One is wheelchair accessible. From the lofty location atop a high ridge behind town, it's a 10-minute walk to the waterfront.

78 Old Blue Rocks Rd. ☎ *902-640-3344. Fax: 902-640-3345.* www.lunenburg oceanview.com. *Rack rates: One-bedroom cottage C$139 (US$118.20), two-bedroom cottage C$229 (US$194.70). MC, V.*

Spinnaker Inn
$$–$$$ Lunenburg

Water views and central location are the good news. The bad news is there are only four units, so you will need to book well in advance for summer. The highlight of the rooms are the big windows and the expansive views (the best in town). The rooms themselves are simply furnished with antique-style beds and hardwood floors, and the bathrooms have been thoroughly updated. The more expensive units are split-level and have a jetted tub and kitchenette (although Suite 4 has limited views). The Spinnaker is one of the fewer small inns open year-round; rates drop as low as C$69 (US$58.80) in winter.

126 Montague St. ☎ *902-634-4543. Fax: 902-640-2022.* www.spinnakerinn.com. *Rack rates: C$99–C$170 (US$84.20–US$144.50) double. AE, MC, V.*

Dining in Lunenburg

Big Red's
$–$$ Lunenburg   FAMILY DINING

If you're traveling with a family in tow and looking for an inexpensive meal, it's hard to beat Big Red's, a big restaurant with great views. Of course there's seafood, but you can also choose from hamburgers, pizza, and an extensive kid's menu.

80 Montague St. ☎ *902-634-3554. Main courses: C$9–C$21 (US$7.70–US$17.90). AE, DC, MC, V. Open: Daily 9 a.m.–10 p.m.*

Old Fish Factory
$$–$$$$ Lunenburg SEAFOOD

Overlooking Lunenburg Harbour from a converted fish factory (also home to the fisheries museum), this touristy yet stylish restaurant has a varied menu, with plenty of seafood choices. Mussels or oysters are a good choice to start, with mains ranging from fish cakes with baked beans to a seafood platter for two (C$80/US$68.20) that comes with a full lobster. The pricing is a little higher than comparable seafood restaurants, but the tables on the enclosed patio are a pleasant place to relax over an evening meal.

68 Bluenose Dr. ☎ 902-634-3333. Reservations recommended for dinner. Main courses: C$16–C$32 (US$13.60–US$27.20). AE, DC, DISC, MC, V. Open: Daily 11:30 a.m.–9 p.m.

Rissers
$$–$$$ Downtown SEAFOOD/MODERN CANADIAN

Rissers is away from the water, which isn't necessarily a bad thing — you're not paying for a view and the atmosphere is distinctly more mellow than down the hill. Dining is in a casually elegant room or on a tiered patio. The quality of food is equal to anywhere else in town, with choices running the gamut of Canadian cuisine from lamb to lobster. Rissers has no dessert menu. Instead, samples of each are presented to your table, which makes them almost impossible to resist.

Lunenburg Arms Hotel, 94 Pelham St. ☎ 902-634-3333. Main courses: C$13–C$24 (US$11–US$20.40). AE, DC, MC, V. Open: Daily 7:30 a.m.–10 p.m.

Rum Runner Restaurant
$–$$$ Lunenburg SEAFOOD

Set on the lower level of the Rum Runner Inn, this restaurant is a little bit old fashioned in décor and cuisine, but the menu is well priced and the unobstructed harbor views are unbeatable. The prime seats are outside on the covered verandah. Local seafood takes precedence on the menu. Lobster is served in various ways, including in a bisque. A seafood platter for two is only C$42 (US$35.80), or take your pick from any of a variety of non-seafood mains, like chicken curry and Vienna schnitzel.

66 Montague St. ☎ 902-634-9200. Main courses: C$9–C$25 (US$7.70–US$21.30). AE, DC, MC, V. Open: Daily 11 a.m.–9 p.m.

Exploring Lunenburg

Lunenburg's biggest attraction is the town itself, so take some time to stroll around and appreciate its historic architecture. Or, soak up authentic Maritimes fishing culture at the Fisheries Museum. If you run out of things to do in town, there's plenty to see and do out on the water or at any of the nearby attractions — this section's got it all covered.

Fisheries Museum of the Atlantic
Downtown

If wandering along the waterfront doesn't give you a good enough feeling for the region's heritage, this harborside museum in a former fish-processing plant will. As the name suggests, it highlights the fishing industry, using exhibits of boat-building (including a shop where you can watch carpenters at work), whales and whaling, commercial fishing equipment, and rum-running during the era of prohibition. In the Millennium Aquarium, commercially important fish species, super-sized lobsters, and a variety of crabs reside in large tanks, and a touch tank allows you to get up close and personal with tidal pool species such as starfish. And the museum takes advantage of its harborfront location — a small fleet of historic vessels is tied up out front, including the *Teresa E. Connor,* a wooden schooner that spent her life on the famous Grand Banks fishery. You can also take your pick from a busy schedule of daily events such as knot-tying and seafaring storytelling out on the dock.

68 Bluenose Dr. ☎ *902-634-4794.* www.museum.gov.ns.ca/fma. *Admission: C$9 (US$7.70) adults, C$7 (US$6) seniors, C$3 (US$2.60) children. Open: May–Oct daily 9:30 a.m.–5:30 p.m., Nov–Apr Wed 9:30 a.m.–4 p.m.*

Historic buildings of note

Some buildings in the oldest part of town (known as Old Town) date to the 18th century, but most are pre-1900. Aside from the colorful palate of paint, restoration work is unpretentious (no fancy woodwork or fake facades). What you see is what you would have seen a century ago, which creates a real visual sense of history. Although most of the restoration has been done by individual owners, the town as a whole achieved the ultimate accolade in 1995 — when the Old Town was declared a World Heritage Site by UNESCO for being "the best example of a British colonial settlement in North America."

While it was Old Town as a whole that was recognized by UNESCO as a World Heritage Site, the following individual buildings are especially noteworthy:

- ✔ **Scotia Trawler Shipyard.** The *Bluenose* was built at this sprawling complex at 250 Montague St. (☎ **902-634-4914**). Today, it also incorporates boat construction and repair with the Yacht Shop, primarily serving the needs of local seamen but with a range of marine-themed souvenirs unlike anything in the more touristy shops. The actual shipyards are off-limits, but access to the adjacent Government Wharf is permitted.

- ✔ **Knaut Rhuland House.** Aside from commercial enterprises, this historic home at 125 Pelham St. (☎ **902-634-3498**) is the only historic building in Old Town Lunenburg open to the public. Considered to be the finest example of Georgian architecture anywhere in the Maritimes, it's open June to early October Monday to Saturday 11 a.m. to 4 p.m. Admission costs C$2 (US$1.70).

✔ **Bailly House.** Built in 1780, this privately owned home at 134 Pelham St. is the oldest building in Lunenburg. It's owned by the brother of artist Earl Bailly, whose work is displayed in civic buildings (including the library and museum) throughout town.

✔ **St John's Anglican Church.** Tragically destroyed by fire in November 2001, this 1753 Lunenburg landmark on the corner of Duke and Cumberland Streets has been carefully rebuilt in its gothic revival grandeur.

✔ **Lunenburg Academy.** This striking building at 97 Kaulbach St. is a rare example of a large wooden school. Dating to 1895, it still operates as a center for education. The black and white turreted structure is easy to recognize from anywhere around the harbor.

Other cool things to do in and around Lunenburg

In addition to browsing nautically themed shops and walking the fairways of **Bluenose Golf Club** (☎ **902-634-4260**), here are a few other activities to keep you busy in and around Lunenburg.

The *Bluenose*

The dime is the only Canadian coin that doesn't feature one of the country's flora or fauna. It depicts the *Bluenose*, a famous sailing ship that represents east coast nautical traditions and is about as Canadian as the maple leaf. Built as a fishing schooner, the *Bluenose* was actually designed for winning the International Fishermen's Trophy, an America's Cup–style racing series between working ships from Canada and the U.S. After its launch from Lunenburg in 1921, the *Bluenose* enjoyed a tremendously successful career, retiring from racing after 17 undefeated years, and was then ingloriously lost on a reef off Haiti in 1946.

Back in Lunenburg, construction of the *Bluenose II* began in the 1960s, using the original plans to create an exact replica of her predecessor, right down to the sails and rigging. The *Bluenose II* now spends June through September mixing public cruises with appearances at festivals and events around the Nova Scotian coast. The public cruise portion of her schedule is divided between Lunenburg and Halifax. Half of all tickets are allotted for advance sales (☎ **866-579-4989** or 902-634-4794), with the remainder sold dockside 90 minutes prior to sailing. For tickets in Lunenburg, go to the fisheries museum; in Halifax, look for the booth on the waterfront beside the Maritime Museum of the Atlantic. The cost is C$25 (US$21.30) adults, C$10 (US$8.50) children. The *Bluenose II* sailing schedule is posted on the Web site, www.museum.gov.ns.ca/bluenose. To ensure a spot, you will either need to make advance reservations at least three months prior to sailing or be in line for the standby tickets at least two hours before the posted departure time. Don't say I didn't warn you.

Wondering where the boat's unusual name originated? So do the experts, but I like one theory in particular — local fishermen would wipe their noses when wearing blue mittens, and in the cold, wet conditions onboard, the dye would often run.

Boat tours

If the *Bluenose II* is out of port, or you missed a spot, don't despair, there is another option. The ***Eastern Star,*** a classic 15m (48-foot) wooden ketch, departs Lunenburg up to four times daily for a sailing trip around the harbor (the 7 p.m. Sunset Cruise is two hours and travels to Ovens Natural Park). Buy tickets from the dockside booth at the foot of King St. (☎ **902-634-3535**). The cost is C$22 to C$25 (US$18.70–US$21.30) adults, C$11 to C$12 (US$9.40–US$10.20) children.

Exactly as the name suggests, **Lobstermen Tours** (☎ **902-634-3434**), are trips in a working fishing boat. Led by local fishermen, you get to learn first-hand about lobsters and the industry from the experts before pulling traps (hopefully) filled with lobsters. The two-hour tour departs four times daily from the foot of King St., and the cost is C$28 (US$23.80) adults, C$14 (US$11.90) children.

If you're not planning on traveling as far as Digby or Cape Breton Island, then Lunenburg is the next best option for a whale-watching trip. **Lunenburg Whale Watching Tours** (☎ **902-527-7175**) has an excellent record for spotting humpback, finback, minke, and pilot whales. Regular sightings of sunfish, turtles, porpoises, dolphins, seals, and puffins round out what can be a very exciting tour. The cost is C$45 (US$38.30) adults, C$30 (US$25.60) children.

Blue Rocks

In this picturesque hamlet, you'll find a jumble of fishing cottages clinging to a rocky shoreline, with small fishing boats in a protected bay, and the shoreline dotted with fishing nets and lobster traps. In other words, this is exactly what Nova Scotia is supposed to look like — minus the crowds of Peggy's Cove. Take Pelham St. eastbound through Lunenburg and follow Blue Rocks Rd.

Ovens Natural Park

The "ovens" are sea caves that have been carved into cliffs over thousands of years by the ocean's waves. A trail leads to various overlooks, while another ends at the mouth of one of the larger caves. Also at the site are a small gold rush museum and a restaurant. To get to this commercialized natural attraction, take Route 332 south from Lunenburg for 16km (10 miles) (☎ **902-766-4621**). Admission is C$6 (US$5.10) adults, C$3 (US$2.60) seniors and children. A guided walk costs an additional C$3 (US$2.60), or view the caves from sea level on a boat tour for C$20 (US$17.10) adults, C$15 (US$12.80) children. Open: Mid-May to early October daily 8 a.m. to 9 p.m.

Shelburne

The small South Shore town of Shelburne is as attractive and interesting as its better-known counterparts to the north, but because it's that much farther from Halifax, it remains untouristy.

Founded in 1783, by 1900 Shelburne had grown into one of the most important shipbuilding centers in North America. Local boat builders were renowned for quality wooden boats, with some of the world's first and fastest yachts coming from local shipyards (some consider Shelburne the birthplace of the yacht). The waterfront remains remarkably unchanged from its halcyon years.

Getting there

Take Exit 26 from Highway 103 to access downtown Shelburne. This turn-off is 133km (83 miles) southwest of Lunenburg and 123km (76 miles) east of Yarmouth.

Staying in and around Shelburne

Loyalist Inn
$ Shelburne

Don't anticipate too much from this 200-year-old hotel. You'll get the basics — budget rooms with private bath, television, and air-conditioning. On weekends, request a room as far away from the downstairs bar as possible if you want a good night's sleep. The in-house dining room is open Tuesday to Sunday 7:30 a.m. to 8:30 p.m., or use the money you've saved on a room for dinner at Charlotte Lane Café.

*160 Water St. ☎ **902-875-2343**. Fax: 902-875-1473. Rack rates: C$65 (US$55.30) double. MC, V.*

Whispering Waves Cottages
$$$ Ingomar

If you want a modern, well-equipped cottage with panoramic ocean views, Whispering Waves is hard to beat. Beautifully located on the ocean south of Shelburne, the property runs right down to the rocky shoreline, with sandy beaches and mackerel fishing within easy walking distance. The cottages are in three subtle themes — wilderness, seaside, and romance — and are carefully designed to take advantage of ocean views while also offering a certain amount of privacy. Inside, the practical layout includes a separate bedroom, small kitchen, and living area with electric fireplace.

Sliding doors open to a verandah. Congenial hosts Jo-Anne and Paul Goulden will go out of their way to make you feel comfortable. They will organize sea kayaking with a local operator, tee times at the local golf course, appointments at a nearby spa, and evening beachside bonfires. When I'm on the the road researching a book, there's no time for golfing or the like, but I did take the Goulden's up on one option — a lobster dinner (complete with strawberry shortcake) delivered to my cottage.

Black Point Rd., Ingomar (take Exit 27 or 28 from Highway 103). ☎ *866-470-9283 or 902-637-3535.* www.whisperingwavescottages.com. *Rack rates: C$150–C$165 (US$127.50–US$140.30) double. AE, MC, V. One cottage is wheelchair accessible.*

Dining in Shelburne

Charlotte Lane Café
$$–$$$ Shelburne   SEAFOOD/FUSION

Tucked between Shelburne's main street and the waterfront, this delightful dining room is a great find. The Swiss chef concentrates on combining local seafood with cooking styles from around the world. Starters range from a rich but simple chowder (with real scallops and shrimp) to a creative East-meets-West fish sampler, which includes smoked salmon and sushi. The biggest concern is finding room for dessert (the almond fruit torte is a must).

13 Charlotte Lane. ☎ *902-875-3314. Main courses: C$13–C$21 (US$11.10–US$17.90). Open: Tues–Sat 11:30 a.m.–2:30 p.m. and 5–8 p.m.*

Exploring Shelburne

Head down to Dock Street, which runs along the waterfront, and you'll find yourself in the middle of **Shelburne Historic District,** which is the largest concentration of wooden buildings from the late-1700s remaining in Canada. Many are private residences, while others are still home to a variety of boat-building endeavors. Four buildings are open to the public. Admission to each is C$3 (US$2.60), or buy a combined pass for C$8 (US$6.80). They are as follows:

- ✔ **Shelburne County Museum,** 8 Maiden Lane (☎ **902-875-3219;** June–mid-Oct 9:30 a.m.–5:30 p.m., mid-Oct–May Mon–Fri 10 a.m.– noon and 2–5 p.m.), is the best place to learn about the earliest Loyalist settlers and the subsequent years of shipbuilding fame.

- ✔ **Dory Shop,** 11 Dock St. (☎ **902-875-3219;** June–Sept daily 9:30 a.m.– 5:30 p.m.), has been churning out dory boats since the 1880s, when they were first used on the Grand Banks to help lay fishing nets from a mother ship.

- ✔ **Muir-Cox Shipyard,** south end of Dock St. (☎ **902-875-5310;** June–Sept daily 9:30 a.m.–5:30 p.m.), has been in continuous operation since 1820. Inside, the Shipbuilding Interpretive Centre describes the history of the industry while the Boatshop, which once turned out enormous full-rigged barques, now takes orders for smaller wooden boats (viewing year-round Mon–Fri 8 a.m.–4 p.m.).

✔ **Ross-Thomson House,** 9 Charlotte Lane (☎ **902-875-3141;** June–mid-Octo daily 9:30 a.m.– 5:30 p.m.), a general store built by Loyalist brothers in 1784. The interior recreates the time (complete with staff in period costume behind the counter) when locals flocked in to purchase goods such as salted cod and tobacco.

La Côte Acadienne

The French place names, the soaring church spires, and the numerous Acadian flags (red, white, and blue strips with a yellow star) tell you that this is Nova Scotia's largest Francophone enclave. La Côte Acadienne (Acadian Coast) is home to descendents of Acadians who resettled here after returning from their 1755 expulsion, which you'll learn all about up the road at Grand-Pre National Historic Site (see later in this chapter).

Getting there

La Côte Acadienne stretches for 50km (31 miles) along the Bay of Fundy between Yarmouth and Digby. Highway 101 zooms through the region, but you'll want to take coastal Highway 1 to hit the highlights detailed below.

Staying along La Côte Acadienne

La Côte Acadienne is decidedly untouristy, but scattered through the small towns are a number of roadside motels like the **Bluefin Motel,** along Highway 1 in Meteghan (☎ **902-645-2251**), which falls into the $$ price range and has a restaurant.

Cape View Motel & Cottages
$$ **Mavillette**

What would normally be a rather nondescript complex of 10 motel rooms and 5 self-contained cottages is enlivened by sweeping water views and an adjacent provincial park that protects a sandy beach. Across the road is an affiliated restaurant where the menu includes locally inspired dishes such as a lobster omelet.

Mavillette Beach. ☎ *800-876-1960 or 902-645-2258. Fax: 902-645-3999.* www.cape viewmotel.ca. *Rack rates: C$80–C$135 (US$68–US$114.80) double. MC, V. Open: mid-May–mid-Oct.*

Dining along La Côte Acadienne

You'll find small cafés in most towns along La Côte Acadienne, and restaurants in the motels, but for a fully Acadian dining experience, nowhere beats Rapure Acadienne.

Rapure Acadienne
$ Point de Église ACADIAN

More of a bakery than a restaurant, this roadside outlet specializes in *rappie* pie, a simple and hearty Acadian dish. The filling — shredded potato, chunks of chicken, and bacon — is delicious, but it has an unusual texture that may take some getting used to. The pies here are massive (plan on sharing one between two people) and come with a side of molasses. Order at the inside window and plan on eating at one of the outdoor picnic tables off to the side.

1443 Hwy 1, Point de Eglise. ☎ *902-769-2172. Main courses: C$6 (US$5.10). Open: Mon–Sat 8 a.m.–5:30 p.m.*

Exploring La Côte Acadienne

The drive along Highway 1 is scenic, and also takes in each of the attractions described below, which are detailed from south to north.

- ✔ **Mavillette Beach Provincial Park.** La Côte Acadienne's nicest stretch of sand is within this small park on the south side of Mavillette. The sun warms the shallow water on summer days, but swimming isn't compulsory — you can also comb the beach for seashells and follow a boardwalk that leads across a salt marsh.

- ✔ **Smuggler's Cove Provincial Park.** The name is a giveaway. From a clifftop parking lot, a path leads down through a wind-blown coastal forest to a cove where it is said rumrunners stored their goods during the Prohibition era.

- ✔ **La Vielle Maison.** This homestead in Meteghan has been restored and converted to a museum. It allows a glimpse inside an Acadian home, with furnishings dating back 200 years and interpreters in traditional dress. It's along Highway 1 (☎ **902-645-2389**). Open: July to August daily 9 a.m. to 7 p.m. and admission is by donation.

- ✔ **Église de Sainte-Marie.** This, the tallest wooden church in North America, towers above all else in the aptly named village of Church Point. Completed in 1905, the church is laid out in the shape of a cross, with the steeple rising 56m (175 feet). Inside is a small museum open weekdays through summer.

Digby and Digby Neck

Best-known for its plump, sweet-tasting scallops, this bustling town of 2,300 has been an important fishing center since its founding by Loyalists in 1783.

Getting there

Digby is near the entrance to the Annapolis Basin, just off Highway 101, halfway between Yarmouth and Wolfville.

Bay Ferries (☎ **888-249-7245** or 902-245-2116; www.nfl-bay.com) operates the *Princess of Acadia* year-round between Saint John (New Brunswick) and Digby, with one or two departures in each direction daily. The crossing takes between two and three hours. Depending on the time of year (July to early Oct is high season) the one-way cost is C$22 to C$37 (US$18.70–US$31.50) adults, C$18.50 to C$26 (US$15.75–US$21.20) seniors, and C$15 to C$21 (US$12.80–$17.90) children aged 5 to 17. The fare for vehicles under 6.4m (21 feet) is C$75 to C$92 (US$63.90–US$78.30) one-way.

Staying in and around Digby

Bayside Inn
$–$$ **Digby**

Overlooking the bay and within walking distance of downtown Digby, you won't go wrong at this small lodging that has been taking in guests for over 100 years. Historic character blends with modern touches in the 11 rooms, some outfitted with antiques and others in a floral theme. Every room has a television and ensuite bathroom, while an enclosed porch awaits you downstairs. Rates include a cooked breakfast.

115 Montague Row. ☎ *888-754-0555 or 902-245-2247.* www.baysideinn.ca. *Rack rates: C$58–C$98 (US$49.40–US$83.50) double. AE, DC, DISC, MC, V.*

Brier Island Lodge
$–$$ **Brier Island**

Nature lovers should plan on spending at least one night on Brier Island, preferably at Brier Island Lodge, perched atop sea cliffs and surrounded by native woodlands. Staying here, you can spot whales from your room, go birdwatching, or hike down to a narrow cove where seals haul themselves onto the rocks. The 40 motel-like rooms are a little plain, but they are clean and comfortable and most have ocean views. The more expensive rooms have either a king-size bed or a jetted tub.

Meals are taken in a casual restaurant (7 a.m.–9:30 p.m.) featuring lots of exposed wood and snappy-colored fabrics. Mains are mostly under C$20 (US$17.10), including smoked pollock, a local delicacy that is poached in milk and served with a creamy white sauce.

Westport, Brier Island. ☎ *800-662-8355 or 902-839-2300. Fax: 902-839-2006.* www.brierisland.com. *Rack rates: C$70–C$139 (US$59.50–US$118.30) double. MC, V. Open: Apr–Oct.*

Mountain Gap Inn
$$–$$$$ Smith's Cove

Set along the edge of Annapolis Basin, this sprawling resort does a good job of keeping guests occupied. Activities include hiking, biking, tennis, and swimming at the beach or in the outdoor heated pool; or you can just relax in the hot tub or at tables spread throughout the grounds. Most units were revamped in 2003, including the regular motel rooms and older cottages, many with kitchens and water views. The dining room is contained in the original 1915 lodge building and is open daily 7:30 a.m. to 9:30 p.m. For something more casual, pick up seafood at the fish market in Digby and boil or grill it at one of the resort's barbeque areas.

Smith's Cove (Exit 25 from Highway 101 east of Digby). ☎ *800-565-5020 or 902-245-5841. Fax: 902-245-2277.* www.mountaingap.ns.ca. *Rack rates: C$138–C$340 (US$117.30–US$289) double. AE, MC, V. Open: May–Oct.*

Olde Village Inn
$–$$ Sandy Cove

An attractive inn with panoramic views; you won't need to go anywhere for a meal — breakfast is included and the in-house restaurant does wonders with local seafood. Accommodations range from cabins that share bathrooms to a spacious modern suite in the main building with a balcony and water views. It's located along Digby Neck, 30km from Digby.

387 Sandy Cove Rd., Sandy Cove. ☎ *800-834-2206 or 902-834-2202. Fax: 902-834-2927.* www.oldevillageinn.com. *Rack rates: C$85–C$130 (US$72.30–US$110.50) double. MC, V. Open: June–mid-Oct.*

Dining in Digby

Fundy Restaurant
$$–$$$ Digby   SEAFOOD

With a harbor full of trawlers, finding fresh seafood in Digby is not an issue. What really matters is the view, and the Fundy Restaurant wins hands down. Located right on the harborside boardwalk, choose from an upstairs dining room that opens to a wide deck or the downstairs Dockside Restaurant with tables spread right to the water's edge. For an evening meal, stick to the upstairs section. The menu is scallop-centered, whether you're looking for breakfast (scallop omelet), lunch (scallop wrap), or dinner (scallop stir-fry, fettucini, or casserole).

34 Water St. ☎ *902-245-4950. Main courses: C$14.50–C$21 (US$12.40–US$17.90). MC, V. Open: Daily 7 a.m.–11 p.m.*

O'Neil's Fundy Fish Market "Best Seafood"
$–$$ Digby   SEAFOOD

Primarily a fish market, a few tables are set aside for in-house dining at this family-run business that also operates a fleet of fishing boats. Scallops (pan- or deep-fried) and chips is the obvious choice, but you can also order steamed mussels, lobster, or a platter of fish, scallops, and shrimp. The market also sells a wide variety of seafood (fresh scallops are around C$12/US$10.20 per pound), perfect if you are staying somewhere with cooking facilities. Otherwise, grab Digby chicks (smoked herring) for C$1 (US85¢) each and eat them on the go.

Prince William St. ☎ 902-245-6528. Main courses: C$6–C$15 (US$5.10–US$12.80). Open: Mon–Fri 9 a.m.–5:30 p.m., Sat 10 a.m.–5 p.m.

Exploring Digby

Although Digby offers a couple of worthwhile sights, the main local attraction is the drive out along Digby Neck.

Along the harborfront

The **Admiral Digby Museum,** an 1850s home at 95 Montague Row (**☎ 902-245-6322**), documents a local history dominated by the ocean. On display are model ships, recreated 1880s living quarters, and a large collection of photographs. Open: Mid-June to August daily 9 a.m. to 5 p.m.

Around the world in 1,160 days

Born near Digby in 1844 and raised on Brier Island, **Joshua Slocum** left home at 16 for a life on the high seas. After a distinguished career as captain, he set off on April 24, 1895, in the 11m (37-foot) sloop *Spray* on a journey that would make him famous well beyond the sailing community. He was at sea for over three years, returning to his starting point on June 27, 1898, thus becoming the first person to sail single-handedly around the world.

Although Slocum remains one of the world's best-known sailors of all time, his feat is not well-promoted in Annapolis County — a plaque on Brier Island makes note of his Nova Scotian links; the ferry to Brier Island is named in his honor, as is a bar at Mountain Gap Inn; and the one-room school he attended in Hanley is now a museum. You won't find his grave around these parts — he was lost at sea in the southern Atlantic in 1909.

In front of the Fundy Restaurant at 34 Water St., the *Lady Vanessa*, a retired wooden scallop boat, is open for inspection June to September daily 9 a.m. to 7 p.m. In addition to simply clambering over and into the boat, a video shows footage of fishermen at work, and displays include the claws of a 20-kilogram (45-pound) lobster. Admission is a worthwhile C$2 (US$1.70).

Driving Digby Neck

Digby Neck is a narrow finger of land that extends around 50km (31 miles) into the Bay of Fundy. Most visitors are drawn to the end of the road by its diversity of wildlife.

Along the way, you'll encounter a string of villages. The most picturesque is **Sandy Cove,** overlooking a beach with good swimming. Ask directions to the local waterfall, one of the highest in the Maritimes.

Highway 217 reaches right to the end of Digby Neck. From there it's a short ferry ride to **Long Island,** then an 18km (11-mile) drive to another ferry that crosses to **Brier Island.** Both ferries run 24 hours per day, year-round. Departures are timed to link up with drivers who don't stop in-between. The fare on either ferry is C$3 (US$2.60) round-trip, per vehicle (including passengers).

The ferry from the mainland docks on Long Island at Tiverton, a small fishing village with a couple of whale-watching operations and a museum. Around 2km (1.2 miles) beyond the village is a trail to the **Balancing Rock.** This striking natural feature is an outcrop of igneous (volcanic) rock that rises 7m (22 feet) from a narrow ledge above the ocean. The 2km (1.2-mile) trail leading to the lookout platform is somewhat tricky to negotiate, but the round-trip can easily be made in 90 minutes.

If you're feeling hungry as you approach the far end of Long Island, make a stop in Freeport at **Lavena's Catch Café** (☎ **902-839-2517;** mid-May to mid-Dec daily 9 a.m.–8 p.m., until 11 p.m. in summer) for well-priced fresh seafood without a deep fryer in sight.

The ferry from Freeport docks at **Westport,** the only settlement on **Brier Island.** The island is renowned for high populations of seabirds and excellent hiking.

Whale-watching

The Bay of Fundy teems with plankton, which attracts an abundance of marine life — fish, whales, and dolphins are all common in the area. Of course, that means the whale-watchers aren't far behind. Finback, minke, and humpback are the most common types of whales, but right and sperm whales are also present. The main whale-watching season is June through October, with August considered the prime month.

A number of companies based along Digby Neck and on the two islands take people to see the whales. Most use ex-fishing boats, with the captains keeping in contact with each other by radio to help track down the whales. Trips last three to five hours (depending on how quickly whales are found) and cost C$25 to C$35 (US$21.30–US$29.80) adults and C$15 to C$20 (US$12.80–$US17.10) children. Operators include: **Freeport Whale & Seabird Tours,** at Freeport, Long Island (☎ 866-866-8797 or 902-839-2177); **Brier Island Whale and Seabird Cruises,** at Westport (☎ 800-656-3660 or 902-839-2995); and **Mariner Cruises,** also at Westport (☎ 800-239-2189 or 902-839-2346). Tours with **Ocean Explorations,** at Tiverton (☎ 877-654-2341 or 902-839-2417; www.oceanexplorations. ca), are led by biologist Tom Goodwin in large, stable Zodiac boats. The advantage of this type of craft is speed — reaching the whales takes less time. In August, when North Atlantic right whales (the world's rarest whale) congregate in the middle of the Bay of Fundy, this is the only company that can get out far enough to see them. Tour cost is C$50 (US$42.50) adults, C$30 (US$25.60) children.

Annapolis Royal

The site of Canada's first permanent settlement, Annapolis Royal is under the grand delusion that it is still the Victorian era. The French and British fought for control of this town for over a century. In 1710, the British finally took control and renamed it in honor of Queen Anne. Despite its age, less than 1,000 people call Annapolis Royal home, although the streets swell with summer visitors wandering the compact downtown core.

Getting there

Annapolis Royal is 29km (18 miles) northeast of Digby Neck. Take Exit 23 from Highway 101 to follow the Annapolis Basin shoreline to town or Exit 22 for a more direct approach.

Staying in Annapolis Royal

Garrison House Inn
$$ Annapolis Royal

Unlike most local bed and breakfast inns, the 1854 Garrison House was designed originally as a guesthouse. Careful renovations have restored its Victorian-era feel. In total, there are seven guest rooms, each with a private bathroom and shower, and some with canopy beds. Choose Room 2 for its spaciousness and views across to Fort Anne, or Room 4 for its quiet, nicely cozy feel. The in-house restaurant is Annapolis Royal's premier dining room.

350 St. George St. ☎ 902-532-5750. Fax: 902-532-5501. www.garrisonhouse.ca. *Rack rates: C$109–C$149 (US$92.80–US$126.70) double. AE, MC, V. Open: May–Oct.*

Queen Anne Inn
$$–$$$ Annapolis Royal

Named for the Queen of England at the time the British were ceded Acadia, this 1865 landmark lodging is set back from the road and surrounded by expansive gardens. A grand stairway leads from the lobby and parlor to 10 guest rooms, all of which are extremely spacious (except Number 10). While furnishings and fabrics reflect the Victorian era, the rooms have been thoroughly modernized, some featuring amenities like a jetted tub. An adjacent carriage house holds an additional two units, each with two bedrooms. Rates include a full breakfast and nice touches, such as plush bathrobes and the use of a DVD player on request.

494 St. George St. (across from the Historic Gardens) ☎ *877-536-0403 or 902-532-7850. Fax: 902-532-2078.* www.queenanneinn.ns.ca. *Rack rates: C$109–C$169 (US$92.80–US$143.80) double. AE, MC, V. Open: April–Nov.*

Dining in Annapolis Royal

Fort Anne Café
$–$$ Annapolis Royal   CAFÉ FARE/SEAFOOD

The décor might not have changed since the 1970s, but that's not a concern to the locals who gather here for hearty and well-priced, no-frills food. Served until noon, breakfast choices include a three-filling omelet for just C$4.50 (US$38.30); even the biggest, meanest cooked breakfast is only C$7 (US$5.95). The rest of the day, tuck in to a clam burger for C$6 (US$5.10) or pay C$13.50 (US$11.50) for a pile of juicy Digby scallops.

298 St. George St. ☎ *902-532-5254. Main courses: C$5–C$16 (US$4.30–US$13.60). Open: Daily 8 a.m.–8 p.m.*

Garrison House
$$–$$$ Annapolis Royal   SEAFOOD/GLOBAL

At this lovely three-room restaurant in the lodging of the same name, seafood and local produce are served in all kinds of creative ways. The menu changes every few weeks, but usually includes a rich Acadian seafood chowder and mains ranging from the simple (pan-fried haddock) to Greek-inspired (Digby scallops, feta cheese, and olives on a bed of pasta) to Asian (chicken and shrimp coconut milk curry). Most dishes are accompanied by local, farm-fresh produce.

350 St. George St. ☎ *902-532-5750. Main courses: C$15–C$23 (US$12.80–US$19.60). AE, MC, V. Open: Daily 5:30–8:30 p.m.*

Exploring Annapolis Royal

Make your first stop the generating station, home to the **Annapolis Royal Tourist Information Centre** (☎ **902-532-5769**; May–mid-Oct daily 9 a.m.–5 p.m.). Here you can pick up the brochure *Footprints with Footnotes,* an excellent reference for a self-guided tour of **St. George Street,** one of Canada's oldest streets. Of dozens of historic buildings, the most notable is the **Sinclair Inn,** at 230 St. George Street. Built in 1710, it's the oldest wooden building in Canada.

Annapolis Tidal Generating Station
North of downtown

The Bay of Fundy's record-breaking tides are used to generate electricity at the world's second-largest tidal generating station (actually, there's only three, but it's bigger than the one in Russia) on a causeway north of Annapolis Royal. Although it continues to generate electricity, the station was originally built as an experiment, a precursor to a more ambitious project that has been stalled by environmental concerns. An upstairs interpretive center explains the generation process in a straightforward manner, with large picture windows allowing views of the holding pond.

Prince Albert Rd. (Highway 1). ☎ *902-532-5769. Admission: Free. Open: Mid-May–mid-Oct daily 9 a.m.–5 p.m.*

Fort Anne National Historic Site
Downtown

Preserving the site of settlements dating back to 1629, this accessible attraction is centrally located on a low rise beside the main street. Star-shaped earthen fortifications and a moat dating to 1702 are the oldest visible remains of 200 years of struggles between the French and British. In a more modern building is a mid-sized museum with rooms representing different eras, including the period between 1713 and 1749 when the settlement was the capital of Nova Scotia. If you are staying overnight in town, ask at the museum about entertaining night-time tours of the Garrison Graveyard, led by a top-hatted "undertaker."

St. George St. ☎ *902-532-2397. Admission: C$4 (US$3.40) adults, C$3.50 (US$3) seniors, C$2 (US$1.70) children. Open: Mid-May–mid-Oct 9 a.m.–6 p.m.*

Historic Gardens
Downtown

These "historic" gardens were actually created in the 1980s, but they have been laid out to represent distinct eras in the history of Annapolis Royal, including Acadian (pre-1700s), British (early 1700s), and Victorian (late 1880s). Also on the grounds is a rose garden that comes alive with color in midsummer, a small maze that will keep children on their toes, and a marshland trail dotted with interpretive panels explaining Acadian dyking techniques. A restaurant with a pleasantly shaded patio serves lunch.

441 St. George St. ☎ *902-532-7018.* www.historicgardens.com. *Admission: C$8.50 (US$7.30) adults, C$7.50 (US$6.40) seniors and children. Open: Mid-May–mid-Oct daily 9 a.m.–5 p.m. (until dusk July–Aug).*

Keji what?

Pronounced "Kedge-im-a-*koo*-jik" (and sensibly known simply as "Keji"), **Kejimkujik National Park** protects a remote inland region of Nova Scotia scarred by glacial action from the last Ice Age.

A single road penetrates the park, branching off Highway 8 halfway between Annapolis Royal and Liverpool. Along its length are numerous easy hikes, a lookout tower with expansive views, a large campground, and supervised swimming at Merrymakedge Beach. The park's extensive system of shallow lakes and rivers is ideal for canoeing. Rentals are available at **Jakes Landing,** 8km (5 miles) from Highway 8 (☎ 902-682-2196) for C$5 (US$4.30) per hour and C$25 (US$21.30) per day, including paddles and life jackets.

Stop at the **Visitor Reception Centre** by the park entrance (☎ 902-682-2772; www.pc.gc.ca; daily 8:30 a.m.–4:30 p.m., until 9 p.m. in summer) for schedules of guided walks and paddles and the evening interpretive program. A Day Pass costs C$6 (US$5.10) adults, C$5 (US$4.30) seniors, C$3 (US$2.60) children.

Port-Royal National Historic Site

This is the actual site of Canada's first permanent settlement, which was founded in 1605 by French explorer Samuel de Champlain. Destroyed by the British eight years later, the fort has been reconstructed using Champlain's original plans, complete with costumed interpreters. One of the most interesting exhibits describes how the Mi'Kmaq helped the settlers adapt to the new land.

Follow Granville Rd. for 10km (6.2 miles) from the north side of the causeway ☎ *902-532-2898. Admission: C$4 (US$3.40) adults, C$3.50 (US$3) seniors, C$2 (US$1.70) children. Open: Mid-May–mid-Oct 9 a.m.–6 p.m.*

Continuing toward Halifax from Annapolis Royal

From Annapolis Royal, Highway 101 continues to make its way along the southern edge of the Bay of Fundy. It's just over 200km (125 miles) back to Halifax along this direct route. A more enticing option is Highway 1, which heads in the same direction, but at a more relaxing pace. The following are easily reached from both highways:

> ✔ **Cape Split.** Reaching the end of this narrow finger of land extending almost across the Minas Channel entails an 8km (5-mile) one way hike, but you will be rewarded with magnificent views down to the Bay of Fundy. On the protected eastern side of the spit, **Blomidon Provincial Park** protects an impressive lineup of red cliffs. To get to either spot, take Exit 11 from Highway 101 and follow the signs from Highway 358.

✔ **Wolfville.** This university town has an impressive array of Victorian-era homes, the **Randall House Museum** at 171 Main St. (☎ **902-542-9775**), which catalogs the colonists who came after the Acadians had been expelled, and a pleasant waterfront area where interpretive boards describe the natural and human history of Minas Basin. Built by an apple baron, **Victoria's Historic Inn** at 600 Main St. (☎ **800-556-5744** or 902-542-5744; www.victoriashistoric inn.com) can be an inexpensive overnight stop or a decadent splurge, depending on your room choice. Regardless of how much you pay, everyone enjoys the same gourmet breakfast. Rates are C$108 to C$245 (US$91.90–US$208.60), which is in the $$ to $$$$ range.

✔ **Grand Pré National Historic Site.** Once the principal population center of Acadia, this outdoor museum east of Wolfville off Highway 1 (☎ **902-542-3631**) remembers the expulsion of Acadians in 1755. Although the English burned their villages, the clever dyking system Acadians developed to farm land below sea level is still present. Also on the grounds are a church, various statues and monuments, and a blacksmith's shop. While the outdoor attractions are the main draw, it is well worth also spending time in the main interpretive center to learn a little about Acadian culture and the deportation. Admission C$6.50 (US$5.50) adults, C$5.50 (US$4.70) seniors, C$3.25 (US$2.80) children. Open: Mid-May to October daily 9 a.m. to 6 p.m.

✔ **Howard Dill Enterprises.** If you're tiring of history, maybe it's time for a detour to one of Nova Scotia's quirkiest, yet most impressive, attractions. Howard Dill is famous for developing pumpkin seeds that go on to produce some of the world's largest pumpkins, including the current world record of 656 kilograms (1,446 pounds). He's no slouch himself in the growing department, with four world records in the books. The best time to visit his farm at 400 College Rd. (☎ **902-798-2728**) is late September through early October, when the pumpkins are at their biggest.

Chapter 13

Central Nova Scotia

In This Chapter
▶ Watching the tidal bore in Truro
▶ Poking around Pictou
▶ Exploring the wild and rugged Eastern Shore

"**C**entral" Nova Scotia is a somewhat arbitrary designation that encompasses the region north of Halifax and extends east to Cape Breton Island. This portion of the province is served by main highways that lead to major population centers like Truro, New Glasgow, and beyond. In this chapter, I encourage you to explore towns and attractions that lie beyond the highways but are still close at hand. Highlights are as varied as watching the tidal bore created by massive tides in the Bay of Fundy, clambering over a replica of the boat that transported early Scottish settlers to North America, and learning to surf in the Atlantic Ocean.

Truro

Two major highways merge at Truro, Nova Scotia's third largest city, but many tourists pass right on by. That's a shame, because the Truro area offers a few notable attractions that make a visit worthwhile.

Getting there

Highway 102 from Halifax (90km/56 miles to the south) passes west of Truro, while the east-west Trans-Canada Highway, here called Highway 104, passes north of it. To get downtown from Highway 102, take Exit 14; if you're on Highway 104, take Exit 15 to Highway 102 and then Exit 14.

Staying in Truro

Truro lodgings are designed to fill the needs of overnighting highway travelers. You'll find some decent, well-priced motel rooms along the roads linking downtown to the main highways.

Comfort Inn Truro
$$ Truro

This low-slung, two-story chain motel is handy to Highway 102, but far enough away from it for traffic noise to be at a minimum. The mid-sized rooms come with lots of amenities (in-room coffee, hairdryers, ironing facility), and a light breakfast is included in the rates.

12 Meadow Dr. (Exit 14 from Highway 102). ☎ *902-893-0330. Fax: 902-897-0176.* www.choicehotels.ca. *Rack rates: C$119 (US$101.20). AE, DC, DISC, MC, V.*

Palliser Motel
$ Truro

It's certainly not the older-style rooms that are the attraction here: It's quite simply the location. Set on a low bluff above the Salmon River, this is the prime local spot for viewing the tidal bore (the river in front of the motel is lit at night for this purpose). The Palliser also has a restaurant, where motel guests are offered a complimentary hot buffet breakfast.

Tidal Bore Rd. (Exit 14 from Highway 102). ☎ *902-893-8951. Fax: 902-895-8475. Rack rates: C$65–C$74 (US$55.30–US$62.90) double. AE, DC, MC, V.*

Dining in Truro

Give all the usual chain restaurants on the outskirts of Truro a miss, and take the time to search out the only local restaurant I recommend.

Murphy's
$ Truro SEAFOOD   "Best Sea Food"

Who says it's all about location? One of Nova Scotia's best-known seafood restaurants is in Truro, which isn't even on the ocean — and it's in a strip mall to boot. Inside, the fish nets, model boats, and bright maritime murals leave no one guessing at this restaurant's specialty. The menu offers a wide range of all the usual seafood suspects, but it's the perfectly cooked deep-fried fish (usually cod) that brings in a constant flow of locals and travelers in the know.

112 The Esplanade. ☎ *902-895-1275. Main courses: C$10–C$22 (US$8.50–US$18.70) dinner. MC, V. Open: Daily 11 a.m.–8 p.m.*

Exploring Truro

Start your visit at the local **information center** (Victoria Square; ☎ **902-893-2922**), and take a downtown walking tour that focuses on an unfortunate history with a silver lining. A few years back, Dutch elm disease struck many of the stately elm trees lining Truro's streets. While trees afflicted with the same disease in other towns were destroyed, an imaginative group of locals commissioned a wood carver to create art from the trunks. Today, over 30 tree-trunk sculptures dot the downtown streets. Ask for a map detailing each at the information center.

There aren't many reasons to linger too long in Truro, though. See the tidal bore, and then hit the road for some quick out-of-town sight-seeing.

Tidal Bore
Truro

Some of the world's highest tides rise through the Bay of Fundy. When the ocean water in the bay is forced up adjacent low-lying rivers, a wall of water surges across the mudflats and funnels into the local river systems, and you can actually see the water changing direction. Truro's location beside the Salmon River at the far end of the "funnel," combined with easy access from the highway, make the local **Tidal Bore Park** a favorite viewing spot for this intriguing sight.

Tides change just over every six hours, so the bore occurs twice daily. It arrives approximately 50 minutes later each day, so be sure to check at the local visitor center (☎ **902-893-2922**) for tide times.

South Tidal Bore Rd. (Exit 14 off Highway 102 or west from downtown along Prince St.). Admission: Free.

Balmoral Grist Mill
Balmoral Mills

Step back in time at this underrated, off-the-beaten-path attraction that was built in 1874 and has been restored to working order. Within a bright-red wooden building nestled in a lush valley, water tumbles through a waterwheel linked by a pulley system to a solid granite millstone that grinds wheat and oats. Various demonstrations take place daily, with the finished product used in a variety of baked goodies sold at the site. Not only is Balmoral Grist Mill worth visiting for its historical interest, the location is delightful. Plan on enjoying a picnic lunch in the adjacent park.

38 kilometers (24 miles) north of Truro off Hwy. 311. ☎ 902-637-3016. Admission: C$4 (US$3.40) adults, C$3 (US$2.60) seniors and children. Open: June–mid-Oct, Mon–Sat 9:30 a.m.–5:30 p.m., Sun 1 p.m.–5:30 p.m.

Glooscap Trail
West from Truro

Named for a mythical Mi'Kmaq spirit who controlled the tides, this route (Highway 2) follows the northern shoreline of Cobequid Bay and Minas Basin west from Truro to Parrsboro before taking a jog north to rejoin the Trans-Canada Highway (104) near Springhill. Although the Glooscap Trail is in the geographical center of the Maritimes, it passes through a relatively remote region, with verdant forests running down to sea cliffs and tiny fishing villages.

An obvious attraction along this stretch of highway is the scenery, but the most interesting features are less obvious. In the 1980s, this region came into the paleontological spotlight when more than 100,000 bone fragments from dinosaurs were unearthed. The **Fundy Geological Museum** in Parrsboro (☎ **902-254-3814**) explains the importance of the 200-million-year-old fossil beds. In addition, agate and amethyst are common along this stretch of coast. **Parrsboro Rock and Mineral Shop** (☎ **902-254-2981**), operated by local legend Eldon George, displays various dinosaur fossils (including thumbnail-sized dinosaur footprints) along with lots of gemstones. Eldon will sell you rock-collecting gear or, if he's not busy, will take you out to his favorite collecting grounds for around C$30 (US$25.60) per person.

The **Maple Inn,** at 17 Western Ave. in Parrsboro (☎ **902-254-3735**) is a good overnight choice for travelers looking to soak up local history. Rates are C$90 to C$150 (US$76.50–US$127.50) double, including breakfast.

Pictou

In 1773, about 250 hardy Scottish settlers stepped ashore at Pictou Harbour after a treacherous trans-Atlantic journey aboard the *Hector*. They were brought to the area by a Philadelphia company looking to fulfill the terms of a land grant. Few people from North America were willing to move to the area, so the company began to look farther afield; Acadia was renamed Nova Scotia ("New Scotland" in Latin) in a desperate effort to attract Scots.

Getting there

Pictou lies on a protected harbor 12km (7.5 miles) north of Highway 104. The road to Pictou is busier than you might expect, because it continues through town to the Caribou ferry terminal, one of two gateways to Prince Edward Island.

Staying in Pictou

This town has a good selection of historic properties that offer comfortable lodging without going over the top in décor or price.

Consulate Inn
$$–$$$ **Pictou**

This ivy-covered 1810 building was once a consulate for the United States, and later a prominent local judge called it home for 50 years. Perhaps as a result, it has a somewhat jaded air of having been-there, done-that. The cheaper rooms may not be designer-chic, but you'll get a good night's rest. The Lower Garden Suite with basic cooking facilities is good value, but has a low ceiling. Rooms in the modern annex all have a jetted tub and varying water views. Out back, the garden runs all the way to the water's edge, with outdoor furniture, a gazebo, and a barbeque area. For families on a budget, the adjacent house can be rented through the Consulate Inn for C$119 (US$101.20).

115 Water St. ☎ _800-424-8283 or 902-485-4554. Fax: 902-485-1532._ www.consulate inn.com. _Rack rates: C$75–C$159 (US$63.80–US$135.20) double. AE, MC, V._

Pictou Lodge Resort
$$–$$$$ East of Pictou

This sprawling resort occupies a prime position on Northumberland Strait. Pictou Island is visible in the distance and water surrounds the property on three sides, with a man-made pond thrown in for good measure. Activities include canoeing, sea kayaking lessons, horseback riding, hiking along nature trails, biking, or just relaxing on the private beach. The oldest units date to the 1920s; some have been given a thorough going-over (the one-bedroom deluxe cottages, complete with a kitchen and screened verandah, are my favorite), but more modern motel units and snazzy log cabins have the better views. A summer activity program makes the lodge a great place for families.

Braeshore Rd. (5km/3.1 miles east of Pictou). ☎ _888-662-7484 or 902-485-4322. Fax: 902-485-4945._ www.maritimeinns.com. _Rack rates: C$125–C$249 (US$106.30– US$211.70) double. AE, DISC, MC, V. Open: Mid-May–mid-Oct._

Dining in Pictou

Pictou Lodge Resort Dining Room

Even if you're not staying here, it's worth the short drive just for a meal. While the rest of the resort has undergone numerous upgrades through the years, the restaurant hasn't, which is a good thing. Breakfast and lunch are taken on the screened-in verandah, while the main dining room, with its high ceiling, exposed log work, and massive fireplace, has a distinctly historic charm. The menu also reflects an earlier era, with steak, chicken, and seafood dishes cooked to perfection and served without frills. The salmon, basted in maple syrup and herbs and broiled on a cedar plank, is a real treat. Sunday brunch is also popular.

Braeshore Rd. ☎ _902-485-4322. Reservations recommended for dinner. Main courses: C$24–C$30 (US$20.40–US$25.60). AE, DISC, MC, V. Open: Mid-May–mid-Oct. daily 7 a.m.–9 p.m._

Exploring Pictou

Pictou's biggest draw is the waterfront. Plan on spending at least half a day poking around the harbor.

Hector Heritage Quay
Pictou

This harbor complex is anchored by a full-sized floating replica of the 33.5m (110-foot) _Hector_, the sailing ship that transported Nova Scotia's first Scottish settlers across the Atlantic. The three-masted ship was constructed using traditional tools and techniques, making it the most faithful reconstruction project of its kind ever undertaken in North America. Admission includes access to the ship itself, but it's also worth spending time "on land," reading interpretive panels that narrate the story of the original ship and its passengers and watching blacksmiths and carpenters at work in their dockside shops. It's perfect for families — interesting for adults, but the kids will have fun, too.

33 Caladh Ave., Pictou. ☎ 902-485-6057. Admission: C$5 (US$4.30) adults, C$4 (US$3.40) seniors, C$2 (US$1.70) children 6–12. Open: June–Aug Mon–Sat 9 a.m.– 5 p.m., Sun 10 a.m.–5 p.m., the last two weeks of May and Sept–mid-Oct Mon–Sat 9 a.m.–5 p.m., Sun noon–5 p.m.

Northumberland Fisheries Museum
Pictou

At one time, this red-brick railway station was the eastern end of the rail line across Canada. Now it's an unassuming museum that's actually pretty interesting. You'll find an impressive collection of exhibits on diverse ocean-related topics ranging from local marine life to the whaling and fishing industries and racing boats. Kids will love the model boats and tank of live lobsters. It's easy to spend an hour at this museum, even if you're not a maritime buff.

71 Water St., Pictou ☎ 902-485-4972. Admission: C$4.50 (US$3.80) adults, C$3.50 (US$3) seniors, C$2 (US$1.70) children 6–12. Open: Mid-June–mid-Oct Mon–Sat 9 a.m.–7 p.m., Sun noon–5 p.m.

Not Jost another winery

Everyone loves promoting a local product — that's why you'll see wines from **Jost Vineyards** (pronounced "yost") featured in many Nova Scotia restaurants. Though it's situated well away from Canada's better-known wine-producing regions, Jost has produced some award-winning products. They're only available in Nova Scotia, so be sure to get a sample while you're here, especially of their award-winning **ice wine**. Frost is the enemy in most vineyards, but at Jost it is a vital part of the ice wine process. The frozen grapes are left on the vines for a few days, then gently pressed to extract just a few drops of concentrated juice from each grape. The result of this low-yield process is an intense, sweet wine that pairs well with dessert. Ice wine is only a small part of the Jost repertoire. Many classic European varietals that reflect the owner's German roots, including a classic Riesling, are picked at a more traditional time of year to produce bottles of wine in the C$11 to C$40 (US$9.40–US$34) range.

Free winery tours are offered daily at noon and 3 p.m. throughout the summer. Afterward, you can browse the wine shop, pick up some gourmet goodies at the deli, and enjoy a picnic on the patio.

Jost Vineyards is at Malagash, east of Pictou along Highway 6 (☎ **902-257-2636**; www.jostwine.com). Open: Mid-June to Sept. daily 9 a.m.–6 p.m.

Touring along Northumberland Strait

East of Pictou, Northumberland Strait is bordered by a convoluted coast-line that extends all the way to Canso Causeway, gateway to Cape Breton Island. Highway 104, the main route to Cape Breton, sensibly follows a direct route well away from the coastline, leaving a variety of options for casual touring. Here are some suggested detours along the way:

✔ **New Glasgow.** East of Pictou along Highway 104, this sprawling town has a pleasant downtown core centered on a river. An 1841 building constructed from ship ballast has been converted to the **Dock, Food, Spirits, and Ales** pub. Its historical origins are ignored by most patrons, who gravitate to the sun-drenched patio.

✔ **Stellarton.** New Glasgow and Stellarton are separated by Highway 104, though linked by commercial sprawl. Take Exit 24 on Highway 104 to get to Eastern Canada's largest museum, the **Nova Scotia Museum of Industry** (☎ 902-755-5425). This may not sound like an exciting stop, but kids will love every minute of it. In keeping with the theme, you must punch a time card upon entry. Allow at least an hour to explore. Open: Mon to Sat from 9 a.m.to 5 p.m. (closed Sat in winter). Admission: C$7 (US$6) adults, C$4 (US$3.40) seniors, C$3 (US$2.60) children.

✔ **Antigonish.** Pronounced An-*tee*-gun-ish, this busy highway town becomes even busier during the middle weekend of July for the **Highland Games,** the biggest and oldest such games outside of Scotland. Heavyweight events like tug-o'-war and caber-tossing are balanced by pipe-bands and performances by some of the biggest names in Celtic music.

✔ **Arisaig Provincial Park.** This park protects coastal cliffs that tell the 400-million-year-old story of a time when Nova Scotia was part of a shallow sea. What makes this place particularly interesting to scientists is that layers of sediment laid down over millions of years have become exposed along a single cliff line, revealing a neck-straining time line of ancient life on Earth. Digging into the cliff for fossils is not permitted, but you are allowed to search through fallen rubble along the beach.

Eastern Shore

Promoted as the **Marine Drive** (Highway 7, then Highways 211 and 316), the route between Halifax and Canso looks relatively tame on a big map, but when it comes to negotiating the narrow, winding 320km (200-mile) route you should allow a full day — *without* stops. But don't let the pace put you off: The slow going is the perfect excuse to take your time and spend the night in one of the charming villages enroute.

Getting there

From Dartmouth, across the harbor from downtown Halifax, take Exit 7 from Highway 111. The highway is occasionally in sight of the ocean, but the most scenic areas are along side roads. Consult a good map, and enjoy!

Staying along the Eastern Shore

The Eastern Shore has a few excellent lodging options, but make sure you've reserved ahead of time or you'll end up spending the night in a nondescript roadside motel.

Liscomb Lodge
$$–$$$ Liscomb Mills

Its location halfway between Halifax and Canso makes Liscomb Lodge a good place for an overnight stop. Standard rooms are comfortable but unexceptional. It's worth paying extra for the much larger cottages, even if you don't have a family in tow. Activities like hiking and boating will tempt you to stay longer. The resort restaurant is one of the few dining choices along this stretch of coast, so it's worth enquiring about meal packages when booking a room.

Highway 7, Liscomb Mills ☎ *800-665-6343 or 902-779-2307. Fax: 902-779-2700.* www.signatureresorts.com. *Rack rates: C$135–C$160 (US$114.80–US$136) double. AE, DISC, MC, V. Open: Mid-May–late Oct.*

Salmon River House Country Inn
$$ Salmon River Bridge

Less than an hour's drive from Halifax, this lodging has been a popular getaway for almost 100 years. The rooms have been modernized, but décor remains a bit old-fashioned. Still, the additions of ensuite bathrooms and televisions aren't a bad thing. Close-up river views and a wonderful restaurant are the real reason this place makes the cut. The self-contained guesthouse may appeal to those looking for a little more privacy.

Highway 7, Salmon River Bridge. ☎ *800-565-3353 or 902-889-3353. Fax: 902-889-3653.* www.salmonriverhouse.com. *Rates: C$94–C$144 (US$79.90–US$122.40) double. AE, MC, V. Open: April–Oct.*

Seaboard Bed and Breakfast
$$ East Lawrencetown

Popular with active travelers on a budget, this converted 1912 farmhouse is less than 1km (0.6 miles) from the waves of Lawrencetown Beach. Guests are welcome to use bikes or the canoe the hosts leave at a lake across the road. You'll find basic, comfortable accommodations, a communal television room, a small library, and a lounge with fireplace.

A hearty breakfast with lots of homemade baked goodies will get you going in the morning.

2629 Crowell Rd. ☎ *902-827-3747.* www.seaboardbb.com. *Rack rates: C$100–C$115 (US$97.80) double. AE, MC, V.*

St. Mary's River Lodge
$–$$ Sherbrooke

The six rooms in this renovated residence all have private bathrooms and television, and all but one are air-conditioned. The rooms are a little cutesy for my liking, but the price is right and it's handy to historical Sherbrooke Village, which is right next door. Rates include a cooked breakfast.

21 Main St., Sherbrooke. ☎ *902-522-2177. Fax: 902-522-2626.* www.river lodge.ca. *Rack rates: C$68–C$96 (US$57.80–US$81.60) double. MC, V.*

Dining along the Eastern Shore

J. Willy Krauch & Sons Ltd.
$ Tangier   SEAFOOD

You'll often see salmon in restaurants referred to as "Krauch" salmon, and this is where it comes from. Krauch salmon is cold-smoked, which means the fish has been salted and then smoked for up to a week at very low temperatures. The process is very different from normal smoking, where the fish literally cooks as it is smoked. Cold-smoking creates a subtle, savory flavor and a firm texture — perfect for slicing thinly and serving on crackers (it is the most divine smoked salmon you will ever taste). If you're worried about consuming your purchase before it makes it home, you'll be pleased to know that the company ships worldwide.

Highway 7, Tangier. ☎ *902-772-2188. Open: Mon–Fri 8 a.m.–6 p.m.*

Lobster Shack
$$–$$$ Salmon River Bridge   SEAFOOD

Ahoy, matey! Even landlubbers are made to feel at home in this small-town restaurant with a big-time reputation. The dining room is part of the Salmon River House Country Inn, and has a pleasant riverside deck. The interior walls are decorated in all manner of maritime memorabilia — the sort of stuff you'd expect to find washed up on the beach after a big storm. As the name suggests, lobster is a menu feature. To start, choose from super-creamy lobster chowder or rich seafood dip with pita bread. If you're serious about your lobster, choose one from the tank and order it as a main course. Boiled lobster is boiled lobster; what sets the Lobster Shack apart from other restaurants is the variety of sizes — up to 5 pounds on my last visit (I was told they often hold them up to 10 pounds).

Highway 7, Salmon River Bridge. ☎ *902-889-3353. Main courses: C$13–C$25 (US$11.10–US$21.30). AE, MC, V. Open: April–Oct 8 a.m.–9 p.m.*

Exploring the Eastern Shore

Like the rest of the province, the Eastern Shore has a long and interesting history, which can be relived at numerous attractions. But it is the smell of salt in the air, the long stretches of sandy beach, and the quiet coves that are the real draw.

Fisherman's Life Museum
Jeddore Oyster Pond

Life for an East Coast fisherman and his family 100 years ago was not easy. This museum re-creates the simple, self-sufficient lifestyle of one such family. Ervin Myers, the husband, spent long days at sea while his wife Ethelda raised 13 daughters in this small green and white house. Details such as the family's woodstove and small pipe organ and the surrounding gardens planted with root vegetables add to the museum's authentic quality.

58 Navy Pool Loop, Jeddore Oyster Pond. ☎ *902-772-2344. Admission: C$3 (US$2.60) adults, C$2 (US$1.70) seniors and children. Open: June–mid-Oct Mon–Sat 9:30 a.m.–5:30 p.m., Sun 1 p.m.–5:30 p.m.*

Canso Islands National Historic Site
Canso

The Canso Islands, within sight of the small town of Canso, have a long and colorful history, but today sit empty beyond the end of one of Nova Scotia's most remote roads. The British established an outpost on one of them, Grassy Island, in the early 1700s, harvesting and processing 8 million cod annually. They also made a lackadaisical attempt at fortifying the settlement, but were unable to protect it against a 1774 attack by the French, who destroyed the entire town. The National Historic Site has two parts; stop by the Visitor Reception Centre along Union St. in Canso to learn more about the history, then take the free 15-minute boat ride across to the island, where an interpretive trail leads past various foundations and a well. It's an interesting trip for the stark, end-of-the-world feel surrounding the site.

Access by boat from Canso ☎ *902-366-3136. Admission: Donation of C$5 (US$4.30) includes admission to the Visitor Reception Centre and boat ride. Open: June– mid-Sept daily 10 a.m.–6 p.m.*

Sherbrooke Village
Sherbrooke

What makes this historic park stand out from others is that the village is an actual community, with real live Nova Scotians going about their daily business. Sherbrooke was the site of an 1860s gold rush, and many of the original buildings have been faithfully restored in the style of this era. Costumed guides are on hand to talk about the village and its history, or to give demonstrations of traditional crafts such as candle-making and old-time photography. One of the most interesting displays is the work-shop, where carpenters combine traditional skill with modern technology to produce reproductions in demand at historic sites across the province. On Thursday at 7:30 p.m., the village courthouse hosts Celtic concerts.

Highway 7, Sherbrooke. ☎ *888-743-7845 or 902-522-2400.* www.museum.gov.ns. ca/sv. *Admission: C$9 (US$7.70) adults, C$7.25 (US$6.20) seniors, C$3.75 (US$3.20) children. Open: June–mid-Oct daily 9:30 a.m.–5:30 p.m.*

More cool things to do along the Eastern Shore

While the historic sites are worth a stop, it's the ocean that takes center stage along the Eastern Shore. Apart from the coastal scenery, it's a great area for trying your hand at surfing or sea kayaking, and boasts some great beaches:

- ✔ **Surfing:** After surfing on both coasts of Canada, I'm not sure if it's possible to say one is better than the other. One thing is for certain, though: Lawrencetown Beach, a half-hour drive from Halifax, is Canada's best-known surf spot. Waves break along a rocky point as well as on the beach, with the biggest swells rolling though in winter. DeCane Sports (☎ **902-431-7873**) charges around C$50 (US$42.50) per day for rental of surfboard and wetsuit (you'll need one, even in summer). Lessons are also offered from their beach-side outlet.

- ✔ **Sea kayaking:** Even if you've never been near a sea kayak, the guides at **Coastal Adventures,** based at Tangier (☎ **902-772-2774;** www.coastaladventures.com), will make you feel comfortable in the water. The full-day beginner course (C$110/US$93.50 per person) is as much a tour as a lesson, with an introduction to basic paddling skills followed by a trip to an uninhabited island and lunch. You're in safe hands with co-owner Dr. Scott Cunningham, who could write a book on the subject — and in fact has (*Sea Kayaking in Nova Scotia*).

- ✔ **Beach walking:** Okay, this activity is a little less adventurous than the others, but there's nothing like feeling sand between your toes and breathing in the smells of the ocean. Best of all, it's free. As Canada's longest stretch of sand (5km/3.1 miles), **Martinique Beach,** south of Musquodoboit Harbour, is a good option for an extended beach walk. It is protected as a provincial park and is dotted with day use areas and access paths. Continuing north from Martinique Beach, **Taylor Head Provincial Park** protects a narrow spit of land lined by glorious white-sand beaches along its pro-tected eastern side.

Chapter 14

Cape Breton Island

● ●

In This Chapter

▶ Taking in the life and times of Alexander Graham Bell at Baddeck
▶ Driving the Cabot Trail through Cape Breton Highlands National Park
▶ Stepping back in time at the Fortress of Louisbourg

● ●

Cape Breton Island is a Maritimes gem. It offers plenty of breathtaking coastal scenery and a dash of Canadian history, coupled with that unmistakable down-home East Coast charm you've heard so much about. Joined to the mainland by a causeway, the island is renowned for its rugged coastline, while mountains, lakes, and salmon-filled rivers add to the diversity inland. The Cabot Trail, a 300km (186-mile) road that winds its way around Cape Breton Highlands National Park, is the island's top attraction.

History buffs will be satiated at Canada's largest historical reconstruction, the Fortress of Louisbourg National Historic Site, which reminds us that the French once held sovereignty to the island after ceding the rest of the province to the British in 1713.

A big part of this region's appeal is the people ("Cape Bretoners"), many of them proudly descended from Scots who were attracted by the island's strong resemblance to their homeland. The island's most famous resident was born in Scotland himself: Alexander Graham Bell, like so many others, was captivated by this unique part of the country and called Baddeck home for much of his life.

You need your own vehicle to make the most of a visit to Cape Breton Island.

Plan on spreading the wealth around when it comes to lodging. One night at a historic inn at Baddeck and another at a beachy resort along the Cabot Trail would be the perfect combination for a two-night stay.

Cape Breton Island

Baddeck

Halfway up the island, the delightful resort town of Baddeck is a good central location to plan an overnight (or longer) stay. The town's most famous resident was Alexander Graham Bell, who spent summers and then the last three decades of his life at a stately waterfront mansion across the bay from Baddeck. The home is owned by Bell's descendants, but in town one of the province's best museums tells his interesting life story. Down on the waterfront, a free ferry shuttles visitors to Kidston Island for hiking and swimming, while other tour boats can take you to search out nesting bald eagles.

Getting there

Take Highway 105 north from the Canso Causeway, and in less than an hour you'll be greeted by a bombardment of Baddeck billboards.

Staying in Baddeck

Whether you're looking to spend your day at a waterfront resort or a character-laden historic lodging, you'll find something in Baddeck.

Summer is very busy in Baddeck, so reservations are necessary for local lodging. If you do arrive without having booked a room, stop at the centrally located **Baddeck Welcome Centre** (☎ 902-295-1911) for suggestions.

Bethune's Boathouse Cottage
$$ Baddeck

The name says it all: This small cottage is a converted boathouse on the Baddeck waterfront. Inside, you'll find a double bed, bathroom, and living area with a television and radio. Cooking is done on an outside barbeque. The cottage sits on its own small lot, but is not particularly private. If you feel like getting away, simply take to the water in the complimentary rowboat.

49 Water St. ☎ *902-295-2687. Rack rates: C$110 (US$93.50) double. No credit cards. Open: Mid-May–mid-Oct.*

Inverary Resort
$$–$$$$ Baddeck

Kids in particular will enjoy this resort on the south side of Baddeck. It's not really within walking distance of town, but why would you want to leave when you've got tennis courts, a spa facility, an indoor pool, a fitness center, a large playground, boat and kayak rentals, and sailing trips aboard a boat once owned by Alexander Graham Bell? The rooms vary from those in an original building to modern, fully equipped suites with private balconies. The resort also has two restaurants and a lounge. Golf and meal packages can be a good deal.

Shore Rd. ☎ *800-565-5660 or 902-295-3500. Fax: 902-295-3527.* www.capebreton resorts.com. *Rack rates: C$110–C$390 (US$93.50–US$331.50) double. AE, DISC, MC, V. Open: Apr–Dec.*

Telegraph House
$–$$$ **Baddeck**

Built in 1861 and now run by the fifth generation of the same family, this imposing gray-and-white inn on a main street was once a telegraph office. Rooms in the main lodge are basic and some are very small, but all are clean and comfortable, and the location couldn't be more central. Alexander Graham Bell often stayed in Room 1 when in town — do you need a better recommendation? Behind the main lodge is a wing of more modern motel rooms decorated in a vaguely Victorian décor. They may lack the history of those in the original building but are good value, especially the extra-large ones which are ideal for families.

9 Chebucto St. ☎ *888-263-9840 or 902-295-1100. Fax: 902-295-1136.* www.baddeck. com/telegraph. *Rack rates: C$75–C$199 (US$63.80–US$169.20) double. AE, MC, V.Open: Daily.Serve meals only between June 1-Oct 30.*

Water's Edge Inn
$$–$$$ **Baddeck**

Water's Edge Inn overlooks the lake and Kidston Island, and is just a couple of blocks downhill from the main street. It is well worth paying extra for one of the four rooms with private balconies and water views, although all six are well appointed and come with modern niceties such as DVD players. The inn is also home to a café and an art gallery.

22 Water St. ☎ *866-439-2528 or 902-295-3600. Fax: 902-295-1382.* www.thewaters edgeinn.com. *Rack rates: C$140–C$170 (US$119–US$144.50) double. AE, MC, V. Open: May–Oct.*

Dining in Baddeck

Restaurants line the main street through Baddeck, but some of the better dining choices are associated with local lodgings.

Baddeck Lobster Suppers
$$ **Baddeck**   **SEAFOOD**

In typical lobster-supper style (or lack of it), this traditional Maritimes feast is replayed for tourists in a dining hall across from the waterfront. At dinner, pay C$27 (US$23) for one full lobster and all-you-can-eat mussels, chowder, dessert, and non-alcoholic drinks. Lunch offers similar choices from a regular menu.

Ross St. ☎ *902-295-3307. Lobster supper: C$27 (US$23). MC, V. Open: June–Oct daily 11:30 a.m.–1:30 p.m. for lunch and 4 p.m.–9 p.m. for dinner.*

Lakeside Café
$$ Baddeck   GLOBAL

Drive down through the Inverary Resort to reach this casual waterfront restaurant, which has lots of outdoor tables. The lunch menu is made up of fancy sandwiches such as a Lobster Clubhouse and appetizers from the dinner menu. The evening menu takes its roots from around the world, with an emphasis on local produce. Choose from dishes such as a Thai stir-fry tossed with scallops, or go Greek with grilled halibut topped with feta cheese and olives.

Inverary Resort, Shore Rd. ☎ *902-295-3500. Main courses: C$12–C$20 (US$10.20–US$17.10). AE, MC, V. Open: May–Oct daily 11:30 a.m.–3:30 p.m. and 4:30–10 p.m.*

Lynwood Inn Dining Room
$$–$$$ Baddeck   CANADIAN

Tucked inside a historic residence that has been converted to an inn, this smallish dining room features subtle Victorian furnishings with the modern addition of a deck wrapped around two sides. For starters, the menu covers all bases, with nachos, mussels, and chicken soup (with loads of chicken). Entrées are no less diverse, with choices ranging from a charbroiled T-bone to grilled rainbow trout splashed with a corn salsa.

23 Shore Rd. ☎ *902-295-1995. Main courses: C$12.50–C$21 (US$10.60–US$17.90). AE, MC, V. Open: Daily 11 a.m.–9 p.m.*

Exploring Baddeck

Baddeck isn't big on traditional official "sights," but that doesn't mean it's not a delightful town to visit. Chebucto Street is the main thorough-fare, but walk one block down Jones Street to reach the waterfront and you'll find yourself in the real heart of the town.

Alexander Graham Bell National Historic Site
Baddeck

Like most kids, I learned in school that Alexander Graham Bell invented the telephone, but it wasn't until I'd spent a few hours in this museum that I realized the extent of his contribution to the world of science and engineering. The first exhibit explains Bell's achievements in teaching the deaf (including Helen Keller) to speak, using a phonetic alphabet developed by his father. Spend some time at this display, as the interpretive panels go on to explain how this early work was inextricably linked to his later experimenting with transmitting sound along wire using voice pulsations.

Cape Bretoners and their music

You'll hear Celtic-based music wherever you travel on Cape Breton Island. It's incredibly popular with the local population, and so catchy that you can't help but be captivated by its spirit and energy. Cape Bretoners Natalie MacMaster, Ashley MacIsaac, The Rankins, and the Irish Descendents have introduced this music to the world, but there's no place like the island itself to immerse yourself in the traditions of Celtic song and dance. To find the best place to go for a night out, ask a local, check entertainment listings in newspapers, or simply wander the streets listening for live music.

One event worth noting is the **Celtic Colours International Festival** (☎ 877-285-2321 or 902-562-6700; www.celtic-colours.com), which is held the second week of October with the magnificent backdrop of fall's blazing colors. Celtic musicians from around the world perform in over 40 island towns in churches, halls, and theaters.

This, of course, led to Bell's patenting of the world's first telephone in 1876. The rest of the museum is devoted to his lesser-known inventions, such as the world's first hydrofoil and first seaplane. Among the various replicas and original parts on display is the *Silver Dart*, with which Bell broke the world speed record on Bras d'Or Lake. As a symbol of Bell's work with children, part of the museum is set aside for kids, with puzzles, experiments, and kite-making.

Chebucto St. ☎ *902-295-2069.* www.pc.gc.ca/lhn-nhs/ns/grahambell. *Admission: C$6.50 (US$5.50) adults, C$5.50 (US$4.70) seniors, C$3.25 (US$2.80) children. Open: June daily 9 a.m.–6 p.m; July–mid-Oct daily 8:30 a.m.–6 p.m.*

Other cool things to see and do in Baddeck

Relax at an outdoor café, wander down to the waterfront or, if you're feeling more active, consider one of the following:

- ✔ **Set Sail.** The *Elsie* (☎ 902-295-3500) is a gracious sailing boat once owned by Alexander Graham Bell. It departs the Inverary Resort daily at 10:30 a.m. and 2:30 p.m. for a three-hour tour on Bras d'Or Lake. Keep an eye out for Alexander Graham Bell's mansion, and you may spy a bald eagle along the way. The cost is C$65 (US$55.30) per person.

- ✔ **Paddle over to Kidston Island.** Protected as a park, this uninhabited island lies just across a narrow channel from Baddeck. It has a beach, nature trails, and even a lighthouse. A free ferry departs Government Wharf for the island every 20 minutes, but it's more enjoyable to rent a canoe or kayak from **Harvey's,** beside Government Wharf (☎ 902-295-3318), and reach the island under your own steam.

- ✔ **Take a drive through the Margaree Valley.** West of Baddeck, the southernmost section of the Cabot Trail follows the Margaree River, famed in fishing circles for its high concentrations of salmon. At the **Margaree Salmon Museum** in North East Margaree (☎ **902-248-2848**) you can learn about the salmon's lifecycle from guides or on your own. It's open mid-June to mid-October daily 9 a.m. to 5 p.m., and entry is just $1 (US85¢). North of the museum, potter Bell Fraser sells her distinctive ocean-inspired pieces at **Cape Breton Clay** in the village of Margaree Valley (☎ **902-235-2467**).

✔ **Dance the night away.** The **Baddeck Gathering Ceilidhs** is a nightly performance by local musicians in St. Michael's Parish Hall on Main St. (☎ **902-295-2794**). Entry costs just C$8 (US$6.80); tea, coffee, and oatcakes are each $1 (US85¢), and all the action gets under way at 7:30 p.m., July and August only.

Cape Breton Highlands National Park and the Cabot Trail

It is impossible not to fall in love with this spectacular national park, which stretches across the top of Cape Breton Island. Sea cliffs and rocky coves dominate the west side and long sandy beaches run down the east side, with a vast plateau of wilderness in between. The Cabot Trail, one of Canada's most scenic drives, loops through the park and weaves along both coasts, ensuring you miss nothing. Wildlife viewing is excellent: Most visitors spot moose, whales, and bald eagles, often without even leaving their vehicles.

Getting there

Unless you're planning to traverse the Cabot Trail by bike, you'll need your own vehicle. To reach the main park gate, turn off Highway 105 south of Baddeck.

Paying entrance fees

The **park entry fee** of C$6 (US$5.10) adults, C$5 (US$4.30) seniors, C$3 (US$2.60) youths, to a maximum of C$12 (US$10.20) per vehicle, is good until 4 p.m. the day following its purchase. Passes can be purchased at the information center north of Chéticamp or at the tollbooths at both park entrances. If you have a **National Parks of Canada Pass** (see Chapter 5), you'll be waved right on through.

Arriving at the park's main entrance

Make your first stop the **Chéticamp Visitor Centre** (☎ **902-224-2306**), 5km (3.1 miles) north of Chéticamp. It's open June and September to mid-October daily 9 a.m. to 5 p.m., July to August daily 8 a.m. to 8 p.m. Inside, natural history exhibits provide a good introduction to the park, and posted activities schedules will help in planning your time. Friendly staff at the information desk supply free maps and will help you decide which hiking trails best suit your abilities. Off to one side is **Les Amis du Plein Air** (☎ 902-224-3814), a bookstore that stocks park-related literature and a wide selection of general outdoor and nature guides.

Staying along the Cabot Trail

Cliff Waters Wilderness Retreat
$$–$$$ **Pleasant Bay**

Cliff Waters comprises just three units, and each is very different: The three-bedroom Main House (perfect for families); the Spinning Jenny Guest Cabin, an old tool shed that has been transformed into a contemporary space; and the Luxury Tent, which has an en suite bathroom. The emphasis throughout the property is on eco-friendliness (think solar-powered lanterns, organic coffee, and more).

1773 Red River Rd., 9km north from Pleasant Bay ☎ *902-224-1130. Fax: 902-422-1711.* www.cliffwaters.com. *Rack rates: C$100–C$200 (US$170) double. AE, MC, V. Open: mid-May–mid-Nov.*

Glenghorm Beach Resort
$$–$$$$ **Ingonish**

Set on a sprawling property that extends from the Cabot Trail to a beautiful sandy beach, this resort has activities for the whole family and accommodations to suit all tastes. It offers canoe and kayak rentals, an outdoor pool, volleyball courts, a large playground, a fitness room, an esthetics salon, and nightly beachside bonfires. The least expensive units are roadside motel rooms. Older cottages come with a kitchen and up to two bedrooms; some are within sight of the ocean. The Deluxe Suites are among the best guest rooms in all of the Maritimes: Luxuriously appointed, they still manage to maintain a casual air — you can happily tramp sand in without feeling guilty. Each air-conditioned unit has a private verandah or balcony, separate sleeping quarters, a jetted tub, a kitchen, and comfortable couches set around a gas fireplace. Resort dining includes a restaurant open for three meals and a downstairs bar with live Celtic music most nights.

Ingonish Beach. ☎ *800-565-5660 or 902-285-2049. Fax: 902-285-2395.* www.cape bretonresorts.com. *Rack rates: High season C$107–C$395 (US$91–US$335.80) double, low season C$87–C$295 (US$74–US$250.80) double. AE, MC, V. Open: May–Oct.*

Keltic Lodge
$$$–$$$$ **Ingonish Beach**

Sharing a narrow peninsula that juts into Ingonish Bay with the famous Highland Links golf course, the Keltic Lodge is one of Canada's most fashionable resorts. A short drive from the Cabot Trail leads to the perfectly positioned main lodge, on an isthmus high above the ocean and with water views to the north and south. The nationalistic red and white exterior contrasts starkly with the surrounding blues and greens. Dating to the 1940s, this is the original lodge, with older rooms, a restaurant and lounge, and the main lobby. Guests also have the use of a heated outdoor pool, and the concierge can make bookings for tennis, whale-watching, and fishing. You don't need to be a registered guest to get a tee time at Highland Links or to hike out to the tip of Middle Head, but you'll feel more like you belong if you are. Price-wise, you may expect more from the rooms. On the other hand, you'll find yourself enjoying the outdoors for much of your stay. Rooms in the main lodge are a little old-fashioned, while those in the Inn at Keltic are motel-like, but air-conditioned and just steps away from a grassy area with a gazebo and colorful Adirondack chairs. The four-bedroom cottages can be rented as an entire unit or with guests sharing a communal living area.

Ingonish Beach. ☎ *800-565-0444 or 902-285-2880. Fax: 902-285-2859.* www. signatureresorts.com/keltic. *Rack rates: High season C$190–C$320 (US$161.50–US$272) double, low season C$100–C$150 (US$85–US$127.50) double. AE, DISC, MC, V. Open: June–Oct.*

Parkview Motel
$$ Chéticamp

Choose from older rooms or upgrade to air-conditioned creek-side deluxe rooms at this motel complex within walking distance of the park information center. The on-site restaurant and lounge save you from having to drive anywhere.

West entrance, 5km (3.1 miles) north of Chéticamp. ☎ *902-224-3232. Fax: 902-224-2596.* www.parkviewresort.com. *Rack rates: C$89–C$109 (US$75.75–US$92.70) double. AE, MC, V. Open: June–mid-Oct.*

Seascape Coastal Retreat
$$$ Ingonish

Set on a grassy slope that ends at a private beach on Ingonish Bay, this resort is a little piece of heaven beside the busy Cabot Trail. The well-tended grounds are dotted with outdoor seating and a hot tub. In one corner, a garden produces vegetables and herbs used in the adjacent restaurant. The cottages have solid, modern furnishings; amenities such as jetted tubs and fireplaces; and special touches like bathrobes add to their charm. All cottages have a verandah with an ocean view. Prices include seafood hors d'oeuvres upon arrival, a cooked breakfast, and the use of kayaks and mountain bikes.

36083 Cabot Trail, Ingonish. ☎ *866-385-3003 or 902-285-3003.* www.seascape coastalretreat.com. *Rack rates: High season C$189–C$209 (US$160.70–US$177.70) double, low season C$149–C$159 (US$127–US$135.20) double. MC, V. Open: May–Oct.*

Dining along the Cabot Trail

It's seafood and more seafood along the Cabot Trail. If you feel like a break from the catch of the day, try the major resorts, most of which have restaurants with wide-ranging menus.

Atlantic Restaurant
$$–$$$ Ingonish Beach   SEAFOOD/CANADIAN

Looking in, this place could be an up-market family restaurant anywhere in North America. Looking *out*, the drop-dead gorgeous ocean view through big windows could only be Cape Breton. Low prices are the only real surprise on the seafood-dominated menu. You can order favorites like beer-battered fish and chips for as little as C$10 (US$8.50), but I encourage you to be more adventurous. The grilled halibut, bookended by crab cakes to start and a slice of blueberry shortcake for dessert, will set you back around C$35 (US$29.80).

Keltic Lodge, Ingonish Beach. ☎ *902-285-2880. Main courses: C$10–C$22 (US$8.50–US$18.70). AE, DISC, MC, V, DC. Open: June–Oct 11 a.m.–9 p.m.*

Chowder House
$ Neil's Harbour   SEAFOOD   ''Best Seafood''

This is casual Cape Breton dining at its very best. The Chowder House is in a weather-beaten building on a headland through the village of Neil's Harbour. Don't be put off by the pine-paneled décor: The food is super-fresh and very well priced. The clam chowder is chockablock with juicy clams and costs just C$4.50 (US$3.80) per bowl; a lobster burger will set you back C$10 (US$8.50); or you can order the most expensive item on the menu board, a full lobster with fries and coleslaw, for C$20 (US$17.10). Once you've made a decision, order at the counter and listen for your number. The restaurant is totally enclosed, which is a bit of a shame — if it's a nice day, I'd recommend spreading a blanket out on the grassy headland.

Neil's Harbour, beside the lighthouse. ☎ *902-336-2463. Main courses: C$7–C$20 (US$6–US$17.10). Open: May–Sept 11 a.m.–8 p.m.*

Muddy Rudder
''Best Seafood''
$–$$ South Ingonish Beach   SEAFOOD

The delightfully named Muddy Rudder is part restaurant, part attraction, and totally unique. It's simply a roadside shanty at the head of Ingonish Harbour with a few plastic outdoor table settings off to one side. Choose from lobster, crab, mussels, or clams, all of which are cooked to order in big pots of boiling water out front. Prices are a little higher than you'd pay at a local seafood market, but a lot lower than at a regular restaurant. While researching this book, my wife and I enjoyed the biggest plate of mussels I've ever seen (C$7/US$6), followed by a full crab that came with tea cakes and coleslaw (C$17.50/US$14.90), and we just happened to have a bottle of red from Jost Vineyards (see Chapter 13) in the car, which the owner happily opened for us.

Cabot Trail, South Ingonish Beach. ☎ *902-285-2266. Main courses: C$7–C$17.50 (US$6–US$14.90). Cash only. Open: May–Sept 10 a.m.–7 p.m. (later if the owner doesn't have other engagements).*

Restaurant Acadian
$–$$ Chéticamp ACADIAN

Attached to a craft shop, this casual restaurant is a wonderful place to try Acadian cuisine. Adding to the charm, the women who work there all dress in traditional clothing. Mains like *Croquettes de Morue* (cod fish cakes) and *Chaudrée au Poisson* (haddock chowder) are mostly under C$10 (US$8.50). Plan on saving room for dessert — the raisin pudding (C$3.25/US$2.80) is as good as it gets.

774 Main St. Chéticamp. ☎ *902-224-3207. Main courses: C$8–C$14 (US$6.80–US$11.90). MC, V. Open: Mid-May–late Oct daily 7 a.m.–9 p.m.*

Seascapes Restaurant
$$$ Ingonish SEAFOOD

Attached to the resort of the same name, it's easy to miss this small ocean-front dining room as you scoot along the eastern side of the Cabot Trail. There is no menu as such; the chef simply uses available seafood to create a half-dozen dishes (along with at least one vegetarian option), which are written up on a blackboard. I picked a creamy lobster linguini (C$21/US$17.90), and the lobster was boiled especially for my order. A rather refined-looking couple seated next to me were gleefully tucking into snow crab — complete with bibs (on them, not the crabs).

Seascape Coastal Retreat, 36083 Cabot Trail, Ingonish. ☎ *902-285-3003. Reservations Recommended. Main courses: C$17.50–C$26 (US$14.90–US$21.10). MC, V. Open: May–Oct. daily 6–9 p.m.*

Exploring the Cabot Trail

The Cabot Trail, parts of which have already been covered in this chapter, is a 300km (186-mile) route that takes in not just Cape Breton Highlands National Park, but also the coastal drive south from the park to St. Ann's and on to Baddeck, then through the Margaree Valley to Chéticamp. The spectacular 110km (68-mile) section inside the park is detailed here.

Highlights along the way

Although it's only a little over 100km (62 miles) between Chéticamp and Ingonish, you should allow at least one full day for this stretch of highway, simply due to the number of interesting stops enroute. The road is steep and narrow in some sections but is not difficult to drive. Pullouts and viewpoints are spaced along the entire route. Do not use the narrow shoulder as your personal parking space.

My description of the Cabot Trail follows a clockwise direction. It could have gone either way, but by following this course, you'll hit the main information center first up and complete the drive on the east side of the peninsula, where most of the recommended accommodations and restaurants can be found.

The most dramatic section of the entire Cabot Trail is the 45km (28-mile) stretch along the west coast. The scenery kicks off in a big way almost immediately, with the road hugging the shoreline, ascending precipitous sea cliffs, and then dropping back down to sea level. Stop at as many overlooks as your time allows; take in the scenery and read the interpretive boards.

One particularly scenic overlook is the **Veterans Monument,** 18km (11 miles) north of the park entrance. When I last made the stop, a moose and her calf were grazing in the open meadows below while a whale could be seen in the ocean beyond and a black bear foraged on the high hills behind.

Once you reach **Wreck Cove,** the road ascends steeply via a series of switchbacks to reach sea level at **Pleasant Bay,** just outside the park boundary. This small village, which was in existence well before road access was possible, now takes full advantage of summer traffic with a variety of tourist services. It tries hard to function primarily as a fishing village, but the harbor is filled with whale-watching boats and sea kayakers. The **Whale Interpretive Centre (☎ 902-224-1411;** open mid-May–Oct daily 9 a.m.–6 p.m.) has displays on the various species you may see out on a whale-watching trip. Admission is C$5 (US$4.30) for adults, C$4 (US$3.40) for seniors and children.

From Pleasant Bay, the Cabot Trail begins its ascent to a high plateau, re-entering the national park after a few minutes' drive. Just inside the boundary is **Lone Shieling,** the stone replica of a Scottish crofter's hut. It is also the starting point for a short trail leading to a grove of 350-year-old sugar maple trees. Continuing eastward, the road traverses a stunted *taiga* (mostly evergreen) forest before reaching a turn off to **Cape North.** This side road skirts **Aspy Bay,** where a plaque and statue commemorate John Cabot's 1497 landfall. It then crosses to the northern tip of the island and the picturesque fishing communities of **Bay St**. **Lawrence, Capstick,** and **Meat Cove** — Cape Breton living in its rawest state.

After a side trip to Cape North, you have no choice but to backtrack before rejoining the Cabot Trail for its final push across the peninsula. Although the landscape on the east coast is less dramatic than the west, it is no less captivating, with long stretches of sand broken by rocky headlands. Highlights include the beach at **Black Brook Cove** and **Lakies Head Lookout.** Continuing south, the Cabot Trail leaves the park again. Along this section, it passes four villages with Ingonish in their names, although in reality, they merge into one long strip broken only by

Middle Head, a narrow peninsula that holds one of Canada's finest golf courses and the grand Keltic Lodge. Beyond Ingonish, the Cabot Trail leaves the national park for a final time, making its last grand ascent to **Cape Smokey,** one of the most dramatic lookouts along the entire trail.

Hiking the highlands

You can enjoy the park's spectacular scenery from the inside of your car easily enough, but to really appreciate the place, you need to get out onto the hiking trails. Stray away from the road to experience the park's natural beauty on any of these trails:

- **Le Buttereau Trail:** Here's an easy one to get you started. This 2km (1.2-mile) loop starts just north of the tollbooth, with views across a large lagoon. Plan a dawn walk for the best bird watching, or wait until dusk to watch the sun set over the Gulf of St. Lawrence.

- **Skyline Trail:** The Skyline is a high ridge with a long but easy trail leading to a magnificent viewpoint where whales can often be spotted frolicking below. The trailhead is on the left as the Cabot Trail heads inland beyond French Mountain. Allow at least three hours for the 12km round-trip.

- **Benjie's Lake Trail:** This small lake is easily reached in 30 minutes from a parking lot 6km (3.7 miles) beyond the Skyline Trail. As most visitors spend their time along the coastline, visiting this lake is a good way to escape the crowds — and you may even spy moose along the way.

- **Fishing Cove Trail:** Two trails make the steep descent to this small bay along an otherwise inaccessible stretch of coastline. The first, beginning 3km (1.9 miles) north of Benjie's Lake Trail, is 8km (5 miles) each way. Further north, another trail is much shorter (4km/2.5 miles) but a lot steeper. Either way, you should pack lunch and something to drink.

- **Jigging Cove Lake Trail:** On the park's east coast, 4km (2.5 miles) south of Neil's Harbour, this lake lies just out of sight of the highway. It is encircled by a 3km (1.9-mile) trail which can be hiked in well under an hour.

- **Jack Pine Loop:** Escape the crowds at Black Brook Cove by scrambling through the boulders at the north end of the beach to reach the beginning of this 3km (1.9-mile) loop which weaves through coastal forest. You'll be back on your beach towel in less than an hour, even if you stop to read the interpretive boards along the way.

- **Middle Head Trail:** Drive as far as you can through the grounds of the Keltic Lodge, then walk for 2km (1.2 miles) and you'll find yourself at the very end of a narrow peninsula surrounded by dramatic cliffs. If you're staying at the Keltic Lodge, join a 9:30 a.m. guided walk to learn about the flora and fauna as you go.

✔ **Freshwater Lake Loop:** As the trailhead is Ingonish Beach, one of Canada's finest stretches of sand, you may find that motivating yourself to leave the beach is the hardest part of taking this easy 2km (1.2-mile) loop trail. Walking the path at dusk is a good opportunity to watch beavers hard at work — and you won't feel so bad about not being on the beach.

Other cool reasons to stop along the Cabot Trail

Apart from driving and hiking, consider the following options:

✔ **Whale-watching:** From the village of Pleasant Bay, you can take a tour boat to see whales frolicking along the coast. Commonly sighted species are pilot, humpback, and minke whales. The following operators are Coast Guard-certified, have partly-covered vessels, and are run by experienced captains who have a wealth of knowledge: **Captain Mark's Whale & Seal Cruise** (☎ **888-754-5112** or 902-224-1316), **Fiddlin' Whale Tours** (☎ **866-688-2424**), and **Highland Coastal Nature Tours** (☎ **866-266-4080** or 902-224-3103). Typically, tours last 90 minutes and cost C$25 (US$21.30) per person. Fiddlin' Whale Tours costs a few dollars extra, but Celtic fiddlers keep passengers entertained along the way. Each operator has a booth along the marina at Pleasant Bay, but advance reservations are recommended. All cruises are weather permitting — if the captain decides not to go sail because of rough seas, you probably don't want to be out on the water anyway.

The advantage of choosing a whale-watching trip at Pleasant Bay over other locations throughout the Maritimes is that it's only a short ride to where the whales are, so you get to spend more time watching and less time traveling.

✔ **Sea-kayaking:** The protected water of St. Ann's Bay, south of Ingonish, is an ideal place to kayak. You're likely to spot eagles and whales while visiting inaccessible-by-foot beaches, sea caves, and tidal pools. Twice daily, **North River Kayak Tours** (☎ **888-865-2925** or 902-929-2628; www.northriverkayak.com) offers a half-day (actually, around 3 hours) trip for C$55 (US$46.80) and a full-day for C$100 (US$85). I recommend the full-day option. Great for first-timers and families, you'll learn basic paddling techniques and then head off to a sea cave; keep a lookout for eagles and mink along the way. The turnaround point is a remote beach where lunch is prepared. The cost includes kayak rental, instruction, lunch (steamed mussels if you're lucky), and maybe a friendly wave from the lighthouse keeper as you pass his posting. Overnight and multi-day trips explore more remote waters, or opt for the Rough It and Romance overnight excursion, which includes camping gear, all meals, and guidance to a remote beach.

✔ **Beaching it:** The best beaches are on the eastern side of the park. **Black Brook Cove** is somewhat protected from wind and ocean swells, creating a safe swimming spot. This sandy beach is backed by a grassy picnic area. Continuing south, **Ingonish Beach** is a long stretch of sand, well protected by Middle Head. The shallow water is warm, and a short section is patrolled through summer daily from noon.

✔ **Golfing:** A 1939 Stanley Thompson layout, **Highland Links,** near Ingonish (☎ **800-441-1118** or 902-285-2600; www.highlandlinks golf.com) is consistently rated as one of the world's top 100 courses by *Golf Magazine.* Although not overwhelming by today's standards, it is a classic links-style course with a dramatic coastal setting. In keeping with the Scottish theme, each hole has a name, with both English and the Gaelic translation signed at the teebox (Hole 6, for example, is Mucklemouth Meg, the nickname for a girl with a big mouth, in reference to a pond that swallows wayward golf balls). Greens fees are C$70 to C$83 (US$59.50–US$70.60) during peak season, dropping to just C$42 (US$35.70) for twilight golfing during the shoulder season (June and Oct).

Shopping

Shopping? In a national park? Well, sort of. Cape Breton Island is known for its artists and, with the large number of tourists, many have set up shop in the tiny villages that lie on the edge of the park. Most are open long hours through summer, shorter hours during the shoulder seasons, and then close completely for winter.

I list the following in a clockwise direction from Chéticamp: Beyond the top of the park at Dingwell, **Arts North** (☎ **902-383-2732**) showcases the pottery of owner Linda Doyan, the jewelry of Johanna Padelt, and the hooked rugs of Maggie Miller. One of the island's best-known painters is Christopher Gorey, whose oil and watercolor landscapes are sold at **Lynn's Craft Shop & Art Gallery,** at Ingonish (☎ **902-285-2845**). **Tartans and Treasures** at South Harbour (☎ **902-383-2005**) claims to have North America's largest collection of tartan scarves and blankets. Most products come directly from the mother country, so you know you're buying the real thing. **Iron Art & Photography,** south of Ingonish at Tarbot (☎ **902-929-2821**), combines the hand-forged ironwork of Gordon Kennedy with the striking hand-tinted black and white photography of his wife, Carol, to make a worthwhile stop on the road back to Baddeck.

Louisbourg

It's been over 250 years since the French were driven from the lonely outpost of Louisbourg, on the remote eastern tip of Cape Breton Island. Today, it is one of the most interesting historical sites in all of the Maritimes, with lodging and other tourist services in an adjacent town of the same name.

Getting there

Louisbourg is 45km (28 miles) southeast of Sydney along Highway 22. No public transportation reaches the town.

Staying in Louisbourg

Even though it's at the end of the road, Louisbourg has several comfortable lodgings within walking distance of the fort, including these two recommendations.

Cranberry Cove Inn
$$–$$$ **Louisbourg**

It's impossible to miss this three-story, cranberry-red inn as you head out to the fortress. Inside, the décor is a little tamer. Each of seven guestrooms has its own theme. The top-floor Captain's Den, for example, has a quirky layout (thanks to the gabled roof), a subtle maritime color scheme, a gas fireplace, and a jetted tub. Not all the rooms have televisions. Downstairs is a parlor, in which three generations of the same family used to spend their evenings during the inn's former life. Breakfast is included in the rates and is served on the sunny side of the house.

12 Wolfe St. ☎ *800-929-0222 or 902-733-2171.* www.louisbourg.com/cranberry cove. *Rack rates: C$105–C$160 (US$89.30–US$136) double. MC, V. Open: May–Oct.*

Point of View
$$–$$$ **Louisbourg**

This modern oceanfront property hogs the prime spot on a high headland within walking distance of both the town and the fortress. It sprawls over 1.6 hectares (4 acres) of well-maintained grounds, with a private beach at one corner of the property. Inside, the units have a sleek, contemporary styling, hardwood floors, and sliding doors that open to either a balcony or verandah. The apartments are much larger than the suites and come with a full kitchen.

At the front of the property is a beach house where the owners host a nightly lobster supper. It's a casual gathering of guests, who are served steamed lobster and crab with all the trimmings and entertained with story-telling or a sing-along. Breakfast isn't included in the rates, but is available, eggs, bacon and all, for just C$5 (US$4.30).

15 Commercial St. Extension ☎ *888-374-8439 or 902-733-2080.* www.louisbourg pointofview.com. *Rack rates: C$125 (US$106.30) suites, C$199 (US$169.20) apartments. MC, V.*

Dining in Louisbourg

Plan on eating lunch at one of the three restaurants at the Fortress of Louisbourg. If you're staying at Point of View Suites, you'll want to reserve a spot at their nightly lobster supper. If not, the single recommendation below is a good one.

Grubstake Restaurant
$$–$$$ Louisbourg SEAFOOD

It's now been over 30 years since a group of well-traveled friends got together and opened this restaurant that serves local cuisine to visitors from around the world. Not much has changed since, and no one seems to mind. The restaurant is casual and cozy, and the seafood is done without a deep fryer in sight. If you order the seafood linguini with a creamy lobster sauce, plan to give dessert a miss; or, for something lighter, try halibut poached in milk and white wine, , fish cakes with baked beans, or a vegetarian stir-fry. The adjacent cocktail lounge is a popular gathering spot for Fortress workers.

7499 Main St. ☎ 902-733-2308. Main courses: C$10–C$25 (US$8.50–US$21.30). MC, V. Open: Daily noon–8:30 p.m., later in July and Aug.

Exploring Louisbourg

Even if you don't like history lessons, a little background is necessary to set the scene for a visit to the Fortress of Louisbourg National Historic Site. After the 1713 Treaty of Utrecht, all the French were left with in the Maritimes were Prince Edward Island and Île Royale (Cape Breton Island), the latter a base for a lucrative cod-fishing industry. Wary of an attack on their sovereignty, the French established a massive fortress around the Louisbourg village to repel an attack from the ocean, but in 1745, the British came from behind and took it in a little more than six weeks. After the fortifications changed hands on two more occasions, the British destroyed them and burnt the village to the ground in 1760. Two hundred years later, with many Cape Breton coal mines closing, the federal government decided to begin the daunting task of rebuilding the entire village and fort as a make-work project. The result is Canada's largest historical reconstruction — a must-see for anyone traveling around Cape Breton Island.

Fortress of Louisbourg National Historic Site

Plan on spending the better part of a full day on the grounds. Start by watching the video at the interpretive center, and then catch the shuttle to the back of the fort to get going on your exploration of the site. Every detail of the original fort and village has been re-created, down to the construction techniques and materials. Even the social structure is historically correct, with ostentatious homes of the rich filled with fine china and French wines, while ramshackle working-class abodes have earthen floors and wood stoves for heating. Around 100 costumed interpreters do a wonderful job of playing their parts. Actually, if you ask them, they won't admit they're playing a part at all — a military officer may sternly ask if you're spying for the British, or a carpenter will complain about how much harder it is to get materials in Canada than back in France, while vendors peddle their wares on cobblestoned streets.

Traditional menus and costumed servers depict 1700s life at three eateries. **Hotel de la Marine** is where regular folk eat; no meat is served on days of abstinence (Fri and Sat), and customers eat with only a large spoon. Wealthy citizens (and visitors wanting to live the high life) eat and gossip at **L'Épée Royale,** where fancier European cuisine is served and diners have the privilege of using silver cutlery. If you've arrived at the settlement with limited funds, head to **King's Bakery,** where a loaf of heavy bread and a hunk of cheese cost less than a single appetizer at L'Épée Royale.

Louisbourg. ☎ *902-733-2280.* www.pc.gc.ca/lhn-nhs/ns/louisbourg. *Admission: C$15 (US$12.80) adults, C$12.75 (US$10.80) seniors, C$7.50 (US$6.40) children. Open: Mid-May–June and Sept–mid-Oct daily 9:30 a.m.–5 p.m.; July and Aug. daily 9 a.m.–6 p.m.*

Fast Facts: Cape Breton Island

ATMs

ATMs aren't as common as they are elsewhere in Nova Scotia. Most towns have at least one, including Baddeck (Royal Bank) and Ingonish (Scotiabank).

Emergencies

Dial ☎ **911** for all emergencies.

Hospitals

Options include **Cape Breton Regional Hospital,** 1482 George St., Sydney (☎ **902-564-5566**), and **Victoria County Memorial Hospital,** Baddeck (☎ **902-295-2112**).

Information

Make your first stop over Canso Causeway at the provincial **Visitor Information Centre,** Port Hastings (☎ **902-625-4201**). It's open June–Sept daily 9 a.m.–5 p.m. The **Baddeck Welcome Centre** (☎ **902-295-1911**) maintains similar hours through the summer season.

Internet Access

You can retrieve your e-mail at **Cape Breton Regional Library,** 526 Chebucto St., Baddeck (☎ **902-295-2055**).

Police

For emergencies, dial ☎ **911;** the non-emergency number in Baddeck is ☎ **902-295-2350.**

Post Office

The post office in Baddeck is on Chebucto St.

Weather

Environment Canada maintains a Web site at www.weatheroffice.ec.gc.ca with links to the forecast for major Cape Breton Island towns.

Part IV
New Brunswick

The 5th Wave
By Rich Tennant

I love how you've handled the lighting in here.

In this part . . .

New Brunswick is a quiet achiever — though it's the biggest of the Maritimes provinces, it's not so familiar to outsiders as a tourist destination. Spend any time there and, like me, you will wonder why it's not more popular. Here, I cover New Brunswick's three main cities: Moncton, with its distinct Acadian flavor; historic Saint John, Canada's oldest city; and the stately provincial capital, Fredericton. Follow my lead and you'll be swimming in the warm waters off the Acadian Coast, fishing for lobsters in Northumberland Strait, searching out the "kissing bridges," and marveling at the Fundy tide phenomenon.

Chapter 15

Moncton and the Acadian Coast

. . . .

In This Chapter

▶ Finding your way to and around Moncton
▶ Deciding where to stay and eat
▶ Hitting the town
▶ Soaking up the sunshine of Shediac
▶ Immersing yourself in Acadian culture

. . . .

*M*oncton, which due to its location at the geographic center of the Maritimes serves as a transportation and business hub, began in the 1720s as an Acadian settlement. Today, a third of its 68,000 residents are French-speaking, and it is the only officially bilingual city in Canada. You will see and hear the influence of Acadian culture everywhere you go — all signage is in both English and French, and you'll be greeted in both languages by residents. Moncton University is the largest French university outside Quebec in Canada.

The nearest stretch of coastline is along Northumberland Strait, near the resort town of Shediac, which is renowned for long beaches and warm water. The region north of Shediac is known as the Acadian Coast for its long association with Acadians who returned to the Maritimes after being expelled from Nova Scotia by the British in 1755. The city itself has two quirky natural attractions: a tidal bore, which moves up the Petitcodiac River twice daily, and a hill with a seemingly magnetic pull.

Getting To Moncton

Moncton is an excellent starting point for a Maritimes vacation. In addition to its location at the geographic center of the region, flights there are often cheaper than they are to Halifax, which is just a three-hour drive to the southeast. You can also roll into the city by rail or bus.

New Brunswick

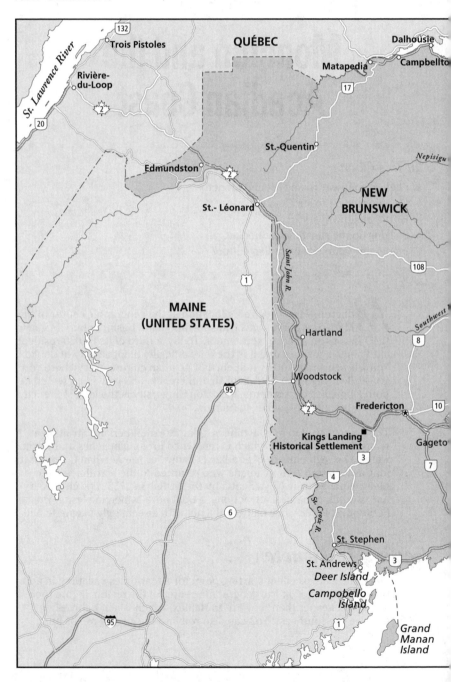

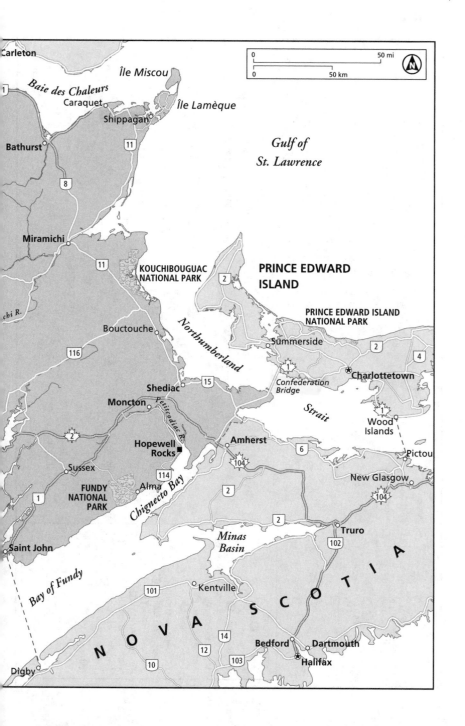

Moncton

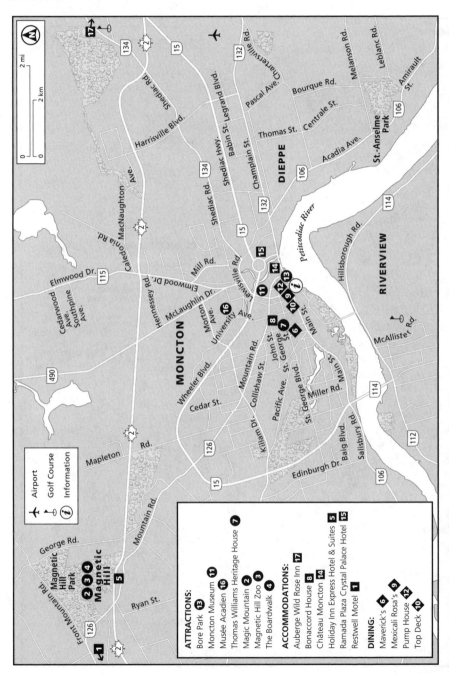

ATTRACTIONS:
Bore Park **13**
Moncton Museum **11**
Musée Acadien **16**
Thomas Williams Heritage House **7**
Magic Mountain **2**
Magnetic Hill Zoo **3**
The Boardwalk **4**

ACCOMMODATIONS:
Auberge Wild Rose Inn **17**
Bonaccord House **8**
Château Moncton **14**
Holiday Inn Express Hotel & Suites **5**
Ramada Plaza Crystal Palace Hotel **15**
Restwell Motel **1**

DINING:
Maverick's **6**
Mexicali Rosa's **9**
Pump House **12**
Top Deck **10**

By plane

Greater Moncton International Airport (www.gma.ca) is off Champlain St. (Route 132), about 8km (5 miles) from downtown. It is served by Air Canada, CanJet, and WestJet (see the Appendix for toll-free numbers and Web sites), with direct flights originating in Halifax, St. John's, Montreal, Toronto, and Calgary. Fares between airlines are generally competitive, but it pays to check each for specials.

All passengers departing Greater Moncton International Airport must contribute C$15 (US$12.80) to the Airport Improvement and Reconstruction Fund. Make your payment at a booth inside the main terminal.

Moncton's public bus system, operated by **Codiac Transit** (☎ 506-857-2008), runs between the airport and downtown Monday through Saturday. **Air Cab** (☎ 506-857-2000) is one of many local cab companies. You won't need to call, as taxis always wait out front of the main terminal. The fare to downtown is C$15 (US$12.80). Avis, Budget, Hertz, and National have desks at the airport (see the Appendix for the toll-free numbers and Web sites of major car-rental agencies).

By car

If you're driving around the Maritimes, chances are you'll pass through Moncton at some stage of your travels. Here's how to enter the city from a variety of directions:

- ✔ **Route 2 from Nova Scotia:** Take Exit 467 for downtown or Exit 450 for Magnetic Hill.

- ✔ **Route 15 from Shediac and the Confederation Bridge:** Pass under Route 2 and follow the signs right into downtown.

- ✔ **Route 114 from Hopewell Rocks:** Cross the Petitcodiac River via one of two bridges — the first to reach downtown, the second to loop around the western edge of the city to Magnetic Hill.

- ✔ **Route 2 from Fredericton:** Take Exit 466 (Route 128) for downtown or Exit 450 for Magnetic Hill.

By train or bus

VIA Rail's *Ocean* train passes through Moncton on its daily (except Tues) run between Montreal and Halifax. The station is off Main Street, on the southwest side of downtown (☎ 888-842-7245; www.viarail.ca).

Acadian (☎ 800-567-5151 or 506-859-5060; www.acadianbus.com) buses arrive and depart from a centrally located depot at 961 Main St. (corner of Bonaccord St.). The building is open Monday to Friday 7:30 a.m. to 8:30 p.m. and weekends 9 a.m. to 8:30 p.m. Some destinations linked to Moncton that are served by Acadian include the Acadian Coast, Prince Edward Island, Halifax, Fredericton, and Saint John.

Getting Around Moncton

Except for morning and evening weekday rush hours, driving around Moncton is easy. The downtown core spreads out around a bend in the Petitcodiac River. Main Street, which runs parallel to the river, is the main thoroughfare. To the east is suburban Dieppe, while south across the Petitcodiac is Riverview. The city's fun sights are 9km (5.6 miles) northwest of downtown at Magnetic Hill, on the north side of Route 2.

Parking

Finding parking in downtown Moncton isn't too difficult if you know where to look. The best bet for a spot is Moncton Market, on Westmorland Street south of Main Street, where a spot costs C$1 (US85¢) per hour to a maximum of C$7 (US$6) per day (free on weekends). Metered street parking is C$1 (US85¢) an hour, but it is not monitored weekdays after 6 p.m. or on weekends.

Cabbing It

Hailing a cab from the street is possible, but it's easier in front of a major hotel such as the Delta Beausejour, 750 Main St. (at Westmorland St.). From downtown, expect to pay around C$15 (US$12.80) to reach either Magnetic Hill or the airport. Cab companies include:

- ✔ **Air Cab** (☎ 506-857-2000)
- ✔ **Trius Taxi** (☎ 506-858-0000)
- ✔ **White Cab** (☎ 506-857-3000)

Taking transit

Codiac Transit (☎ 506-857-2008) serves Moncton with a bus network running Monday through Saturday 6:30 a.m. to 7 p.m. (extended to 10:30 p.m. on Thurs and Fri). Buses run east along Main Street to a major interchange at Champlain Place, from where they head out in all directions, including to the airport. Bus fare is C$2 (US$1.70) per sector for all passengers aged over 4.

Staying in Moncton

As the hub of the Maritimes, Moncton can meet every lodging need and budget. Accommodations are available all over the city, with the two main concentrations being downtown and out on Route 2 near Magnetic Hill.

As in the rest of the Maritimes, July through August is high season in Moncton — this is when lodging is in most demand and rates are highest.

As always, if you're planning on staying in a chain hotel, check its Web site for package deals and discounted rates.

Auberge Wild Rose Inn
$$–$$$$ Lakeville

The Auberge Wild Rose Inn is set on 15 hectares (38 acres) of beautifully landscaped gardens on the north side of Route 2. The inn has a dignified ambience, but is far from formal. The 16 guest rooms have modern amenities, such as cable TV and Internet access, as well as thoughtful touches, like bathrobes and plush comforters. Those in the C$135 to C$150 (US$114.80–US$127.50) range, with jetted tubs and either a private entrance or balcony, are the best deal. On the premises is a restaurant that serves full breakfasts (included in the rates) and four-course, fixed-price dinners in a French provincial atmosphere.

See map p. 192. 17 Baseline Rd. (off Route 134), Lakeville. ☎ *888-389-7673 or 506-383-9751. Fax: 506-870-7547.* www.wildroseinn.com. *Rack rates: C$99–C$229 (US$84.20–US$194.70) double. AE, DC, MC, V.*

 ## Bonaccord House
$ Downtown

Centrally located Bonaccord House is halfway between downtown and the university campus. The 100-year-old home has a common lounge area with fireplace and four guest rooms with private bathrooms.

See map p.192. 250 Bonaccord St. (at John St.). ☎ *506-388-1535. Fax: 506-853-7191. Rack rates: C$70 (US$59.50) double. V.*

Château Moncton
$$–$$$$ Downtown

It's difficult to miss this downtown hotel with its bright red roof. The rooms have a vaguely European feel and are comfortably sized. Some have up-close views of the Petitcodiac River, which flows right by the back door. All guests can enjoy views of the river and the tidal bore from Le Galion, a first-floor lounge with a south-facing deck that catches the afternoon sun. A light breakfast is included in the rates, but no other meals are served.

See map p. 192. 100 Main St. ☎ *800-576-4040 or 506-870-4444. Fax: 506-870-4445.* www.chateau-moncton.nb.ca. *Parking: free. Rack rates: C$129–C$239 (US$109.70–US$203.20) double. AE, MC, V.*

 ## Holiday Inn Express Hotel & Suites
$$–$$$ Magnetic Hill

This modern lodging comes exactly as you'd expect from the well-known chain — a handy highway location; an indoor pool, sauna, and hot tub; spacious rooms packed with basic amenities; and a complimentary breakfast bar off the lobby. A few rooms are themed especially for children, and a family-style Italian restaurant is open Mon–Sat at 5 p.m. From Route 2, take Exit 450; from downtown Moncton, follow Mountain Road northwest for 9km (5.6 miles).

See map p. 192. 2515 Mountain Rd., Magnetic Hill. ☎ *800-595-4656 or 506-384-1050. Fax: 506-859-6070.* www.hiemoncton.com. *Rack rates: C$115–C$185 (US$97.80– US$157.30) double. AE, DISC, DC, MC, V.*

Ramada Plaza Crystal Palace Hotel
$$$–$$$$ **Dieppe**

This modern hotel, which is part of the Crystal Palace Amusement Park complex and a short walk from the largest shopping mall in the Maritimes, is popular with vacationing Maritimers year-round — so don't expect any great off-season bargains. The surroundings are parking-lot plain, but the hotel itself is centered around a tropical atrium with a pool. The business rooms are adequately appointed, while 12 "Fantasy Suites" are devoted to diverse themes ranging from rock 'n' roll to the Victorian era.

See map p. 192. 499 Paul St., Dieppe. ☎ *800-561-7108 or 506-858-8584. Fax: 506-858-5486. www.crystalpalacehotel.com. Parking: free. Rack rates: C$159–C$229 (US$135.20–US$194.70) double. AE, DISC, DC, MC, V.*

Restwell Motel
$–$$ **Magnetic Hill**

This nondescript roadside motel close to Magnetic Hill provides better value than the nearby chain hotel properties. Some rooms share bathrooms, but the more expensive ones are surprisingly attractive and overlook pleasant grounds with a small outdoor pool and barbeque area. To get there, take Exit 450 (Magnetic Hill) north from Route 2, then go 4km (2.5 miles) west along Ensley Road.

See map p. 192. 12 McFarlane Rd., Magnetic Hill. ☎ *506-857-4884.* www.restwell motel.com. *Rack rates: C$50–C$100 (US$42.50–US$85) double. MC, V. Open: May–Oct.*

Dining in Moncton

Moncton bustles with chain restaurants, which can be found along all major arteries and concentrated around Magnetic Hill. For something more original, head to Main Street, the busy thoroughfare that runs through downtown Moncton. You'll find it lined with pubs, cafés, and restaurants, many with tables set out on the sidewalk.

Maverick's
$$–$$$$ **Downtown   STEAK**

Finding this lovely restaurant is well worth the effort. Away from the main restaurant strip and a little pricey for the college population, it is mostly the haunt of locals in the know. The winsome menu combines the best cuts of beef with local seafood — lobster-stuffed mushrooms to start, for example, and then rib eye with a side of garlic prawns. The wine cellar is one of the best in town, while the weekday lunch buffet gets rave reviews.

See map p. 192. 40 Weldon St. ☎ 506-855-3346. Reservations recommended. Main courses: C$17–C$29 (US$14.50–US$24.70). AE, MC, V. Open: Mon–Fri 11:30 a.m.– 2 p.m., daily 5–10 p.m.

Mexicali Rosa's
$–$$ **Downtown   MEXICAN**

A central location and inexpensive food make this place hugely popular with the college-aged crowd. The décor is bright and attractive, blending red brick walls with orange paint and head-high cactuses. The menu is mostly Mexican, with a "California influence" (their words, not mine) and a tip of the hat to Italy (pasta dishes served with tortilla chips). The kitchen prepares a delicious Mexicali dip as well as combo platters for around C$16 (US$13.60). Save room for the deep-fried ice cream.

See map p. 192. 683 Main St. ☎ 506-855-7672. Reservations recommended on weekends. Main courses: C$8.50–C$18 (US$7.20–US$15.30). MC, V. Open: Daily 11:30 a.m.–10:30 p.m.

Pump House
$–$$ **Downtown   PUB FARE**

Locals come to this brewpub for its convivial atmosphere and well-priced food and drink. The menu is mostly pub fare, with the usual westernized Mexican dishes good for sharing and the single-serve pizzas from a wood-fired oven. Explore the pub before settling down at a regular table — choices include booths contained within cut-off wine barrels, a sunny sidewalk deck, and tables in front of the brew tanks.

See map p. 192. 5 Orange Lane. ☎ 506-855-2337. Reservations not necessary. Main courses: C$8–C$17.50 (US$6.80–US$14.90). AE, MC, V. Open: Daily 11 a.m.–10 p.m.

Top Deck
$$–$$$ **Downtown   NORTH AMERICAN**

Hotel restaurants are the same the world over. They offer wide-ranging menus that don't offend anyone, they are open long hours, and the service is efficient. Which, along with river views, is exactly what you get at the Top Deck on the ninth floor of the newly renovated (in 2006) Crowne Plaza Hotel. This is one of the best places in town for breakfast; expect to pay around C$10 (US$8.50) for a cooked breakfast.

See map p. 192. 1005 Main St. ☎ 506-854-6340. Main courses: C$13–C$26 (US$11.10– US$22.10). AE, DC, MC, V. Open: Daily 6:30 a.m.–2 p.m. and 5–10 p.m.

Exploring Moncton

Moncton's location makes it a perfect base from which to explore the region. It's central to the beachy resort town of Shediac, the culturally intriguing Acadian Coast (both covered later in this chapter), and the Bay of Fundy (see Chapter 16).

The city itself features two interesting natural phenomena (maybe a little less exciting than the tourist brochures claim, but interesting nevertheless), as well as a mix of museums and cultural pursuits.

Downtown

Bore Park, home to the main visitor information center, is the best starting point for exploring downtown. West of the park, Main Street has been the focus of a rejuvenation program in recent years — red brick sidewalks, ornate benches, old-fashioned lampposts, and the like.

Bore Park
Downtown

Twice daily, the Petitcodiac River drains dry of water as the huge Fundy tide recedes; then the tide turns, literally, and water rushes up the muddied riverbed, led by a "wave" up to 50 centimeters (20 inches) high. The river takes an hour to fill completely. The phenomenon is interesting rather than exciting, but well worth watching. You can see the bore anywhere along the river (as well as many other places, including Truro in central Nova Scotia), but Bore Park is the most accessible and has interpretive boards describing the how's and why's of the tide. Look for the clock at the park's Main Street entrance to see when the bore is next due.

Bore Park is linked to the **Riverfront Promenade,** a wheelchair-accessible walkway extending east to Hall's Creek and west to the Gunningsville Bridge, a total distance of 2km (1.2 miles). Take the path upstream and you'll quickly leave the city high rises behind and be rewarded with panoramic views across the river to undeveloped wetlands.

The park is also home to Moncton's main **Visitor Information Centre** (☎ **800-363-4558** or 506-490-5946; open June–Aug daily 9 a.m.–8 p.m., the rest of the year Mon–Fri 8:30 a.m.–4:30 p.m.).
See map p. 192. Main St. (at Lewis St.). Admission: Free.

Moncton Museum
Downtown

Housed in the former city hall, the Moncton Museum gives a good general overview of local history. Its displays concentrate on the region's first inhabitants, the Mi'Kmaq First Nations people, as well as industries such as shipbuilding that have long since disappeared. The museum also hosts several touring exhibits a year.

Beside the museum is the Free Meeting House, used by various religious congregations. Dating to 1821, it's Moncton's oldest remaining building.

See map p. 192. 20 Mountain Rd. (at Belleview St.). ☎ *506-856-4383. Admission: donation. Open: July–Aug daily 9 a.m.–5 p.m.; Sept–June Mon–Sat 9 a.m.–4:30 p.m., Sun 1–5 p.m.*

Musée Acadien
North of downtown

Founded by Father Camille Lefebvre in 1886, this museum focuses on historic events and aspects of Acadian life. Over 35,000 pieces are on display, making it Canada's largest collection of Acadian culture. The oldest is an ax dating to 1645, which was recovered from the site of a trading post along the Acadian Coast. Of special historical importance is the original Acadian flag; also of interest are the original register of donated pieces and displays of Acadian art and religious sculptures. The museum is on the sprawling grounds of Moncton University, well worth walking around in summertime for the peaceful student-free setting.

See map p. 192. Clément-Cormier Building, Moncton University ☎ *506-858-4088. Admission: C$2 (US$1.70) adults, C$1 (US85¢) children. Open: July–Aug Mon–Fri. 10 a.m.–5 p.m., Sat–Sun 1–5 p.m.; Sept–June Tues–Fri 1–4:30 p.m., Sat–Sun 1–5 p.m.*

Thomas Williams Heritage House
Downtown

Tucked away on a quiet residential street eight blocks from downtown is a grand home built in 1883 for Thomas Williams, treasurer of the Intercolonial Railway. Period furnishings and gardens reflect the Victorian era. The house is worth visiting for afternoon tea alone, which is served on the verandah. It's not particularly traditional (coffee and muffins, by golly!), but the park-like setting and unpretentious ambience lend to an enjoyable time out from sightseeing.

See map p. 192. 103 Park St. (at Highfield St.). ☎ *506-856-4383. Admission: free. Open: July–Aug Mon–Sat 9 a.m.–5 p.m., Sun 1–5 p.m.*

Magnetic Hill

Take Exit 450 from Route 2 or follow Mountain Road northwest from downtown to reach the Magnetic Hill area, a crunch of commercialism that has grown around an optical oddity.

Upon arrival, you must first take care of business and pay C$3 (US$2.60) per vehicle at the tollbooth. Continuing a short distance along a rural-type stretch of road, you will be directed by signage to come to a complete stop. Then, when you take your foot off the brake, your vehicle seemingly rolls *uphill*. The illusion is compelling: Basically, the entire lower hillside of a larger mountain is tilted at an angle to the surrounding countryside, creating the impression that the top of the hill is lower than the bottom. It has puzzled folks for generations, including early farmers who were forced to pull their wagons "down" the hill to town.

A magnet for commercial attractions

The magnetic appeal of Magnetic Hill extends well beyond one quirky stretch of road. Many local entrepreneurs have set up theme-park style businesses around the bottom (or is that the top?) of the hill. Here are the highlights:

✔ **Magic Mountain** (☎ 506-857-9283) is the largest waterpark in the Maritimes. Expect wild water rides, a wave pool, kid slides, and an oversized hot tub. Admission is C$24 (US$19.60) adults, C$18 (US$15.30) seniors and children aged 4 to 11. It's open mid-June through early September daily 10 a.m. to 8 p.m.

✔ **Magnetic Hill Zoo** (☎ 506-877-7718) is home to around 100 species of mostly exotic animals. It also has a small petting zoo of farm animals. Admission is C$8.75 (US$7.40) adults, C$5.75 (US$4.90) children. It's open mid-June through mid-September daily 9 a.m. to 8 p.m.

✔ **The Boardwalk** (☎ 506-852-9406) features go cart rides, batting cages, mini-golf, a golf driving range, and butterflies flying freely in their domed habitats. It's open June through mid-September daily 10 a.m. to 10 p.m.

Nightlife

Despite its outwardly staid appearance, Moncton has a number of happening pubs and clubs. You can find entertainment listings through **Tourism Moncton** (☎ 800-363-4558 or 506-853-3590; www.gomoncton.com). This organization also publishes a list of annual festivals and events.

Bars and live music

Le Galion, an elegant lounge in the Château Moncton at 100 Main St. (☎ 506-870-4444), is a pleasant place to get away from it all. This bar opens to a deck overlooking the Petitcodiac River.

The stretch of Main Street between Botsford St. and Lutz St. comes alive after dark, with crowds of college-aged drinkers spilling onto sidewalk tables. **Doc Dylan's** at 841 Main St. (☎ 506-382-3627) awaits, with one of the best ranges of draught beer in town and bands on some nights. A half block off Main, the **Pump House Brewery,** 5 Orange Lane (☎ 506-855-2337), brews a delicious range of beers, which can be enjoyed indoors or out on a small porch with parking lot views. For something a little different, try the Blueberry Ale, which comes complete with floating blueberries. The **Rattlesnake Saloon,** in the back of the Lone Star Café at

644 Main St. (☎ **506-384-7772**), is a Texas-themed bar that is generally quieter than those facing the main street.

For live music, head to **Kramer's Corner** at 702 Main St. (☎ **506-857-9118**) on Saturdays. In the same building, the **Cosmopolitan Club,** 700 Main St. (☎ **506-857-9117**), attracts the under-25 crowd with Moncton's largest dance floor. The music is as hip as it gets in New Brunswick, with a crowd to match. Open Wednesday through Sunday only. **Ziggy's,** 730 Main St. (☎ **506-858-8844**), is another place that beckons you with live music, stand-up comedy, and pool tables.

The arts

The **Capitol,** at 811 Main St. (☎ **506-856-4379**), is an old vaudeville house that has been devotedly restored to its 1920s grandeur, right down to gold-leaf stenciling and renovated opera boxes. It provides a home for Theatre New Brunswick and the New Brunswick Symphony, as well as a stage for a wide range of touring acts. Check a schedule at their Web site, www.capitol.nb.ca.

Acadian Coast

The French-flavored Acadian Coast stretches north from Moncton along Northumberland Strait. Separating Prince Edward Island from the mainland, this narrow waterway is lined along the New Brunswick side by beaches galore, where shallow water warms quickly under the summer sun. The center of beach culture is Shediac, while the place to get away from the crowds is to the north in Kouchibouguac National Park.

Shediac

Beach lovers will feel right at home in laid-back Shediac. The coast here borders Northumberland Strait, a shallow stretch of water between the mainland and Prince Edward Island, where the water reaches a pleasant 22°C (72°F) in summer. So even when it's foggy around the Bay of Fundy, or the water along the Nova Scotia coast is too cold for swimming, the stretch of coast fronting Shediac sparkles in the sun. But don't expect to have the place to yourself through the warmest months of the year — the town gets packed with college students on summer break and retirees who can afford to kick back for a few months.

Getting there

From Moncton, follow Route 15 in a northeasterly direction for 20km (12 miles) to Exit 31B. Head north along Route 11 for a 400m (0.5 miles), and then take Exit 1. This road leads past the main information center and Shediac Harbour, then along the long main street. The turn-off to Parlee Beach is through the town to the east.

Expulsion, then a cultural explosion

Most of the French-speaking population in the Maritimes today is Acadian, a culture that differs from that of its better-known francophone cousin, Quebec, not only in history but in dialect, cuisine, and customs.

When the French began colonizing the Maritimes in the 1630s, most settled in the Annapolis Valley, which came to be known as Acadia (and its settlers, hence, as Acadians). In 1713, the British claimed sovereignty to Nova Scotia, and the Acadians were encouraged to swear an oath of allegiance to England. Most refused, and in 1755 the British reacted by confiscating their property and expelling them. With no place to call home, the Acadians scattered — some returned to France, others moved west to Quebec, and some settled in Louisiana (where they became known as Cajuns); a small percentage escaped into the remote forests of what is now New Brunswick and to the far corners of Prince Edward Island.

A decade after their expulsion, many who had been exiled came out of hiding and returned to the region. They resettled and built new communities as far from the British as possible. In 1884, at an Acadian convention held in Miscouche, Prince Edward Island, these once displaced people officially adopted their own flag and anthem ("Ave Maris Stella") — the seeds of a distinct and unique culture that thrives to this day.

New Brunswick, Canada's only bilingual province, has a large Acadian population centered in Moncton and stretching up the coast. Acadian heritage and traditions remain strong, and visitors are offered many opportunities to experience it firsthand through museums, historical re-enactments, and, of course, the food!

Staying in Shediac

Many of the accommodations near the water are rented by the week or the month, making them impractical for the casual visitor. If hanging out at the beach for a week fits into your schedule, **Domaine Parlee Beach Chalets & Suites,** a short walk from the water at 642 Main Street (☎ **800-786-5550** or 506-532-5339; www.domaineparleebeach.ca) is the place to do it. Cottages rent for C$1,100 (US$935) per week; suites are C$1,200 to $1,450 (US$1,020–US$1,232.50), with daily rates offered from September through June.

Auberge Belcourt Inn
$$ Shediac

This stately residence was built in 1911 for a local doctor and was the home of a former New Brunswick premier for a time. Today, it provides a refined and relaxing retreat from the sun and sand (spend some time on the covered verandah for the full effect). The seven guest rooms are filled with Victorian charm and period antiques. All have en suite bathrooms. The rate includes a full breakfast.

310 Main St. ☎ 506-532-6098. Fax: 506-533-9398. Rack rates: C$95–C$110 (US$80.80–US$93.50) double. AE, DC, MC, V. Open: Feb–Dec.

Dining in Shediac

Lobsters can be enjoyed at most restaurants along the main street, or buy them live or cooked from **Shediac Lobster Shop,** a seafood market at 261 Main St. (☎ **506-532-4302**). Expect to pay around C$12 (US$10.20) per pound.

Captain Dan's
$–$$ Shediac   SEAFOOD

This boisterous restaurant/bar is away from the best beaches but attracts hordes of tanned bods for fresh seafood, cold beer, and live music nightly throughout the summer (Sun from 2 p.m.). The food is exactly what you'd expect from a seafood house, with prices that may pleasantly surprise you: For example, the substantial three-piece fish-and-chips entrée comes with freshly made tartar sauce for under C$9.50 (US$8.10). The lobster bisque and maritime chowder are also both under C$10 (US$8.50). Take a table either downstairs, upstairs on the tiered deck — with views across to the marina — or in the Lobster Hut, where you can order full lobster, chowder, coleslaw, and dessert for just C$28 (US$23.80).

Pointe-du-Chêne Wharf. ☎ 506-533-2855. Main courses: C$8–C$17.50 (US$6.80–US$14.90). AE, MC, V. Open: Daily 11 a.m.–10 p.m.

Cool things to do in and around Shediac

Don't come to Shediac looking for cultural stimulation. This is a place to lie on the beach, swim in the warmest ocean water north of Virginia, and feast on lobster.

The swimming season is short — July and August only. **Parlee Beach,** accessed from the east side of town, is by far the most popular spot for sunning and swimming. A large complex behind the dunes holds change rooms, a concession, and a lively bar/restaurant with a huge deck. Mid-May through mid-September, beach access costs C$9 (US$7.70) per vehicle (it's free the rest of the year). Further east, **Ocean View Beach** and **Gagnon Beach** are quieter and just as pleasant.

When you've had enough sun, sand, and salt, consider the following:

 ✔ **Visit Shediac Island.** Lying just offshore, this forested island is laced with nature trails, including a boardwalk over fragile marshland and a walking path through a mixed forest of spruce, fir, and maple. The island is ringed by some appealing beaches. Get there by boat from the **Shediac Island Interpretation Centre** at the foot of Pleasant St. (☎ **506-532-7000**) The hourly shuttle to the island costs just C$4 (US$3.40) per person.

✔ **Go lobster fishing.** With Eric LeBlanc at the helm, **Shediac Bay Cruises** (☎ **888-894-2002** or 506-532-2175; www.lobstertales.ca) takes visitors on a 2.5-hour fishing trip that culminates in an on-board lobster feast. The cost is C$60 (US$51) adults, C$40 (US$34) children. Call for times and directions.

✔ **Drive to Cape Jourimain.** The easternmost point of New Brunswick, 80km (50 miles) east of Shediac, is protected by a national wildlife area that is home to 170 species of birds. A system of hiking trails branches out from a large nature center (☎ **506-538-2220**; open mid-June through early Sept daily 8 a.m.–9 p.m.). One trail ends at the cape itself, where views extend north along the Confederation Bridge. Admission is C$6 (US$5.10) adults, C$5 (US$4.30) seniors, C$4 (US$3.40) children.

✔ **Climb on the world's largest lobster.** This 10m (33-foot)-long cast-iron crustacean stands guard at the mouth of the Scoudouc River, at the west entrance to town. Kids will love clambering over its massive claws, while adults are usually content with a photograph.

Bouctouche and beyond

Imagine spending the morning exploring a seemingly endless sand dune, followed by an afternoon immersing yourself in Acadian culture in a make-believe island village. You can do this at Bouctouche, a small coastal town 20km (12 miles) north of Shediac along Route 11.

Staying in Bouctouche

Accommodation in Bouctouche is limited. If the recommendation below doesn't sound like your scene, continue north to the Acadian Peninsula, or plan on visiting the region as a day trip from Moncton.

Bellevue sur mer
$$ Bouctouche

A small inn catering to guests who value a homey atmosphere over a room full of fancy amenities, this lodging is in an 1820s farmhouse that was home to three generations of the same Acadian family. Set on the water, it's a five-minute drive from La Dune de Bouctouche, so you can rise early and enjoy the spit before the crowds arrive, or walk to Le Pays de la Sagouine. The four guest rooms are decorated with soothing pastel colors and each has an en suite bathroom. Rates include cooked breakfasts such as crepes with maple syrup.

539 Route 475 ☎ *506-743-6575. Rack rates: C$85 (US$72.30) double. V.*

Exploring Bouctouche

It may not be much more than a lot of sand, but **La Dune de Bouctouche** is one of the natural highlights of New Brunswick. It is an extremely narrow spit of sand, extending 12km (7.5 miles) into Northumberland Strait. Plant life, such as beach heather, has a stabilizing effect, but tidal action and wind still manage to move the sand around, ever so slowly extending the spit while also making it narrower. To learn more about the unique ecosystem, stop by **Irving Eco Centre,** along Route 475 at the start of the spit (☎ **506-743-2600;** open July–Aug 10 a.m.–8 p.m.). To protect the fragile environment from over-use in the busiest months (July and Aug), only the first 2,000 visitors to arrive each day after 10 a.m. are allowed access. A boardwalk extends for the first 2km (1.2 miles); to continue farther, walk along the high tide mark.

Located on a small island in the Bouctouche River, **Le Pays de la Sagouine,** accessed by footbridge from Acadie St. (☎ **506-743-1400**), is a fun place to immerse yourself in the rich culture of Acadia. Part theme park, part learning experience, it is centered on a fictional Acadian village created by writer Antonine Maillet. Costumed performers put on musical and theatrical presentations throughout the day. Storytelling neighbors, young pranksters, and Acadian bands encouraging singalongs are just a taste of what you can expect. Admission is C$14 (US$11.90) adults, C$13 (US$11.10) seniors, C$10 (US$8.50) children. Nightly (except Mon) is a dinner theater for C$65 (US$55.30) adults, C$32 (US$27.20) children, which includes general park admission.

Kouchibouguac National Park

Although the entire Acadian Coast offers similar coastal scenery, the section between Bouctouche and Miramichi is particularly appealing because it is protected as a national park and, therefore, remains in its natural state. Kouchibouguac (pronounced *Koo*-she-*boo*-gwack), meaning "river of long tides," is dominated by a ribbon of barrier islands composed entirely of sand. Extending for 25km (15.5 miles), these islands have formed lagoons that attract a wide variety of bird life (over 200 bird species have been recorded in the park). The rest of the park is a mix of forest, slow-flowing rivers, peat bogs, and marshland. Deer, moose, black bears, and beavers are all resident, while seals are often spotted in the surrounding waters.

To experience the best of Kouchibouguac, you will want to explore beyond the paved roads. Here's how:

  ✔ **Hiking.** This isn't the place for grueling all-day hikes. Instead, visitors have a choice of short trails, many lined with interpretive panels describing the surroundings. If you take just one trail, make it **Kelly's Beach Boardwalk,** which crosses a lagoon to sand dunes and open water. Don't be perturbed by the name of the Bog Trail — a boardwalk leads through the marshland.

✔ **Biking.** You'll find a 60km (37-mile) system of crushed-gravel bike trails. The main loop — taking in the river, the forested interior, and the coast — is 23km (14 miles). Complete the circuit in two hours, or spend all day stopping at its points of interest. Bikes can be rented at **Ryan's Rental Centre,** based at Ryan's day-use area (☎ **506-876-8918**), for C$6 (US$5.10) per hour or C$30 (US$25.60) per day.

✔ **Canoeing.** If you are comfortable out on the water on your own, canoes can be rented from Ryan's (see above), which is beside the calm waters of the Kouchibouguac River. Just as enjoyable is joining park staff on a three-hour guided paddle in a large voyageur canoe, which seats up to 9 people. The cost is C$30 (US$25.60) adults, C$15 (US$12.80) children. Reserve a seat at the visitor center (☎ **506-876-2445**).

✔ **Swimming.** The water on the ocean side of the dunes at Kelly's Beach is supervised throughout the summer. Although the water temperature is comfortable, it's even warmer to the south at Callender's Beach, along a tidal lagoon.

Get to the park by taking Exit 75 from Route 11, 35km (21 miles) north of Bouctouche. Just inside the park boundary is the **Visitor Reception Centre** (☎ **506-876-2445**), holding displays on the park ecosystem and including a small theater, a gift shop, and an information desk. This is also the place to pick up a park **day pass,** which costs C$6 (US$5.10) adults, C$5 (US$4.30) seniors, C$3 (US$2.60) children, to a maximum of C$12 (US$10.20) per vehicle. The center is open mid-May through mid-October daily 9 a.m. to 5 p.m., with extended hours in July and August of daily 8 a.m. to 8 p.m. Access to the park is possible year-round, but everything closes down in mid-October, and the entry fee isn't collected out of season.

Check the bulletin board at the visitor center for a schedule of events, which may include interpretive hikes, campfire talks, slide presentations, and a puppet theater.

Acadian Peninsula

Extending northeast from Miramichi along Baie des Chaleurs, the Acadian peninsula is a hotbed of Acadian culture. You can experience this unique culture by exploring local museums, sampling the cuisine, or simply taking a drive through the many small villages where traditions run deep.

At Miramichi, you are presented with two options for onward travel: either cut south through the heartland of New Brunswick to Fredericton, or follow Route 11 around the Acadian Peninsula, which is dotted with farms and fishing villages.

Staying on the Acadian Peninsula

Use Miramichi as a base for a daytrip around the Acadian Peninsula, or push on and spend the night at the recommended accommodations in Caraquet (the region's largest town) or Miscou Centre.

Governor's Mansion Inn
$-$$ Miramichi (Nelson)

The lovely location and budget-priced rooms alone would make this lodging a good choice. But best of all is the historic atmosphere — pull up a chair on the covered verandah, look across to the river, and imagine yourself transported back in time. Formerly the home of a provincial lieutenant governor, this stately 1860 mansion has been given a bright yellow coat of paint on the outside and undergone a rigorous restoration inside. Rooms are divided between the main home and the adjacent Beaubear Manor. Antiques and convivial hosts make up for slightly threadbare furnishings. Some rooms share bathrooms (the Eagles Eyrie, with water views, is the pick of these), but at just C$79 (US$67.20) for the most expensive (the Lord Beaverbrook Room, which comes complete with a 4-piece bath and fireplace), you can afford to splurge. Within sight of the inn is Beaubears Island; tours depart the nearby dock Tuesday and Thursday at 6:30 p.m. and Sunday at 1:30 p.m.

62 St. Patrick's Dr. ☎ *877-647-2642 or 506-622-3036. Fax: 506-622-3035.* www. governorsmansion.ca. *Rack rates: C$49–C$99 (US$41.70–US$84.20) double. AE, MC, V.*

Hotel Paulin
$$$-$$$$ Caraquet

Modern development has encroached on the water views at this 1891 hotel, but it still offers a level of intimacy you just can't get at a motel. Operated for three generations by the same family, the Paulin has a Christmasy red and green exterior and a cheerful interior to match. The 12 guest rooms have been given a serious overhaul and feature a contemporary slant on the heritage theme, comfortable beds, and en suite bathrooms. The top-floor suites are massive and come with upgraded everything.

143 St-Pierre Blvd., Caraquet. ☎ *866-727-9981 or 506-727-9981.* www.hotel paulin.com. *Rack rates: C$195–C$315 (US$165.80–US$267.80) double. AE, MC, V.*

Plage Miscou Chalets
$$ Miscou Centre

Situated on Miscou Island, which is linked to the mainland by a bridge, this complex is part cottages, part campground, and all fun. It lies behind a long sandy beach, with water warm enough for swimming. There are plenty of other things to keep everyone busy — fishing trips, canoeing (rentals available), volleyball, mini-golf, horseshoes, and more. The six cabins each have two bedrooms and a fully equipped kitchen, making them excellent value.

22 Allée Alphonse, Miscou Centre. ☎ *506-344-1015. Fax: 506-344-7444. Rack rates: C$95 (US$80.80) double. MC, V. Open: mid-June–mid-Sept.*

Rodd Miramichi River
$$–$$$ **Miramichi (Chatham)**

Located right on the Miramichi River, this modern motel has a distinctive lodge feeling to its rooms, which are decorated in earthy tones and have fish prints on the walls. The specialty at the in-house Angler's Reel Restaurant is salmon, while the adjacent lounge spreads onto a riverside deck. You'll want to request a room with a river view when booking.

1809 Water St., Chatham. ☎ *800-565-7633 or 506-773-3111. Fax: 506-773-3110.* www.rodd-hotels.ca. *Rack rates: C$110–C$155 (US$93.50–US$131.80) double. AE, DC, MC, V.*

Dining on the Acadian Peninsula

Most villages have a choice of cafés or restaurants, and you may consider taking a chance at any of them. I recommend two very different restaurants that both showcase the charm of the region in their own unique ways. As alternatives, the Hotel Paulin or Rodd Miramichi River, both recommended above as places to stay, have dining rooms worthy of a visit.

La Fine Grobe Sur Mer
$$–$$$ **Nigadoo   FRENCH**

Translating to "fine grub by the sea," this fine restaurant provides some of the best cooking in New Brunswick, with spectacular views of Chaleur Bay. The seasonal menu offers a great variety of traditional French dishes, relying on local seafood and produce from the garden to create a memorable meal. The chateaubriand and herb-crusted leg of lamb are both noteworthy. For dessert, the cheese plate will tempt you, but, seriously, can you choose anything but the chocolate cake?

289 Main St., Nigadoo (north of Bathurst). ☎ *506-783-3138. Main courses: C$16–C$25 (US$13.60–US$21.30). AE, DC, MC, V. Open: Daily 5–10 p.m.*

Old Town Diner
$ **Miramichi (Chatham)   DINER**

Chances are you'll be the only out-of-towner at this small-town, super-friendly diner on the south side of the Miramichi River in Chatham. The menu is exactly what you might expect — breakfast served all day, deep-fried seafood, and a couple of token salads. A full-cooked breakfast costs just C$5 (US$4.30), including bottomless coffee.

1724 Water St., Chatham. ☎ *506-773-7817. Main courses: C$6–C$9.50 (US$5.10–US$8.10). Open: Daily 7 a.m.–7 p.m.*

Exploring the Acadian Peninsula

To fully appreciate the peninsula's natural and cultural appeal, plan on spending at least a day in the region. Visiting the two top Acadian attractions detailed below will alone fill the better part of a day.

Route 11 parallels the Gulf of St. Lawrence all the way from Miramichi to Bathurst, a total distance of 170km (106 miles). From Bathurst, it's a short hop back across the peninsula to Miramichi.

Village Historique Acadien
Route 11 west of Caraquet

Definitely a highlight of the Acadian Coast, this park re-creates Acadian life between 1770 and 1890. The 40 restored buildings include simple homes, a chapel, a farmyard, a schoolhouse, various workshops, a lobster hatchery, and a tavern. The village is brought to life by costumed staff who go about their daily business — tending to their animals, overseeing auctions, spreading gossip, attending marriages, and more. Visitors can also watch as artists ply their trade, or dine on Acadian food in one of two restaurants.

Route 11 between Caraquet and Grand-Anse. ☎ *506-726-2600. Admission: C$14.40 (US$12.20) adults, C$12.50 (US$10.60) seniors, C$9.50 (US$8.10) children. Open: June–late Sept daily 10 a.m.–5 p.m.*

Acadian Museum
Caraquet

Founded by Acadians fleeing the British in 1755, the village of Caraquet has evolved into the unofficial center of the peninsula's French-speaking community. This small museum does a wonderful job of representing the town and its residents, many of whom have donated items to display. It's also worth taking in the water view from the second floor balcony.

15 St-Pierre Blvd., Caraquet. ☎ *506-726-2682. Admission: C$3 (US$2.60) adults, C$1 (US85¢) children. Open: June–mid-Sept Mon–Sat 10 a.m.–6 p.m., Sun 1–6 p.m.*

Newcastle

Now incorporated as part of Miramichi, this bustling river town is more attractive than at first glance. Make your way down to **Ritchie Wharf** (Leddon St.) and let the children go wild on the Maritime-themed playground; take lunch at one of the cafes; and learn more about the region at the riverside information center.

In the heart of downtown is a memorial to Lord Beaverbrook (1879–1964), a British press baron who spent his childhood in Newcastle. His boyhood home, at 518 King George Highway, is a few blocks west of the memorial (☎ **506-624-5474**). It's open to the public June to August Monday to Friday 9 a.m. to 5 p.m. and Saturday 10 a.m. to 5 p.m. Admission is free.

From the south, cross the Miramichi River via Route 8 and follow King George Highway to the southeast.

Fast Facts: Moncton

ATMs

Most banks have ATMs, including the **Bank of Montreal** at 633 Main St., **CIBC** at Church and Main Sts, and **Scotiabank** at 780 Main St.

Emergencies

Dial ☎ **911** for all emergencies.

Hospital

Moncton Hospital is at 135 MacBeath Ave. (☎ **506-857-4150**).

Information

Tourism Moncton (☎ **800-363-4558** or **506-853-3590**; www.gomoncton.com) operates an information center at Bore Park, Main St. It's open June–Aug daily 9 a.m.–8 p.m., the rest of the year Mon–Fri 8:30 a.m.–4:30 p.m.

Internet Access

Moncton Public Library, 644 Main St. (☎ **506-869-6000**), has free public Internet access.

Pharmacy

Drugstore Pharmacy is at 165 Main St. (☎ **506-857-7240**).

Police

For emergencies, dial ☎ **911**. For other police matters, call ☎ **506-857-2400**.

Post Office

The main post office is at 281 St. George St. (at Highfield St.).

Restrooms

The main Visitor Information Centre, in Bore Park, has public restrooms.

Taxis

Reliable cab companies include **Air Cab** (☎ **506-857-2000**) and **White Cab** (☎ **506-857-3000**).

Transit Info

Public buses are operated by **Codiac Transit** (☎ **506-857-2008**) daily, except Sunday.

Weather

For the local weather forecast, call **Environment Canada** at ☎ **506-851-6610** or check the Web site www.weatheroffice.ec.gc.ca.

Chapter 16

Saint John and the Fundy Coast

. . . .

In This Chapter

▶ Getting to Saint John and finding your way around the city

▶ Deciding where to stay and dine

▶ Seeing the sights and spending a night on the town

▶ Visiting St. Andrews and exploring Fundy National Park

. . . .

*S*aint John is a gritty industrial city with a striking waterfront enhanced by the Harbour Passage, a municipal beautification project. With a population of 75,000, it is New Brunswick's largest city and offers all the benefits of big-city life — like upscale accommodations and creative dining — at affordable small-town prices.

Established in 1785 by Loyalists (American colonists who wished to remain loyal to the British crown after the birth of the United States), Saint John was Canada's first incorporated city, prospering as a port and shipbuilding center. In 1877, a fire destroyed almost the entire downtown, which was then rebuilt with fine brick and stone buildings, most of which remain today.

Saint John is always spelled out. It is never abbreviated to "St. John," thereby avoiding confusion with St. John's, Newfoundland.

Saint John may be the biggest name on the map, but there are plenty of reasons to explore the rest of the Fundy Coast. Take Route 1 west from Saint John to reach St. Andrews, a one-time retreat for the wealthy that now welcomes everyone. Up the Bay of Fundy from Saint John, a rugged section of the coast is protected by Fundy National Park. Beyond the park is Hopewell Rocks, intriguing towers of sandstone that have become separated from the mainland.

Saint John

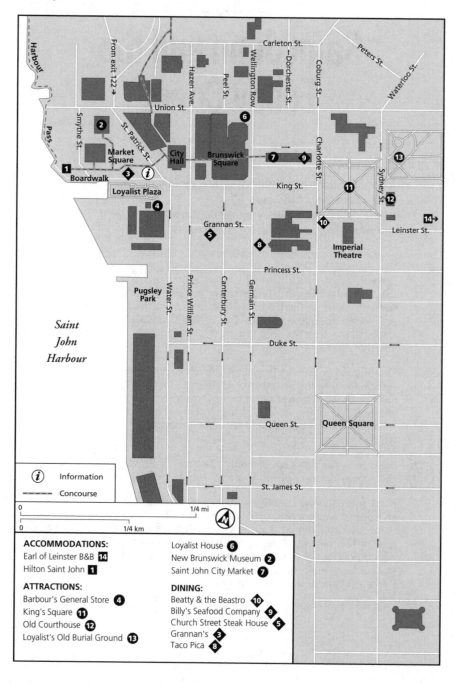

ACCOMMODATIONS:
Earl of Leinster B&B **14**
Hilton Saint John **1**

ATTRACTIONS:
Barbour's General Store **4**
King's Square **11**
Old Courthouse **12**
Loyalist's Old Burial Ground **13**

Loyalist House **6**
New Brunswick Museum **2**
Saint John City Market **7**

DINING:
Beatty & the Beastro **10**
Billy's Seafood Company **9**
Church Street Steak House **5**
Grannan's **3**
Taco Pica **8**

Getting To Saint John

You'll probably arrive in Saint John by road, but options include flying in or coming from Nova Scotia by ferry.

By plane

Saint John Airport (Internet: www.saintjohnairport.com) is along Route 111 toward St. Martins, 16km (10 miles) east of downtown. Air Canada flies into Saint John from Halifax, Toronto, and Montreal. Rental-car companies with desks at the airport are Avis, Budget, Hertz, and National.

The least expensive way to travel between the airport and downtown is on a **Saint John Transit** bus (☎ **506-658-4700**). The service costs C$2.25 (US$1.90), exact change only. The cab fare between the airport and downtown is C$30 (US$25.60) for the first person, and C$2 (US$1.70) for each additional person.

All passengers departing Saint John Airport are required to pay a **Passenger Facility Fee** of C$15 (US$12.80). The fee is incorporated into the ticket price.

By car

The most direct route between Moncton and Saint John is Route 1, a distance of 155km (96 miles) that should take you about 90 minutes to drive. A more scenic option is Route 114 along the Bay of Fundy, which passes two of New Brunswick's most appealing natural attractions — Hopewell Rocks and Fundy National Park. Taking this route doubles the driving time.

The provincial capital of New Brunswick, Fredericton, is 105km (65 miles) north of Saint John via Route 7. If you are willing to do a longer course with scenic appeal, take Route 102 via Gagetown.

By ferry

If you're planning on visiting both southwestern Nova Scotia and New Brunswick, it makes sense to take advantage of the ferry service between Digby and Saint John. **Bay Ferries** (☎ **888-249-7245** or 506-649-7777; www.nfl-bay.com) runs this passage year-round, up to three times daily in each direction. The fare is C$22 to C$37 (US$18.70–US$31.50) adults, C$18.50 to C$26 (US$15.70–US$24.70) seniors, C$15 to C$21 (US$12.80–US$17.90) children aged 5 to 17, and C$75 to C$92 (US$63.80–US$78.20) for vehicles under 6.4m (21 feet) long. Reservations for the 3-hour trip are highly recommended in summer.

Getting around Saint John

Saint John is very spread out, with downtown (and the best attractions) centered on a peninsula at the mouth of the Saint John River. Exit 122 from Route 1 leads right into the heart of downtown. Immediately west, Route 1 crosses the Saint John River via the Harbour Bridge (C$.25 toll) and heads out toward Irving Nature Park.

Ferries from Digby arrive in Saint John West, from where signage directs you to Exit 120 of Route 1. From this point, head east over the Harbour Bridge to downtown.

 Note that many streets of Saint John West have the same names as those downtown. To avoid confusion, they are designated as "West," as in Church St. W.

Parking

To park downtown, take Exit 122 from Route 1 and then turn down the first street to the right to have a choice of outside parking for C$1 (US85¢) per hour, or slightly more for underground parking.

Grabbing a cab

You can hail a cab anywhere downtown, but if you're having trouble, walk through the Market Square and wait for one at the Saint John Hilton. Local companies include:

- ✔ **Century Taxi** (☎ 506-696-6969)
- ✔ **Coastal Taxi** (☎ 506-635-1144)
- ✔ **Diamond Taxi** (☎ 506-648-8888)
- ✔ **Royal Taxi** (☎ 506-652-5050)

Taking transit

Saint John Transit (☎ 506-658-4700) is a highly efficient bus system that operates along 30 routes to all corners of the city, including out to the airport. Many buses run at 10-minute intervals from the main downtown pick-up point at King's Square. The fare is C$2.25 (US$1.90), exact change only.

Staying in Saint John

Saint John has a number of historic inns, the best of which are within walking distance of downtown. Concentrations of mid-priced chain motels lie along Route 1 east and west of the city.

A string of cheap motels is spread along Manawagonish Road, west of downtown. Among the least expensive are the **Balmoral Court Motel,** at 1284 Manawagonish Rd. (☎ **506-672-3019**), and **Island View Motel,** 1726 Manawagonish Rd. (☎ **888-674-6717** or 506-672-1381). Both these places charge around C$70 (US$59.50) double and are in the $ price category.

 ## Coastal Inn Fort Howe
$$ Downtown

Across Route 1 from the heart of downtown, the Coastal Inn is a good choice for families — more appropriate for children than a bed and breakfast, within walking distance of most attractions, and free for children under 18. The property itself is large and blockish, but that is of little consequence if you're looking outward from a harbor view room. Amenities include an indoor pool and a sauna, while a downstairs café and a top-floor restaurant are other worthy options. Coming from the west, take Exit 121 and turn right onto Chelsey Drive, then right again onto Main Street. From the east, take Exit 123 and follow Paradise Row onto Main.

10 Portland St. (at Main St.). ☎ *800-943-0033 or 506-657-7320. Fax: 506-693-1146. Internet:* www.coastalinns.com. *Rack rates: C$119–C$139 (US$101.20–US$118.20) double. AE, DC, MC, V.*

Dufferin Inn
$$$–$$$$ Saint John West

If you don't need to be right downtown, consider the Dufferin Inn, across the harbor from downtown and within walking distance of the Carleton Martello Tower (and a two-minute drive from the ferry terminal). Once the home of a provincial premier, the grand old home has been converted to a professionally operated bed and breakfast, with four gust rooms, various sitting areas, and a restaurant that gets rave reviews from even the harshest food critic. All rooms have TVs, phones, and high-speed Internet, and even the smallest has ocean views. You'll rise to a steaming pot of coffee and freshly baked pastries, which is just a warm up to a cooked breakfast that may include pancakes topped with real cream and berries or a cheese and proscuitto pancake.

357 Dufferin Row, Saint John West. ☎ *866-383-3466 or 506-635-5968. Fax: 506-674-2396.* www.dufferininn.com. *Rack rates: C$155–C$285 (US$131.80–US$242.30) double. MC, V.*

Earl of Leinster B&B
$$ Irving Nature Park

Inside this red brick downtown building, you will find seven inviting guest rooms, each with a smallish en suite bathroom, phone, fridge, and television. Those out back in a converted coach house have kitchenettes.

Guests have access to a games room and laundry, and a cooked breakfast is also available (C$13/US$11.10 per person).

See map p. 212. 96 Leinster St. ☎ 506-652-3275. Parking: on the street. Rack rates: C$92–C$102 (US$78.20–US$86.70) double. AE, DC, MC, V.

Hilton Saint John
$$$–$$$$ Downtown

Located right on the water and linked by a covered walkway to Market Square, this hotel has the best location of any downtown Saint John accommodation. The 197 rooms are spacious and comfortable, and most have water views. You won't find any surprises on the menu at the Turn of the Tide Restaurant, but it offers good solid, contemporary Canadian cooking, while the Brigantine Lounge is one of the best places in town to enjoy a quiet drink. Both the restaurant and lounge have water views. The hotel also has a swimming pool and exercise room.

See map p. 212. 1 Market Square. ☎ 800-445-8667 or 506-693-8484. Fax: 506-657-6610. www.hilton.com. *Parking: C$10 (US$8.50). Rack rates: C$180–C$280 (US$153–US$238) double. AE, DC, DISC, MC, V.*

Homeport Historic Bed & Breakfast
$$–$$$ West of downtown

This large and luxurious bed and breakfast lies on a high ridge overlooking the harbor and is within walking distance of downtown via the Harbour Passage promenade. The creation of the inn, a subtle amalgamation of two side-by-side mansions built for shipbuilding brothers, was a labor of love for owners Ralph and Karen Holyoke. The inn is full of appropriate antiques sourced by Ralph throughout the Maritimes; big windows, high ceilings, and ornate furnishings add to the grandeur. The ten guest rooms are all very different, but each is outfitted with a large bathroom. The Veranda Room (C$125/US$106.30) is my favorite. The centerpiece of this unit is an 1850s walnut bed, while the adjacent sitting area has views across to Saint John Harbour. The parlor is a popular place to relax, especially in the afternoon when refreshments are laid out. A big breakfast will get you going each morning.

60–80 Douglas Ave. ☎ 888-678-7678 or 506-672-7255. Fax: 506-672-7250. www. homeport.nb.ca. *Rack rates: C$90–C$165 (US$76.50–US$140.30) double. AE, MC, V.*

Inn on the Cove & Spa
$$$ Irving Nature Park

This sprawling property well away from the bustle of the city has 11 stylish guest rooms, all with stunning ocean views and some with private balconies. Centered on a 1907 mansion that has been thoroughly modernized by gracious owners Ross and Willa Mavis, the place is sophisticated but has a wonderfully carefree feeling about it. The perfect way to follow up a walk in the adjacent Irving Nature Park (which was once part of the estate) is with time spent in the inn's day spa. A gourmet breakfast is included in the rates, while dinner, available Monday to Saturday, revolves around seafood and seasonal produce (reservations required).

1371 Sand Cove Rd. (take Exit 119A from Route 1). ☎ 877-257-8080 or 506-672-7799. Fax: 506-635-5455. Internet: www.innonthecove.com. *Rack rates: C$149–C$225 (US$126.70–US$191.30) double. MC, V.*

Dining in Saint John

In Saint John, many of the better restaurants are tucked away and easy to overlook. One place you can't miss is Market Square, down on the waterfront, where a string of restaurants take full advantage of summer warmth by setting out tables along a cobbled plaza.

Beatty & the Beastro
$$–$$$ Downtown EUROPEAN

This restaurant overlooks King's Square from beside the historic Imperial Theatre. Lunch is extremely popular — mussels steamed open in white wine, "Beast of the Day" soup, Caesar salad, and a curried chicken wrap are all good. In the evening, the curry of the day is a local favorite (as is the accompanying freshly-made mango chutney), but my last visit coincided with a delivery of spring lamb from a local farm, so choosing anything else wasn't even an issue.

See map p. 212. 60 Charlotte St. ☎ 506-652-3888. Reservations recommended. Main courses: C$21–C$25 (US$17.90–US$21.30). AE, DC, MC, V. Open: Mon–Fri 11:30 a.m.– 3 p.m. and 5–9 p.m., Sat 5–10 p.m.

Billy's Seafood Company   "Best Seafood"
$$–$$$$ Downtown SEAFOOD

Tucked away at the back of the Saint John City Market, Billy's enjoys a stellar reputation for fresher-than-fresh seafood, which can also be bought market-style at the front counter. The restaurant itself is a sleek, old-fashioned room with comfortable booths, dim lighting, and lots of dark polished wood. You could start by sharing steamed mussels and crab cakes with Cajun mango dipping sauce, and then move on to cedar plank salmon, broiled halibut in oyster cream sauce, or a full lobster. The wine list complements the food well but is a bit on the expensive side. A lunchtime visit would be a good time to try the lobster roll, packed with a combination of the delicious meat and mayonnaise.

See map p. 212. 49 Charlotte St. (Old Market Square). ☎ 506-672-3474. Reservations recommended. Main courses: C$17–C$30 (US$14.50–US$25.60). AE, DC, DISC, MC, V. Open: Mon–Thurs 11 a.m.–10 p.m., Fri–Sat 11 a.m.–11 p.m., Sun 4–9 p.m.

Church Street Steak House
$$–$$$$ Downtown STEAK

Saint John is a long way from the rangelands of Alberta, but this popular steakhouse does an excellent job of sourcing the best cuts of beef and cooking them exactly as you ordered them. The appetizers are mostly seafood-oriented, a perfect complement to a beef entrée. The setting is an historic red brick building that remains virtually unchanged in appearance since it was built following the 1877 fire that destroyed most of downtown.

See map p. 212. 8 Grannan St. ☎ 506-672-3463. Reservations recommended. Main courses: C$16–C$32 (US$13.60–US$27.20). AE, MC, V. Open: Mon–Sat 4 p.m.–11 p.m., Sun 4 p.m.–10 p.m.

Grannan's
$$–$$$$ Downtown SEAFOOD

My favorite of the many Market Square restaurants. Grannan's has lots of outdoor seating, but the interior is also appealing, with a stylish mix of maritime-themed artifacts, including brass ship lamps and an antique diving suit. A blackboard menu is the place to search out seasonal seafood, but you won't go wrong with a pick from the Captain's Choices section of the regular menu (my blackened salmon was delicious). For a splurge, consider the Seafood Brochette, a lobster tail with skewered scallops and shrimp sautéed at your table.

See map p. 212. Market Square ☎ 506-634-1555. Reservations recommended for dinner. Main courses: C$15–C$37 (US$12.80–US$31.50). AE, DC, MC, V. Open: Mon–Wed 11 a.m.–11 p.m., Thurs–Sat 11:30 a.m.–midnight, Sun noon–10 p.m.

Taco Pica
$–$$ Downtown GUATELAMALAN/MEXICAN

Look no further than Taco Pica for a unique and inexpensive meal in cheerful surroundings. You'll be impressed by the flavor of such dishes as pepian, a spicy beef stew, and chimichanga, a minty-flavored pork tortilla. Seafood offerings include a Spanish-style paella and a garlic shrimp dish. The dessert menu goes beyond the confines of Central America to include Pavlova, an Australian meringue cake topped with cream and fruit.

See map p. 212. 96 Germain St. ☎ 506-633-8492. Reservations recommended. Main courses: C$8.50–C$18 (US$7.20–US$15.30). AE, DC, MC, V. Open: Mon–Sat 10 a.m.–10 p.m.

Exploring Saint John

Now that you've chosen somewhere to stay and have an idea of dining options, it's on to the real reason you will want to spend time in Saint John — to soak up the sights, sounds, and smells of a port city that has changed little in appearance in over 100 years.

All of the attractions discussed in this section (except Carleton Martello Tower) are within walking distance of each other. Pick up the *Three Historic Walking Tours* brochure (free) from the information center to learn more about the most notable buildings as you explore downtown.

Barbour's General Store
Downtown

This late 1800s shop is preserved as a museum, its shelves stocked with merchandise sold a century ago, like candy and tobacco.

See map p. 212. Market Square. ☎ *506-658-2939. Admission: free. Open: Mid-June– early Sept daily 9 a.m.–6 p.m.*

Carleton Martello Tower
Saint John West

Built in 1812 to protect the then-fledgling Loyalist city of Saint John from attack, the tower is similar in design to circular towers built along the British coastline during the Napoleonic Wars. Over the years, this solid stone structure has also been used for ammunition storage, as a soldiers' barracks, as a detention center for deserters, and as an anti-aircraft position. Today, protected as a National Historic Site, it's all tourist attraction.

545 Whipple St. (at Fundy Dr.; take Exit 120 from Route 1). ☎ *506-636-4011. Admission: C$4 (US$3.40) adults, C$3.50 (US$3) seniors, C$2 (US$1.70) children. Open: June–Sept daily 10 a.m.–6 p.m.*

Fort Howe Lookout
North of Downtown

The best place to get a feel for the layout of Saint John is Fort Howe Lookout, a 2-minute drive north of downtown, off Main Street. The Loyalists established a fort here in 1778 to defend their new settlement against attack by Americans. Looking out to the mouth of the harbor, which affords unobstructed views of incoming vessels, it's clear why they chose this lofty location.

Magazine St. off Main St.

King's Square
Downtown

From the waterfront, it's a steep walk up King Street to reach King's Square, which was laid out in the shape of a Union Jack to reflect the loyalty to the British monarchy held by those who escaped the American Revolution to settle in Saint John. The most intriguing of numerous monuments is a lump of melted metal salvaged from a hardware store that was destroyed by the fire that raced through downtown in 1877.

Walking the walk

Harbour Passage, along Saint John's downtown foreshore, is an ambitious project that will eventually see the entire waterfront area linked by pathways and dotted with green space, benches, and interpretive panels that extend all the way to Reversing Falls. At this stage, the 2.3km (1.4-mile) paved trail extends around the harbor from the Hilton Saint John to a pavilion with sweeping city views. Along the way it passes by the Gathering Garden, planted with species used by natives; the site of a 1600s Acadian fort; and a power substation with interpretive panels describing what goes on behind the wires.

Across Sydney Street from King's Square are a couple of other historic diversions. Inside the 1829 County Courthouse, at King and Sydney Streets, is a massive spiral staircase built of unsupported stones. Across King Street is the Loyalist's Old Burial Ground, the final resting place of the city's founding fathers.

See map p. 212. At King and Charlotte Streets.

Loyalist House
Downtown

Dating to 1810, this Georgian-style Loyalist House is Saint John's oldest building and is well worth visiting. Lived in by six generations of the same family, it is furnished with authentic Georgian antiques and has a total of eight fireplaces, an indication of the wealth of its original owner, David Daniel Merritt.

See map p. 212. 120 Union St. ☎ 506-652-3590. Admission: C$3 (US$2.60) adults, C$1 (US$0.85) children. Open: June Mon–Fri 10 a.m.–5 p.m., July–mid-Sept daily 9 a.m.–5 p.m.

New Brunswick Museum
Downtown

One of the largest museums in the Maritimes, this modern facility is part of the Market Square complex down on the harborfront. Every gallery has something different and interesting: The Shipbuilding Gallery catalogues the city's first industry, the Hall of Great Whales is dominated by a full-size right whale skeleton, the Birds of New Brunswick Gallery features displays describing some of the province's 370 recorded species, and the Discovery Gallery is filled with kid-friendly learning experiences.

See map p. 212. Market Square. ☎ 506-643-2300. Admission: C$6 (US$5.10) adults, C$4.75 (US$4) seniors, C$3.25 (US$2.80) children. Open: Mon–Sat 9 a.m.–5 p.m. (Thurs until 9 p.m.), Sun noon–5 p.m.

Saint John City Market
Downtown

The 1876 City Market, the oldest in Canada, occupies a full block between Charlotte and Germain Streets. The handsome building was designed by local shipbuilders, whose influence is obvious when you look up at the inverted-keel ceiling. The collection of stalls is varied — there's an old-fashioned butcher, fruit produce, fresh seafood, and touristy knick-knacks. Instead of eating at the unappealing food court along one side, choose some cheeses from the dairy bar, some smoked salmon and a cooked lobster from the seafood counter, and some crusty rolls from the bakery and then head out to Irving Nature Park for a picnic lunch.

See map p. 212. 47 Charlotte St. ☎ 506-658-2820. Admission: free. Open: Mon–Thurs 7:30 a.m.–6 p.m., Fri 7:30 a.m.–7 p.m., Sat 10 a.m.–5 p.m.

Other cool things to see and do
Once you've finished exploring downtown, expand your horizons and consider the following attractions.

Reversing Falls
Another Fundy phenomenon, this is Saint John's most hyped natural attraction. As the massive Fundy tide rises, the flow of the Saint John River reverses as ocean water pushes upstream. When the tide recedes, the water flows in the opposite direction. The "falls" are a series of rock ledges at the base of a narrow gorge, which form rapids where the water tumbles in opposite directions just before and after low tide. You really need to visit at both high and low tides to appreciate the difference in water level — 4.4m (14.5 feet).

To get to Reversing Falls from downtown, cross Route 1 via Main Street and take Chesley Drive off to the left. You can also get there by taking Exit 119 from Route 1 and turning right onto Bridge Road.

Overlooking the gorge is the **Reversing Falls Visitor Centre,** part of a restaurant complex at 200 Bridge Rd. (**☎ 506-658-2937**). Displays describe the effect of the tides, out back is an observation platform, and you can watch a film about the falls (C$2.50/US$2.10). The center is open from mid-May through early October, daily 8 a.m. to 8 p.m. Or cross to **Fallsview Park,** on the east side of the gorge. Access is via Douglas Avenue.

Only when the tide reaches a certain level and the current slows are boats able to safely navigate the gorge. The only people who avoid this "slack" tide are folks at **F1 Reversing Falls Jet Boat Rides** (**☎ 506-634-8987**), who wait until the rapids are at their roughest to take you out for an exhilarating ride through the churning water. The cost is C$31 (US$26.40) adults, C$26 (US$22.10) children. The departure point is Fallsview Park. The same company runs a regular one-hour boat tour through the gorge and around the harbor for C$31 (US$26.40) adults, C$26 (US$22.10) children. These trips depart from downtown's Market Square to coincide with calm slack tide.

Rockwood Park

Canada's largest urban park (810 hectares/2,000 acres) encompasses native forests and numerous lakes northeast of downtown Saint John. There's plenty for everyone to do, including:

- ✔ **Monkey around** at **Cherry Brook Zoo,** Foster Thurston Rd. (☎ 506-634-1440), where you can see lions, tigers, and over 30 other exotic species. It's open 10 a.m. to dusk, and admission is C$6.50 (US$5.50) adults, C$5.50 (US$4.70) seniors, and C$5 (US$4.30) children.

- ✔ **Take a hike** along 25km (15.5 miles) of pathways. One trail begins from Lake Dr. S and encircles pretty Crystal Lake.

- ✔ **Aim for the water hazard** at **Rockwood Park Golf Course,** on Sandy Point Rd. (☎ 506-634-0090), which has the Maritimes' only aquatic driving range. Greens fees are C$32 (US$27.20).

- ✔ **Swim and splash** in one of the park's 12 lakes. **Fisher Lakes,** off Lake Dr. S, has supervised swimming, canoe rentals, and a sandy stretch of beach.

The easiest way to get to Rockwood Park is to take Foster Thurston Drive north from Exit 128 of Route 1, 3km (1.9 miles) east of downtown. This road leads all the way around the park. If you're feeling confident in your route-finding ability, cross Route 1 via Somerset St. and hook a right on Churchill Boulevard. For park information, dial ☎ 506-658-2883.

Irving Nature Park

A rocky peninsula jutting into busy Saint John Harbour has escaped development and is protected as Irving Nature Park. This 240-hectare (600-acre) park has a sandy stretch of beach near the entrance, rocky coves, pleasant hiking trails, and tidal pools filled with colorful critters. Along the **Squirrel Trail,** near the information booth, an observation tower offers sweeping views back across the mud flats linking the peninsula to the mainland. Between early June and late October the park becomes home to hundreds of seals, which haul themselves out of the water and onto the rocky shoreline. Bird life is prolific year-round — over 200 species have been recorded in the park.

Irving Nature Park is west of downtown. To get there, take Exit 119 from Route 1 and follow Bleury St. and then Sand Cove Rd. into the park. Cross the mud flats to reach an information booth that is staffed late May through October. For park information, call ☎ 506-653-7367. Admission is free.

Night Life

If you feel like enjoying a tipple and some local music but want to avoid the hard-drinking, dimly-lit downtown bars, there are plenty of options. Stop by either of the city information centers for a schedule of what's on, or check with **Tourism Saint John** (☎ 866-463-8639 or 506-658-2855; www.tourismsaintjohn.com) directly.

Pubs and clubs

All the restaurants in Market Square, including **Grannan's** (☎ 506-634-1555), have a section of the public plaza cordoned off for outdoor seating. You're welcome to stop by for just a refreshing drink in the sun at any of these places. Also here is **Saint John Ale House** (☎ 506-657-2337), with British-style beers on tap. In the vicinity, the **Brigantine Lounge** in the Hilton Saint John at 1 Market Square (☎ 506-693-8484) has unobstructed harbor views.

The Trinity Royal area, up King and Princess Streets, is a good place to look for local color and live music. **O'Leary's Pub,** 46 Princess St. (☎ 506-634-7135), is a jumping Irish pub, with Guinness on tap and Celtic bands most nights. **Tapps Brew Pub,** 78 King St. (☎ 506-634-1957), attracts an older crowd.

The arts

The **Imperial Theatre** on King's Square (☎ 506-633-9494) is a meticulously restored 1913 vaudeville theater. It is home to local theater, opera, ballet, and music productions, with programs that usually run through the winter months. Theater tours are available in summer Monday through Saturday 10 a.m. to 6 p.m.

Fundy Coast

Beyond Saint John, you can head west to the resort town of St. Andrews, back toward Moncton via Fundy National Park, or inland to the provincial capital of Fredericton. The following sections detail the first two options, while Fredericton is covered in the next chapter.

Fundy National Park

The massive Fundy tides are the most dramatic aspect of this popular coastal park northeast of Saint John, but it's the rugged interior dotted with lakes along with the network of hiking trails that brings in the summertime crowds. The park even has a covered bridge, which lies near the end of Point Wolfe Road.

Wildlife is prolific on the land, in the air, and out in the Bay of Fundy. At dawn or dusk you have an excellent chance of spying moose, beavers, or black bears, while birdwatchers delight in spotting peregrine falcons.

Getting There

You'll need a vehicle to reach Fundy National Park. It is bisected by Route 114, which branches off Route 1 84km (51 miles) northeast of Saint John. From this junction, it's 25km (15.5 miles) to the park gate and a further 17km (10.6 miles) to the main facility area.

Park entry fees

The daily entry fee to Fundy National Park is C$6 (US$5.10) adults, C$5 (US$4.30) seniors, C$4 (US$3.40) children, to a maximum of C$12 (US$10.20) per vehicle. Fees are collected at booths located at both park entrances.

Gathering more information

The main **Visitor Centre** (☎ **506-887-6000;** www.pc.gc.ca) is just inside the east park gate. It's open mid-June through August daily 8 a.m. to 10 p.m. and from mid-May to mid-June and September to mid-October daily 8 a.m. to 4:30 p.m.

If you're coming in from the west, make a stop at the **Wolfe Lake Visitor Centre,** open mid-June through September daily 10 a.m. to 6 p.m.

Staying in Fundy National Park

Most people staying in Fundy camp out in one of four park campgrounds. Indoor accommodations are limited, so you will want to reserve a room as far in advance as possible.

Fundy Highlands Inn & Chalets
$$ Fundy National Park

Perched on a grassy slope 2km from the main facility area, this comfortable lodging offers views across the Bay of Fundy that make it worth every cent of the already reasonable rates. Units within the main complex are slightly dated, but each comes with cooking facilities and opens to a large patio with ocean views. The chalets are smaller, but have kitchenettes as well as a little more character.

Route 114, Fundy National Park. ☎ *888-883-8639 or 506-887-2930. Fax: 506-887-2453.* www.fundyhighlandchalets.com. *Rack rates: C$84–C$99 (US$71.40–US$84.20) double. MC, V. Open: May–Oct.*

Fundy Park Chalets
$$ Fundy National Park

These fresh little cottages lie in a grove of trees adjacent to hiking trails, the swimming pool, the golf course, a restaurant, and the main information center. Each has basic cooking facilities and a bathroom. In the shoulder seasons, you can enjoy accommodations, a round of golf, and a lobster dinner for just C$70 (US$59.50) per person. Book well ahead for July and August.

Route 114, Fundy National Park ☎ *506-887-2808. Fax: 506-887-2282. Internet:* www.fundyparkchalets.com. *Rack rates: C$90 (US$76.50) double. MC, V. Open: May–mid-Oct.*

Dining in Fundy National Park

The park has just one restaurant, but as both accommodations have cooking facilities, preparing your own meal is an easy option. In adjacent Alma, **Butland's Seafood** on Main St. (☎ **506-887-2190**) sells cooked lobsters for around C$10 (US$8.50) per pound, with the price clearly displayed in black marker on their claws. You can also buy fresh shrimp, mussels, scallops, and a variety of fish.

Seawinds Dining Room
$$–$$$ Fundy National Park   SEAFOOD

This restaurant is exactly what you'd expect in the popular park — family-friendly and informal, with well-priced, unfussy food. Three massive chandeliers, a large stone fireplace, and a 6-kilogram (13.5-pound) lobster shell dominate the main dining room. The menu is short and simple, ranging from a traditional roast beef dinner to sautéed scallops. All children's dishes are under C$6 (US$5.10).

Route 114, Fundy National Park ☎ *506-887-2098. Reservations not necessary. Main courses: C$12–C$23 (US$10.20–US$19.60). MC, V. Open: May–Oct daily 11 a.m.–9:30 p.m.*

Exploring Fundy National Park

The main facility area, just inside the east gate, is a good place to get oriented. Stop by the visitor center for a park map and hiking trail description brochure and then wander down to the water's edge for panoramic views across the Bay of Fundy.

Hiking

Within the park are 120km (74.6 miles) of hiking trails designed for all fitness levels. Head to either visitor center for a trail map and to ask advice about which trails would suit your fitness level and interests.

At low tide, you can walk along the beach below the main visitor center, but don't expect to have it to yourself. To escape the crowds, drive west along Point Wolfe Rd. From the end of this road, a 0.6km (0.4-mile) path leads through a lush spruce forest to **Point Wolfe Beach** at the braided mouth of the Point Wolfe River. From the same trailhead, the **Coppermine Trail** leads 2.3km (1.4 miles) further west along the coast to the site of an abandoned mine. Allow two hours for the round trip. Backtrack along Point Wolfe Rd. and then take Herring Cove Rd. to reach **Herring Cove Trail,** a 15-minute jaunt down to a rocky cove with a tidal cave off to one side. From the cove, the **Matthews Head Trail** leads off to the south, traversing to a high headland with stunning ocean views. Allow 90 minutes for this 4.5km (2.8-mile) circuit.

An easy introduction to the park's interior forest is the **Caribou Plain Trail,** a 3.4km (2.1-mile) circuit that loops around a beaver pond. The trailhead is just east of Bennett Lake. **Third Vault Falls** tumbles over a 16m-high (52.5-foot-high) ledge in the eastern portion of the park. The falls are reached via a 3.7km (2.3-mile) trail that braches off Laverty Road. Allow 60 to 70 minutes each way.

Other things to do and see in Fundy National Park

Hiking is the major attention-getter in the park, but you can also do the following:

- ✔ **Swim.** A unique **saltwater pool** is filled with water pumped up from the Bay of Fundy and then heated to a comfortable temperature. Entry is C$3 (US$2.60) adults, C$2.50 (US$2.10) seniors, C$1.50 (US$1.30) children. It's open July through August, 11 a.m. to 7 p.m.

- ✔ **Golf.** The fairways of a short nine-hole golf course wind their way along Dickson Brook, beside the main facility area. A pro shop (☎ **506-887-2970**) rents clubs and collects greens fees of C$17 (US$14.50).

- ✔ **Paddle.** Rent a canoe (C$9/US$7.70 per hour) at **Bennett Lake,** halfway along the park road, to explore the shoreline of this tranquil body of water.

- ✔ **Watch the tide.** Okay, it's not very exciting watching tidal movements, but at low tide, **Alma Harbor** is devoid of water, leaving fishing boats high and dry on the ocean floor.

Hopewell Cape

Around halfway between Fundy National Park and Moncton, Route 114 rounds Hopewell Cape. Turn here to reach Hopewell Rocks, a cluster of rock towers that were once part of the mainland but became separated by erosion caused by the tides. Known as "flower pots" (many have trees and shrubbery growing on top), they are partly covered at high tide, but when the massive Fundy tide recedes, they rise starkly from the muddy shoreline.

Plan on arriving one to three hours before low tide. Tidal charts are published in all local newspapers and are available at information centers. The visitor's guide to Fundy National Park (you'll be given one at the park entrance) has a tide chart on the center page.

Staying and dining at Hopewell Cape

Most visitors to Hopewell Rocks spend two to four hours poking around and then move on to Moncton or Fundy National Park. Alternatively, you can stay overnight at the Hopewell Rocks Motel & Country Inn, within walking distance of the attraction.

Hopewell Rocks Motel
$$ Hopewell Cape

Located at the entrance to Hopewell Rocks, this adequate motel has large air-conditioned rooms and a small outdoor pool. The hanging baskets of colorful flowers out front are a nice touch. Rooms 11 through 20 face away from the road and are quieter.

Ignore your hunger pangs down at Hopewell Rocks and plan on taking a meal back out on the highway at this motel's Log Cabin Restaurant. The lobster dinner is well priced; or choose one of the daily specials, which are discounted from the main menu. The dining room is open May through October, daily 8 a.m. to 9 p.m.

Route 114. ☎ *888-759-7070 or 506-734-2975. Fax: 506-734-2252. Internet:* www. hopewellrocksmotel.com. *Rack rates: C$75–C$95 (US$63.80–US$80.80) double. AE, MC, V. Open: May–Oct.*

Exploring Hopewell Rocks

At the end of the access road off Route 114 are a massive parking lot and a fee station where the entry charge is collected. Admission is C$8 (US$6.80) adults, C$7 (US$6) seniors, C$6 (US$5.10) children.

The gates are open mid-May to mid-June 9 a.m. to 5 p.m., mid- to late June 8 a.m. to 7 p.m., July to mid-August 8 a.m. to 8 p.m., mid- to late August 8 a.m. to 7 p.m., September to mid-October 9 a.m. to 5 p.m., and are closed the rest of the year.

Beyond the fee station, make your way down to the large **interpretive center.** This is a good place to get an overview of these geological oddities, as well as to learn more about the Fundy tides.

The rock towers are scattered along a 2km (1.2-mile) stretch starting immediately below the interpretive center, but the most impressive concentration is a 30-minute walk away, along a wooded trail. The alternative to walking is to catch a ride in an oversized golf cart. This costs just C$1.25 (US$1.10) each way; buy tickets at the main entrance or at the cart turn-around point.

At the end of the trail/cart path, a steep metal stairway descends to the muddy shoreline and the **Flower Pot Rocks.** To escape the summer crowds, walk west along the beach (to the right from the bottom of the stairs). Hoses are provided back at the top to clean the sticky, red mud from the soles of your shoes.

The time of day you visit is restricted by the tide, but early morning is best if you want to avoid the crowds. For shutterbugs, an early-morning visit also offers more favorable light for photography.

St. Andrews

On the Fundy Coast west of Saint John, St. Andrews is New Brunswick's most famous resort town. Laid out by Loyalists in 1783, the oldest part of town has remained remarkably untouched by modern encroachment and is protected as a National Historic Site.

St. Andrews was mainly a port city until it was discovered in the late 1880s by wealthy Americans looking to escape the summer heat of the Eastern Seaboard. They stayed in grand resorts like the Algonquin or in their own private estates, and St. Andrews was transformed.

Today, St. Andrews is popular not only with vacationing New Englanders, but also with Canadians who come to celebrate special occasions, spend time out on the water, or simply stroll the streets browsing through the many galleries and boutiques.

Getting there

Although St. Andrews is across the St. Croix River from Maine, access from the United States is via the Calais/St. Stephen border crossing, 24km (15 miles) northwest.

From elsewhere in New Brunswick, the most direct access to St. Andrews is Route 1 west along the Bay of Fundy from Saint John, a distance of 100km (62 miles). From Fredericton, 133km (82.6 miles) away, the most direct way is Route 3 via St. Stephen.

Just before entering the town proper, make a stop at the **St. Andrews Welcome Centre,** in a converted residence at 46 Reed Ave. (☎ **506-529-3556**). It's open May through September daily 9 a.m. to 6 p.m. (and until 9 p.m. in July and Aug).

Staying in St. Andrews

Many of St. Andrews' lodgings are upscale inns and bed and breakfasts, priced higher than elsewhere in the Maritimes. I've included the best of these and dug out a cheapie and a family favorite to keep everyone happy.

Inn on Frederick
$$$–$$$$ **Downtown**

This centrally located structure started life in the 1840s as home to a Loyalist family. Now beautifully restored to create a historic and welcoming ambience, the building is also home to a fine-dining restaurant (open for dinner daily 5–9 p.m.). The seven guest rooms are big and bright, with even the smallest featuring a canopy bed and luxurious bathroom. Rates include a cooked breakfast.

58 Frederick St. ☎ *877-895-4400 or 506-529-2603. Fax: 506-529-4460.* www.innon frederick.ca. *Rack rates: C$195–C$495 (US$165.80–US$420.80) double. AE, DISC, MC, V.*

Kingsbrae Arms
$$$$ **Downtown**

Staying at this country estate, the only Relais & Chateaux property in the Maritimes, is an unforgettable experience. Built by a Boston businessman in 1897, the Kingsbrae was originally part of a sprawling estate that is now Kingsbrae Garden (see below). Today, the gracious home is still surrounded by beautifully landscaped grounds, and has been converted to an inn with an impeccable pedigree. The eight rooms have marble bathrooms, gas fireplaces, and canopy beds, topped with luxurious linens. Although bed-and-breakfast rates are offered, most guests stay as part of a package that includes a memorable cooked breakfast, picnic lunch, and four-course table d'hôte dinner, inclusive of wine.

219 King St. ☎ _800-470-4088 or 506-529-4210. Fax: 506-529-4311._ www.kingsbrae. com. _Rack rates: C$615–$1100 (US$522.80–US$935) double. AE, MC, V. Open: May–Oct._

Picket Fence Motel
$$ **North of downtown**

If all you want is a regular motel room, consider this hotel on the edge of town.

102 Reed St. ☎ _506-529-8985._ www.picketfencenb.com. _Rates: C$80 (US$68) double. AE, MC, V. Open: May–Oct._

Seaside Beach Resort
$$ **Downtown**

Located at the far end of the main street, this is a good choice for families who are looking for a waterfront setting at a reasonable price. Each unit in this historic miscellany of cottages and apartments is different, but most have cooking facilities and bright, practical furnishings. The two-bedroom Seagull apartment is right on the water and opens to a boardwalk dotted with Adirondack chairs, while the Sandpiper cottage is a cozy space set back from the water. Barbeques and picnic tables dot the grounds.

339 Water St. ☎ _888-506-8677 or 506-529-3846. Fax: 506-529-4479._ www.seaside. nb.ca. _Rack rates: C$100–C$150 (US$85–US$127.50) double. AE, MC, V. Open: Apr–Dec._

Treadwell Inn
$$–$$$$ **Downtown**

The seven-room, olive and burgundy-colored lodge, built in the 1820s for a ship chandler, combines a waterfront setting with comfortable rooms to make it one of the nicest places to stay in St. Andrews. The current owner's faultless taste shines through without taking away from the historic charm. Of the well-furnished rooms, only two don't have ocean views. My fave? Room 5 (C$185/US$157.30), with a king-sized bed, a bathroom with a soaker tub, and wide doors that open to a private balcony with sweeping views across Passamaquoddy Bay.

129 Water St. ☎ 800-529-1011 or 506-529-1011. Fax: 506-529-4826. Rack rates: C$145–C$250 (US$212.50) double. MC, V.

Dining in St. Andrews

Dining in St. Andrews compares favorably with much larger centers across the Maritimes — a combination of an abundance of seafood and a century of demand from well-heeled visitors.

The Gables
$$–$$$ Downtown SEAFOOD

This restaurant lies down a narrow alley, beyond a giant wood carving of a lobster. It is a casual affair, liberally decorated with netting and the like, all salvaged from the sea. Seating is inside or out on a deck that extends to above the high tide mark. The cooking is simple but tasty. Plan on starting with a plate piled high with steamed mussels. For mains, peruse the blackboard offerings, which feature whatever seafood is in season — lobster, scallops, halibut, and haddock are all staples. The Gables opens for breakfast in summer, with full cooked breakfasts costing a reasonable C$7 (US$6).

143 Water St. ☎ 506-529-3440. Reservations recommended for dinner. Main courses: C$14–C$20 (US$11.90–US$17.10). AE, MC, V. Open: July–Aug daily 8 a.m.–11 p.m., Sept–June daily 11 a.m.–9 p.m.

Niger Reef Tea House
$$–$$$ Downtown CANADIAN

This historic teahouse is my favorite spot in St. Andrews for lunch, although I have dropped by just for a piece of the melt-in-your-mouth strawberry shortcake. Choose to dine in a cozy room and enjoy the wonderful aromas that waft in from the kitchen, or sit out on the weathered deck and take in the view across Passamaquoddy Bay. In the evening, you can indulge in the rich seafood chowder or skewered scallops, grilled with a ginger and curry glaze. If you weren't here at lunch, end your meal with the shortcake; otherwise, go for the triple chocolate brownie sundae. The salmon eggs Benedict (C$12.50/US$10.60), served at Sunday brunch, is to die for.

1 Joe's Point Rd. ☎ 506-529-8007. Reservations recommended for dinner. Lunch: C$7–C$13 (US$6–US$11.10). MC, V. Open: Mid-June–mid-Sept daily 11 a.m.–5 p.m.

Windsor House
$$–$$$ St. Andrews CONTINENTAL

The cooking at this upscale establishment in a 1798 Georgian-era home is among the best in St. Andrews. Starters include pâté, made in-house, and a salad of greens harvested from the garden. The mains vary, depending on what's in season, but may include a pan-seared duck breast smothered in cranberry chutney, or beef tenderloin stuffed with Stilton cheese and doused in a red wine demi-glaze. You can dine in one of two elegant rooms, both with fireplaces, or in the walled courtyard. If you want to stay here, there are six beautiful rooms for C$225–C$300 (US$191.30–US$255). Sunday brunch choices include the most delicious eggs Benedict you could imagine.

132 Water St. ☎ _506-529-3330. Reservations essential. Main courses: C$26 (US$22.10). AE, DC, DISC, MC, V. Open: May–Dec daily 6–9 p.m., and Sun 11 a.m.– 2 p.m. (closed Mon and Tues in spring and fall)._

Exploring St. Andrews

If you'd like to take a self-guided walking tour of St. Andrews, pick up a map highlighting points of interest from the Welcome Centre. If you're heading out on your own, here are some sights you won't want to miss.

Atlantic Salmon Interpretive Centre

Very different from St. Andrews' historic attractions, this is the public portion of a research station that studies one of Canada's most important fishing exports. The modern interpretive center nestles in a lush forest, right over a stream where salmon spawn. Inside the timber-frame building are displays on the lifecycle of the salmon and the ongoing fight to save its habitat, as well as some old fly-fishing equipment. A trail leads downstream to Chamcook Harbour and upstream to shallow gravel beds where the fish spawn.

Route 127 (6 km/3.7 miles toward Saint John). ☎ _506-529-1384. Internet:_ www.asf.ca. _Admission C$6 (US$5.10) adults, C$4 (US$3.40) children. Open: Mid-May–mid-Oct daily 9 a.m.–5 p.m._

Kingsbrae Garden

Once part of the sprawling Kingsbrae Arms Estate, this 11-hectare (27-acre) plot is generally regarded as one of the top 10 gardens in Canada. The Rose Garden, filled with fragrant old varieties, is from the original estate; the White Garden is composed entirely of white and silver blossoms; and the Scents and Sensitivity Garden allows visually impaired visitors to experience distinct smells and textures up close. And new gardens are always being added — the Gravel Garden addresses modern environmental concerns by using a minimum of water. In other parts of the grounds, you'll find a scaled-down working windmill, a wooden maze, and fish-filled ponds. Complement your visit with a bowl of steaming seafood chowder in the Garden Café. Kingsbrae is a 10-minute walk up King Street from the waterfront.

220 King St. ☎ _506-529-3335. Admission C$8.50 (US$7.20) adults, C$7 (US$6) seniors and children. Open: Mid-May–mid-Oct daily 9 a.m.–6 p.m._

Minister's Island

Once the summer retreat of William Van Horne, the driving force behind the completion of Canada's transcontinental railway, this small island holds one of the finest private residences you are likely to come across in Canada. Built of locally quarried sandstone, the mansion is notable for its 50 rooms, including a massive drawing room and a billiard room with the original table. On the grounds is a sandstone bathhouse with a tidal swimming pool.

Getting to the island is an adventure in itself. The only access is at low tide (ask at the visitor center or dial ☎ 506-529-5081 to hear a recorded message with exact tide and tour times), at which time everyone meets at the end of Bar Road from where an escort is provided across the dry sea floor to the island. You must have your own vehicle.

Bar Rd. (off Mowat Dr.). ☎ 506-529-5081. Admission C$5 (US$4.30) adults, C$2.50 (US$2.10) children. Tours: June–mid-Oct; times vary with the tide.

Ross Memorial Museum

Formerly the summer retreat of a wealthy American family named Ross, this 1824 home was deeded to the town to help preserve local history. It offers a glimpse into the life of the Rosses, with rooms that remain much as they left them, filled with fine furnishings and original paintings.

188 Montague St. ☎ 506-529-5124. Admission: donation. Open: July–Sept Mon–Sat 10 a.m.–4:30 p.m.

Other cool things to do in and around St. Andrews

Several companies run sightseeing trips on Passamaquoddy Bay, or you can go whale watching or kayaking. The **Day Adventure Centre,** beside Market Wharf (☎ **506-529-2600**), represents various operators, or choose from one of these options:

- ✔ **Whale watching: Fundy Tide Runners,** Market Wharf (☎ **506-529-4481**), uses a stable Zodiac to reach whale-watching grounds out in the Bay of Fundy. Tours last two hours and cost C$50 (US$42.50) adults, C$35 (US$29.80) children. The whale-watching season is June through September.

- ✔ **Sea kayaking:** Even if you've never kayaked before, the guides at **Seascape Kayak Tours,** 165 Water St. (☎ **506-529-4866**), will make you feel at ease on a two-hour introductory paddle from their seafront headquarters; C$45 (US$38.30) per person.

- ✔ **Tide watching:** Walk north along Water St. to reach St. Andrews Blockhouse National Historic Site. Built in the early 1800s to protect the town from attack, the grassy bank in front of this wooden building is the perfect place to watch the tide receding.

✔ **Golfing:** It will *feel* like you're out at sea as you stand on the 12th tee at **Fairmont Algonquin Golf Club,** Brandy Cove Rd. (☎ 506-529-7142), aiming for a tiny patch of green perched on a nub of land surrounded by water. High season greens fees are C$125 (US$106.30).

Shopping

Artisans will say they're attracted to St. Andrews for the inspiration of its scenic setting, and there's no denying the area is beautiful, but the more cynical may say it's because of affluent U.S. residents and visitors with pockets full of greenbacks. Regardless, the end result is a street lined with galleries and boutiques, including the following:

✔ **Jarea Art Studio,** 166 Montaque St. (☎ 506-529-4936), displays the unusual art of Geoffrey David-Slater, whose work features a single line that changes color but remains unbroken.

✔ **Serendipin' Art,** 168 Water St. (☎ 506-529-3327), features colorful hand-blown glass fish.

✔ **Boutique la Baleine,** 173 Water St. (☎ 506-529-3926) is highlighted by stylish whale woodcarvings.

✔ If you want to find that perfect nautical-themed painting, start your search at the **Seacoast Gallery,** 174 Water St. (☎ 506-529-0005).

✔ **Gumushel's Tartan Shop,** 183 Water St. (☎ 506-529-3859), sells tartan ties, berets, and jackets — but you guessed that from the name, didn't you?

✔ **St. Andrews Hardware,** 189 Water St. (☎ 506-529-3158), is filled to the rafters with a hodgepodge of hardware and nautical-themed knick-knacks.

✔ Since 1915, local knitters have sold their hats, blankets, sweaters, and dolls at **Cottage Crafts,** 209 Water St. (☎ 506-529-3190). You can also buy a great variety of yarns.

Fundy Isles

Time spent on one or more of the Fundy Isles is a unique and memorable addition to your travels along the Fundy Coast. The three main islands, Deer, Campobello, and Grand Manan, are all linked to the mainland by ferry and easily visited in a day. You can explore the islands or, if you prefer, head out to the water to marvel at marine life or try your hand at some of the area's popular water sports.

Deer Island

It may be named for a land mammal, but life on this small island revolves around the ocean. The importance of the lobster industry is clear — you'll see the pounds used to hold live lobsters scattered around the shoreline. To get to the island, catch the free ferry (departures year-round, every 30 minutes) from Letete, south of St. George. You can explore the island in just a few hours, but allow two extra hours to take a whale-watching trip with **Cline Marine Tours** (☎ **800-567-5880** or 506-747-0114). **Sunset Beach Cottage & Suites,** on the west side of the island (☎ **888-576-9990** or 506-747-2972; www.cottageandsuites.com), is right on the beach and has an outdoor pool; rates for the five kitchen-equipped suites and one cottage are C$70 to C$100 (US$59.50–US$85) double, which is in the $–$$ range.

Campobello Island

A summer-only ferry links Deer and Campobello Islands, but most visitors cross to the island by bridge from Lubec, Maine — even those visiting from New Brunswick, as St. Stephen is just 70km (43 miles) away by road. Franklin Roosevelt's family were perhaps the most notable of the many wealthy people who have spent their summers here. His 34-room cottage is protected as part of **Roosevelt Campobello International Park** (☎ **506-752-2922**) and is open for inspection late May through mid-October daily 10 a.m. to 6 p.m. Admission is free.

An adjacent property, once owned by Roosevelt's cousin, has been converted to **Lupine Lodge** (☎ **888-912-8880** or 506-752-2555; www.lupine lodge.com), with 11 woodsy rooms in two log cottages. Rates are C$65 to C$125 (US$55.30–US$106.30) per unit ($–$$). The restaurant here is recommended. A good source of island information is the Web site www.campobello.com.

Grand Manan Island

Grand Manan is larger than the other Fundy Isles and much farther from the mainland. Birdwatchers in particular are drawn to the island — famed naturalist John James Audubon spent time here painting. Other draws are whale and seal watching, biking, hiking, and a string of sandy beaches.

Coastal Transport (☎ **506-662-3724;** www.coastaltransport.ca) operates ferries year-round, four to seven times daily between Blacks Harbour (take Exit 60 from Route 1) and the island. The crossing takes two hours. The roundtrip fare is C$10.10 (US$8.60) adults, C$5 (US$4.30) children, C$30.20 (US$25.70) vehicles. Reservations are only taken for the return journey from the island to the mainland.

Don't look further than the **Swallowtail Inn,** at 50 Lighthouse Road near the ferry dock (☎ **866-563-1100** or 506-662-1100; www.swallowtail inn.com), for a gorgeous setting high atop a rocky bluff. Formerly a lighthouse keeper's residence, the guest rooms (C$85–C$125/ US$72.30–US$106.30; $$) have ensuites and ocean views.

Island Coast Whale Tours (☎ **877-662-9393** or 506-662-8181) takes visitors on five-hour boat tours searching out humpback, finback, and minke whales. Whale sightings are guaranteed through the July to mid-September season. The cost is C$50 (US$42.50) adults, C$25 (US$21.30) children. **Sea Watch Tours** (☎ 877-662-8552 or 506-662-8552) have onboard naturalists who are especially knowledgeable about local bird life. **Adventure High,** based near the ferry dock (☎ 506-662-3563), takes visitors kayaking (C$55/US$46.80 per half day) and rents bikes (C$20/US$17.10 per day). In addition to being a wonderful way to explore the island, using a bike means you don't need to bring a vehicle across on the ferry, saving both the expense and, more important, a possible long wait in line to board.

Fast Facts: Saint John

ATMs

All banks along King St. have ATMs accessible 24 hours daily.

Emergencies

Dial ☎ 911 for all emergencies.

Hospital

Saint John Regional Hospital is at 400 University Ave. (☎ 506-648-5000).

Information

Tourism Saint John (☎ 866-463-8639 or 506-658-2855; www.tourismsaintjohn.com) operates an information center downtown in Market Square (open daily 9 a.m.–6 p.m., July–Aug until 8 p.m.) and along Route 1 as you approach the city from the west (open mid-May–mid-Oct daily 9 a.m.)

Internet Access

Internet access is free at **Saint John Public Library,** in Market Square (☎ 506-643-7220); closed Sunday.

Police

For emergencies, dial ☎ 911. For other police matters, call ☎ 506-757-1020.

Post Office

Downtown drugstores such as the one in Brunswick Square have postal services. The main post office is at 125 Rothesay Ave.

Restrooms

Public restrooms are located at street level in Market Square.

Taxis

Local cab companies include **Diamond Taxi** (☎ 506-648-8888) and **Royal Taxi** (☎ 506-652-5050).

Transit Info

Saint John Transit (☎ 902-490-6600) is discussed earlier in this chapter under "Orienting Yourself."

Weather

The **Environment Canada** Web site (www.weatheroffice.ec.gc.ca) has links to the Saint John forecast.

Chapter 17

Fredericton

● ●

In This Chapter

▶ Getting to Fredericton

▶ Finding your way around the city

▶ Deciding on the best places to stay and dine

▶ Seeing the downtown sights and exploring the Saint John River Valley

● ●

*F*redericton (population 47,000), the capital of New Brunswick, is an appealing and practical stopping place with classic Victorian architecture, interesting museums, riverfront pathways, and an excellent range of lodging and dining options.

In 1793, at the end of the American Revolution, around 2,000 Americans loyal to the British crown made their way north into the Saint John River Valley and set up camp at a site that had been the one-time capital of Acadia. These Loyalists set out to create a gracious town, and this sense of style remains today.

Getting to Fredericton

Fredericton is accessible by plane and bus, but most people arrive by automobile, driving in via an excellent provincial highway system.

By plane

Greater Fredericton Airport (www.frederictonairport.ca) is 14km (8.7 miles) southeast of downtown via Route 102. Air Canada and its subsidiary Air Canada Jazz fly in daily from Halifax, Toronto, and Montreal. Delta Air Lines links Fredericton with Boston.

Taxis line up out front of the main terminal and charge around C$18 (US$15.30) to take you downtown. Rental-car companies that maintain desks at the airport are Avis, Budget, Hertz, and National.

Fredericton

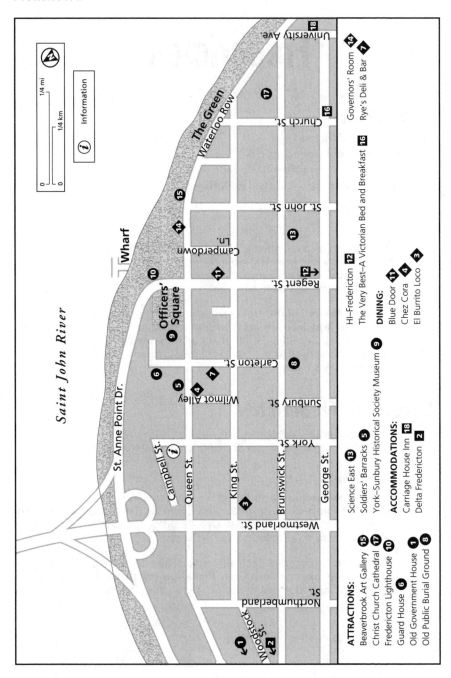

ATTRACTIONS:
Beaverbrook Art Gallery **15**
Christ Church Cathedral **17**
Fredericton Lighthouse **10**
Guard House **6**
Old Government House **1**
Old Public Burial Ground **8**
Science East **13**
Soldiers' Barracks **5**
York-Sunbury Historical Society Museum **9**

ACCOMMODATIONS:
Carriage House Inn **18**
Delta Fredericton **2**
HI-Fredericton **12**
The Very Best–A Victorian Bed and Breakfast **16**

DINING:
Blue Door **11**
Chez Cora **4**
El Burrito Loco **3**
Governors' Room **14**
Rye's Deli & Bar **7**

Information

By car

Route 2 (the Trans-Canada Highway) is the main highway from Moncton and all points east, including Halifax. The drive from Moncton is 174km (108 miles), or a little under 2 hours.

Entering New Brunswick near Edmundston, **Route 2** follows the winding Saint John River all the way to Fredericton for 290km (180 miles), which means you should allow at least four hours.

If you're traveling up the Acadian Coast from Moncton, take **Route 8** from Miramichi south through the heart of New Brunswick to reach Fredericton in 2 hours.

Route 7 is the most direct road between Saint John and Fredericton (105km/65 miles), but **Route 102** along the Saint John River is a more scenic alternative.

By bus

Acadian (☎ **506-458-6007**) buses arrive at 101 Regent St. (at Brunswick St.), on the same block as a Discount car rental agency (☎ **506-458-1118**) and within walking distance of many downtown hotels.

Getting Around Fredericton

Downtown Fredericton lies on the inside of a bend in the Saint John River. King and Queen Streets, running parallel to the river, are the main thoroughfares. North Fredericton, on the north side of the river, is mostly residential. It is linked to downtown by the Westmorland St. Bridge. Further east, the Trail Bridge, starting at the corner of Brunswick Street and University Avenue, is for pedestrians only. Even if you don't need to get to the other side, it's worth crossing the bridge just for the views that extend back across downtown, where you can see the higher buildings rising above the tree-lined riverbank.

Parking

You've gotta love a city that welcomes visitors with free parking. At the visitor center at the corner of Queen and York Streets, show proof that you are from out of province — such as a driver's license — and the staff will issue you a two-day parking permit valid at all parking meters and at the lot at the north end of York Street, immediately behind the visitor center.

Catching cabs

Hailing a taxi is easy along Queen and King Streets. If you're really stuck, you can always go to the Lord Beaverbrook Hotel and have the front desk attendant call one for you. Among the local companies are **Checker Cabs** (☎ **506-450-8294**), **Loyal Taxi** (☎ **506-455-6789**), and **Standard Taxi** (☎ **506-450-4444**).

Transit tips

Fredericton Transit (☎ **506-460-2200**) operates city buses along seven routes Monday through Saturday 6:30 a.m. to 11 p.m. The fare is C$1.75 (US$1.50) per sector (children 6 and under ride free). Exact change is required.

Staying in Fredericton

The following recommendations are my preferences in various price categories. Downtown accommodations are within walking distance of the riverfront and most major attractions.

Room rates here don't tend to fluctuate as much as elsewhere, but offer good value year-round. If you're just looking for a regular motel room, consult the provincial tourism guide, or cruise the arterial roads for posted vacancies (start along Route 105, across the river from downtown). The friendly staff at the City Hall visitor center will be more than happy to help you find a last-minute room.

Carriage House Inn
$$ Downtown

Built in 1875 for a one-time mayor of Fredericton, this three-story Queen Anne-style mansion lies one block from a riverfront pathway leading right to downtown. The ten medium-sized guest rooms are decorated in a subtle Victorian theme and filled with antiques. A cooked breakfast, served in a sunny side room, is included in the rates.

See map p. 238. 230 University Ave. ☎ *800-267-6068 or 506-452-9924. Fax: 506-452-2770.* www.carriagehouse-inn.net. *Rack rates: C$95–C$105 (US$80.81–US$89.30). AE, MC, V.*

Delta Fredericton
$$–$$$ Downtown

This 206-room property, Fredericton's largest, rises above the Saint John River on the west side of downtown (about a ten-minute walk to City Hall). All the amenities of a full-service hotel are available — room service, high-speed Internet, a lounge/restaurant, and so on — as well as a few bonuses: free parking, indoor and outdoor pools, and a summer-only poolside bar and grill. The rooms aren't particularly large but are smartly designed. Request one with a river view when booking.

See map p. 238. 225 Woodstock Rd. ☎ *800-325-3535 or 506-457-7000. Fax: 506-457-4000.* www.deltahotels.com. *Rack Rates: C$159–C$199 (US$135.20–US$169.70) double. AE, DC, MC, V.*

Fort Nashwaak Motel
$ North Fredericton

This motel is situated beside a restored fort, where the Nashwaak and Saint John Rivers meet. The rooms are fairly large but plainly furnished; what makes this place stand out from the 30-odd other roadside motels scattered around the city is its location, a pleasant 15-minute walk from downtown via the pedestrian-only Trail Bridge.

15 Riverside Dr. (at Route 10). ☎ *800-684-8999 or 506-472-4411. Fax: 506-450-8586. Parking: Free. Rack rates: C$75 (US$63.80) double. AE, MC, V.*

HI–Fredericton
$ Downtown

Nestled on a peaceful tree-lined street six blocks up Regent Street from downtown, this hostel is in a converted residence hall. Thoughtful renovations have created more atmosphere than you may imagine a hostel would offer. All the expected amenities are available, including a communal kitchen, laundry, and lockers. Beds are available in both dormitories and private rooms, but outside of summer, you could find yourself a private room for the price of a dorm. Check-in is 7 a.m. to noon and 6 to 10 p.m.

See map p. 238. 621 Churchill Row. ☎ *506-450-4417. Fax: 506-462-9692.* www. hihostels.ca. *Parking: Free. Rack rates: C$16 (US$13.60) members of Hostelling International, C$20 (US$17.10) nonmembers. MC, V.*

On the Pond
$$ Mactaquac

Set on a forested waterfront property well beyond city limits, this European-style country lodge is inviting and relaxing rather than luxurious. Stress-reducing facilities include a wide range of spa services and a beautiful library. You can also grab a bike or canoe and pedal or paddle to your heart's content. The eight spacious guest rooms are richly handsome in an old-fashioned kind of way. Breakfast and dinner are served in the dining room. Check the Web site for packages that include meals and activities.

Route 615 (off Route 105 21 km/13 miles west of Fredericton). ☎ *800-984-2555 or 506-363-3420. Fax: 506-363-3479.* www.onthepond.com. *Rack rates: C$145 (US$123.30). MC, V.*

Ramada Fredericton
$$ North Fredericton

Yes, it's part of a chain, but the Ramada Fredericton is excellent value. It's also right by the river and adjacent to a par three golf course and a complex of tennis courts. The 116 rooms are set around a tropical atrium that contains a swimming pool, hot tub, and poolside bar. The standard guest rooms face the atrium and have small balconies. They are tastefully decorated, and you'll find coffeemakers, irons, and comfortable couches in all units. Executive rooms are larger and overlook the golf course. The on-premise restaurant serves typical hotel fare in a Mediterranean setting.

480 Riverside Dr. (Route 105). ☎ 800-596-4656 or 506-460-5500. Fax: 506-472-0170. www.ramadafredericton.com. Rack Rates: C$105–C$145 (US$89.30–US$123.30) double. AE, DC, MC, V.

The Very Best — A Victorian Bed and Breakfast
$$ Downtown

On a quiet street at the eastern edge of downtown, this elegant 1840 home, run by friendly owners Yolande and Sam Rubenstein, is a wonderful retreat from the surrounding city. Inside, welcoming public areas open onto guest rooms that mix modern conveniences like air conditioning and super-comfy beds with antiques and historic charm. The sunny rear garden has a heated pool and plenty of space to stretch out and relax. You can have your breakfast in the formal dining room or outdoors under a gazebo.

See map p. 238. 806 George St. (at Church St.). ☎ 506-451-1499. Fax: 506-454-1454. Rack rates: C$119–C$129 (US$101.20–US$109.70) double. AE, MC, V.

Dining in Fredericton

You can indulge in a surprising range of cuisine in this outwardly staid city, thanks in part to the population of worldly university students. Outdoor dining is a treat that locals take full advantage of throughout the summer.

Blue Door
$–$$$ Downtown FUSION

It's difficult to miss this casual and colorful downtown restaurant — just look for the historic brick building with bright red shutters, distinctive white trim and yes, a blue door. In good weather, enjoy your meal (or just a martini) on the large patio. The young owners have brought their West Coast experiences to Fredericton, offering dishes that combine Canadian produce with spices and cooking styles from around the Pacific Rim. You'll be hooked on the flavorful jambalaya, which is full of shrimp, mussels, chicken, and sausage. Other choices are varied: Try the maple Dijon salmon or a Mexi burger topped with tangy blackened corn and tomato salsa. Non-meat eaters (as well as meat-eaters) will love the pad Thai, a filling noodle dish.

See map p. 238. 100 Regent St. ☎ 506-455-2583. Reservations recommended for dinner. Main courses: C$8–C$18 (US$6.80–US$15.30). AE, MC, V. Open: Mon–Sat 11:30–10 p.m., Sun 5:30–9:30 p.m.

Chez Cora
$–$$ Downtown BREAKFAST

Best Inexpensive Dining

The story sounds good — a Quebec woman makes good with a local café that serves up healthy breakfasts in a cheery environment, then franchises the concept across eastern Canada. In reality, you get a Denny's-style breakfast with a couple of slices of fruit on the side. Your best bet is the crêpes, which range from an adventurous spinach/cheddar combo to a sweet and creamy Strawberry Satisfaction. This place stands out because of its bright color scheme, fun-loving furnishings (lots of stuffed chickens), and walls graffitied with the names of dishes. Kids will love the fun atmosphere, and parents will fall for the reasonable prices. Breakfast is served all day; lunch is from 11 a.m. until the mid-afternoon closing.

See map p. 238. 476 Queen St. ☎ 506-472-2672. Reservations not taken. Main courses: C$7–C$12.50 (US$6–US$10.60). AE, MC, V. Open: Mon–Sat 6 a.m.–3 p.m., Sun 7 a.m.–3 p.m.

El Burrito Loco
$–$$ Downtown   MEXICAN

Locals are drawn in droves to this smallish restaurant for one reason: the authentic Mexican cooking of owner Perez Huerta. Everything from the guacamole to the taco shells is created in-house. In warmer weather, you'll need to reserve ahead to snag a table on the patio. Occasional live entertainment creates a fun vibe.

See map p. 238. 304 King St. ☎ 506-459-5626. Reservations recommended. Main courses: C$8–C$14.50 (US$6.80–US$12.30). AE, MC, V. Open: Daily 9:30 a.m.–10:30 p.m.

Governors' Room
$$$–$$$$ Downtown   CONTINENTAL

The intimate setting and consistently high quality of food make the Governor's Room popular with locals celebrating a special occasion and business travelers dining on expense accounts (it's ensconced in a bustling business hotel). The kitchen concentrates on classic European cooking. For starters, try shrimp bisque topped with brandied croutons. Then move on to grilled venison topped with black currant and port sauce, or roasted rack of lamb brushed with Dijon mayonnaise. End the meal with a rum-based, nut-topped ice cream Bananas Foster.

Also in the hotel is the informal **Terrace Dining Room,** with a wide-ranging hotel menu and a large deck overlooking the river. The hotel's **James Joyce Irish Pub** is the place to tuck into a hearty bowl of Irish stew or a generous piece of cottage pie.

See map p. 238. Crowne Plaza Fredericton, 659 Queen St. ☎ 506-455-3371. Reservations essential. Main courses: C$18–C$38 (US$15.30–US$32.30). AE, DC, MC, V. Open: Daily 6–9:30 p.m.

Rye's Deli & Bar
$–$$ Downtown   DELI/PUB FARE

The combination of healthy deli food and traditional pub fare may seem a little strange, but Rye's does it well. The interior is pub-like, but if the weather is warm, you'll want to be on the streetfront trellised patio. The specialty is smoked meat on rye or in a wrap (all under C$10/US$8.50), a perfect lunchtime meal, although the portions are huge and could pass for dinner. Other notable offerings include Cajun-spiced chicken nachos and a tangy Thai chicken and bacon burger. The most popular breakfast dish — with good reason, as I found out after dining here — is huevos rancheros.

See map p. 238. 73 Carleton St. ☎ 506-472-7937. Reservations not necessary. Main courses: C$7.50–C$17 (US$6.40–US$14.50). AE, MC, V. Open: Mon–Fri 8 a.m.–11 p.m., Sat from 9 a.m., Sun from 10 a.m.

Exploring Fredericton

Queen Street, one block from and running parallel to the Saint John River, is lined with historic sights and attractions. Most major sights are within walking distance of the City Hall at 397 Queen Street, which houses the **Visitor Information Centre** (☎ **506-460-2129**), open mid-May through mid-October daily 8 a.m. to 5 p.m. (July and Aug until 8 p.m.).

Historic Garrison District

Due to its status as the capital of New Brunswick and to the proximity of the United States border, Fredericton was the headquarters to a large contingent of British military personnel. After Confederation in 1867, the military moved on, but much of the character remains within the walls of the old military compound, now protected as the Historic Garrison District National Historic Site, located right downtown. Inside the precinct's wrought-iron fence are a number of historic buildings. In addition to the two attractions discussed below, one room in the imposing Soldiers' Barracks is open to the public (July and Aug daily 10 a.m.–7 p.m.). The cellars of this same building provide a summer home for local artists selling their wares.

Guard House
Downtown

The interior of this solid stone building looks much as it did when occupied by garrison guards in the mid-1800s, complete with muskets at the ready and uniforms hanging along one wall. The adjacent windowless cellblock is also open for inspection. Try to time your visit with the outdoor musical presentations, which take place on the verandah through summer on Wednesdays at 12:30 p.m.

See map p. 238. Carleton St. ☎ 506-460-2129. Admission: Free. Open: July–Aug daily 10 a.m.–6 p.m.

York-Sunbury Historical Society Museum
Downtown

Finding a home in the Officer' Quarters, this old-fashioned museum spills from room with an eclectic display of memorabilia. Much of the space is devoted to telling the story of the Mi'Kmaq and the early European settlers, but expect a couple of surprises, including a stuffed 17-kilogram (37-pound) frog.

See map p. 238. Carleton St. ☎ *506-455-6041. Admission: C$4 (US$3.40) adults, C$3 (US$2.60) seniors, C$2 (US$1.70) children. Open: Mon–Sat 10 a.m.–5 p.m., Sun noon–5 p.m.*

Other Fredericton sights

Beaverbrook Art Gallery
Downtown

A gift to the city from the late press baron Lord Beaverbrook, this is one of Canada's premier art galleries. The building's rather dour exterior belies the treasures inside, most notably Salvador Dali's *Santiago el Grande.* The gallery is also home to an impressive collection of works by other European masters — J.M.W. Turner, John Constable, and Augustus John, as well as works of Canada's best known artists from all eras, including Emily Carr.

Kids are encouraged to try their hand at painting and drawing in a special summer program operated by the gallery. Children aged 5 to 8 are invited to the 10 a.m. session, while those aged 9 to 12 attend the 2 p.m. sitting. Classes last around two hours and cost C$14 (US$11.90) per child.

See map p. 238. 703 Queen St. ☎ *506-458-8545.* www.beaverbrookart gallery.org. *Admission: C$6 (US$5.10) adults, C$5 (US$4.30) seniors, C$3 (US$2.60) children. Open: June–Sept Mon–Fri 9 a.m.–6 p.m., Sat–Sun 10 a.m.–5 p.m.; Oct–May Tues–Fri 9 a.m.–5 p.m., Sat 10 a.m.–5 p.m., Sun noon–5 p.m.*

Christ Church Cathedral
Downtown

For over 150 years, the single spire of this compact Gothic revival church has dominated the Fredericton skyline. Rising regally from the surrounding residences and the tree-lined riverbank, the building was modeled on the 1340 St. Mary's Church in the village of Snettisham, Norfolk.

The most beautiful of many stained-glass windows is on the east side and is best viewed from the nave. From this central location, the morning sun illuminates a seven-paneled scene depicting Christ on the cross, flanked by three apostles on either side. Facing the nave from the northern transept is a massive organ comprising 1,500 pipes.

See map p. 238. 168 Brunswick St. ☎ *506-450-8500. Internet:* www.christchurch cathedral.com. *Church tours (free) are offered mid-June through Aug Mon–Fri 9 a.m.–6 p.m. July–Aug chamber music recitals are held every Fri at 12:10 p.m.*

Old Government House
Downtown

An impressive stone structure set on the banks of the Saint John River, this mansion was built in 1826 as the official residence of the governor, and served as such until 1892. In the ensuing years, it housed a school for the deaf, functioned as a hospital, and was the headquarters of the RCMP in New Brunswick. In the late 1990s, a massive overhaul of the grand old building saw it return to its original use as the home of the lieutenant governor, the representative of the Queen Elizabeth II in New Brunswick. Great care was taken in the restoration work to properly replicate the original look, right down to the carpet and draperies. The governor's living quarters are on the top floor, away from the eyes of the public, but the rest of the building is open for tours throughout the year. Rooms restored to their former look include the library, formal dining room, and drawing room.

See map p. 238. 51 Woodstock Rd. ☎ *506-453-2505. Admission: Free. Open: Mid-June–mid-Sept daily 10 a.m.–5 p.m., mid-Sept–mid-June Mon–Fri 10 a.m.–4 p.m.*

Science East
Downtown

Set in a stone jail that dates to 1840 and was used as a prison until 1996, this fun attraction will keep enquiring minds occupied for at least a few hours. Everywhere you turn are interesting displays and interactive activities — an oversized kaleidoscope, an insectarium, and the chance to create a mini-tornado are the more popular ones. Outdoor amusements center on a large playground. The building's former life has been preserved in the grim dungeon, where displays describe the most notorious inmates and tell the story of the last hanging.

See map p. 238. 668 Brunswick St. ☎ *506-457-2340.* www.scienceeast.nb.ca. *Admission: C$5 (US$4.30) adults, C$3 (US$2.60) children. Open: Mon–Sat 10 a.m.–6 p.m., Sun 1–5 p.m.*

Other cool things to see and do in Fredericton

Fredericton has a well-marked trail system, good for walking or biking. The downtown section extends east from the front of the Fredericton Sheraton to the Princess Margaret Bridge. Along the way is the Trail Bridge, originally built for trains but which now provides a pleasant link to North Fredericton for cyclists and pedestrians.

You can also take a break from sightseeing to:

- ✔ **Climb a lighthouse.** The nationalistic red and white **Fredericton Lighthouse,** at the foot of Regent St. (☎ **506-460-2939**), was built as a tourist attraction. To climb to the top costs C$2 (US$1.70) adults, C$1.50 (US$1.30) seniors and children. At street level is a booking desk for attractions throughout the region. You can also rent bikes and canoes here. It's open July and August daily 10 a.m. to 9 p.m., September daily noon to 7 p.m.

- ✔ **Take a river cruise.** The *Carleton II* takes up to 100 passengers on one-hour cruises along the downtown shoreline. The cost is a very reasonable C$10 (US$8.50) adults, C$5 (US$4.30) children. The departure point is the wharf near the foot of Regent St. (☎ 506-454-2628). Tours run June through August, up to five times daily.

✔ **Explore an urban forest.** At 175-hectare (430-acre) **Odell Park,** ducks frolic on a small pond, trails lead through various forest environments, and large grassy areas are perfect for stretching out and doing absolutely nothing. In the southern section (access from Waggoner's Rd.) is an arboretum containing all of New Brunswick's native tree species.

✔ **Wander among headstones.** Walk up Carleton St. to Brunswick St. to reach the **Old Public Burial Ground,** the final resting place of the city's earliest residents.

✔ **Head back to school.** Founded in 1785, the **University of New Brunswick,** Bailey Dr. (☎ 506-453-4666), is North America's oldest public university. Feel free to walk the grounds.

✔ **Go golfing.** Picturesque **Kingswood Park Golf Course,** south of downtown along Hanwell Rd. (☎ 800-423-5969 or 506-443-3333), stretches over 7,000 yards from the back markers. Big bunkers, rolling fairways, and a 10m (33-foot) waterfall on the signature 14th hole define the layout. Greens fees are C$75 (US$63.80).

Shopping

You may be surprised at the diversity of shops in the downtown area, especially along the lower end of York St., where an old-fashioned drug store, trendy import stores, and secondhand clothing shops sit side by side.

Fredericton has mall shopping along Prospect Street, including the **Fredericton Mall,** at 1150 Prospect St. (☎ 506-458-9226).

Antiques

Old Tyme Collectibles, 40 Main St. (☎ 506-451-9218), is the largest of Fredericton's antique shops. Across the road is **This Old Thing Antiques,** at 173 King St. (☎ 506-454-4317). Both have solid collections of Maritimes furniture and knick-knacks from the late 1800s and early 1900s.

Arts and crafts

The centrally located **Gallery Connexion,** at 453 Queen St. (☎ 506-454-1433) is an artist-operated, not-for-profit outlet where artists work in-situ. Also within the Garrison Historic District is **River Valley Fine Crafts,** a string of vendors with summer-only outlets on the lower level of the Soldier's Barracks (☎ 506-460-2837). Look for handmade soaps and candles, jewelry, knitted clothing, and more. **Aitkens Pewter** has a more traditional setting, at 408 Queen St. (☎ 506-453-9474), along with free tours of their workshop. The **New Brunswick Crafts Council** displays an eclectic range of its members' work at a gallery on 87 Regent St. (☎ 506-450-8989).

Gallery 78, at 796 Queen St. (☎ 506-450-8989), housed in a converted century-old residence just a few blocks east of the main downtown core, is worth visiting to view the building itself. But the art is worth a peek too — the gallery sells mostly contemporary Canadian work at prices that aren't as high as you might expect.

Books

Westminster Books, 445 King St. (☎ 800-561-7323 or 506-454-1442) is Fredericton's premier independent bookstore. You can pick up everything from the latest bestsellers to local fiction, along with maps and specialty guidebooks. For secondhand and rare books, browse the floor-to-ceiling shelves at **Owl's Nest Bookstore,** at 390 Queen St. (☎ 506-458-5509).

Market

The **W.W. Boyce Farmer's Market,** 665 George St. at Regent St. (☎ 506-451-1815), is open year-round, Saturday 6 a.m. to 1 p.m. It attracts hordes of locals who come for fresh produce, meats, and cheeses, as well as local arts and crafts.

Night Life

Fredericton isn't particularly known for its nightlife, but warm summer nights keep numerous decks and patios busy, while the populations of two universities keep the downtown spots busy the rest of the year.

Pubs and clubs

Most pubs and clubs are within walking distance of each other in the downtown core. Here are a few options:

- ✔ The **Lunar Rogue,** 625 King St. (☎ 506-450-2065), is an English-style pub with lots of draught beer choices. The patio hops on hot nights.

- ✔ **Rye's Deli & Bar,** 73 Carleton St. (☎ 506-472-7937), has a small outdoor patio, and books jazz and blues music acts on weekends.

- ✔ **Dolan's Pub,** 349 King St. (☎ 506-454-7474), has a traditional pub atmosphere and live east coast music.

- ✔ The **Dip Pool Bar,** set beside an outdoor swimming pool, is located in the Delta Fredericton at 225 Woodstock Rd. (☎ 506-457-7000), and offers a resort atmosphere.

- ✔ **Upper Deck,** 1475 Piper's Lane (☎ 506-457-1475), is your typical sports bar, with big-screen televisions, pool tables, nightly drink specials, and bands on weekends.

- ✔ **Liquid,** 375 King St. (☎ 506-457-1475), is one of the city's hottest nightclubs.

The arts

Fredericton Playhouse, at 686 Queen St. (☎ **506-458-8344;** www.the
playhouse.ca), is the capital's main venue for performing arts and live
music. Symphony New Brunswick and Theatre New Brunswick regularly
perform here.

A troupe of costumed performers lead theatrical walking tours of the historic precinct three times daily in July and August. The meeting point is
the Soldiers' Barracks, at Queen and Carleton Streets. Call ☎ **506-460-2129**
for times.

Side Trips from Fredericton

The Saint John River flows past Fredericton, draining into the Bay of
Fundy at Saint John. If you're traveling between these two cities, the
detour to pretty Gagetown is well worthwhile.

Upstream of Fredericton are a string of historic riverside towns, along
with Kings Landing Historical Settlement, which re-creates a Loyalist village from 200 years ago.

Gagetown

Historic Gagetown is regarded by many as one of the picturesque villages in all of the Maritimes. Laid out by Loyalists in 1783, the streets lie
parallel to Gagetown Creek and are lined with stately trees and carefully
restored buildings, some over 200 years old. The surrounding countryside is equally appealing — think apple orchards, grazing cattle, and the
wide Saint John River dotted with islands.

To get to Gagetown from Fredericton, follow Route 2 (Trans-Canada
Highway) east for 50km (31 miles) and take Exit 330 to the south.
Following Route 102 from the capital takes a little longer, but the scenery
is more eye-catching.

In the center of the village, Queens County Museum is a whitewashed
home at 69 Front St. (☎ **506-488-2966**) filled with Loyalist antiques.
It's open June to mid-September daily 10 a.m. to 5 p.m. Admission is
C$2 (US$1.70). Gagetown is a fertile ground for shopping. One of my
favorites stores is **Jugglers Cove Fine Arts & Crafts,** 32 Tilley Rd.
(☎ **506-488-2574**), which displays a colorful range of pottery and
paintings. **Loomcrafters,** 23 Loomcraft Lane (☎ **506-488-2400**), located
in a structure dating to 1761 at the east end of Tilley Rd., is the place to
pickup handmade woven items.

Mactaquac and area

The highlight of the Mactaquac area, west of Fredericton, is King's
Landing Historical Settlement, but **Mactaquac Provincial Park** is also
worth exploring. Protecting the shoreline of a reservoir formed by the

Mactaquac Dam, which spans the Saint John River, activities on offer include canoeing (rentals available), golfing (☎ **506-363-4926**), and hiking. To get to the park, cross the Saint John River via Fredericton's Westmorland St. Bridge and follow Route 105 west for 24km (15 miles). Access to the park costs C$7 (US$6) per vehicle per day.

From the park, retrace your path and drive south across the Mactaquac Dam to reach Route 2.

Kings Landing Historical Settlement
King's Landing

Fleeing the American Revolution in 1783, around 15,000 people loyal to Britain headed north to New Brunswick. They established settlements throughout the region, including Saint-Anne, on the site of present-day Fredericton. King's Landing is a re-creation of one of these villages, historically accurate down to the last detail and fun for the whole family. Over 100 costumed staff "live" here, transporting visitors along dirt roads in horse-drawn carts, tending to crops, picking apples in the orchard, crafting horseshoes in the blacksmith shop, and cooking simple meals for visitors in the King's Head Inn. Children will love the outdoor theater program, while all ages will enjoy the ice cream shop.

King's Landing (Exit 253 from Route 2). ☎ *506-363-4999.* www.kingslanding. nb.ca. *Admission C$15 (US$12.80) adults, C$12 (US$10.20) seniors, C$10 (US$8.50) children. Open: June–mid-Oct daily 10 a.m.–5 p.m.*

Kissing bridges

If your travels include driving around New Brunswick, you'll no doubt notice that an abundance of covered wooden bridges dot the province. Now a symbol of New Brunswick, the enclosures, affectionately referred to as "kissing bridges," were originally created to protect the wood from weathering by sun and rain — not to provide an opportunity for a romantic rendezvous. It was estimated that uncovered bridges lasted around ten years, while those that were covered would last many times longer. The fact that 66 covered bridges remain is a testament to their durability.

Some of the easiest bridges to find are along the upper Saint John River Valley. Heading north from Kings Landing, the **Nackawic Siding Covered Bridge** straddles Route 585 west of Millville, while in Benton, west of Meductic, the **Benton Village Covered Bridge** is in a particularly scenic locale.

Further north, the **Hartland Covered Bridge,** in the town of Hartland, stretches for 390m (1,280 feet) across the Saint John River, making it the world's longest covered bridge. The visitor center on the east side of the bridge has displays telling the story of this and other bridges in the province.

Fast Facts: Fredericton

ATMs

Look for ATMs at all downtown banks. Try **CIBC,** at 448 Queen St., and **Bank of Montreal,** at 505 King St.

Emergencies

Dial ☎ **911** for all emergencies.

Hospital

Dr. Everett Chalmers Hospital is at 700 Priestman St. (☎ **506-452-5400**).

Information

Contact **Fredericton Tourism** at ☎ **888-888-4768** or 506-460-2041; www.fredericton. ca. The main visitor center is in **City Hall,** at 397 Queen St. It's open mid-May–mid-Oct daily 8 a.m.–5 p.m., extended hours July–Aug until 8 p.m.

Internet Access

Fredericton Public Library, at 12 Carleton St. (☎ **506-460-2800**), has free Internet access on a first-come, first-served basis.

Police

Dial ☎ **911** in an emergency. For non-emergencies, dial ☎ **506-452-3400**.

Post Office

The main downtown post office is at 570 Queen St.

Restrooms

Militia Arms Store, Historic Garrison District, Carleton St.

Taxis

Call **Checker Cab** (☎ **506-450-8294**), **Loyal Taxi** (☎ **506-455-6789**), or **Standard Taxi** (☎ **506-450-4444**).

Transit Info

The information line for **Fredericton Transit** is ☎ **506-460-2200**.

Weather

Click through the links at the **Environment Canada** Web site (www.weatheroffice. ec.gc.ca) for local forecasts, or call ☎ **506-446-6244** for a recorded message.

Part V
Prince Edward Island

"THAT'S NOT WHAT I MEANT!"

In this part . . .

Potatoes, lobsters, and an orphan girl named Anne are the best-known exports from Prince Edward Island, a serene oasis unlike anywhere else in Canada. Usually referred to simply as "PEI," it may be the country's smallest province, but for many visitors it is the most memorable. Beyond the historic capital of Charlottetown, a patchwork of fields extends in all directions, ringed by red cliffs that descend to usually calm ocean waters. Dotted through this landscape are painted farmhouses, quaint towns, and fishing villages. The island became more accessible in 1997 with the completion of the Confederation Bridge that lings it to the mainland, yet the atmosphere on the island remains mellow. The short summer visiting season attracts visitors from around the world to Cavendish, the setting for *Anne of Green Gables,* while vacationing families are drawn to surrounding beaches.

Chapter 18

Charlottetown

*W*ith a population of 35,000, Charlottetown is Canada's smallest provincial capital and like no other city in the country. A distinct lack of pretense and an unhurried feel make it decidedly un-capital–like, while its tree-lined downtown streets and incredibly rich history only add to the charm.

In summer, the downtown streets of Charlottetown bustle with activity. Its central location makes it a natural draw for visitors and its well-priced lodgings and cultural events make the city a perfect base for day trips to other island destinations (Cavendish, for example, less than an hour's drive away).

Getting There

Sitting in the central portion of Queens County, Charlottetown is at the hub of a varied road system that includes everything from the major thoroughfares to narrow back roads. Most important of these roads is the Trans-Canada Highway, which links Charlottetown to the mainland by bridge and ferry.

By plane

Air Canada has direct flights to Charlottetown from Halifax, Montreal, and Toronto. **WestJet** flies in from Toronto and **Northwest** connects Charlottetown to Detroit. **Charlottetown Airport** is 8km (5 miles) north of downtown. An Airport Facility Fee of C$15 (US$12.80) is incorporated into the fare for departing flights. Charlottetown has no airport shuttle service, but you'll find a row of taxis waiting out front of the arrivals terminal, charging C$10 (US$8.50) per person plus C$2 (US$1.70) for every extra person for the ride downtown.

Confederation Bridge

Completed in 1997, the Confederation Bridge links Prince Edward Island to the rest of Canada. It's the world's longest single-span bridge — 13km (8 miles) from Cape Jourimain, New Brunswick, to Borden-Carleton, just an hour west of Charlottetown in PEI. Built at a cost of almost C$1 billion (US$850 million), it comprises 44 spans, each as long as a city block, and extends up to 20m (66 feet) above Northumberland Strait.

Driving to the island is free. The toll (C$39.50/US$33.60) is only collected on the return journey.

All major **car-rental** companies have airport desks and vehicles are parked within easy walking distance of the arrivals area. The number of vehicles is limited, so be sure to make reservations as far in advance as possible. For information on contacting major car-rental companies, see the Appendix.

By car

The **Trans-Canada Highway** (Highway 1) crosses to Prince Edward Island via the Confederation Bridge, 60km (37 miles) from the capital. If you cross to the island via the ferry, it's a similar distance from the dock to downtown.

By bus

Acadian (☎ 800-567-5151 or 902-628-6432; www.acadianbus.com) has service three times daily between Moncton and Charlottetown, with connections in Moncton from throughout the Maritimes. The Charlottetown bus depot is at 156 Belvedere Avenue. **PEI Express Shuttle** (☎ 877-877-1771 or 902-462-8177; www.peishuttle.com) offers van service between Halifax and Charlottetown for C$50 (US$42.50) each way. The trip takes five hours, with drop-offs made at major hotels in both cities.

Getting Around Charlottetown

The downtown core of Charlottetown is very compact. Almost all the accommodations recommended here are within walking distance of the best restaurants. Scattered throughout are the main city attractions, including the very central **Province House,** with other buildings of historic interest, the best shops, and the harbor all within six blocks.

Downtown streets are laid out in a grid pattern. Those running northwest to southeast end at Water Street, which runs along the harborfront. At its north end, Water Street merges with the eastbound Trans-Canada Highway. University Avenue is the major northbound artery. North of the university, you can take Malpeque Road to Route 2 towards Cavendish and the North Shore, or head west along the Trans-Canada Highway to the Confederation Bridge.

Prince Edward Island

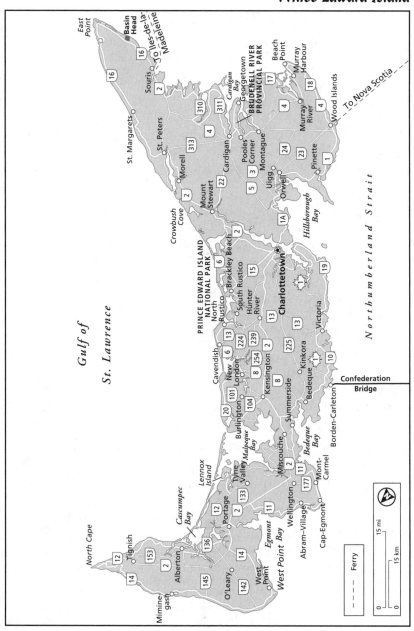

Charlottetown

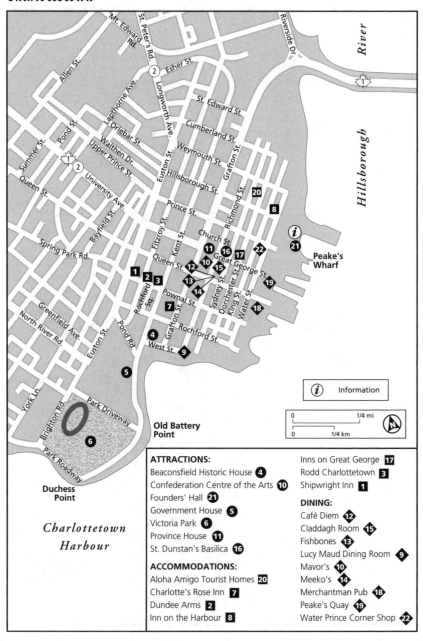

ATTRACTIONS:
Beaconsfield Historic House **4**
Confederation Centre of the Arts **10**
Founders' Hall **21**
Government House **5**
Victoria Park **6**
Province House **11**
St. Dunstan's Basilica **16**

ACCOMMODATIONS:
Aloha Amigo Tourist Homes **20**
Charlotte's Rose Inn **7**
Dundee Arms **2**
Inn on the Harbour **8**

Inns on Great George **17**
Rodd Charlottetown **3**
Shipwright Inn **1**

DINING:
Café Diem **12**
Claddagh Room **15**
Fishbones **13**
Lucy Maud Dining Room **9**
Mavor's **10**
Meeko's **14**
Merchantman Pub **18**
Peake's Quay **19**
Water Prince Corner Shop **22**

Parking

Public parking is spread along Water Street. Parking meters and pay lots cost C$.50 (US$.42) per hour on weekdays. Look for free street parking on the outskirts of downtown (try northeast of Prince St.). Parking is free everywhere on weekends.

The best place to park and start your exploration of the city is the main information center along Water Street at Hillsborough Street. Don't forget to pick up a voucher for one hour's free parking in the adjacent lot at the information center.

Transit and tours

Charlottetown Transit (☎ 902-566-5664) serves mostly residential areas along four routes Monday through Saturday. The fare is C$2 (US$1.70) per sector.

Jump aboard the red double-decker bus operated by **Abegweit Sightseeing Tours** (☎ 902-894-9966) to see all the downtown highlights as well as outlying attractions, such as the Lieutenant Governor's mansion, the University of Prince Edward Island campus, and Victoria Park. The tour takes one hour and is bargain-priced at just C$9.50 (US$8.10). The bus departs June through mid-September up to seven times daily, with pick-up points in front of the Rodd Charlottetown and the Queen Street side of the Confederation Centre of the Arts.

Staying in Charlottetown

Accommodations in Charlottetown are generally well priced and fall within one of two categories: hotels or historic inns. Don't associate the city's lower rates with a lack of services or charm — you get excellent value for your money in Charlottetown, especially during non-summer months.

Because the city is compact, you can plan on walking to all the top attractions and restaurants from your room.

Aloha Amigo Tourist Homes
$ Downtown

Lifetime local Maynard MacMillan has converted two adjacent historic homes into accommodation for travelers on a budget. Each house has a shared bathroom, lounge with cable TV, and fully equipped kitchen. The six guest rooms are brightened by a coat of colorful paint and all are clean and well-maintained. The property is open year round, with discounts outside the summer months.

See map p. 258. 234 Sydney St. ☎ *902-892-9944.* www.alohaamigo.com. *Rack rates: C$50 (US$42.50) double.*

Charlotte's Rose Inn
$$–$$$ **Downtown**

This cozy 1884 Victorian residence is on a quiet, tree-lined street close to everything. The four guest rooms are decorated with period antiques and lots of frilly fabrics. Each has an ensuite bathroom, a TV/VCR combo, original artwork on the walls, and comfortable wingback chairs. The top floor loft apartment has a small kitchen and opens to a private rooftop deck. Downstairs you'll find a parlor stocked with cookies and coffee, and a richly decorated breakfast room. Rates include a full breakfast.

See map p. 258. 11 Grafton St. ☎ *888-237-3699 or 902-892-3699. Fax: 902-894-3699.* www.peisland.com/charlottesinn. *Rack rates: C$139–C$199 (US$118.20–US$169.20) double. AE, MC, V.*

Dundee Arms

$$–$$$ **Downtown**

Built in 1906 as the home of a local entrepreneur, this elaborate Queen Anne Revival building has housed an inn since 1972. It has gone through many changes over the years, including the additions of an English-style pub, a dining room, and a wing of motel rooms. Through it all, the Dundee Arms remains a charming choice for your stay in Charlottetown. Guest rooms in the original building range from cutesy (Anne's Room) to staid (Chandler Suite), but all come packed with niceties, such as bathrobes and Internet access.

See map p. 258. 200 Pownal St. ☎ *877-638-6333 or 902-892-2496. Fax: 902-368-8532.* www.dundeearms.com. *Rack rates: C$145–C$250 (US$123.30–US$212.50) double. AE, DC, MC, V.*

Inns on Great George
$$$–$$$$ **Downtown**

Dating to the early 1800s, three adjoining townhouses bookended by two hotels and a smattering of surrounding buildings make up this grand lodging complex one block from Province House. In its heyday, the Pavilion Hotel at Dorchester Street was the fashionable social center of the city and the accommodation of choice for delegates attending the 1864 Charlottetown Conference. This property now holds the most rooms (24) along with the reception area and a sofa lounge — a comfortable gathering spot where a light breakfast is served each morning. The layout and décor of the guest rooms varies greatly, but all are thoroughly modern (ensuites, air-conditioning, high-speed Internet access, etc.). For a splurge, consider one of the four suites in the Stable House, especially room 222, which features a kitchen, luxurious bathroom, separate bedroom and lounge area with leather furniture and a fireplace. My favorite rooms can be found in the Wellington Hotel, which combines historic charm with modern styling at a reasonable price.

See map p. 258. 58 Great George St. ☎ *800-361-1118 or 902-892-0606. Fax: 902-628-2079.* www.innsongreatgeorge.com. *Rack Rates: C$184–C$349 (US$156.40–US$296.70) double. AE, DC, MC, V.*

Inn on the Harbour
$$–$$$$ Downtown

Opposite Founders' Hall and the main information center, this restored heritage home is close to everything. The stylish heritage-style rooms all have hardwood floors while the more expensive ones come with a fireplace, jetted tub, and water view. A light breakfast is included.

See map p. 258. 3 Hillsborough St. ☎ *877-333-9933 or 902-651-2191. Fax: 902-651-3733.* www.innontheharbourpei.com. *Rack rates: C$120–C$235 (US$102–US$199.80) double. AE, MC, V.*

Rodd Charlottetown
$$ Downtown

A distinctive 1931 red-brick building with grand colonnades flanking its entry, this downtown hotel is perfectly located for the tour group crowd. The marble-floored lobby gives way to 115 elegant guest rooms decorated with period reproductions. Amenities include a largish indoor pool, a fitness room, and a sauna. You can take a break from seafood with the finest cuts of beef in the Carvery Dining Room, or relax with a cocktail in The Provinces lounge before searching out dinner at one of the many nearby restaurants. Weekend discounts are standard year-round, but the best deals are packages advertised on the Rodd Web site.

See map p. 258. 75 Kent St. ☎ *800-565-7633 or 902-894-7371. Fax: 902-368-2178.* www.rodd-hotels.ca. *Parking: Free. Rack rates: C$145 (US$123.30) double. AE, DISC, DC, MC, V.*

Royalty Maples Cottages and Motel
$$ North of Downtown

On the north side of downtown, close to the airport and perfect for getting an early morning start to Cavendish, this lodging is about as un-city-like as you'll ever find. It's comprised of a collection of neat cottages set around a sprawling greenspace — perfect for children. The cottages come with one or two bedrooms and each has a kitchen and cable TV.

Malpeque Rd. (north of the Trans-Canada Hwy.). ☎ *800-381-7829 or 902-368-1030. Fax: 902-566-9242.* www.royaltymaples.com. *Rack rates: motel rooms C$75 (US$63.80) double, cottages C$95–C$105 (US$80.80–US$89.30) double. AE, MC, V.*

Shipwright Inn
$$–$$$$ **Downtown**

The water views that the original owner, a local shipbuilder, enjoyed from this 1860s home are long gone, but the building's solid timber construction — including the original hardwood floors — remains through extensive restoration work. The end result is one of Charlottetown's premier accommodations. Each of the nine guest rooms has its own character and configuration, but what they have in common is a distinct historic charm and a subtle maritime theme. The rooms have amenities you'd expect in a hotel — TV, air-conditioning, telephone — as well as many you wouldn't, like goose down duvets and nautical-themed antiques. Even the smallest unit, the Chart Room (which really isn't that small) has a fireplace, a walnut four-poster bed, and, of course, nautical charts on the walls. Breakfast is taken in a communal dining area, although I found myself sneaking back through the day for the complimentary homemade goodies and freshly squeezed lemonade.

See map p. 258. 51 Fitzroy St. ☎ *888-306-9966 or 902-368-1905. Fax: 902-628-1905.* www.shipwrightinn.com. *Rack rates: C$135–C$280 (US$114.80–US$238) double. MC, V.*

Dining in Charlottetown

Charlottetown's local dining scene is surprisingly vibrant, thanks to a healthy student population and thriving tourism industry.

Café Diem
$ **Downtown CAFE**   *Best Inexpensive Dining*

Of Charlottetown's small selection of cafés, this is the best. You can take advantage of the tree-shaded tables out front or check your e-mail on computer terminals lined along the narrow indoor loft. The blackboard menu is crammed with healthy choices — salads, soups, curries, and more — all under C$10 (US$8.50).

See map p. 258. 128 Richmond St. ☎ *902-892-0494. Lunches: C$6–C$10 (US$5.10–US$8.50). MC, V. Open: Daily 9 a.m.–midnight.*

Claddagh Room
$$$–$$$$ **Downtown SEAFOOD**

Owner/chef Liam Dolan named this restaurant for a fishing village in his Irish homeland, and naturally the menu features mostly seafood with a small selection of other dishes. Choose between lobster-stuffed mushrooms and orange salad with almonds to start, or dive right into typical mains like jumbo shrimp Creole or herb-crusted honey mustard lamb chops. On Friday evening, the crowd comes for prime rib and Yorkshire pudding. A handsome, old-fashioned dining room, sharp service, and a delicious dessert selection round out what many consider to be Charlottetown's finest restaurant.

See map p. 258. 131 Sydney St. ☎ *902-892-9661. Main courses: C$18–C$30 (US$15.30–US$25.60). AE, MC, V. Open: Mon–Fri 11:30 a.m.–2 p.m., daily 5–10 p.m.*

Fishbones
$$–$$$ **Downtown** **SEAFOOD**

This glorified oyster bar is on Victoria Row, a short section of Richmond Street that is designated pedestrian-only throughout the summer months. Choose to dine at tables out on the sidewalk, or inside at regular tables and in very private booths. Malpeque Bay oysters are a natural starter. They sit on a massive bed of ice, accompanied by your choice of sauces for C$2 (US$1.70) each. Other sample starters are bacon-wrapped scallops and steamed mussels broiled in a garlic broth; mains include almond-crusted halibut and delicious chicken and lobster casserole. Lunches are mostly under $12, including tangy lemon-peppered haddock.

See map p. 258. 136 Richmond St. ☎ *902-628-6569. Reservations not necessary. Main courses: C$15–C$23 (US$12.80–US$20). MC, V. Open: Daily 11 a.m.–11 p.m.*

Lucy Maud Dining Room   *ⒷEST Inexpensive Dining*
$$–$$$ **Downtown** **MODERN CANADIAN**

Students at the highly regarded Culinary Institute of Canada prepare lunch and dinner, then enthusiastically serve it to the public as part of their training at this large restaurant. Dining here is a wonderful opportunity to enjoy fine food at reasonable prices. Be sure to snag a window seat to enjoy views that extend over Charlottetown Harbour. The menu changes each semester and is based on seasonal specialties, such as Cornish game hen in the fall. Seafood chowder is a thankful staple. End your meal with one of the extravagant desserts.

See map p. 258. 4 Sydney St. ☎ *902-894-6868. Reservations recommended. Main courses: C$16–C$27 (US$13.60–US$23). AE, MC, V. Open: Tues–Fri 11:30 a.m.– 1:30 p.m., Tues–Sat 6–8 p.m.*

Mavor's
$$ **Downtown** **CONTEMPORARY**

The bland looking Confederation Centre of the Arts is hiding a surprise. Mavor's is an ultra-slick bistro where the fare includes sweet potato fries served with sides of sour cream and mustard mayo dip (a personal favorite), salmon burger topped with mango tartar sauce, and smoked salmon fettuccine. The kitchen hours are given below, but you can order Starbucks coffee daily 8 a.m.–8 p.m., complete with the fancy names.

See map p. 258. 145 Richmond St. ☎ *902-628-6107. Main courses: C$9–C$16 (US$7.70–US$13.60). AE, MC, V. Open: Daily 11 a.m.–2 p.m. and 5–9 p.m.*

A moolicious treat

Wowie Cowie. Deja Moo. Gooey Mooey. These are three of over 30 flavors you'll be confronted with at **COWS,** an island institution whose ice cream holds up against the best Ben & Jerry's can offer (I've "researched" both). COWS uses handmade waffle cones and an old-fashioned recipe that calls for the freshest island cream. Started from a single outlet in Cavendish, the company now has two stores in Charlottetown (one at Queen and Grafton Sts. and another at Peake's Wharf), one in Gateway Village (at the north end of Confederation Bridge), another onboard the Caribou–Wood Islands ferry, and others as far away as Park City (Utah).

The ice cream may be traditional, but the associated COWS fashion line is anything but — the distinctive and colorful t-shirts make a wonderful souvenir. Look for them in all COWS stores or purchase online at www.cows.ca.

Meeko's
$–$$ **Downtown GREEK**

At Meeko's you'll find the best Greek food on Prince Edward Island, served in a nationalistic blue and white room with murals on the walls and mellow Greek music in the background. You can take a break from seafood by choosing a tzatziki and mousakka combo, which will set you back just $20. The same menu is offered all day, with well-priced salad and sandwich choices at lunchtime.

See map p. 258. 146 Richmond St. ☎ *902-892-9800. Main courses: C$10–C$19 (US$8.50–US$16.20). MC, V. Open: Daily 11 a.m.–10 p.m.*

Merchantman Pub
$$ **Downtown PUB FARE**

In an 1850s building across from Confederation Landing Park, the Merchantman is a typical British-style pub — think dim lighting, exposed beams, and red-brick walls — with an ambitious selection of food that goes well beyond the traditional bangers and mash. You can order all sorts of fresh seafood, chicken, and steaks, some prepared with Cajun or Asian influences. While researching this edition I ordered fish and chips followed by sticky raisin pudding in rum sauce, a delicious combination that came to under C$20 (US$17.10).

See map p. 258. 23 Queen St. (at Water St.). ☎ *902-892-9150. Main courses: C$13–C$20 (US$11.10–US$17.10). AE, MC, V. Open: Mon–Sat 11:30 a.m.–11:30 p.m.*

Peake's Quay
$-$$ Downtown   PUB FARE/SEAFOOD

Peake's Quay offers a wonderful waterfront location and well-priced food, though the service is not exactly stellar. This restaurant-cum-bar takes full advantage of its upstairs location with garage-style doors opening to a huge deck overlooking the marina. The menu mixes regular pub food with maritime staples like seafood chowder served in a bread bowl, lobster rolls, and a boiled lobster that comes with all the usual trimmings. Desserts are all around C$5 (US$4.30), or head to the COWS ice cream shop directly below for a scoop to go.

See map p. 258. 1 Great George St. (at Water St.) ☎ *902-368-1330. Main courses: C$9–C$18 (US$7.70–US$15.30). AE, DISC, DC, MC, V. Open: Daily 11 a.m.–10 p.m.*

Water Prince Corner Shop
$-$$$ Downtown   SEAFOOD

Disguised as a corner shop at the corner of Water and Prince Streets, this local favorite dishes up the freshest seafood at very reasonable prices. While not particularly creative, the menu covers all the familiar choices, including boiled lobster dinners, Malpeque oysters, steamed mussels, and seafood chowder. The patio is a popular spot on warm evenings, but this friendly restaurant draws a crowd throughout its limited season.

See map p. 258. 141 Water St. ☎ *902-368-3212. Main courses: C$9–C$22 (US$7.70–US$18.70). MC, V. Open: May–Oct. daily 9:30 a.m.–8 p.m.*

Exploring Charlottetown

As the provincial capital, Charlottetown has a number of major attractions. Most notable among them are Founders' Hall and Province House, both of particular interest to Canadians. One thing that everyone should do in Charlottetown is stroll through the narrow streets between Province House and the waterfront, where the mix of residential and commercial architecture has remained unchanged for over a century.

Beaconsfield Historic House
Downtown

Built in 1877 for local shipbuilder James Peake Junior, this gracious home is one of the finest pre-1900 residences on the island. From the street, it's the sharp yellow exterior and gingerbread trim that will catch your eye. Inside, you'll find an impressive 25 rooms and eight fireplaces. The first two of three floors are furnished, while a narrow stairway leads to the belvedere, a turret with water views. Special events include musical performances and a weekday children's program in the adjacent carriage house. The on-site bookstore has a solid collection of island literature.

See map p. 258. 2 Kent St. (at West St.) ☎ *902-368-6603. Admission: C\$4.25 (US\$3.60) adults. Open: July–Aug daily 10 a.m.–5 p.m.*

Confederation Centre of the Arts
Downtown

This large, boxy structure in the heart of downtown is at odds with surrounding historic buildings, but once inside, you'll find many redeeming features, including the largest art gallery east of Montreal. The Confederation Centre Art Gallery is highlighted by the luminaries of Canadian art through the last 200 years. Many of the names won't be familiar (even to most Canadians), but Gordon Smith sculptures, paintings by the husband-and-wife team of Christopher and Mary Pratt, and works by Robert Harris are standouts. The center also has three theaters (see Night Life later in this chapter), a large library with first editions of *Anne of Green Gables*, a craft shop, a memorial hall, and a café. Through summer, it hosts the Charlottetown Festival, which includes daily lunchtime entertainment at an amphitheater by the main entrance.

See map p. 258. 145 Richmond St. ☎ *902-566-1267.* www.confederation centre.com. *Gallery admission: free. Gallery hours: June–Sept daily 9 a.m.–5 p.m. Oct–May Wed–Sat 11 a.m.–5 p.m., Sun 1–5 p.m.*

Founders' Hall
Downtown

Using innovative state-of-the-art displays, this waterfront attraction transports visitors back in time to the 1864 Charlottetown Conference. It is contained within a historic railway building just steps from where the Fathers of Confederation stepped ashore. You begin your journey by entering the Time Tunnel, stepping back to life in the 1860s. The tunnel opens to the octagonal Hall of the Fathers, which describes the men who met to discuss the formation of the country. Beyond this exhibit is a string of rooms, each dedicated to a province or territory, linking up in the order they joined the Dominion of Canada. Along the way, televisions, computer terminals, headsets, trivia games, and dynamic audiovisual displays enhance the story.

See map p. 258. 6 Prince St. ☎ *902-368-1864.* www.foundershall.ca. *Admission: C\$7 (US\$6) adults, C\$6 (US\$5.10) seniors, C\$3.75 (US\$3.20) children. Open: mid-May–mid-Oct Mon–Sat 9 a.m.–5 p.m., Sun 9 a.m.–4 p.m.; July–Aug Mon–Sat until 7 p.m.*

Walk the walk

Joining a walking tour with the **Confederation Players** (☎ 800-955-1864 or 902-368-1864), a group of eager locals dressed in Confederation-era garb, is a great way to learn a little about Charlottetown while taking advantage of warm summer temperatures. Choose from three tours: a trip back in time along Great George Street; , the Settlers Tour, which recounts locals of note; or Ghostly Realm, an evening stroll through cemeteries and back alleys. All depart Founders' Hall June through mid-September one to three times daily and cost C$5 (US$4.30). Historical re-enactments on the steps of Province House (July through Aug daily at 2:30 p.m.; free) are part of the same program.

Government House and Victoria Park
Downtown

Perched on a slight rise at the edge of downtown, the 1835 Government House is the official residence of the Lieutenant-Governor. The grounds are not open to the public, but the grand mansion is clearly visible through stands of mature white birch.

Beyond Government House, Kent Street passes through Victoria Park, a pleasant green space that ends at the shoreline of Charlottetown Harbour. The best way to enjoy the park is on foot (although you'll be passed by a stream of jogging, skating, and biking locals). Near the entrance to the park, a row of six antique cannons points to the harbor entrance.

See map p. 258. Take Kent St. southwest through downtown.

Province House
Downtown

Still the seat of the provincial legislature, Province House is where the Fathers of Confederation met in 1864 to discuss the formation of the Dominion of Canada. This landmark meeting took place in the second-floor chamber, which has been restored to the way it looked back then, right down to the original furniture, and has an adjacent clerk's office and library. Also on the second floor is the current Legislative Chamber, a smallish room that looks to have changed little in well over a century. Traditions are well entrenched here — the premier gets a small flag on his desk and the ruling party is always seated on the south side of the room, a throwback to the days before central heating when the afternoon sun warmed only this part of the chamber. You can walk through by yourself, but the guided tour is highly recommended.

See map p. 258. 165 Richmond St. (at St. George St.). ☎ *902-566-7626. Admission: free. Open: June–Sept daily 8:30 a.m.–5 p.m., Oct–May Mon–Fri 9 a.m.–5 p.m.*

St. Dunstan's Basilica
Downtown

Distinctive for its twin Gothic spires, St. Dunstan's Basilica is one of Canada's largest churches. The interior is notable for its intricate vaulted ceiling, ornate Italian carvings, and polished marble columns.

See map p. 258. 45 Great George St. ☎ *902-894-3486. Admission: free. Open: Daily 8 a.m.–5 p.m.*

Other cool things to see and do

When you've had your fill of downtown attractions, and are ready for other diversions or sights lying beyond city limits, here are a few possibilities:

- **Peake's Wharf Boat Cruises** (☎ 902-566-4458), departing from Peake's Wharf on Water St. June through September. Choose from harbor tours with full commentaries (1, 6:30, and 8 p.m.; C$18/US$15.30) or a seal-watching excursion (2:30 p.m.; C$25/US$21.30).

- The **Farmer's Market,** on Belvedere Ave., opposite the university. Vendors at this indoor market sell everything from fresh seafood to island-made crafts. It operates year-round Saturday 9 a.m.–2 p.m.

- **Orwell Corner Historical Village,** 30km/18.6 miles east of Charlottetown (☎ 902-651-8510). Experience life in the 1850s at this restored farming community. The village is open late May through mid-October Monday to Friday 9 a.m.– 4:30 p.m., plus weekends in July and August. Admission is C$7.50 (US$6.40) adults, C$3 (US$2.60) children.

- **Port-la-Joye–Fort Amherst National Historic Site,** a pleasant 35-minute drive west, then south, from downtown (☎ 902-566-7626). Not much remains of the island's first European settlement, which was established in 1720, but a visitor center (mid-June through Aug daily 9 a.m.–5 p.m.) at the site tells its story. The surrounding grounds are a great place for a picnic.

Shopping

As the hub of Prince Edward Island, Charlottetown shops cater well to the needs of islanders, with a nod to the tourists down on the waterfront along Water St. For mall shopping, head north from downtown along

University Avenue. Here are some of my favorite shops in Charlottetown (in no particular order):

- ✔ **Anne of Green Gables Chocolates** (102 Queen St., ☎ 902-368-3171) is the place for sweet tooths to pick up edible souvenirs.

- ✔ **Island Crafts Shop** (156 Richmond St., ☎ 902-892-5152) is crammed with arts and crafts, including woodwork and weaved items.

- ✔ **Details Past and Present** (166 Richmond St., ☎ 902-892-2233) displays fine art in the front and an eclectic range of antiques out back.

- ✔ **Pilar Shephard Art Gallery** (82 Great George St., ☎ 902-892-1953) is another fine art gallery. It features island landscapes and Mi'Kmaq artwork.

- ✔ **Gallery 18** (41 Grafton St., ☎ 902-628-8869) holds an impressive collection of antiquarian books, maps, and charts.

- ✔ **Moonsnail Soapworks** (85 Water St., ☎ 888-771-7127) specializes in handmade soaps and other body treats.

- ✔ **PEI Specialty Chip Co.** is based in Marshfield, northeast of Charlottetown (☎ 902-629-1818), but look for their lobster-flavored potato chips at retail outlets throughout the city.

- ✔ **Canada Eh?**, in Founders' Hall (6 Prince St., ☎ 902-368-1864), is crammed with Canadian souvenirs — maple syrup, smoked salmon, wooden fishermen, Canadian flag kites, and more.

Nightlife

No one could ever describe Charlottetown as a hotbed of after-dark action, but still, something is usually going on somewhere.

The Buzz is a free publication with listings of what's happening throughout Charlottetown. It comes out monthly, or check the online version at www.isn.net/buzzon. The Web site www.visitcharlottetown.com lists festivals and events, including all performing arts.

Of course, you can also drop by the Visitor Information Centre on Water St. (☎ 902-368-7795) to find out what's on when you're in town.

Pubs and clubs

Victoria Row, a short section of Richmond Street between Queen and Great George Streets, is designated as pedestrian-only through summer. The local restaurants and bars set tables out across the sidewalk and some have live music.

Most pubs open at 11 a.m. and close at midnight through the week, and at 1 a.m. on weekends.

Around the corner from Victoria Row, the **Olde Dublin Pub,** 131 Sydney St. (☎ 902-892-6992) is a lively Celtic-styled bar, often with live Maritime music and always with pints of Guinness. In the same vicinity, **Gahan House,** 126 Sydney St. (☎ 902-626-2337) is PEI's only brewpub — and it's a good one. Six ales are brewed in-house, including a stout that gets rave reviews. The food is also a cut above pub grub (the beer-battered haddock and chips are delicious). Named for one of the delegates at the Charlottetown Conference, **D'Arcy McGee's** sits in the heart of the city at the corner Prince and Kent Streets (☎ 902-894-3627). Inside is a fun and fittingly British atmosphere, with visitors and regulars mixing easily. Overlooking the harbor, **Peake's Quay,** 1 Great George St. at Water St. (☎ 902-368-1330) has a slightly more touristy feel than the other places.

The club scene in Charlottetown is dominated by **Myron's,** at 151 Kent St. (☎ 902-892-4375), a two-story complex that books bands ranging from rock to country Wednesday to Saturday for the downstairs stage. The upstairs crowd is equally diverse, dancing to everything from hip hop to disco, Thursday through Saturday.

The arts

The **Confederation Centre of the Arts,** at 145 Richmond St. (☎ 800-565-0278 or 902-628-1864; www.confederationcentre.com) hosts the Charlottetown Festival June through September. This theatrical event combines outdoor performances, a children's theater, and two or three musical productions. The star of the show is *Anne of Green Gables—The Musical,* a family-oriented production that brings Lucy Maud Montgomery's most famous character to life. Showtime is Monday to Saturday at 8 p.m. with additional 2 p.m. matinees in July and August on Monday, Wednesday, and Saturday. Expect to pay C$21 to C$64 (US$17.90–US$54.40) adults, half price for children.

Harness racing

Locals who attend harness racing meets at **Charlottetown Driving Park,** 46 Kensington Rd. (☎ 902-892-6823), do so to gamble, so the operators welcome them with open arms — letting everyone in for free. Races are held on Saturdays May through January as well as Thursdays in summer; race time is 7:30 p.m. (call to confirm the schedule).

Fast Facts: Charlottetown

ATMs

Look for ATMs at most banks, including the **CIBC** at Queen and Grafton Streets. A growing number of grocery stores and gas stations also have ATMs, but beware of additional charges.

Emergencies

Dial ☎ 911 for all emergencies.

Hospital

Queen Elizabeth Hospital is at 60 Riverside Dr. (☎ **902-894-2095**).

Pharmacy

Murphy's Pharmacy, at 24 St. Peters Rd. (☎ **902-894-4449**), is open Mon–Fri 8 a.m.–10 p.m., Sat–Sun 9 a.m.–10 p.m.

Information

The **Visitor Information Centre** is at 178 Water St. (☎ **902-368-4444;** www.visit charlottetown.com). It's open July–Aug daily 8 a.m.–10 p.m.; Sept–June Mon–Fri 9 a.m.–4:30 p.m.

Internet Access

Café Diem, at 128 Richmond Street (☎ **902-892-0494**) has public computers with a high-speed Internet connection.

Police

For emergencies, dial ☎ **911**; for general **RCMP** matters call ☎ **902-368-9300**.

Post Office

The main post office is at 135 Kent St.

Restrooms

Public restrooms can be found in Founders' Hall on Water St.

Taxis

Recommended companies include **City Taxi** (☎ **902-892-6567**), **Co-op Taxi Line** (☎ **902-628-8200**), and **Yellow Cab** (☎ **902-566-6666**).

Transit Info

Local bus service is provided by **Charlottetown Transit** (☎ **902-566-5664**). See "Getting Around Charlottetown," earlier in this chapter, for details.

Weather

Environment Canada maintains a website at www.weatheroffice.ec.gc.ca with links to the forecast in Charlottetown, as well as locations around Prince Edward Island.

Chapter 19

Cavendish

Cavendish is known worldwide through the writing of Lucy Maud Montgomery, who used her childhood in the idyllic island setting as inspiration for her timeless tale, *Anne of Green Gables*. The setting for the book was Green Gables, a farmhouse now protected as a National Historic Site, which, along with other spots related to the author and her writing, will keep fans of Anne occupied for at least a full day.

The tranquility of the "Avonlea" that Montgomery wrote about so floridly has mostly gone, thanks somewhat ironically to the popularity of the book. Cavendish's main thoroughfare is lined with theme parks, accommodations, and other touristy offerings. The only thing stopping commercial sprawl from spreading to the adjacent coastline is Prince Edward Island National Park, which protects long stretches of red-sand beach and provides prime habitat for over 100 species of birds.

Cavendish has served as a summer retreat for decades. You need only to take a drive through the rolling rural landscape, spend time down on the beach, or walk the wooded trails to see why families return year after year. The off-season, however, really does mean lights off. November through April almost everything is closed, including most accommodations and all the attractions and restaurants.

Getting There

Cavendish is 40km (25 miles) northwest of Charlottetown. To get there from the capital, take Route 15 to Brackley Beach, then head west on Route 6; or take Route 2 west to Hunter River, followed by Route 13 north through New Glasgow.

Cavendish and Prince Edward Island National Park

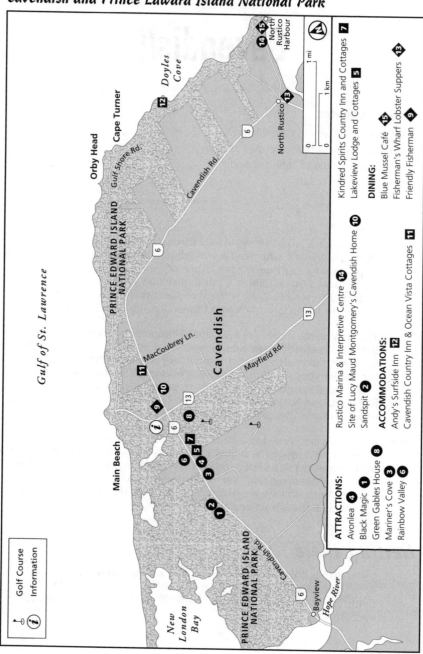

ATTRACTIONS:
Avonlea **4**
Black Magic **1**
Green Gables House **8**
Mariner's Cove **3**
Rainbow Valley **6**
Rustico Marina & Interpretive Centre **14**
Site of Lucy Maud Montgomery's Cavendish Home **10**
Sandspit **2**
Kindred Spirits Country Inn and Cottages **7**
Lakeview Lodge and Cottages **5**

ACCOMMODATIONS:
Andy's Surfside Inn **12**
Cavendish Country Inn & Ocean Vista Cottages **11**

DINING:
Blue Mussel Café **15**
Fisherman's Wharf Lobster Suppers **13**
Friendly Fisherman **9**

Staying in Cavendish

As well as being inundated with visitors from around the world, Cavendish is very popular with families on summer vacation. For travel in July and August, you should reserve accommodations as far in advance as possible. Discounted rooms and a lack of crowds make June and September a fine time to visit Cavendish; in early September, it's still warm enough to swim in the ocean, yet you'll find rooms discounted up to 50 percent.

Andy's Surfside Inn
$ North Rustico

This rambling whitewashed, red-roofed home sits above a pebbly beach 3km (1.9 miles) east of Cavendish. The nine rooms are basic and share bathrooms, but the seaside setting is gorgeous. Guests have use of a kitchen, barbeques, and bikes. Rates include continental breakfast.

See map p. 274. Gulf Shore Rd., between North Rustico and Cavendish. ☎ *902-963-2405. Fax: 902-963-2341. Rack rates: C$50–C$75 (US$42.50–US$63.80) double. MC, V. Open: June–Nov.*

Cavendish Country Inn & Ocean Vista Cottages
$$–$$$ Cavendish

Choose between motel units, bed and breakfast rooms, or lovely wooden cottages at this modern resort within walking distance of both the national park and Cavendish. The cottages (from C$160/US$136) are the best value. Each has a deck with outdoor furniture and a barbeque, while inside, lots of polished wood and comfortable furnishings create an inviting atmosphere. Also on the property is a playground and outdoor heated pool.

See map p. 274. Route 6, 1km (0.6 miles) east of Route 13, Cavendish. ☎ *800-454-4853 or 902-963-2181. Fax: 902-963-3213.* www.cavendishpei.com. *Rack rates: C$109–C$350 (US$92.70–US$297.50) double. AE, MC, V. Open: May–mid-Oct.*

Kindred Spirits Country Inn and Cottages
$$$–$$$$ Cavendish

In the heart of Cavendish, but set well away from the busy main road, this delightful country estate is a world away from the rest of the bustling village. Green Gables Heritage Site is reached along Lover's Lane, a walking trail that remains exactly as described by Montgomery in *Anne of Green Gables*. The local golf course is even closer. Guest rooms in the inn are country cozy and loaded with local antiques. Three price levels are offered: the lower-priced rooms include all the basics, while more expensive rooms add a balcony and a fireplace. Surrounding the inn are 14 luxurious cottages, each with kitchen, color TV, and a deck with a barbeque. The most expensive cottages have a king-size bed, air-conditioning, fireplace, and hot tub. Regardless of the type of accommodation chosen, all guests can enjoy the playground area and outdoor heated pool.

See map p. 274. Memory Lane, off Route 6, Cavendish. ☎ *800-461-1755 or 902-963-2434. Fax: 902-963-2619.* www.kindredspirits.ca. *Rack rates: inn rooms C$120–C$245 (US$102–US$208.30) double, cottages C$185–C$400 (US$157.30–US$340). MC, V. Open: Inn mid-May–mid-Oct, cottages year-round.*

Lakeview Lodge and Cottages
$$–$$$$ Cavendish

Close to everything, this large property features a heated outdoor pool, a barbeque area, a playground, and a variety of room choices. Basic motel rooms can be had for under C$100 (US$85). From June to September, the kitchen-equipped duplex cottages offer the best value for larger groups. Freestanding executive cottages, each with a kitchen and private deck, are a step up in quality (and price) while two modern suites in the main lodge are also well priced. In June and September, Lakeview has great off-season specials with rates reduced up to 50 percent.

See map p. 274. Route 6, Cavendish. ☎ *800-565-7550 or 902-963-2436. Fax: 902-963-2493.* www.lakeviewlodge.cc. *Rack rates: C$91–C$350 (US$77.40–US$297.50) double. MC, V. Open: Late May–early Oct.*

Dining in Cavendish

The Cavendish dining scene reflects that of local accommodations — touristy, mostly overpriced, and always busy. Thankfully, a number of alternatives lie in surrounding villages.

Blue Mussel Café   *"Best Seafood"*
$$–$$$ North Rustico Harbour   SEAFOOD

pg. 307

My favorite dining spot on all of Prince Edward Island is the Blue Mussel Café. The café is terribly small, but that's a good thing if you manage to get a table. Most of the seating is outside, on an old dock that catches the evening sun and has views extending back down the harbor. You can't go wrong with any of the seafood, like creamy chowder or lobster pâté to start, followed by a full lobster or poached fish, such as haddock or salmon. Best of all, the Blue Mussel must be one of the few seafood restaurants anywhere in the Maritimes without a deep fryer.

See map p. 274. Harbourview Dr., North Rustico Harbour. ☎ *902-963-2152. Main courses: C$11.50–C$19 (US$9.80–US$16.15). Open: Late June–Sept daily 11:30 a.m.–8 p.m.*

Fisherman's Wharf Lobster Suppers   *"Best Seafood"*
$$ North Rustico   SEAFOOD

A little more commercialized than the New Glasgow Lobster Supper (a bit later in this chapter), the North Rustico version is otherwise very similar.

Over 400 diners can be seated at once in the cavernous restaurant, which is lined on one side by a long buffet of hot and cold appetizers and desserts. Tables feature paper placemats that describe how lobsters are caught and, more importantly, the best way to eat them.

See map p. 274. Route 6, North Rustico. ☎ *902-963-2669. Lobster supper: from C$28 (US$23.80). AE, MC, V. Open: Mid-June–mid-Oct daily noon –9 p.m.*

Friendly Fisherman
$$ Cavendish BUFFET

I thought I should include at least one restaurant in Cavendish, so I joined the throngs of families and entered the fray to research the Friendly Fisherman, right at the town's main intersection. (It was friendly enough, but there wasn't a fisherman in sight.) Because this buffet restaurant is perpetually busy, the turnover of food is fast, which keeps the salads fresh and the hot food hot. Seafood is limited to a lasagna and a couple of baked fish dishes, but there are plenty of other choices. Beer and wine is extra, but well priced. Pay for a ticket at the front door and wait your turn for a table. Children pay C$1 (US85¢) for every year of age. Breakfast and lunch are served cafeteria-style.

See map p. 274. Route 6, Cavendish. ☎ *902-963-2234. Buffet dinner: C$15 (US$12.80). AE, DC MC, V. Open: Mid-June–mid-Oct daily 8 a.m.–9 p.m.*

Lovin' lobster

Believe it or not, it wasn't that long ago that the supply of lobster exceeded demand so much that islanders used it as fertilizer. Things have changed, though; lobster is now promoted as a delicacy across the Maritimes. The trapping season for lobsters is short, but the lobsters are held live in holding tanks so they can be offered fresh year-round.

Lobsters served in restaurants and at lobster suppers usually weigh around one pound, which provides enough of the rich meat for most people. They are generally served whole, challenging diners to extract as much of the meat as they can using fingers, lobster crackers, and skewers. It can be a messy process, so most places — even upscale restaurants — supply a bib.

One of the best things about lobster is that it tastes best simply boiled, which means you can do the cooking yourself (many accommodations provide big pots especially for this purpose). **Doiron Fisheries,** on the dock at North Rustico (☎ **902-963-2442**), is the best place around Cavendish to buy lobster. Expect to pay around C$10 (US$8.50) per pound, live or precooked. This seafood market is also the place to pick up Malpeque Bay oysters, mussels, clams, and fresh fish. It's open May to early October, daily 8 a.m. to 8 p.m.

New Glasgow Lobster Supper
$$ **New Glasgow** SEAFOOD

Held in community halls and restaurants throughout the province, lobster suppers are informal, fun, and good value. The one at New Glasgow is the oldest, having been in operation since 1958. Here, up to 500 diners can be seated at once in a two-level riverside building with its own lobster holding pond. Chose the size of lobster you want (1–2 pounds) and enjoy all-you-can-eat chowder, mussels, salad, breads, desserts, and non-alcoholic beverages for a set price. If you want to pass on the lobster as a main, breaded scallops, haddock, and roast beef are offered as alternatives. Children under 12 get their own menu, which includes a lobster supper for C$12 (US$10.20), and kids 3 and under eat for free. To get to New Glasgow, take Route 13 southeast from Cavendish. The big building is impossible to miss across the river in New Glasgow.

Route 258, New Glasgow. ☎ *902-964-2870. Lobster supper: from C$26 (US$22.10). AE, MC, V. Open: June–mid-Oct daily 4–8:30 p.m.*

Exploring Cavendish

The sites associated with *Anne of Green Gables* are somewhat overshadowed by amusement parks and tacky tourist traps (although you won't hear any complaints from children). I've divided this section up accordingly, with some suggestions for touring beyond Cavendish sandwiched in between.

Anne attractions

Separating fact from fiction is somewhat difficult when it comes to visiting the childhood haunts of Lucy Maud Montgomery, many of which ended up in her famous novels and are now shrines to fans from around the world.

Anne of Green Gables Museum
Park Corner

Owned and operated by relatives of Montgomery, this museum is housed at Silver Bush, a name given to the home of the Campbell family who appear in two of her novels. The residence is decked out in period furnishings and a selection of the author's personal belongings is on display. The parlor, where Montgomery was married in 1911, is now a popular spot for Japanese couples to say their vows. You can relax in the small tea room, which serves hot drinks and homemade goodies, or enjoy a carriage ride (C$9/US$7.70 per family) along the nearby beach.

Route 20, 24km (15 miles) west of Cavendish. ☎ *902-436-7329. Admission: C$2.50 (US$2.10) adults, C$1 (US85¢) children. Open: May–Oct daily 9 a.m.–4:30 p.m., extended hours July–Aug daily 9 a.m.–6 p.m.*

Anne's land

Anne of Green Gables chronicled the life of Anne Shirley, a lovable character created by Canada's best-known author, Lucy Maud Montgomery (1874–1942). Although the enduring tale of the red-haired orphan girl and her life at Avonlea was fictional, it drew on Montgomery's own experiences growing up in her grandparents' Cavendish home and spending her younger days exploring the rural surroundings.

On the island, the tale has spawned an entire industry. *Anne of Green Gables* has been translated into dozens of languages and has been reprinted over 100 times. The character of Anne has been recreated in a musical and television drama. Half a world away, it is even part of the official curriculum in Japanese schools — and hence Cavendish receives large numbers of Japanese visitors.

If you're an Anne fan, it's worth planning your time in Cavendish to coincide with the **L.M. Montgomery Festival** (www.lmmontgomeryfestival.com), held annually on the second weekend of August. Festivities include readings, a coloring competition at the local schoolhouse, and afternoon high tea, served outdoors at the site of Montgomery's childhood home.

Avonlea
Cavendish

Of the many amusement parks in Cavendish, only Avonlea, which reconstructs Montgomery's version of rural PEI, has any connection to *Anne of Green Gables*. The park comprises a general store, a church, farm animals, old-fashioned games, themed rides, and a chocolate factory (which wasn't in the book, but is a popular spot nevertheless). Throughout the day, costumed performers go about their business: milking cows, leading pony rides, giving dance lessons — and did I mention the chocolate factory?

See map p. 274. Route 6, Cavendish. ☎ *902-963-3050. Admission: C$16 (US$13.60) adults, C$10 (US$8.50) children 6–12. Open: Mid-June –Sept daily 10 a.m.–5 p.m.*

Green Gables House
Cavendish

Within easy walking distance of Montgomery's childhood home is Green Gables, which belonged to her grandfather's cousins. This green and white farmhouse served as the setting for *Anne of Green Gables*. At the main entrance is an interpretive center; inside the picket fence, rooms in the main house have been restored and the barn recreates early farm life. Two of the most loved connections between the property and the book are Haunted Wood and Balsam Hollow, reached by short trails from the house.

See map p. 274. Route 6 (just west of Route 13). ☎ *902-963-7874. Admission: C$7 (US$6) adults, C$5.50 (US$4.70) seniors, C$3.50 (US$3) children. Open: May–Oct daily 9 a.m.–5 p.m., extended hours July–Aug daily 9 a.m.–8 p.m.*

Lucy Maud Montgomery Birthplace
New London

This modest home is where the writer was born in 1874. The interior is decorated in corresponding style. Among personal effects on display is Montgomery's wedding dress, as well as scrapbooks she put together as a child.

New London, southwest of Cavendish on Route 6. ☎ *902-886-2099. Admission: C$3 (US$2.60) adults, C$1 (US$.85) children. Open: Mid-May–mid-Oct daily 9 a.m.–5 p.m.*

Site of Lucy Maud Montgomery's Cavendish Home
Cavendish

This is where the writer lived with her grandparents after the premature death of her mother. All that remains of the home are the foundations, but the well-tended gardens and mature groves of apple trees provide a peaceful retreat from the rest of Cavendish. A small museum and bookstore at the site are operated by members of Montgomery's family.

See map p. 274. Route 6 (just east of Route 13). ☎ *902-963-2231. Admission: C$2 (US$1.70) adults, C$1 (US$.85) children. Open: June–mid-Oct daily 9 a.m.–5 p.m., extended hours July–Aug daily 9 a.m.–7 p.m.*

Cool things for kids to do in Cavendish

Amusement park-style attractions open June through September are strung out along Route 6 between Cavendish and Stanley Bridge. They strongly contrast the idyllic Avonlea so loved by Anne fans — but children will love them, and we all know that's the most important thing. Here's just a sampling:

- ✔ **Sandspit (☎ 902-963-2626)** has old-time fairground rides including a roller coaster, carousel, and ferris wheel, as well as bumper boats and go-carts.

- ✔ **Rainbow Valley (☎ 963-2221)** features many rides for younger children and is extremely popular on hotter days for its waterslides.

- ✔ **Mariner's Cove (☎ 902-963-2242)** is the most challenging of Cavendish's many mini-golf courses.

- ✔ **Black Magic (☎ 902-963-2889)** is mini-golf with a twist — indoors and in the dark.

Touring beyond Cavendish

Once you manage to pry the Anne fan in your family away from Cavendish, you'll discover that the surrounding area is well worth exploring. Take a walk from the village to the natural, rugged beauty of Cavendish's coast or drive east along the shoreline to Tracadie Bay and loop back on Route 6 to take in a mix of coastal and rural scenery.

Prince Edward Island National Park

This narrow park protects a sliver of coastline extending from London Bay in the west to Tracadie Bay in the east, as well as a separate chunk of coastline further east near St. Peters. The park encompasses a varied landscape with wide beaches, attractive red sandstone cliffs, and rolling dunes. It can be accessed from seven different points along Route 6.

Swimming and sunbathing are the big summertime attractions for most visitors. The water is warm enough for swimming in July and August. Trained supervisors watch out for the well-being of those who take to the water at the busiest spots. The best — and busiest — beaches are those near Cavendish.

Gulf Shore Road, which begins as a northern extension of Route 13 through Cavendish, hugs the coastline, passing more park beaches, numerous lookouts (Orby Head is my fave), and a pretty picnic area at Cape Turner.

The section of park east of Rustico Bay is a lot quieter. Here you can enjoy a long beach walk, or take a morning stroll along the marshland behind the dunes in search of local birds, such as piping plovers and northern phalarope. **Brackley Beach,** at the north end of Route 15, has supervised swimming, change rooms, a concession, and an information center.

 Rise early to experience Prince Edward Island National Park in its most picturesque and pristine state. Overnight, wind and water action creates textured herringbone patterns across the beaches and dunes and the rising sun casts an intriguing red glow across the entire park.

A National Park Day Pass costs C$6 (US$5.10) adults, C$5 (US$4.30) seniors, C$3 (US$2.60) children, to a maximum of C$15 (US$12.80) per vehicle. The **Park Information Centre,** just north of the junction of Route 6 and 13 in Cavendish (☎ **902-963-2391**), has park maps, posted weather forecasts, and natural history displays. It's open June through Sept daily 9 a.m. to 5 p.m. (July and Aug until 9 p.m.).

Starving art lovers, tuck in!

If not the most notable island gallery, then **The Dunes,** on Route 15 at Brackley Beach (☎ 902-672-1883), is certainly the most unique. Made up almost entirely of windows, this ultra-contemporary building is part gallery, part restaurant, and all tourist attraction. The island's pre-eminent painters, wood carvers, and sculptors have their work on display in a multi-level, spiral room, with a narrow stairway leading to a fourth-floor lookout. Hungry? The gallery restaurant outdoes itself with dishes such as Vietnamese rice noodle salad with grilled shrimp (C$12/US$10.20) at lunch and a roasted rack of lamb crusted with Indian spices in the evening (C$21/US$17.90). The gallery is open June through October daily 10 a.m. to 6 p.m. while the restaurant hours are 11:30 a.m. to 10 p.m.

North Rustico Harbour

At the entrance to Rustico Bay, the tiny hamlet of North Rustico Harbour comprises a lighthouse and a smattering of trim homes lodged between the beaches of Prince Edward Island National Park and a small harbor packed with fishing boats. The picturesque setting attracts hordes of visitors, but somehow the village maintains a peaceful demeanor.

Down on the dock is **Rustico Marina & Interpretive Centre,** a small facility that catalogs local history. Native displays share space with exhibits on harvesting Irish moss, artifacts from local canneries, and a tank of live lobsters. The story of the Mi'Kmaq, who left middens of shells on nearby Robinsons Island as evidence of 1,500 years of habitation, is most intriguing. Admission is a worthwhile C$3 (US$2.60) adults, C$2.50 (US$2.10) seniors and children.

Court Brothers (☎ 902-963-2322) is one of many local operations that take visitors out to sea fishing for mackerel. Trips last around three hours and cost a reasonable C$25 (US$21.30) adults and C$15 (US$12.80) children, although the catch belongs to the boat. **Outside Expeditions** (☎ 800-207-3899 or 902-963-3366) launches sea kayak tours from a beach right beside the dock. If you've never kayaked before, the 90-minute trip is a great introduction to the sport. The cost is just C$40 (US$34) per person and includes instruction in basic paddling skills and the chance to view a wide range of sea birds while paddling along the calm waters of the bay. If you're feeling adventurous, consider a day trip to Robinsons Island, where a picnic lunch is included in the price of C$100 (US$85).

To get to North Rustico Harbour, take Route 6 east from Cavendish and veer left at the main intersection in North Rustico.

Chapter 20

Prince County

. . . .

In This Chapter

▶ Soaking up Summerside

▶ Exploring Acadian culture

▶ Meandering around Malpeque Bay

▶ Reaching North Cape

. . . .

*M*any visitors only tour the central portion (Queens County) of Prince Edward Island — they cross Confederation Bridge and head straight for Charlottetown, then venture north to Cavendish and maybe loop through Kings County before leaving via the ferry. But, to experience the island's less touristy side, you really should include Prince County, the western third of the island, in your itinerary.

The low-lying landscape of Prince County is mostly rural. It is surrounded by some of the Maritimes' best beaches, long sand dunes, and low, red cliffs. To appreciate the best of the west, stick to the coast wherever possible (Route 14 between West Point and Tignish is the highlight) and give the main thoroughfare — Route 2, which runs through the middle of Prince County — a miss.

Summerside

Summerside (population 16,000), located 71km (44 miles) west of Charlottetown, is the second-largest city on Prince Edward Island and is the gateway to Prince County. Spread around a south-facing harbor, the waterfront is the most appealing section of the city, although a recent rejuvenation extends to commercial buildings adorned with colorful murals.

Getting there

From the Confederation Bridge, take Route 10, then Route 1A, to reach Summerside in less than 30 minutes. The most direct route from Charlottetown is Route 2 through Kensington. Both these routes merge east of Summerside, with a well-signposted exit leading right downtown.

Staying in Summerside

A strip of motels on the eastern approach to downtown (within walking distance of the waterfront) offers well-priced overnight accommodations — just don't expect valet parking and room service.

Baker's Lighthouse Motel
$ Summerside

Rooms at Baker's Lighthouse Motel are no better than similarly priced choices on the east side of downtown, but children will enjoy the playground while you cook up a storm (or a lobster — pots supplied) at the outdoor barbeque area.

802 Water St. East. ☎ *877-436-2996 or 902-436-2992. Rack rates: C$55–C$65 (US$46.80–US$55.30) double. MC, V.*

Quality Inn Garden of the Gulf
$$–$$$ Summerside

The rooms at this chain motel are nothing exceptional, but the downtown location is perfect for an evening stroll along the waterfront and kids will love the choice of outdoor and indoor swimming pools.

618 Water St. East. ☎ *800-265-5551 or 902-436-2295. Fax: 902-432-2911.* www.qualityinnpei.com. *Rack rates: C$139–C$189 (US$118.20–US$160.70) double. AE, DC, MC, V.*

Silver Fox Inn
$$ Summerside

A distinctive 1892 Queen Anne Revival residence, this inn offers six comfortable guest rooms decorated in frilly Victorian style. Tea and cookies are served each afternoon in the large living area. A tiered deck and well-stocked library provide alternate relaxation areas. Rates include a cooked breakfast. Dinner is available with advance reservations.

61 Granville St. ☎ *800-565-4033 or 902-436-1664.* www.silverfoxinn.net. *Rack rates: C$95–C$140 (US$80.80–US$119) double. AE, DC, MC, V.*

Dining in Summerside

Summerside has many restaurants, including a string of places along the waterfront, and none of them will break your bank account. If you plan on just one meal in town, sacrifice the water views and head for the nearby Brothers Two.

Brothers Two Restaurant
$$–$$$ Summerside CANADIAN

Locals love this casual, pine-paneled place for its wide selection of dishes that go well beyond seafood (I had the meatloaf and loved it). Naturally, you can't go wrong with local seafood either. Try pan-fried scallops or a lobster club, or chose two favorites from a list (haddock, salmon, scallops, shrimp, etc.), accompanied by potato, vegetables, and bread for C$21 (US$17.90). Seating choices are tables, booths, or out on a rooftop patio.

618 Water St. ☎ 902-436-9654. Main courses: C$10–C$24 (US$8.50–US$20.40). AE, DC, MC, V. Open: Daily 11 a.m.–9:30 p.m.

Flex Mussels

$ Summerside SEAFOOD ⟨Best Seafood ⟩

Wow! For those who like mussels (the ones you eat), there's no place in the Maritimes like Flex Mussels, a simple harborfront café where this island delicacy is steamed to order in 50 different ways. Take your pick from Bombay (ginger, wine, curry, mango, and cream), Maine (baby clams, white wine, cream, and parsley), Wild Turkey (roast corn, scallions, kumquats, and bourbon), and more, many more. A pound of mussels costs C$7.50 (US$6.40), with fries cut from island potatoes and a freshly baked baguette are extra. If you've always wondered what a growing mussel looks like, check out the Mussel Cam at www.flexmussels.com.

Spinnakers' Landing, 150 Harbour Dr. ☎ 902-754-0022. Main courses: C$7.50 (US$6.40). Open: June–Sept daily 11 a.m.–5 p.m.

Exploring Summerside

Base yourself at the waterfront, where you'll find plenty of free parking, an **information center** (☎ **902-888-8364**), and a lighthouse that you can climb for 360-degree views. Adjacent is the much larger Spinnakers' Landing complex, which has a small interpretive display that tells the story of the once-thriving shipbuilding business. Also here you'll find a pub with a waterfront deck, bike rentals, and summertime weekend entertainment on an outdoor stage.

College of Piping
Summerside

This college, the only one of its type in North America, is for people who want to learn Highland and step-dancing, or how to play the bagpipes. Students from around the world live in residences during the year, but for the casual observer, the college is also worth a visit. July through August, tours of the facility go Monday to Friday 11 a.m. to 5 p.m. This is a great chance to learn about ancient Celtic culture and the skills involved in the various disciplines taught on campus. Mini-concerts, also free, are held daily at 11:30 a.m., 1:30 p.m., and 3:30 p.m. The nightly (July through Aug) ceilidh (pronounced "*kay*-lee") showcases lively Celtic music at 7 p.m. for C$12 (US$10.20) adults, C$11 (US$9.40) seniors, C$5 (US$4.30) children.

619 Water St. ☎ 902-436-5377. www.collegeofpiping.com.

Région Évangéline

The Acadians comprised the first group of Europeans to settle on Prince Edward Island. When the British took control of the island in 1755, many of these French nationals escaped exile by hiding out in the remote western portion of the island. Over time, they resumed normal, mostly rural lives. Their descendents now make up over 15 percent of the island's population and are concentrated along the portion of the island covered in this next section — the southern coastline of Prince County, west of Summerside along Route 11.

Getting there

Route 2 west from Summerside flies right through the middle of Région Évangéline. You can take Route 11 south at Miscouche to follow the coast to Cap Egmont for more scenic views, and then rejoin Route 2 at Mount Pleasant.

Staying in Région Évangéline

If you're looking for regular motel rooms or the services of a resort, plan on staying in Summerside or Charlottetown; for something unique, try my recommendation below.

Hôtel Village sur l'oc
$–$$$ Mont-Carmel

An overnight stay at Hôtel Village sur l'oc, is a wonderful way to immerse yourself in Acadian culture. Guest rooms are unspectacular — choose from those in the main building, a motel-style wing, or small cottages — although many enjoy water views. Aside from exploring local culture, an Acadian restaurant (see below) supplies delicious meals. All ages can relax around the outdoor pool and children will love swimming and shell-collecting on the adjacent beach. Other amenities include bike rentals and a gift shop.

6216 Route 11, Mont-Carmel. ☎ *800-567-3228 or 902-854-2227. Fax: 902-854-2304.* www.levillagedelacadie.com. *Rack rates: C$60–C$180 (US$51–US$153) double. MC, V. Open: June–mid-Sept.*

Dining in Région Évangéline

Cajun Jacques
$–$$ Mont-Carmel   ACADIAN

A meal at Cajun Jacques is a definete high point of a visit to Le Village de l'Acadie. As you'd expect, it specializes in Acadian cuisine, based on recipes using locally available produce that date back many centuries. Be prepared for a hearty meal, including *poutine râpée* (pork wrapped in grated potato), *rappie pie* (meat pie topped with grated potatoes), *frîtes*

(French fries), and chicken *fricot* (chicken stew), all exceptionally well-priced. During July and August the village hosts a nightly dinner featuring Acadian cooking as well as dancing and singing (C$32/US$27.20 per person). Some nights it is presented in English, on others in French; call ahead to confirm.

6216 Route 11, Mont-Carmel. ☎ *902-854-2227. Main Courses: C$8–C$18 (US$6.80–US$15.30). Open: June–mid-Sept Sun–Thurs 8 a.m.–9 p.m., Fri–Sat 8 a.m.–10 p.m.*

Exploring Région Évangéline

Trim homes, impressive churches, and flapping flags are signs that pride in Acadian culture is strong in Région Évangéline. Traditions are also showcased at Musée Acadien — and I've included an eccentric non-Acadian sight as a bonus.

Bottle Houses
Cap Egmont

Think you know the world's most obsessive collector? Think again. Originally put together by the late Edouard Arsenault, over 25,000 bottles have been cemented together to form three buildings, including a church complete with alter and pews, at this unique attraction. The surrounding gardens alone are worth the price of admission.

Route 11, Cap Egmont. ☎ *902-854-2987. Admission: C$4 (US$3.40) adults, C$3 (US$2.60) seniors, C$1 (US85¢) children. Open: June–Sept daily 9 a.m.–6 p.m.; until 8 p.m. in July and Aug.*

Musée Acadien
Miscouche

Protected as a National Historic Site, this museum commemorates the trials and tribulations of the Island's early French settlers. It boasts a permanent display of Acadian history, as well a remarkable audiovisual presentation that tells the story of their mass expulsion from Prince Edward Island in moving detail. Acadians gathered in Miscouche in 1884 to officially adopt the Acadian flag and an anthem, which gives the museum extra appeal.

Miscouche, Route 2. ☎ *902-436-2881. Admission: C$4 (US$3.40) adults, C$2 (US$1.70) children. Open: July–Aug daily 9 a.m.–7 p.m.*

Our Lady of Mont-Carmel
Mont-Carmel

Facing the highway, but sitting atop red cliffs that descend to Northumberland Strait, this magnificent church is the architectural highlight of Région Évangéline. The town's first inhabitants came from the Poitou region of France, and this is reflected in the cathedral's ornate interior. Most visitors are happy to do their admiring from the surrounding grounds, but Sunday mass is open to the public.

Route 11, Mont-Carmel. ☎ 902-854-2260.

Malpeque Bay

The calm waters of Malpeque Bay are famous for oysters, but the area's pleasant beaches, its human history, and its native culture make this massive tidal waterway a worthwhile detour from the drive north through Prince County.

Getting there

If you're coming from Cavendish, follow Route 6 through to Kensington, then take Route 20 north to Cabot Beach or Route 2 around the head of the bay. Tyne Valley, on the western side of the bay, is reached by taking Route 132 from Route 2.

Staying around Malpeque Bay

Lodging around Malpeque Bay is limited, so reserve a room well ahead of time, especially for July and August.

Doctor's Inn Bed and Breakfast
$ **Tyne Valley**

On a rise above the village of Tyne Valley, this rambling 1860s home is more farm than bed and breakfast. It contains only two guest rooms and a single guest bathroom, but it is hospitable hosts Jean and Paul Offer and their wonderful down-home cooking that you'll remember long after you've gotten over having to share a bathroom. A full-cooked breakfast, prepared in the old-fashioned kitchen complete with wood stove, is included in the rates. If you choose to pay the C$45 (US$38.30) per person extra for the four-course dinner, you'll enjoy appetizers and wine in the sitting room, followed by seafood complemented by wonderful salads in the dining room. Freshly baked desserts complete the cosy dining experience. Non-guests are also welcomed for dinner with 24 hours' notice.

Route 167, Tyne Valley. ☎ 902-831-3057. Rack rates: C$60 (US$51) double. MC, V.

Green Valley Cottages
$$–$$$ **Spring Valley**

If you're looking for an escape from touristy Cavendish, you can't do any better than these cottages in a rural setting. Green Valley is close to both Cavendish and the beaches of Malpeque Bay, while a ten-minute drive south is the Kensington Towers theme park. Each modern, woodsy cottage has 1 to 3 bedrooms, a full kitchen, color television, and deck. Children will love the wagon rides and marshmallow cookouts around the bonfire.

The owners also operate **Malpeque Cove Cottages** (304 King St.; ☎ 888-283-1927 or 902-836-1072; www.malpeque.ca), which are perched right on the water beside Cabot Beach Provincial Park. They are rented on a weekly basis only in summer, with nightly rentals in June and September.

1540 Spring Valley Rd., off Route 104 north of Kensington. ☎ *866-526-1332 or 902-836-3327.* www.springvalleycottages.com. *Rates: C$110–C$175 (US$93.50–US$148.80) double. MC, V. Open: Apr–Dec.*

Exploring Malpeque Bay

Prince Edward Island itself is so small that the big foldout tourism map skews distances — you can drive from one end of Malpeque Bay to the other in just two hours.

Lennox Island
North Malpeque Bay

The Mi'Kmaq, the original inhabitants of Prince Edward Island, had their 10,000-year nomadic lifestyle wiped out after Europeans arrived and cleared the land for farming. Around 1800, some had been persuaded to resettle on Lennox Island, which was later purchased for their people. Now linked to PEI by a short causeway, descendents of the Mi'Kmaq still live on the island, living a mostly traditional lifestyle that includes fishing and harvesting peat moss. They share their culture with interested visitors at **Lennox Island Cultural Centre,** down by the main dock (☎ 902-831-2702). It's generally open in summer daily 10 a.m. to 6 p.m., but call ahead to confirm these hours. Across the road is **Indian Art & Craft of North America** (☎ 902-831-2653) where you can purchase Mi'Kmaq baskets, pottery, and jewelry.

Take Route 163 east from Route 12.

Green Park Shipbuilding Museum
Port Hill

If you want to revisit the 1860s, when shipbuilding was Prince Edward Island's main industry, plan on a visit to this sprawling property on the western shore of Malpeque Bay. The mansion of James Yeo, who owned the yards, sits in the heart of sweeping grounds. It is fully furnished in Victorian style, including the top-floor cupola from which Yeo was able to watch over his workers. If you walk down to the site of the actual shipyards, two wooden buildings and the slips are all that remain, although interpretive panels do a good job of describing the once bustling business.

To get to the museum, you pass through **Green Park Provincial Park,** protecting a low peninsula scattered with stunted birch and laced with trails leading along the waterfront.

Route 12, Port Hill. ☎ *902-831-7947. Admission: C$5 (US$4.30) adults, C$2.50 (US$2.10) children. Open: June–Sept. daily 9 a.m.–5 p.m.*

Western Prince County

Western Prince County is an arrow-shaped chunk of land that comes to a point at North Cape. Potato farms dominate the landscape in the central portion of the region while small fishing villages and long stretches of uninhabited coastline lined by sea cliffs beckon to the south and west.

Getting there

Route 2 splits western Prince County neatly in two, but you'll want to steer away from this highway and take the coastal route wherever possible.

Staying in western Prince County

You'll find dozens of cottage-style accommodations in the Prince Edward Island Visitors Guide, but the following three spots stand out.

Rodd Mill River
$$–$$$ Mill River Provincial Park

Families will love this modern resort, the largest in Prince County, for amenities including a waterslide and pool, canoe rentals, and hiking trails. A bonus for golfers is one of Canada's top-rated golf courses. The rooms are adequate with the choice of park or golf course views. Both the main dining room and a casual bistro-café overlook the golf course.

Route 2, Mill River Provincial Park. ☎ *800-565-7633 or 902-859-2486. Fax: 902-859-2486.* www.rodd-hotels.ca. *Rates: C$125–C$225 (US$106.30–US$191.30) double. AE, DC, MC, V. Open: Jan–Oct.*

Tignish Heritage Inn
$$ Tignish

Located in the village of Tignish, this lodging is a good choice if you're looking for inexpensive accommodation close to the cape. Built with locally fired red brick in 1868, a thorough renovation has removed any clinical feel from this former convent. Seventeen guest rooms are available, all with private bathrooms. Rates include a light breakfast and use of a kitchen.

Maple St., Tignish. ☎ *877-882-2491 or 902-882-2491. Fax: 902-882-2500.* www. tignish.com/inn. *Rates: C$80–C$115 (US$68–US$97.80) double. AE, MC, V. Open: Mid-June–mid-Oct.*

West Point Lighthouse
$$ West Point

Have you ever stayed in a lighthouse? Here's your chance. Built in 1875 as a navigational aid to vessels entering Northumberland Strait, West Point is one of the oldest and tallest lighthouses on the island. It has since been converted to an inn with a coveted Tower Room, in the lighthouse itself, in addition to the Light Keeper's Quarters in the adjoining building. All nine guest rooms are furnished with handmade quilts and antiques; a restaurant supplies three meals daily. Book well in advance for the room of your choice.

Route 14, West Point. ☎ *800-764-6854 or 902-859-3605. Fax: 902-859-1510.* www.westpointlighthouse.com. *Rates: C$90–C$135 (US$76.50–US$114.80) double. AE, MC, V. Open: June–Sept.*

Touring through western Prince County

A tour through western Prince County is more about soaking up the scenery than visiting specific sites. The following are highlights of a driving tour that follows Route 2 as far as Mill River Provincial Park, then continues on Route 12 to North Cape, returning along the west coast on Route 14. This entire loop is around 400km (250 miles) and can easily be completed in one day.

- ✔ **Prince Edward Island Potato Museum,** in O'Leary, along Route 142 west of Route 2 (☎ **902-859-2039;** mid-May–mid-Oct Mon–Sat 9 a.m.–5 p.m., Sun 1–5 p.m.). Surrounded by potato farms, exhibits at this small museum catalog the local industry, which dates back to the 1830s when an Irish farmer planted the island's first spuds. Admission is C$5 (US$4.30) for adults, C$2.50 (US$2.10) for children.

- ✔ **Mill River Provincial Park,** beside Route 2 at St. Anthony. This park is best known for its **golf course** (☎ **902-859-2486**), where the river comes into play on many holes. Greens fees are C$60 (US$51).

- ✔ **North Cape,** 16km (10 miles) north of Tignish. Prince County narrows to a point of land at North Cape, with a lighthouse and long reef that becomes exposed at low tide. Nearby is the Atlantic Wind Test Site, where wind turbines generate electricity.

- ✔ **Elephant Rock,** 4km (2.5 miles) north of Norway on Route 182. Detached from high cliffs by erosion, this geological oddity lost its "trunk" in 1998, but the pinnacle of rock and the surrounding barren landscape are well worth the effort to reach it.

- ✔ **Irish Moss Interpretive Centre,** Route 14, Miminegash (☎ **902-882-4313;** June–Sept Mon–Sat 10 a.m.–7 p.m., Sun noon–8 p.m.). A type of seaweed used in the production of ice cream, Irish moss is collected by hand and on horseback from local beaches. This small museum, operated by families involved in the process, tells their story. Admission is C$2 (US$1.70). Attached to the museum is the

Pg. 309

Seaweed Pie Café. Its namesake (C$3.50/US$3 per slice) actually tastes better than you may think.

✔ **West Point Lighthouse,** off Route 14 (☎ **902-859-3605**). Manned from 1875 through to 1963, this historic structure has been converted to an inn (see above) and restaurant, but is well worth just a casual stop. Part of the complex is a small museum describing the structure and its importance to shipping in Northumberland Strait. The lighthouse is within Cedar Dunes Provincial Park, where you can walk the wooded nature trails and try your hand at digging clams.

Chapter 21

Kings County

• •

In This Chapter

▶ Searching out seals in southern Kings County

▶ Striding the fairways of Brudenell River Golf Course

▶ Wandering through the shifting, singing sand of northern Kings County

• •

*L*ike the rest of Prince Edward Island, Kings County is dominated by cleared farmland criss-crossed by rural roads. The biggest difference in the landscape is along the east coast, where the shoreline is more rugged than elsewhere on the island, as the red sea cliffs are replaced by a rocky, forested foreshore.

The region is encircled by a coastal highway that passes through all of the towns and parks detailed in this section of the chapter. From Charlottetown, it follows the Trans-Canada Highway east to Wood Islands, the departure point for ferries to the mainland, then jogs north along the convoluted east coast before returning to the capital as Route 2. The entire loop is 374km (232 miles), easily tackled in one day.

For the purposes of the this chapter, I've broken Kings County in two, with southern Kings County and northern Kings County divided by the Cardigan River, which runs roughly through the center of the county and drains into Cardigan Bay just north of Brudenell River Provincial Park.

Southern Kings County

Mostly rural, the southern portion of Kings County is dotted with picturesque villages, fishing ports, lighthouses, and a number of provincial parks.

Getting there

From Charlottetown, take the Trans-Canada Highway (Route 1) east. After 20km (12 miles), Route 3 branches east to Brudenell River while the main highway heads south toward Wood Islands.

Between May and mid-December, ferries ply Northumberland Strait, linking Caribou (Nova Scotia) with Wood Islands just across the county line from Kings County. In summer, there are eight departures daily in each direction. Service in spring and fall is less frequent and no ferries operate in winter. No reservations are taken, so plan on catching a mid-week, early morning departure to avoid a long wait. The round-trip fare of C$55 (US$46.80) per vehicle, including passengers, is collected upon leaving the island. (If you drive back to the mainland via the Confederation Bridge, a toll is collected there.) The service is operated by **Northumberland Ferries** (☎ **902-566-3838**; www.nfl-bay.com).

Staying in southern Kings County

The lodging scene in southern Kings County is dominated by small bed-and-breakfasts and family-style cottage accommodations. The following are my faves.

Forest and Stream Cottages
$$ Murray Harbour

If you can go without room service and robes, and if you like the idea of cooking your own meals, then this is the spot for you. Set on a small lake, each of five cottages has an older but well-equipped kitchen, a separate bedroom, and a screened porch. Bed and breakfast rooms are also available. Guests have use of rowboats (perfect for an early morning fishing expedition — trout for breakfast, anyone?), a hot tub, and bike rentals. Children will love the shaded playground. Breakfast (C$5/US$4.30 per person) is served on the veranda of the main house.

Route 18, between Murray Harbour and Murray River. ☎ 800-227-9943 or 902-962-3537. Fax: 902-962-3537. Rack rates: C$85–C$125 (US$72.30–US$106.30) double. MC, V. Open: May–Oct.

Rodd Brudenell River
$$–$$$$ Roseneath

This sprawling destination resort takes prime advantage of its bayside setting within the boundaries of Brudenell River Provincial Park. The unequaled choice of activities is what makes this resort a standout — two 18-hole golf courses, indoor and outdoor pools, tennis courts, bike rentals, canoeing and kayaking, horseback riding, and a full spa facility. Kids are catered to with their own activity program and a children's center. The main lodge holds 100 spacious guest rooms decorated in simple, contemporary style. Each has a balcony or patio with water or golf course vistas. Close to the main resort is a cluster of Country Cabins, which look rather boxy from the outside, but are well suited to budget travelers. Finally, each Echelon Gold Cottage has one or two bedrooms outfitted with king beds, a jetted tub, a full-sized kitchen, and a private deck with barbeque. Resort dining and drinking choices include three restaurants and a poolside bar.

Route 3, Roseneath. ☎ 800-565-7633 or 902-652-2332. Fax: 902-652-2886. www.rodd-hotels.ca. Rack rates: C$120–C$330 (US$102–US$280.50) double. AE, DC, MC, V. Open: Mid-May–mid-Oct.

Thought's End
$$ **Panmure Island**

The three motel-like rooms at Thought's End are unspectacular, but the setting is unbeatable — a 5.6-hectare (14-acre) property on remote Panmure Island, which is east of Montague on Route 17 and linked to the rest of PEI by a causeway. The island is ringed by beaches, and those fronting St. Mary's Bay are the most protected. Ask the friendly hosts about local boat tours.

Route 347, Panmure Island. ☎ 866-838-4522 or 902-838-4522. Rack rates: C$79 (US$67.20) double. MC, V. Open: May–Oct.

Dining in southern Kings County

If you've just docked at Wood Islands, there is no better introduction to the region than enjoying a seafood feast — chowder, boiled lobster, or steamed mussels — from **Crabby's Seafood,** right beside the ferry dock (☎ **902-962-3228;** open June–Sept daily noon–7 p.m.) at one of surrounding picnic tables. Further afield, plan on taking a full meal at Rodd Brudenell River (see above), or Windows on the Water in Montague.

Windows on the Water Cafe
$–$$ **Montague   CAFE/SEAFOOD**

This old-fashioned eatery combines country charm with a prime waterfront location overlooking Montague Marina. You can dine inside where the ambience is warm and inviting, but if the sun is shining you'll want to be out on the large deck. I loved the chowder made with homemade fish stock and chock-a-block full of haddock, clams, and scallops. It was lunchtime, so I skipped the mains (whatever seafood is in season, cooked simply) and dived straight into a generous serving of perfectly cooked apple crisp to finish.

106 Sackville St. ☎ 902-838-2080. Main courses: C$8–C$15.50 (US$6.80–US$13.20). AE, DC, MC, V. Open: Mid-May–Sept daily 11:30 a.m.–8 p.m., until 10 p.m. in July and Aug.

Exploring southern Kings County
If you're approaching Kings County from the Trans-Canada Highway, take the coastal route from Charlottetown to Wood Islands, where the ferry from Nova Scotia docks.

East from Wood Islands
From Wood Islands, it's 9km (5.6 miles) to the first worthwhile stop, **Rossignol Estate Winery** on Route 4 (☎ **902-962-4193**), the island's only commercial vineyard. Its eye-pleasing location above Northumberland Strait plays second fiddle to the serious business of producing surprisingly good red and white table wines, as well as fruit-based wines and

maple cider. You can try before you buy at the on-site wine shop, which is open May to Oct, Monday to Saturday from 10 a.m. to 5 p.m., Sun 1 to 5 p.m.

Murray Harbour

This tiny fishing village 10km (6.2 miles) east of Murray River is a little off the beaten track, but is well worth the detour. The **Old General Store** (☎ 902-962-2459) and **Miss Elly's** (☎ 902-962-3555), both on Main Street, hold fine collections of antiques and gifts. Meanwhile, **Marine Adventures Seal Watching** (☎ 902-962-2494) departs the downtown dock up to four times daily for a short boat cruise to a large colony of seals via a mussel farm. The tour costs C$18 (US$15.30) adults, C$15 (US$12.80) seniors, C$12 (US$10.20) children.

Fairways to heaven

Quietly, Prince Edward Island has become one of Canada's premier destinations for golfers. A solid collection of 25 courses makes the most of the rolling rural landscape and picture-perfect coastline, varying from rural nine-hole courses to world-class resort layouts. The best island golf courses are equal in quality and challenge to any others in Canada, yet greens fees (all under C$100/US$85) are a fraction of what you would pay elsewhere.

The Web site www.golfpei.ca details each island course while promoting accommodation packages that make island golfing an even better deal.

Here are my favorite courses:

Belvedere Golf Club (Charlottetown ☎ 902-892-7838) is an old-fashioned layout that nurtured LPGA star Lorie Kane.

Brudenell River (Brudenell River Provincial Park; ☎ 800-235-8909 or 902-859-8873) mixes tree-lined fairways with open riverfront terrain. Thinking golfers are well rewarded at this renowned course.

Countryview (Fairview; ☎ 902-675-2800) is a sporty nine-hole layout with water views. It is surrounded by farmland, yet lies just ten minutes by road from Charlottetown.

Links of Crowbush Cove (Morell; ☎ 800-235-8909 or 902-961-7300) is routed around natural waterways behind North Shore dunes. Crowbush Cove is one of Canada's top courses.

Eagles Glenn (Cavendish; ☎ 866-963-3600 or 902-963-3600), although not overwhelming in length, is a challenging 27-hole, links-style creation through rolling highlands.

Glasgow Hills (Hunter River; ☎ 866-621-2200 or 902-621-2201) is in the middle of the island, but the ocean is in view from its hilly location. Be prepared for major elevation differences between tee and green.

Pooles Corner

Pooles Corner, at the junction of Routes 3 and 4, is in the geographic center of Kings County (you'll often hear it used as a reference point for directions and distances). Friendly staff at the summer-only **Provincial Information Centre** (☎ **902-838-0670**), right at the junction, will help you plan your onward travel.

Northern Kings County

If the weather is good, your time in the northern section of Kings County will be a highlight of your visit to Prince Edward Island. The beaches lining the Gulf of St. Lawrence are as nice as you'll find anywhere around the island, yet tourist crowds are minimal. The entire region is more lightly settled than elsewhere in the province; the largest town, Souris, holds a population of just 1,200.

Getting there

Route 4 is the most direct route between Pooles Corner and Souris, but you'll enjoy the scenic countryside on alternate Routes 311 and 310. From Cavendish, Route 2 enters Kings County near St. Andrews and veers inland to join Route 4 at Fortune Bridge. On any of these approaches, distances are not as long as they may seem from glancing at a provincial map. Souris is 82km (51 miles) from Charlottetown and 70km (43 miles) from Wood Islands.

Staying in northern Kings County

Accommodations in the northern half of Kings County are more spread out than elsewhere on the island, but the choices you do have run the gamut of prices — from one of PEI's best bargains to one of its most upscale (and expensive) inns.

A Place to Stay Inn
$ Souris

Once you get over the name, you'll discover that this inexpensive lodging has everything going for it — comfortable rooms, cooking facilities, television lounges, bike rentals, and a location within walking distance of the Souris waterfront. Beds are in downstairs dormitories or in upstairs bed-and-breakfast rooms that share bathrooms.

9 Longworth St., Souris. ☎ 800-655-7829 or 902-687-4626. Rack rates: C$22 (US$18.70) dorm bed, C$70 (US$59.50) double. MC, V. Open: March–Jan (after mid-Oct by reservation only).

Inn at Bay Fortune
$$$–$$$$ Bay Fortune

Built as a summer retreat for Broadway playwright Elmer Harris, Inn at Bay Fortune is now an upscale, 18-room inn on the calm shores of Bay Fortune. You'll find the lodge and its well-manicured grounds rather aristocratic, and yet the ambience remains unpretentious. The elegant rooms are furnished with a pleasing mix of antiques and island-made furniture; some have wood-burning fireplaces.

The restaurant here has a reputation as one of the finest in the Maritimes. The best views can be seen from the tables along the covered verandah. Enjoy views of the bay in a refined setting while dining on local seafood, carefully prepared using ingredients harvested from the inn's own garden. A full breakfast is included in the rates, or choose a package that includes dinner and a picnic lunch.

Route 310, Bay Fortune. ☎ *902-687-3745. Fax: 902-687-3540.* www.innatbayfortune.com. *Rack rates: C$175–C$325 (US$148.80–US$276.30) double. MC, V. Open: Mid-May–mid-Oct.*

Rodd Crowbush Golf & Beach Resort
$$$$ Morell

In the heart of one of Canada's top-ranked golf courses and adjacent to a magnificent stretch of sandy beach, Crowbush is one of PEI's premier resorts. Guest rooms are spacious and decorated in a casual, contemporary style. All have a private patio or deck and come with niceties such as bathrobes, television and DVD combos, and evening turndown service. Cottages scattered around the property are a luxurious splurge. Tennis courts, an indoor pool, and a restaurant specializing in modern Canadian cooking round out the resort. Although you pay top dollar to stay here, the atmosphere is refined-casual. The staff is service-oriented, friendly, and approachable. Always ask about packages that may include greens fees or meals in the price.

Route 350, Morell. ☎ *800-565-7633 or 902-961-5600. Fax: 902-961-5601.* www.roddhotels.ca. *Rack rates: C$230–C$520 (US$195.50–US$442) double. AE, DC, MC, V. Open: Mid-May–mid-Oct.*

Dining in northern Kings County

Inn at Bay Fortune and Rodd Crowbush Golf & Beach Resort (see above) both feature excellent restaurants that welcome non-guests. You can also dine at one of the following two choices.

Bluefin Restaurant
$–$$ Souris SEAFOOD *Best Inexpensive Dining*

A great place to dig into a hearty seafood meal with the locals. The simple, wide-ranging menu has something to suit everyone — think Caesar salad, roast beef and mashed potatoes, and deep-fried halibut and chips. If you're not lobstered out, head to the downstairs section, where the lobster supper comes with all-you-can-eat seafood chowder and mussels.

10 Federal Ave., Souris. ☎ *902-687-3271. Main Courses: C$9–C$16 (US$7.81–US$13.60). Open: Daily 7 a.m.–8 p.m. MC, V.*

St. Margarets Lobster Supper
$$ St. Margarets SEAFOOD

Unlike the lobster suppers in neighboring Queens County, the St. Margarets version is put on for residents as much as for visitors. It's served up in the local church throughout summer, although because they have no holding pond, the lobster may be frozen. The fixed-price meal includes a full lobster, freshly baked breads, delicious fish chowder, and strawberry shortcake for dessert.

Route 16, St. Margarets. ☎ *902-687-3105. Lobster supper: C$26 (US$19.60). Open: Mid-June–mid-Sept daily 4–9 p.m.*

Exploring northern Kings County
You can easily hit the hotspots of northern Kings County — Souris, East Point, and the eastern end of Prince Edward Island National Park — in a single day, including stops. The road around the peninsula is never more than a few minutes' drive from the water, while rural routes cut across the entire peninsula, opening up various options for exploring the interior.

Souris and area
Souris (pronounced "Surrey"), 39km (24 miles) north of Pooles Corner, has a population of just 1,200, yet is the biggest town in all of Kings County. **St. Mary's Catholic Church,** on Chapel Avenue, soars higher than any other building in town. It was built in 1901 using red-colored island sandstone. At the west entrance to town is a beach and a concession renting kayaks and bikes.

Around 10km (6.2 miles) up the coast from Souris is **Basin Head Fisheries Museum** (☎ 902-357-7233), at the site of an abandoned fish cannery. The original wooden buildings, weathered by sun and salt, hold displays tracing the history of the industry as well as touch tanks and exhibits describing local sea life. The museum is open June to September daily 9 a.m. to 5 p.m. and admission is C$4 (US$3.40) adults, free for children. Below the museum is **Singing Sand Beach,** so named for the squeaking sound when you walk on the sand.

North Shore
The octagonal **East Point Lighthouse** (☎ 902-357-2106) stands on a low knoll at the easternmost point of land on Prince Edward Island. Built in 1867, the timber structure is open for inspection mid-June to August

daily 10 a.m. to 6 p.m. The attached light keeper's residence has been converted to a gift shop with a good selection of seafaring literature.

Take Route 313 west from St. Peters to reach the Greenwich unit of **Prince Edward Island National Park,** which is dominated by massive sand dunes. The unstable dunes are slowly moving inland, burying the coastal woods and leaving bleached tree trunks sticking up through the sand. The access road ends at an interpretive center (☎ **902-963-2391;** open June¢Oct daily 9 a.m.¢5 p.m. and until 8 p.m. July¢Aug) where the unique ecology of the protected peninsula is explained. To see for yourself, take the 4.5km (2.8-mile) **Greenwich Dunes Hiking Trail.** Allow 90 minutes to complete the loop. Admission to the park is C$6 (US$5.10) adults, C$4.50 (US$3.80) seniors, C$3 (US$2.60) children.

Part VI
The Part of Tens

The 5th Wave   By Rich Tennant

"WHAT DO YOU MEAN YOU FORGOT THE WHITE WINE?! YOU KNOW DARN WELL I CAN'T SERVE FISH WITHOUT WHITE WINE!"

In this part . . .

Presented in a top ten format, the following three chapters aren't required reading, but I recommend you give them a look. Find inspiration in Chapter 22, which condenses the best Maritimes experiences. If you want a quick reference of the region's top restaurants (okay, not really — my favorite places to eat), check out Chapter 23. Finally, Chapter 24's rundown will make you the king of trivia, with ten Maritimers of note.

Chapter 22

Ten Maritimes Experiences

*I*n this chapter, I describe experiences that represent the best of the Maritimes — a combination of specific destinations and things to do throughout the three provinces.

A Day in Anne's Land

If you've read *Anne of Green Gables,* you'll want to spend at least a day exploring the area around Cavendish, on Prince Edward Island — the area Lucy Maud Montgomery waxed lyrical about in her famous novel. You can visit Montgomery's birthplace, stroll through the home in which she was married (or even tie the knot yourself), and walk — or skip for the full effect — along Lover's Lane through Balsam Hollow.

Drinking and Dancing

Maritimers love their beer (especially local brews such as Keith's) and they love traditional Celtic music. Combine the two in the surroundings of a local pub, and you're in for an energetic night of fun. Nearly every town throughout the region has at least one pub, each with its regular clientele, but welcoming of visitors. A ceilidh (*kay*-lee) is an organized gathering that combines the two pleasures, often in a community hall or outdoor venue.

Fishing the Miramichi

Serious anglers from around the world are drawn to the wildly remote Miramichi River for spring and summer runs of Atlantic salmon, weighing up to 13 kilograms (30 pounds) each. Fish populations have increased remarkably since a catch-and-release policy was implemented a decade ago. There are still lots up for grabs, but catching them is an art. Better your odds by hiring a local guide, many of whom are associated with riverside fishing lodges.

If the fish aren't biting, head to the Atlantic Salmon Museum in Doaktown and read about other anglers' successes.

Going Golfing

Imagine striding the fairways of one of Canada's finest golf courses, staying the night just a chip and a putt from the 18th green, and then teeing off again the next morning — all for less than you pay for a single round at a top city course elsewhere in North America. Golfing and golf packages are a relative bargain across the Maritimes, but Rodd Crowbush Golf & Beach Resort on Prince Edward Island offers the bonus of activities for everyone in the family — think tennis, horseback riding, hiking, canoeing, and more.

Having a Whale of a Time

Hundreds of whales spend the warmer months feasting in the nutrient-rich waters of the Bay of Fundy. Species such as finback, minke, and humpback are commonly sighted, while the world's rarest whale — the North Atlantic right whale — is spotted by the lucky few. Tour boats depart from Digby Neck (Nova Scotia) and St. Andrews (New Brunswick) throughout the summer, with trips lasting two to three hours. If the whales are playing hide and seek, strike up a conversation with your captain. Most are local fisherman making a little extra money in their downtime, and all are characters with a whale tale or two to tell.

Hiking the Highlands

Views along the Cabot Trail, which winds through Cape Breton Highlands National Park, are stupendous, but this "trail" is for vehicles (or cyclists who take their lives into their own hands by traversing the narrow road by pedal power). You'll best appreciate the park's scenery if you move away from the road and hike along one of the walking trails. The Skyline Trail is a classic. Easily traversed in a half-day, it ends at a magnificent lookout high above the ocean. And if you're lucky, you may spy whales frolicking far below.

Making the French Connection

Acadian culture, which has its roots in the region's early French settlers, can be experienced in many places and in many ways. Visiting a museum — those in Caraquet and Miscouche are best — provides a good introduction to the Acadians and their heroic history. But soaking up the history of Grande Pre National Historic Site, taking in a concert at Village Historique Acadien (Caraquet), or feasting on a rappie pie at Rapure Acadienne (Meteghan) really brings the culture to life.

Sailing into the Sunset

No other boat is better known in Canada than the *Bluenose* (look on the back of the Canadian dime for a scaled-down version), and there is no more romantic way to spend an evening than under sail on the *Bluenose II,* an exact replica of the original. She has a packed summer schedule of public cruises throughout the Maritimes, with regular departures from her home port of Lunenburg as well as from nearby Halifax. You'll need to book well ahead of time to be assured of a spot on board — otherwise you'll be left waving from the dock.

Snapping the Perfect Picture

The combination of colorful subject matter and superlative scenery makes taking good photos in the Maritimes a snap. South of Halifax, picture-taking opportunities line up along the coast — the world's most photographed lighthouse at Peggy's Cove, the trio of bayside churches in Mahone Bay, and the colorful clapboard buildings of Lunenburg. On the rest of your travels, go beyond the obvious. In New Brunswick, have your family stand at a tilt in front of Moncton's Magnetic Hill and snoop around the narrow back streets of Saint John for a historic perspective. On Prince Edward Island, rise early to catch the first flush of light along the red dunes of Prince Edward Island National Park and take to the back roads for rural panoramas.

Walking on the Ocean Floor

Okay, maybe this description is a little overdramatic, but it's true in a literal sense. The action happens at Hopewell Rocks, on the New Brunswick side of the Bay of Fundy. As the massive Fundy tide recedes, it leaves the "ocean floor" bare around the entire bay. What makes this place even more notable is the dozen or so rock towers separated from the mainland by the forces of erosion.

Chapter 23

Ten Places to Eat Great Seafood

· ·

In This Chapter

▶ Checking out the cream of the crop of seafood restaurants
▶ Discovering what makes each place special

· ·

*F*ishophobes beware! Seafood dominates the Maritimes dining scene. Just about every restaurant offers seafood in some form or another, and many specialize in it. The food in major Maritimes cities is comparable in presentation and creativity to that in other North American cities, but it's offered at a fraction of the price. Beside the regular restaurants, many small-town cafés serve up seafood; you can count on the fish being battered, but lobster and mussels are usually boiled, and scallops sautéed. Finally, there are fish markets. Most coastal villages have one, usually down near the harbor, selling a range of fresh seafood — perfect for a home-cooked meal in your cabin.

And so, without further ado, here are the top ten places in the Maritimes to eat seafood.

Blue Mussel Café

Fresh ingredients, locally sourced whenever possible, are prepared at Prince Edward Island's renowned Blue Mussel Café with simple style. The highlight for many diners is what this restaurant *doesn't* have — a deep fryer. One local specialty is the soft-flavored Malpeque Bay oyster. Order them *au naturel* for the full effect. The restaurant setting is as memorable as the food — a cluster of outdoor tables over the water is protected from the wind by a renovated wharf building that serves as the kitchen.

Butland's Seafood

If you're visiting Fundy National Park in New Brunswick, drive through to the adjacent village of Alma, where Butland's Seafood holds a prime position above the small harbor. Inside this lively market is a bathtub-sized container overflowing with cooked lobsters. They are pre-weighed, with prices (around C$10/US$7.10 per pound) marked on the claws. If someone has beaten you to the single picnic table out back, head into the national park and enjoy lunch at any one of its numerous picnic spots.

Chowder House

How does a restaurant that hasn't seen a coat of paint for years and doesn't even offer table service make my top ten? Easy — by serving up huge portions of super-fresh mussels, crab, and lobster at ridiculously low prices. The location helps also, perched on a grassy bluff overlooking the Atlantic Ocean in the village of Neil's Harbour, on Cape Breton Island.

Five Fishermen

In Halifax if you're looking to choose from a wide range of seafood in a stylish setting, make reservations at the Five Fishermen. Ensconced in an 1816 red brick build that was originally a school — and, more infamously, a morgue for bodies of first-class passengers from the *Titanic* tragedy — tables are spread through numerous nautical-themed rooms. A massive wine rack holds pride of place in the center of the restaurant, and a century-old stained glass window is the feature in the main dining room.

Murphy's

Murphy's, in Truro, Nova Scotia, gets my nod for "The Best Maritimes Seafood Restaurant That's Nowhere Near the Ocean." Not only is water out of sight, the strip mall setting is unremarkable. Inside, the distinctly nautical setting includes model ships on the walls and fishnets hanging from the ceiling. Battered fish with a pile of perfectly cooked chips is the specialty, served up by no-nonsense waitstaff.

Muddy Rudder

The Muddy Rudder is nothing more than a ramshackle shed where orders are taken, a gas burner, and a bunch of plastic table settings on a grassed area beside the Cabot Trail. The seafood — crab, lobster, mussels, clams, and more — is dunked in a pot of boiling water to order. A truly unique Maritimes dining experience.

New Glasgow Lobster Supper

Lobster suppers have been held throughout Prince Edward Island for over 50 years. They originated as gatherings in community halls and church basements, often as fundraisers for some local cause or another. The New Glasgow Lobster Supper is one of the best. It attracts quite a few locals, as well as visitors staying in nearby Cavendish. But there's plenty of room for everyone, with over 500 seats on 2 levels. Don't come here for the view (although some tables overlook the River Clyde) or the atmosphere (which is fun and informal). Choose this lobster supper for the food: a fixed-price meal of lobster, complete with all-you-can-eat mussels, seafood chowder, potato salad, and coleslaw. Just make sure to save room for the strawberry shortcake.

O'Neil's Fundy Fish Market

Digby, on the Nova Scotia side of the Bay of Fundy, is renowned for its fleet of scallop boats that harvest the sweetest, plumpest scallops you could ever imagine. At Digby's dockside fish market, they're sold raw to go, or rolled in flour and fried up on the spot. The market also sells Digby chicks, a chewy, jerky-style snack of smoked herring, as well as mussels, oysters, lobsters, and a variety of Fundy fishes such as halibut.

Seaweed Pie Café

At Miminegash, in Prince County, Prince Edward Island, a group of local women have formed a co-operative to harvest and process Irish moss, a type of seaweed that washes up on local beaches in big storms. Irish moss has traditionally been used as a thickening ingredient in ice cream and toothpaste, but the ladies of Miminegash market its nutrient-rich values for health-related products. Not all of it is shipped to outside markets. Some ends up in seaweed pie, a surprisingly delicious dish served up in a small café that is part of a larger interpretive center.

Shediac Bay Cruises

Add a little spice to your seafood feast by helping haul in the catch aboard Shediac Bay Cruises. With Captain Eric le Blanc at the helm, these trips leave daily from Shediac, north of Moncton, New Brunswick. The tour begins with an informative talk about the life cycle of the lobster and harvesting methods. The traps are then lifted onto the boat, the lobsters are extracted, and then they're boiled in preparation of an onboard seafood feast of the freshest proportions.

Chapter 24

Ten Famous People You Probably Didn't Realize Were Maritimers

• •

In This Chapter
▶ Inventing the telephone
▶ Sailing around the world
▶ Cooking french fries

• •

*W*hile the stunning landscape is the Maritimes' most obvious asset, the people (universally known as "Maritimers") themselves are notable. Frank, friendly, and always with a story to tell, they contribute to making the region a great place to visit. The following Maritimers have gone on to greatness beyond their own borders.

Alexander Graham Bell

Prolific inventor Alexander Graham Bell spent his latter years at Baddeck, on Cape Breton Island, where his waterfront home is still owned by the Bell family. At the large museum in town, you can learn about his most famous invention, the telephone, as well as quirky facts, such as why he could never call his mom (she was deaf).

Stompin' Tom Connors

If you're not from Canada, you're probably not familiar with the patriotic tunes written and sung by this legendary musician, who was born in Saint John, New Brunswick, and raised on Prince Edward Island. Stompin' Tom has sold three million albums without ever having a song on the Canadian country charts and without ever releasing a song outside of Canada (who says "Bud the Spud" isn't radio-friendly?).

Samuel Cunard

Born the son of a Halifax carpenter, Samuel Cunard was the man behind Cunard Steamship Limited, the most recognizable name in ocean travel. In 1840, a Cunard ship made the first trans-Atlantic passenger service, marking the start of the company's heyday. Today the company has just one boat in service, the *Queen Mary II*, the largest passenger ship ever built.

Sam Langford

Generally regarded as one of the ten greatest heavyweight boxers of all time, Nova Scotia-born Langford stepped into the ring over 600 times through the first two decades of the 1900s. During his career, he fought in five weight divisions — lightweight through to heavyweight — but makes this list for his final fight, which he fought after having been declared legally blind. The result? He won. By a knockout.

Lucy Maud Montgomery

No other person in Canada has as well-preserved a childhood as this famous writer, who grew up at Cavendish on Prince Edward Island and used her early memories to create the character Anne of Green Gables, a lovable orphan girl. The paths Montgomery walked, the room in which she was married, and the unremarkable but much-visited farmhouse known as Green Gables make up Anne-fan favorites.

The McCain Family

Like thousands of others, the McCain family emigrated from Ireland to the Maritimes in the 1820s, farming hay on a small plot of land alongside the Saint John River. By the mid-1900s, hay had been replaced by potatoes. A half-century later and McCain Foods is the world's largest supplier of frozen french fries. They have 20,000 employees working in 50 factories to process 346,000 kilograms (760,000 pounds) of potatoes every hour. Probably the most amazing fact is that world headquarters is located in the family's hometown of Florenceville, New Brunswick (population 800).

Anne Murray

With sales of 50 million albums and more awards than any other female singer, Anne Murray continues to entertain people worldwide with her sultry voice that blends pop and country. Murray was born in Springhill, Nova Scotia, and retains strong ties to the region through the town's Anne Murray Centre.

John Patch

Patch, a fisherman from Yarmouth, Nova Scotia, developed the screw propeller in 1832. It soon became the preferred method of propulsion in ships, more effective than either sails or paddlewheels. In 1845, a large steamship became the first to cross the Atlantic Ocean using his invention. In the later years of his life, Patch lost the rights to the propeller. He died penniless.

Harry Saltzman

Harry Saltzman had the movie mogul look: tubby, loud, and always brightly dressed. He also had the blockbusters to go with the look. Born in Saint John, New Brunswick in 1915, Saltzman left home to join the circus at the age of 17, ending up in Paris during World War II. After producing *The Iron Petticoat,* which starred the unlikely duo of Bob Hope and Katharine Hepburn, he bought the screen rights to Ian Fleming's James Bond novels and then went on to produce the first nine Bond movies, the biggest espionage thrillers in movie history.

Joshua Slocum

Born and raised around Digby, Joshua Slocum left Nova Scotia for a life on the high seas at a young age. He is remembered today for one particular feat: being the first person to sail solo around the world.

Appendix

Quick Concierge

• •

Fast Facts

AAA

The Canadian affiliate of AAA is the Canadian Automobile Association (www.caa.ca). Check the Web site for the location of regional offices or contact CAA Maritimes at ☎ 800-561-8807.

American Express

American Express has no full-service International Service Centers in the Maritimes. Instead dial ☎ 905-474-0870 for cardholder services. For lost or stolen traveler's checks, call ☎ 800-668-2639.

Area Codes

The telephone area code for Nova Scotia and Prince Edward Island is **902**. The area code for New Brunswick is **506**.

ATMs

The most common place to find bank machines is at the entrance to major banks. Check the back of your debit or credit card to see what network your bank belongs to, and then contact Plus (☎ 800-843-7587; www.visa.com) or Cirrus (☎ 800-424-7787; www.mastercard.com) to find the location nearest to you.

Business Hours

Business hours vary throughout the Maritimes. The following is only a guideline. Banks: Monday through Thursday 9 a.m.–3:30 p.m., Friday 9 a.m.–5 p.m. Retail stores: Monday through Saturday 9:30 a.m.–5 p.m. Mall shops often stay open until 9 p.m. later in the week and open on Sunday from around noon until 5 or 6 p.m. In tourist areas, hours fluctuate greatly, and many shops close completely for the winter.

Credit Cards

For lost or stolen credit cards, contact the following: American Express (☎ 800-668-2639), Diners Club (☎ 800-363-3333), Discover (☎ 800-347-2683), MasterCard (☎ 800-307-7309), or Visa (☎ 800-847-2113).

Currency Exchanges

The best place to exchange money is a bank. Refer to the "Fast Facts" section at the end of each city chapter of this book for bank locations. Airports at Halifax, Moncton, Fredericton, and Charlottetown have currency exchange bureaus. Many Canadian businesses accept U.S. dollars — often gladly, but at a lower rate than a bank would offer you. The Web site www.xe.com/ucc is a good tool for checking the latest rates.

Customs

Representatives of Canada Border Services Agency (☎ 800-461-9999 or 204-983-3500; www.cbsa-asfc.gc.ca) are located at every major border crossing and at airports that receive international flights.

Electricity

Canada's electrical outlets put out 110 volts AC, the same as in the United States.

Emergencies

For ambulance, police, or fire department assistance, call ☎ **911.**

Hospitals

The location of local hospitals is listed in the "Fast Facts" sections of each city chapter.

Internet Access

Public libraries throughout the Maritimes allow visitors to use their computers for Internet access at no cost.

Most major hotels have in-room Internet access or provide access from a "business center." Bed and breakfast owners are often more than happy to let you send e-mail (especially if you say something nice about where you're staying).

Liquor Laws

You must be 19 years old to consume alcoholic beverages in the Maritimes.

A "licensed" restaurant or cafe is one that is licensed by the province to serve alcohol to those 19 years of age and older.

Mail

At the time of publication, stamps for mailing standard letters or postcards cost C$.50 cents, C$.85 cents, and C$1.45.

You can receive mail on the road by having it addressed to your name and "General Delivery," care of the post office in the town of your choice.

Maps

Each of three provincial tourism offices (see "Where to Get More Information" later in the Appendix) offers free information packages, which include a map that is sufficient for general touring.

Map Art (☎ **905-436-2525;** www.mapart. com) publishes a number of excellent regional and city street guides for the Maritimes. Rand McNally produces a soft-cover Atlantic Canada atlas.

The region's only specialty map store is Maps and Ducks, at 1869 Upper Water St. (☎ **902-422-7106**). Independent bookstores and chains such as Chapters (located in all major cities) also carry maps.

Police

Dial ☎ **911** for emergencies.

Safety

The Maritimes is no more or less safe than anywhere else in Canada. You need to take the usual common-sense precautions for your own safety and personal belongings, just like you would when traveling anywhere else.

See Chapter 7 for details about driving in the Maritimes and Chapter 10 for tips on keeping healthy when you travel.

Smoking

Anti-smoking laws in all three provinces limit smoking in public places such as malls, museums, and sporting arenas. In New Brunswick, smoking is not allowed in restaurants and bars. In the other two provinces, many restaurants have set aside an enclosed area for smokers, or have put limits the hours patrons can light up. Hotels often have floors reserved for nonsmokers, while smoking at bed-and-breakfasts is nearly always limited to outdoor areas. Because ordinances vary from province to province and even town to town, you should check before lighting up anywhere.

Taxes

The federal Goods and Services Tax is 7%. Each Maritimes province tacks an additional tax on all purchases except food. The Provincial Sales Tax on Prince Edward Island is 10%, for a total of 17% in taxes. In Nova Scotia and New Brunswick, a provincial tax of 8% is blended with the GST to make a Harmonized Sales Tax of 15%.

The GST paid in Prince Edward Island and the HST paid in Nova Scotia and New Brunswick are refundable on accommodations and most consumer goods (except meals and gas) for non-Canadians. See Chapter 4 for details on getting a refund.

Time Zones

All three provinces are located in the Atlantic Standard Time zone (AST), 1 hour ahead of New York and 4 hours ahead of Los Angeles. From the first Sunday in April through to the last Saturday in October, daylight saving time is observed throughout the region,

along with the rest of Canada (except Saskatchewan). In 2007 and beyond, daylight saving will be extended by one month, with clocks being moved forward one hour on the second Sunday in March and turned back on the first Sunday in November.

Tipping

Tipping in the Maritimes is no different to anywhere else in Canada or in the United States. See Chapter 5 for details.

Weather Updates

The best online source of weather reports, complete with long-range forecasts, satellite pictures, and historical tidbits of meteorological data, is the Environment Canada Web site at www.weatheroffice.ec. gc.ca. If your hotel room has cable television, it will probably be tuned in to Canada's Weather Channel.

Toll-Free Numbers and Web Sites

Major airlines serving the Maritimes

Air Canada
☎ 888-247-2262
www.aircanada.com

Air Canada Jazz
☎ 888-247-2262
www.flyjazz.com

CanJet
☎ 800-809-7777
www.canjet.com

Continental
☎ 800-231-0856
www.continental.com

Delta
☎ 800-221-1212
www.delta.com

Northwest
☎ 800-225-2525
www.nwa.com

WestJet
☎ 800-538-5696
www.westjet.com

Major car-rental agencies in the Maritimes

Avis
☎ 800-272-5871
www.avis.com

Budget
☎ 800-268-8900
www.budgetcanada.com

Discount
☎ 800-263-2355
www.discountcar.com

Dollar
☎ 800-800-4000
www.dollar.com

Enterprise
☎ 800-325-8007
www.enterprise.com

Hertz
☎ 800-654-3131
www.hertz.com

National
☎ 800-227-7368
www.nationalcar.com

Rent-A-Wreck
☎ 800-327-0116
www.rentawreck.ca

Thrifty
☎ 800-847-4389
www.thrifty.com

Major hotel and motel chains in the Maritimes

Best Western
☎ 800-528-1234
www.bestwestern.com

Cape Breton Resorts
☎ 800-565-5660
www.capebretonresorts.com

Coastal Inns
☎ 800-665-7829
www.coastalinns.com

Comfort Inns
☎ 800-424-6423
www.choicehotels.ca

Country Inns and Suites
☎ 800-456-4000
www.countryinns.com

Days Inn
☎ 800-325-2525
www.daysinn.com

Delta Hotels
☎ 877-814-7706
www.deltahotels.com

Fairmont Hotels and Resorts
☎ 800-257-7544
www.fairmont.com

Holiday Inn
☎ 800-465-4329
www.ichotelsgroup.com

Hostelling International–Canada
www.hihostels.ca

Maritime Inns and Resorts
☎ 888-662-7484
www.maritimeinns.com

Ramada
☎ 800-272-6232
www.ramada.com

Rodd Hotels & Resorts
☎ 800-565-7633
www.rodd-hotels.ca

Signature Resorts
www.signatureresorts.com

Super 8
☎ 800-800-8000
www.super8.com

Wandlyn Inns
☎ 800-561-0000
www.super8.com

Where to Get More Information

You'll find most of what you need to know for your Maritimes trip in this book, but if you're thirsting for more, try the following resources.

Tourist Information

Each of the three provincial tourism offices operates visitor information centers at the major gateways to their respective provinces.

Provincial tourism bureaus offer free information packages and maps that'll boost your pre-trip planning. To get the goods, contact the following:

- ✔ **Tourism Nova Scotia** (☎ **800-565-0000** or 902-425-5781; www.novascotia.com)

- ✔ **New Brunswick Tourism** (☎ **800-561-0123**; www.tourismnewbrunswick.ca)

- ✔ **Prince Edward Island Tourism** (☎ **888-734-7529** or 902-368-4444; www.gov.pe.ca/visitorsguide)

These Web sites dish out information on specific cities, parks, and traveling in Canada beyond the Maritimes:

- ✔ **Canadian Tourism Commision:** www.keepexploring.ca

- ✔ **Fredericton Tourism:** www.city.Fredericton.nb.ca

- ✔ **Parks Canada:** www.pc.gc.ca

- ✔ **The Capital Commission:** www.visitcharlottetown.com

- ✔ **Tourism Halifax:** www.halifaxinfo.com

- ✔ **Tourism Moncton:** www.gomoncton.com

- ✔ **Tourism Saint John:** www.tourismsaintjohn.com

Other Guidebooks

Frommer's Nova Scotia, New Brunswick & Prince Edward Island complements this book perfectly. It covers destinations not included in these pages and offers a different perspective on those that are. *Frommer's Canada* is the preferred option for travelers planning on exploring the rest of the country. Another excellent resource is www.frommers.com, which offers travel tips, online booking options, and a daily e-mail newsletter filled with travel specials.

Index

• *H* •

Notes

Notes

Notes

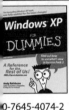

SPORTS, FITNESS, PARENTING, RELIGION & SPIRITUALITY

0-7645-5146-9

0-7645-5418-2

Also available:

- The Bible For Dummies
  0-7645-5296-1
- Buddhism For Dummies
  0-7645-5359-3
- Catholicism For Dummies
  0-7645-5391-7
- Curling For Dummies
  1-894413-30-X

- Pilates For Dummies
  0-7645-5397-6
- Rugby For Dummies
  0-470-83405-6
- Teaching Kids to Read For
  Dummies 0-7645-4043-2
- Weight Training For Dummies
  0-7645-5168-X

TRAVEL

0-470-83398-X

0-7645-5453-0

Also available:

- Alaska For Dummies
  0-7645-1761-9
- Cancun and the Yucatan For
  Dummies 0-7645-2437-2
- Cruise Vacations For Dummies
  0-7645-6941-4
- Europe For Dummies
  0-7645-5456-5
- Ireland For Dummies
  0-7645-5455-7

- Las Vegas For Dummies
  0-7645-5448-4
- London For Dummies
  0-7645-4277-X
- New York City For Dummies
  0-7645-6945-7
- Paris For Dummies
  0-7645-5494-8
- Walt Disney World & Orlando
  For Dummies 0-7645-6943-0

NETWORKING, SECURITY, PROGRAMMING & DATABASES

0-7645-3910-8

0-7645-5784-X

Also available:

- A+ Certification For Dummies
  0-7645-4187-0
- Access 2003 All-in-One Desk
  Reference For Dummies
  0-7645-3988-4
- Beginning Programming For
  Dummies 0-7645-4997-9
- C++ For Dummies
  0-7645-6852-3
- C For Dummies 0-7645-7068-4
- Firewalls For Dummies
  0-7645-4048-3

- Home Networking For
  Dummies 0-7645-4279-6
- Network Security For
  Dummies 0-7645-1679-5
- Networking For Dummies
  0-7645-1677-9
- TCP/IP For Dummies
  0-7645-1760-0
- VBA For Dummies
  0-7645-3989-2
- Wireless All-in-One Desk
  Reference For Dummies
  0-7645-7496-5

HEALTH & SELF-HELP

0-470-83370-X

0-7645-4149-8

Also available:

- Alzheimer's For Dummies
  0-7645-3899-3
- Asthma For Dummies
  0-7645-4233-8
- Controlling Cholesterol For
  Dummies 0-7645-5440-9
- Depression For Dummies
  0-7645-3900-0
- Fertility For Dummies
  0-7645-2549-2

- Fibromyalgia For Dummies
  0-7645-5441-7
- Improving Your Memory For
  Dummies 0-7645-5435-2
- Pregnancy For Dummies
  0-7645-4483-7
- Quitting Smoking For
  Dummies 0-7645-2629-4
- Relationships For Dummies
  0-7645-5384-4
- Thyroid For Dummies
  0-7645-5385-2

EDUCATION, HISTORY & REFERENCE

0-470-83656-3

0-7645-2498-4

Also available:

- Algebra For Dummies
  0-7645-5325-9
- British History For Dummies
  0-7645-7021-8
- English Grammar For
  Dummies 0-7645-5322-4
- Forensics For Dummies
  0-7645-5580-4

- Italian For Dummies
  0-7645-5196-5
- Latin For Dummies
  0-7645-5431-X
- Science Fair Projects For
  Dummies 0-7645-5460-3
- Spanish For Dummies
  0-7645-5194-9
- U.S. History For Dummies
  0-7645-5249-X